Religious Education in a Psychological Key

Religious Education in a Psychological Key

JOHN H. PEATLING

Religious Education Press
Birmingham, Alabama

Library of Congress Cataloging in Publication Data

Peatling, John H.
Religious education in a psychological key.

Includes bibliographical references and index.
1. Christian education—Philosophy. 2. Christian education—Psychology. I. Title.
BV1464.P4 207 81-8678
ISBN 0-89135-027-6 AACR2

Religious Education Press, Inc.
1531 Wellington Road
Birmingham, Alabama 35209
10 9 8 7 6 5 4 3 2

Religious Education Press publishes books exclusively in religious education and in areas closely related to religious education. It is committed to enhancing and professionalizing religious education through the publication of serious, significant, and scholarly works.

PUBLISHER TO THE PROFESSION

DEDICATED TO:

ESTHER AND JOHN, WHO BORE ME AND LOVED ME;

JANE AND LUCIE, WHO BORE WITH ME YET LOVED ME;

JANE ELLEN, KAREN ANN AND MARY ELIZABETH,
WHO WERE LOVED, WHATEVER THEY MAY HAVE THOUGHT;

EDWARD, JENNIFER, BRENDAN AND PATRICK,
WHO ARE LOVED, ALTHOUGH THEY MAY NOT KNOW IT YET.

Contents

Preface

Over twenty-five years ago my late father-in-law decided to take a hand in my postgraduate practical education. He thought my clerical internship and residency had not quite been complete. So he set out to do something about it. Specifically, he proceeded to give me opportunities to know the community of sober alcoholics which meant a very great deal to him. It was a remarkable experience. It made the idea of a community of faith real in ways that normal congregational life only hesitatingly and tentatively suggested. It was a gift that enriched, formed, and encouraged me in the callings I could acknowledge and, so, helped me face into what was then an unknown history.

One of the things I learned from those encounters was the value of stating (1) how you understand yourself and (2) what you think you are about. That is why I want to record how I understand myself and what I think I am about in this book. However, in order to do that I must address two broad and somewhat philosophical queries: Who am I? What am I doing?

WHO AM I?

I want to approach an answer to that broadly probing, quasi-theological question in three steps. Each one of those steps will consist of a statement that is true of me now in this created reality, as it appears under the sun.[1]

I. A First-Step Statement

Question: Who am I?
Statement: I am a Christian by baptism, commitment, and conviction.

This first statement identifies that I am a Christian. In addition, it refers to two past actions (baptism and confirmation) and one present action. As an infant, my paternal grandfather baptized me by the pouring of water and the invoking of the name of God the Father, God the Son, and God the Holy Spirit. Later, as an early adolescent, I joined the Methodist church in which I had grown up. Still later, as a young adult, I was confirmed at the hands of Bishop Richard S. Emrich in Detroit, Michigan, before witnesses (a seminary classmate and two of my aunts). Presently, as an older adult, conviction is an apt description of my existential action in this place within this creation. Such conviction is both a sign and a symbol of past actions and of a now present action.

II. A Second-Step Statement

Question: Who am I?
Statement: I am a Christian who, by calling and vocation, is a husband, father, theologian, religious educator, developmentalist, and researcher.

This second statement identifies that I am a Christian with certain acknowledged roles. However, the statement explicitly identifies each of those roles as a matter of calling and vocation, concepts of particular meaning to a Christian, who is likely to understand them as responses to the deity's intention or permission. Thus, while each role must be judged by very human criteria, each is also a carrier of deity's intention or permission. As a result, each one has both an obviously human and a less obvious, inferred religious dimension. I acknowledge both dimensions.

III. A Third-Step Statement

Question: Who am I?
Statement: I am a Christian who was ordained by good and faithful men, successors to an apostolic faith and tradition, to serve and to celebrate the Christian mysteries with and for my fellow Christians and all of humankind.

This third statement identifies that I am a Christian in a quite specific and particular way. I have been ordained deacon and priest in the church of God. I have been committed to both service and celebration, and I remain so committed. True, my ministries of service have been nonparochial for almost twenty years. However, it is also true that I have exercised my ministry of celebration in the midst of a congregation week after week across the intervening years. I must, and I do, acknowledge the formative effect of repeatedly offering eucharist for those present and absent, for the living and the dead, and for all of creation.

As Paul of Tarsus maintained of himself a very long time ago, so must I maintain, "By God's grace I am what I am."[2] In fact, it is because I understand myself in the way that I do that I have written as I have about an often denigrated, ignored, or simply assumed task, Christian religious education. But that task is too important to be accepted placidly. Christian religious education is a sacramental effort that requires not only time but scholarship, not only good fortune and coincidence but close attention to the human subject, for it is a strange mixture of inferred divine action and observed human behavior in an ever-changing situational context.

However, Christian religious education is not magic. Rather, like all sacramentals, it is firmly located within this creation. That is an important point. In fact, it is one that is basic to those mysteries Christian faith and tradition affirm to be efficacious, but not magical.[3]

WHAT AM I DOING?

Across the backstairs and down the hallways of history one cry reverberates, picks up harmonics, and, periodically, is reinforced in a hundred tongues in each and every present. Although the cry is often directed toward children, they have no monopoly on it. It is directed at both youth and adults as well. Age per se explains neither the cry nor the crier. In many ways, it is an aural/oral approximation of the philosopher's stone, possession of which would open remarkable possibilities. However, just as successful alchemists are rare indeed, so are the possessors of an answer to this cry. Therefore, there is far more hope than anticipation in it. Yet in almost any present it can be heard, if one attends to the specifics of quite simple human living.

What *are* you doing?

That is the cry, and it is still uttered.

Parents, good friends, classmates, spouses, colleagues, relatives, and co-workers are all potential criers. In fact, it may be as close to a universal as the day-by-day experience of humankind provides. We utter it or hear it so frequently that we hardly notice what we are seeking. Concretely, we are asking for a simple statement accurately describing an ongoing action. Formally, we are making an urgent request for a rationale for such an action.

Oddly enough, given its frequency, we rarely receive a thoroughly accurate description of any triggering action. Even less often do we receive an acceptable and understandable rationale. For the most part, we receive a shrug or some similarly opaque verbalism. Yet the cry echoes through the passageways of human history. We have little reason to believe that it will not continue into unknown futures.

What *are* you doing?

Actually, any reader has a right to that cry. However, that is a hard thing for authors to acknowledge. After all, they are very like subcreators in this creation and, so, value their creations.[4] They often do not take kindly to an urgent request for yet another statement about the statement which their subcreation is. Metaphorically, their work is like a child they have spawned, raised, acknowledged, and valued. Thus, it is difficult for authors to be objective, and often objectivity is neither attempted nor achieved. Yet the cry is a reader's right.

That is why I want to attempt a response.

I. The General Organization

This book is divided into twelve chapters, which are grouped into three sections. However, the chapters vary in their length, for I have generally modeled this work after Kurt Lewin's *Principles of Topological Psychology*.[5] That was the book in which I first encountered and appreciated a writer who presented his conceptual units in the space he thought they required. No more, and no less. I have tried to do the same thing here. Thus, I hope the reader will be able to appreciate the why as well as the what of these twelve units. However, if appreciation proves elusive, perhaps these chapters will at least be provocative and cognitively challenging.

II. The General Purpose

This book addresses three aspects of a general topic, Christian religious education. The first such aspect is the *context* of a Christian's religious education. That is what chapters 1 through 4 are all about, for it is my belief that the context must be an acknowledgedly Christian understanding of deity and this creation. The second aspect is the *subject* of a Christian religious education. That is what chapters 5 through 8 are about, for it is my considered opinion that the effort exists for its subject, a human creature capable of learning and loving and acting in its present situation. The third aspect concerns an all-too-infrequently-used and all-too-often-flawed *procedure*, research. It is my conviction that a Christian religious education intends a very great good. However, I do believe that without research the association between that intent and the often painfully obvious result is quite random. Flipping unbiased coins would tell us as much. Thus, chapters 9 through 12 are about the not-so-simple yet very useful procedure we humans call *research*.

III. Some Subthemes

In addition, a number of subthemes can be heard in this book. One such is the idea of human *freedom*. As a creature in this creation, I am both attached to the idea and convinced of its possibility. That is why I think of myself as a libertarian. I am concerned about the preservation of human freedom, both as a possibility and as an acceptable existential state, especially in these decades of the late twentieth century. For me, freedom is a religious matter as well as a creaturely characteristic.

Of course, other subthemes can also be heard. One such is the idea that humans are both blessed with and, often, misinformed by *perception*. What we perceive is certainly seen but, often, it is not all there is to what we can see. Another subtheme is the idea that *choice and decision* are not only possible but, actually, highly probable in many common human situations. Therefore, human responsibility for choice and decision is part of what it means to be a free human creature. Yet another subtheme is the importance of cognition—*thinking*—for any understanding of the human creature. However, like the creature, thinking is subject to the vagaries of development, a concept as complex as it is important. In fact, *development* is yet another subtheme.

IV. Some Repeated Points of Reference

Finally, six contemporary or near contemporary persons are repeatedly used as conceptual points of reference in this book. Fuller, Godel, Piaget, Seuss, Skinner, and Tolkien appear regularly. So do John and Paul, although they hardly qualify as even near contemporaries. However, this is not one more rehearsal of the New Testament warrants for a Christian religious education. Instead, it is a personal, informed consideration of some of the contemporary bases for a positive rationale for the effort. Thus, it may not look like many books concerned with a Christian religious education.

What *are* you doing?

I am often painfully aware of Murphy's law, which states that if anything can go wrong, it will. Yet this book is not a thesis in advanced Murphology. Quite the contrary. Rather than accept the cynicism of Grossman's misquote of H. L. Mencken, which has it that complex problems have simple, easy-to-understand wrong answers, I want to advance some complex ideas about a very real challenge.[6] For example, I want to suggest that a Christian religious education deserving of the name is a process of helping creatures positively and joyfully accept, explore, and discover their very considerable potential in this creation, on this planet, and within the situations that are theirs.

Now, that is a complex challenge. It is also an opportunity. Moreover, it is a basically religious problem. Responding to that challenge, opportunity, and problem will require our best thought and our best efforts. There is no need for simple, easy-to-understand wrong answers . . . and I have not attempted to provide them.

What *are* you doing?

That is what I am doing.

Notes and References

1. For the importance of reality, as it appears under the sun, see J. R. R. Tolkien, "On Fairy-Stories," in *The Tolkien Reader* (New York: Ballantine Books, 1966), p. 55.

2. 1 Cor. 15:10. This and all other biblical quotations in this book, unless otherwise noted, come from *The New English Bible* (New York: Oxford University Press & Cambridge University Press, 1970).

3. For the author's understanding of magic, see Evelyn Underhill, *Mysticism*, 17th ed. (London: Methuen & Co., 1911/1949), p. 162.

4. For this idea that authors are or may be subcreators, see Tolkien, "On Fairy-Stories," pp. 37, 70.

5. Kurt Lewin, *Principles of Topological Psychology* (New York: McGraw-Hill Book Co., 1936/1966).

6. For Murphy's law and Grossman's misquote of H. L. Mencken, see Arthur Bloch, *Murphy's Law Book Two* (Los Angeles: Price/Stern/Sloan Publishers, 1980), pp. 14, 15.

1

God! What a Problem

Once upon a time, close to twenty years ago as humans count off their lives, my parenting became a cognitive challenge. The period of nonphilosophical, albeit linguistically important, questioning had been relatively easy, for I had chewed upon and tolerably well masticated the Gesell studies of infancy and early childhood.[1] But there came a time when a small child recycled to some of those whys and wheres and hows. At the time, I was probably too naive about what was really going on. Yet the challenge was undoubtedly good for my soul. At least, it was a real challenge to that then young parent!

Admittedly, I cannot image the time and place. But the memory is not a mere figment of my imagination. I can recall a young child asking in the midst of a mealtime conversation about safely prosaic matters the questions, "Who is God?" I can also recall that her parents judged this query to be cognitively necessary, not just another linguistic exercise. Thus, she required an answer. There could be no delay, and there should be no avoiding of the issue, not this time.

The blessedness of fallible human memory prevents me from recalling exactly what I said to that young child in the midst of the meal. Whatever it was, I am certain I had no intention of compressing Philosophical Theology 9737 into a quick and simple answer. But I can still recall the desire to be both responsible and responsive to a legitimate early question. Her parents knew a teachable moment when they encountered one, and this was one. For that small child, it was a part of her early Christian religious education. In fact, it was also a challenging part of her parents' own continuing Christian religious education.[2]

Whatever a much younger me may have said then, I now want to use that memory of a common family experience to initiate a consideration of my daughter's early and still challenging question. I want to address that query because it is one that keeps recurring. Small children are not alone in asking, "Who is God?" Older children, adolescents, young adults, and older adults often come back to the same query: "Who *is* God?" In addition, the ideal of a Christian religious education across the life cycle must be built upon a readiness to encounter that query again and again . . . and discover a sequence of "answers."[3]

TRYING TO GET A FEW THINGS STRAIGHT

Who *is* God?

It takes no great intellect to parse the question. There are only three words, plus a question mark. The first word is a pronoun that implies the question, what person? The second word is a verb, the third person singular present indicative of the word *be*. The third and last word is usually regarded as a noun that refers to the one supreme being, the creator and ruler of the universe. The final question mark makes a query of those three words. That much is clear to almost anyone.

However, what does take a good bit of intelligence is an answer to that question which is either appropriate to the questioner or more than an authoritative formula. An answer truly appropriate to another human's existential state requires a kind of knowledge that is all too rare. An answer that is more than a repetition of an authoritative formula requires either personal knowledge or considerable thought. Thus, it is more than likely that the question will be "answered" quite inappropriately, very possibly by some partially remembered authoritative formula.

Actually, we must not be excessively rigorous. Clearly authoritative formulae exist, and have existed for at least a hundred human generations. Good, honorable, and trusted authority support such formulae. Moreover, such formulae often purport to answer the question; they help us all respond to the child's query, "Who is God?" Thus, we have no need to deny such formulae. What we do need to do is simply to (a) remember them accurately, and (b) understand them as best we can. Unfortunately, neither of those two needs is easy or automatic.

It is not wrong to rely on an authoritative formula. To think that it is wrong to do so is to hold humankind to an unhuman standard; it is to commit what the late C. S. Lewis once called the angelic fallacy.[4] However, relying upon authority must not be mistaken for the result of experience or, even worse, confused with the result of personal thought. Authority and authoritative formulae are often useful and sometimes quite necessary, but they are always a crutch for an aching cognitive inability in some present. We must not forget that humans periodically encounter situations in which they suffer a severe mental failure. All too often, the childish query, "Who is God?" is just such a situation.

If we do not admit as much, we risk *hubris*, which the ancient Greeks well knew was not a good thing.[5] That is, unless we acknowledge our own inability, we are readily tempted to an arrogant excess of self-confidence.[6] We assume that we know what we really do not know, or that we have done the hard thinking necessary to reach a conclusion when, in fact, we have not. Yet it is not *hubris* to try and understand an authoritative formula sufficiently to be able to put into our own words that which the formula sought to say in another time and place. Nor is it *hubris* to be unwilling to relax into the cognitive comfort of simple acceptance when, actually, we do not understand. But it is *hubris* to use our minds for nought but the prosaic, safely detailed, and commonly accepted processes of daily living and expect to have some kind of genuine answer to a small child's query. We almost certainly do well in our everyday arenas, but it only takes a child's question to expose the intellectual poverty of our arrogant self-confidence.

Unfortunately, a simpleminded yet rigorous forswearing of any and all recourse to authoritative formulae is also nothing more than 100 percent *hubris*. Frankly, that is a patent absurdity! We cannot reasonably require that we recapitulate the entire intellectual history of humankind before we acknowledge that we have as much sense as our parents. Minimally, such an idea is the sign of an obsessive filial devotion that fails to realize that there is a very important difference between a child's almost total dependence and that loving, concerned independence that characterizes most adult-parent relationships. To insist that we consciously rethink all that has been thought, or rediscover all that has been discovered, is a form of arrogant self-confidence. In addition to its practical difficulty, there is the basic question of its necessity: our authoritative formulae exist to make such total recapitulations infrequently useful and only rarely necessary.

There is an option to *hubris*, although it may seem unsophisticated and even a bit retrograde. That is, we can be honest.[7] When we have no firmly personal knowledge, we can admit as much to ourselves and then to others. When we have decided to accept some authoritative formula, we can acknowledge that decision and fool no one about what we have done, least of all ourselves. Unfortunately, we are almost as likely to try to deceive ourselves as we are to attempt to foist such a deception on others. Self-deception *is* something humans do with remarkable ease, as almost any pastor, counselor, clinical psychologist, therapist, or psychiatrist knows full well. But there is no reason to continue the practice. Specifically, there is no religious reason to avoid honesty and prefer some self-deceptive illusion. There is no real reason to pretend to a knowledge of the great mysteries of human existence, when all we have is a knowledge of what some other human has said or written.

Part of the option of honesty is the simple, albeit difficult, admission that, at some point, most humans depend upon a clearly authoritative formula. Interestingly, that is true of most of us; and it really does not matter whether we think of ourselves as workers or managers, artists or professors, priests or parishioners, theorists or practioners. We do tend to accept some authoritative formula: for most of us, some source simply *is* authoritative.[8] As near as anyone can know, that seems to be an inescapable part of what it means to be a human creature in this creation.

But what are we to say to that child's question: Who *is* God?

Clearly, obviously, we have no need for more *hubris*. Equally clearly, we have a very real need for honesty and an existential realism that will let us say to young children any of several things. For instance, such an existential realism could legitimate each of the following reasonably honest parental answers to a young child's query, "Who *is* God?"

1. I really do not know for certain, but those whom I trust have said that God is . . . (some authoritative formula).[9]
2. Well, I believe that God is . . . (some authoritative formula).[10]
3. Well, as best as I can understand it, God is . . . (a personal statement of what an authoritative formula meant in another time and place).[11]
4. Well, God is the one to whom we give thanks at the beginning of a meal, say our prayers to at night, and sing songs about at church.[12]
5. I am glad you asked that question. God is very like your grandparents, who love you very much and want only the very best for you, even if they do not see you all that often.[13]

An existential realism would not ask which of those five was best. It would ask only whether or not the parental answer was honest and appropriate. Those are the real and present standards. Moreover, a theologically informed and honest parent could respond in any of those five ways to a young child's query. Somehow we need to acknowledge at least that much, or we are in real danger of *hubris:* that is, thinking we are what we very well may not be, yet. Far too often we do not think honesty is an appropriate response to the recurring question about who God is!

ATTEMPTING TO LOCATE SOME REFERENTS FOR AN ANSWER

The question, "Who *is* God?" involves a hidden, often overlooked assumption. That is, the assumption that any answer will inevitably be in terms of some person. In this instance, our very language can easily cause us to overlook an importantly prior query: *Is* God a person?

Dictionaries speak of God as a supreme being, and they credit that being with the creation and rule of the universe. Yet it is our present, quite human understanding of a linguistic, cultural, and religious heritage that translates a supreme being into a supreme person. More precisely, it is our often idiosyncratic understanding of that heritage which permits us to assume that a supreme being must be a supreme person.

Strange as it may seem, our all-too-common ideas of God's personhood probably owe as much to Sigmund Freud's quasi vendetta in *Moses and Monotheism* as they do to anything else.[14] While Freud was not an authoritative biblical scholar nor a good textual critic, his general thesis that God is simply a classic projection (that is, humankind writ large enough to seem supreme) has come to us all, in one way or another. It really doesn't matter *how* the idea permeated our set of assumptions! What really matters is that we recognize that the Freudian idea of projection is no more than a simple, human hypothesis and, so, open our minds to the possibility of another option.

Perhaps God is neither a projection nor a person, at least not in anything like what common sense means by either the word or the concept *person*. Holding onto that possibility is very important. Without it we will almost certainly misunderstand authoritative formulae that literally beg to be considered.

I. Some Selected Referents from the Books of Moses

What I want to do is analogous to navigating a body of water under sail. There is a destination (which is known) and the intervening forces of wind and current (which, before they are actually encountered, cannot really be known). Having acknowledged the necessity of clearly authoritative formulae, I now want to refer to several such formulae.

Whether we are Jew or Gentile, Hebrew or Greek, or in all honesty simply the heirs of Gaul, Celt, Goth, Arabian, Egyptian, Persian, Mongol, Indian, Ethiopian, or the Middle Kingdom, *if* we claim the Judeo-Christian heritage we are likely to acknowledge that some or all of *The Book* is an authoritative source. Therefore, it is to that authoritative source that I now want to refer.

A. The Stories of Creation in the First Book of Moses

At the very beginning of the First Book of Moses there are two stories of creation. This has been known for generations, but its reality has worked its way into our collective consciousness very slowly. What I want to do is to refer to the first of those two stories, which in a Christian's Bible is Gen. 1:1–2:4. The second story follows in Gen.

2:5–3.24, and is a tale about Adam and Eve and a garden in which they lived for a while, before being expelled for breach of contract. Unfortunately, that second story is a fascinating tale that is quite often imprinted upon the quasi-credulous mind. However, since at least the late nineteenth century, the first story has been recognized as the more abstract, more philosophical of the pair that earliest Judaism saved for posterity.

If we can avoid getting caught up in the matter of the "days" of creation, it is amazing how little person-language there is in the first biblical creation tale. The English trigram G-O-D is obviously active and responsive to its own activity, but there is little that qualifies for the accursed epithet *anthropomorphism*. At the end of that tale, G-O-D has distinguished light from dark, sky from ground, seed from plant, night from day, visible from invisible creatures, the animals we do domesticate from those we regard as wild, and homo sapiens from other terrestrial creatures. Then the tale concludes with a note to the effect that G-O-D "ceased from all the work he had set himself to do."[15]

Aside from those two words *he* and *himself*, there is little in this first story of creation that is either anthropomorphic or sexist. True, the trigram G-O-D is active, but the person G-O-D is barely discernible. If we could but be honest with ourselves, we might well admit that this first story is not about a person at all. It is assuredly about a supreme being, but it is not about a supreme person.

While I do not want to get into proof-texting games, I am enough of a writer to suspect that introductions set a tone for what follows. Thus, I cannot avoid the suspicion that too many of us put our minds in neutral or, worse, reverse when we read the first biblical tale. As a result, we do wind up functioning very much like Freud thought all of us necessarily functioned. That is, we project humanity up, out, otherward, and so let our God be humankind writ large enough to seem supreme.

B. The Visit to Abraham of Three Strangers

In the very beginning of the eighteenth chapter of the First Book of Moses there is an enigmatic tale of nomadic hospitality which includes the preposterous forecast that a ninty-year-old man's equally ancient wife shall bear a child. This visit of three strangers to Abraham by the oaks of Mamre is a theophany, an encounter with G-O-D. The scene became a superb iconographic pattern in the hands of the Russian Orthodox artist Rublëv, a veritable sign and symbol of G-O-D as Trinity. While the textual critique of Gen. 18:1–15 is quite complex, I want to emphasize the description of the three visitors as strangers; that seems to come close to the heart of whatever a theophany may be as an experience. Whatever the eyes might have told Abraham, this ancient tale preserves an essential aspect of G-O-D's relation to humankind by putting the forecast of Sarah's child into the mouth of "the stranger." Whatever G-O-D is, there is an irreducible strangeness when G-O-D and humans encounter one another. Otherness is a way of saying much the same thing. God is other. Nothing really overcomes that.

I refer to this tale of Abraham and his visitors simply as a way of suggesting that the apersonhood of G-O-D is not a new idea. In fact, it is an old, overlooked idea. Moreover, the tale suggests that whatever G-O-D is does not prevent encounter or involvement, blessing or promise, or dialogue. All are a part of that tale, and none require that a theophany be an encounter with a supreme person.

C. Moses' Request for Credentials

Early in the Second Book of Moses there is a vignette that (minimally) provides no support for the personhood of God and (maximally) undermines the whole idea. The story occurs as Moses is presumedly conversing with G-O-D during the burning bush theophany. Being quite human, Moses wants to know who it is that wants him to go off to Egypt and "free" the Israelites.

Moses presumes, as humans tend to do, that it is a "who"; otherwise his query makes little sense. However, the response in Exod. 3:13–14 fails to meet the assumption. It is not given in terms of who-ness but of being, pure and simple. To Moses' question G-O-D replies, "I AM; that is who I am." The alternative reading is even less personal: "I will be what I will be."

While Moses is charged with an important task—he is to be G-O-D's representative to Egypt—his thoroughly human who-question receives a strange answer. No name; only an affirmation of sheer being. However, let us be careful. We need not censure Moses for not knowing any better. What he asked is a normal, thoroughly human, utterly natural request. Which of us, in that innermost core where we know that we are a reasonably representative sample of the genus, would not ask, "Who says so?"[16]

Moses asked an important question. The response was less than satisfactory. Moses asked, "Who says so?" G-O-D replied with an affirmation of being. In a word, G-O-D finessed. Thus Moses was left knowing a being, but not a person. Insofar as we are committed to the Judeo-Christian heritage, that is right in the midst of it: G-O-D *is*, but beyond that we know no "name." What we do know is just what Moses knew: the action of G-O-D.

If we will but accept those facts, as apparently Moses did, we may acknowledge G-O-D's is-ness and G-O-D's action without fooling ourselves that we know any more. That is, of course, a big step. It means acknowledging a profound mystery, admitting a paradox, and ceasing to let our minds simply project otherward either our hopes or our fantasies or our best dreams. It does not mean we are atheists or, in any traditional sense, even agnostics: we have not denied encounter, involvement, or communication. Only an all-too-human analogy, personhood, has slipped away.

That is less of a loss than we might believe.

II. A Few Referents from the Prophets

If we considered the canonical prophets as a type, we might begin to wonder at the repeated claim that it was simply "the Word of the Lord" that came to them. No theophany, just communication, that most abstract and fragile of things, that process by which a relationship can be maintained without touch or sight. Time and again that communication came and particular humans responded, obeyed, spoke, and at times suffered. It was "the Lord" that spoke and, we presume, also enlivened and enabled. But "the Word of the Lord" is little or no better than our English trigram G-O-D.

Anyone can go through the *New English Bible* and discover, early in the first chapter of each of the prophetic books, the claim that "the

Word of the Lord" validates the message. It is true of the writings credited to Amos, Ezekiel, Hosea, Isaiah, Jeremiah, Joel, Jonah, Malachi, Micah, Nahum, Zechariah, and Zephaniah. Only Obadiah varies the formula slightly. The phrase is, of course, almost certainly a formula. However, that formula conveys no more of an answer to our who-question than Moses received. The referent remains a being, known via action but not via name.

The prophetic writings certainly suggest something about the nature of G-O-D, but always an analogy from action. Those actions are sometimes obvious and contemporary, but sometimes they are less than obvious and in the then-not-yet. We can deduce persistence and intention from the actions referenced to the Lord, but the deduction is ours. We can also learn from the prophetic writings that G-O-D relates to this creation in several ways, and regards certain human responses as appropriate. However, it is our human action that clusters such things into an inference that G-O-D has a personality. We must remember what we have done.

A theme running through the prophetic writings is peculiarly apropos, the denunciation of "false" prophets. Whoever they may have been, their falsity apparently consisted in being too well attuned to their time and place and, so, speaking more of human wisdom than the oftentimes strange "Word of the Lord." They may have been enthusiasts who let their projections otherward blind them to the Other. Or they may have been rationalists who doubted the existence of that Other and, so, spoke only what they knew would be heard. Whatever their state or whatever their rationale, the prophets remind us that they were wrong. We might not be far off the mark if we imagine that they were unwilling to live with the Mosaic paradox, they were not content with the ambiguities of G-O-D's answer to Moses' who-question. They were prepared to manufacture an answer and, in so doing, they wandered willy-nilly into falseness. Unfortunately, the manufacture of a personhood for G-O-D leads right into some version of the Freudian hypothesis: the process involves projecting humankind otherward, magnifying the perceived virtues, and thinking that the result is G-O-D. It wasn't, and there was no reason to believe it would be. If nothing else, that process creates no strangeness.

III. Some Referents from the Books of the Christian Covenant

However we resolve the knotty problem of dating the books in the Christian's New Testament, there are two places in those writings where the event of Jesus of Nazareth is put into the broadest context. In a sense, whether those places are early or late is secondary to whether or not they are legitimate interpretations. At the very least, their retention within the Christian canon is an indication that they are (or were) acceptable. Thus, they may still be useful in this present.

A. The Prologue to the Gospel of John

In John's introduction, the prophetic formula's central communicative idea of "the Word of the Lord" finds a remarkable expansion.[17] There that Word is posited to be (1) preexistent, (2) equivalent to G-O-D, (3) the agent of creation, and (4) the source of life. Moreover, the event of Jesus of Nazareth is equated with an entry of that Word into the world in the most concrete of terms: "The Word became flesh."[18]

The Johannine Prologue concludes with the flat assertion, "No one has ever seen God; but God's only Son, he who is nearest to the Father's heart, he has made him known."[19] This sentence affirms what we might have suspected: G-O-D had not been seen before, and certainly had not been known as a person. The being that communicated with Moses or the prophets was made known within the particularities of time and space by an appearance of the Word. Thus, if there is an answer to Moses' normal, natural, human who-question, this Prologue affirms that it is only in terms of the event of Jesus of Nazareth. Only because of that event do we have some reason to posit that G-O-D is anything like a person. Unless we exercise our set of assumptions upon these words and, so, modify them to conform to our definitions of acceptability, they stand as a stark affirmation of a unique event.

Although the Gospel according to John continues on for some twenty-four chapters, which detail a story of the actions of Jesus of Nazareth from the time of his baptism by John the Baptizer to three postresurrection appearances, the author clearly indicates the nature of those tales (at least to his mind!) by his final introductory words: "God's only Son, he who is nearest to the Father's heart, he has made him known."

The context is set in the Prologue; the specifics follow as examples.

Read in this light, we can recognize that the Gospels provide person-bound examples of the action of G-O-D. Different, of course, from earlier prophetic indicators, but still essentially the stuff from which humans can relate to a being not known, except through action. The fundamental response to Moses' query remains only slightly expanded: G-O-D is, and G-O-D acts. Beyond that, only in a time-extensive event called Jesus of Nazareth have we any more information than Moses had at the theophany of the burning bush. We are only a very little closer to an answer to Moses' question, "*Who* says so?"

Still, the author of the Johannine Prologue does offer a tantalizing clue as to why G-O-D communicates via action with us: we, and all things created, are life-bearers. There is in that complex concept of life a clue to a relationship and, apparently, also a clue to why a life-giving creator might be at all interested in that which had been accomplished. That is, we live because we share in some way the life of the Word, the posited creative agent. Admittedly, that is not much beyond Moses' answer, but perhaps even that much is important, at least to us. Life per se is a clue, a hint, a possible reason for crediting to G-O-D being and action and a continual communicative effort, an attempt to mold a relationship between life-source and life-bearer. But we should clearly recognize that this is *our* use of that clue; it is our inference from an authoritative formula.

B. A Letter to Hebrews

The vocabulary of John's Gospel is reflected in the first chapter of a Letter to Hebrews, for the author affirms that "in this final age he (G-O-D) has spoken to us in the Son . . . through whom he created all orders of existence."[20] The event of the Son is firmly located as an act of communication, while the Johannine thesis that the Son-Word was the creative agent is also affirmed. For Christians, *the Son* is a clear reference to the event we know as Jesus of Nazareth. But in this passage that entire event is subsumed in the communicative action of G-O-D.

The whole of the person-bound actions of Jesus of Nazareth are here included in a single phrase: "when he brought about the purgation of sins."[21] The context for the writing, then, is set within the affirmation that G-O-D acted and, as a result, humans have some appropriate response as life-bearers to the life-source.

The male words *he* and *Son* are used, but our present concern for sexist language could divert us from a recognition that this passage presumes a "being" far, far more than it provides any information about a gendered "who." Moreover, that being is remarkably similar to the being glimpsed in the Johannine Prologue. This passage affirms much the same thing as Moses found out with his who-question: G-O-D is, and G-O-D is active. The difference is that here an action is held to be extraordinarily important, largely because of the nature of the active agent. We can ignore this point. Or we can interpret it away. Or we can accept it as yet another strange action. But *we* do each of those things and, thereby, affirm more about us than we do about the author's point.

Interpretations always presume an interpreter!

Somewhat later in the fourth chapter of a Letter to Hebrews, there is a passage that seems to echo the prophetic validating formula and, as well, spells out an awesome implication of the relation between the life-bearer and the life-source. The author says, "The word of God is alive and active. . . . It sifts the purposes and thoughts of the heart. There is nothing in creation that can hide from him; everything lies naked and exposed to the eyes of the One with whom we have to reckon."[22] Here G-O-D is and G-O-D is "the One with whom we have to reckon." We cannot hide. Inescapably, we are responsible. While the context is awesome, and while *we* might very well prefer other terms for a relationship, there is also a fundamental affirmation of our freedom in the sheer responsibility of having to "reckon" with such an alive and active being.

C. Several Other Considerations

Although neither the Johannine Prologue nor a Letter to Hebrews lead us to the idea that G-O-D is a supreme person, they add an important affirmation. They identify the event of Jesus of Nazareth as an appearance of G-O-D's creative agent, that life-source to which all life-bearers are related. Moreover, if we humans can accept it, in our responsibility to "reckon" with G-O-D we have a confirmation of our freedom. These two ideas parallel the two possible readings of G-O-D's response to Moses. Like the being queried during the burning bush theophany, we can affirm (1) "I am," for we are life-bearers, as well as (2) "I will be what I will be," for we are free, responsible beings. Yet we are creaturely beings. At best, in J. R. R. Tolkien's phrase, we may be subcreators within this creation.[23]

What most of us overlook is that in the Gospels we have the record of an action which, in the words of the Nicene Creed, was "for us and for our salvation." The specifics of that time-extended and person-bound action are the stuff from which we, as generations before us have done, construct a vision of G-O-D. But that vision is our construction. We work upon the stuff provided by the Books of Moses or the prophetic writings or the Gospels or the Acts of the Apostles or the Letters or the Revelation of John. But we are the ones who work upon that existent stuff!

1. The First Letter of John

We construct a vision that satisfies us or, perhaps, our standards of what is reasonable, possible, or probable. It is *our* action. We are Tolkienian subcreators! Yet we often overlook, forget, or, worst of all, deny what we have done. When we deny our constructive action, we not only deny our responsibility but, all too often, find we are at one another's throats. This denial seems to render us incapable of either appreciating or living out the remarkable third paragraph of the fourth chapter of the First Letter of John.[24] We find ourselves unable to love, so what is meant as a positive exhortation becomes an unbearable judgment. Being free and ingenious beings, we usually bear that judgment by ignoring (as best we can) or by denying (often stridently) or by confusing lust and love.

While we may recall the idea that "God is love," we tend to overlook the author's utter honesty four sentences later. It is as if we had to tame a mystery by denying it! Yet the author of the First Letter of John could, and did, affirm a profound mystery when he wrote, "Though

God has never been seen by any man, God himself dwells in us if we love one another; his love is brought to perfection within us."[25] Only our familiarity with the idea can keep us from recognizing in those words as profound a mystery as that encountered by Moses, or that completely strange action implied in the tale of Abraham's hospitality to the strangers. Only the iceberg's tip of that mystery involves the author's conviction that a being unseen, albeit existent and active, somehow resides in those who manage to love one another. Not yet a supreme person, but an encounterable reality whose sign, symbol, and icon is our love for one another. It is as if we were invited to recognize in other life-bearers a sign of the life-source and, thereby, transform our relationship with one another.

2. The Letter of Paul to the Galatians

Sometime around A.D. 55, probably from the commercial city of Ephesus near the bay where the Cayster River flows into the Aegean Sea, the tent-maker Paul of Tarsus wrote an astringent letter to some early Christians in the general area of the capital of modern Turkey. In the fifth chapter of the Letter of Paul to the Galatians, the themes of freedom and love are joined, and the idea of the Spirit of G-O-D's Son is used to explicate what it means to have a transformed relationship with one another.[26] Paul says, "You, my friends, were called to be free men; only do not turn your freedom into license for your lower nature, but be servants to one another in love." He acknowledges that in interpersonal relationships there is only one standard: "Love your neighbor as yourself." He contrasts behaviors indicative of "the lower nature" and those indicative of that standard, which he suggests are the "harvest of the Spirit." Thus, Paul uses the idea of the Spirit to identify love, joy, peace, patience, kindness, goodness, fidelity, gentleness, and self-control as signs of an encounter between a life-bearer and the life-source. The mystery Paul specifies in terms of interpersonal relationships is no less profound than that alluded to by the author of the First Letter of John.

The idea of the Spirit enables Paul to talk about the human effects of an encounter with that unseen being identified by our English trigram G-O-D. Yet it is our constructions that make of the Pauline Spirit a person. If we attend closely to the concept itself, we will recognize our conceptual handiwork. Moreover, if we are both honest and rigorous, we will admit that such a recognition in no way denies the reality of the effect, or that the effect permits an inference that a life-bearer *is* related to its source. It is only our traditions, poorly understood, which tempt us to project personality otherward for the Spirit. But this is not the first age to be so tempted. Much of the early theological debate during the third and fourth centuries centered upon this and related issues.

IV. Some Referents from the Fourth Century A.D.

Approximately 170 years after Paul's letter to the Christians in Galatia, the first ecumenical council met in Nicaea.[27] The last great persecution of the Christians by the Roman Empire was two decades in the past; church and state had reached an accommodation. But the relation of G-O-D to the event of Jesus of Nazareth remained in controversy.

The actual argument that led directly to the convening of a council at Nicaea was one within the Egyptian diocese of Alexandria. Arius, an enormously successful popular preacher, was in charge of one of the principal churches in Alexandria. While there is little of his writing left, he is reputed to have been a writer of something like popular gospel songs, which we know only by name as the "Thaleia." Most of what we do know about Arius's doctrine we learn from the writings of Athanasius, a bright young theologian attached to the local bishop's staff. It was Arius's inability to agree with his own bishop, Alexander, that led directly to the Council of Nicaea in A.D. 325. There the theological disagreement between the preacher who wrote popular songs and a subtle thinker by the name of Athanasius was argued out. However, ecclesiastical politics were even more complex in the fourth century than they were in the twentieth, if we can believe it. Not until almost two generations later, at the second ecumenical council at Constantinople, was the issue even provisionally settled.

During the period between the councils at Nicaea and Constantinople, three bishops in an administrative area east and south of

Galatia, the district of Cappadocia, contributed greatly to that conciliar settlement. All three were alumni of the university at Athens. Ultimately all three were canonized. Basil, called the Great, was bishop of Caesarea in Cappadocia. Gregory was bishop of Nazianzus. Another Gregory was bishop of Nyssa. Together they are known in church history as the Cappadocian Fathers. Some scholars give them credit for bringing the Arian controversy to an end. If that judgment be true, they accomplished that feat by carefully explicating the meaning to be attached to the basic words in the original Nicaean formula: *homoousios* and *hypostasis*.

At Nicaea the decision had circled around the relation of G-O-D (the Father) and Jesus of Nazareth (the Son). Arius wished to affirm merely that the Son was *like* the Father, because he was a creation of the Father's grace and, so, a creature that was somehow subordinate to the Father. Alexander, Athanasius, and the Council of Nicaea wished to affirm a "yet more." They wanted to follow out the Johannine Prologue's flat assertion that the Word-Son was G-O-D. Their code word for that idea in Greek was *homoousios*, while Arius's code word for his idea was *homoiousios*.

The older historians of Christian doctrine used to say that the argument at Nicaea boiled down to a single Greek letter, an iota. However, the issue was far more important than that. The issue was whether in the event Jesus of Nazareth G-O-D and humankind had an actual encounter, however paradoxical it might seem, or however profound a mystery might be involved in that affirmation. Something less would have been easier to understand, considerably more reasonable by fourth-century standards, and far less strange. The Council of Nicaea opted for a strange, paradoxical, mysterious affirmation: G-O-D (the Father) is *homoousios* with Jesus of Nazareth (the Son-Word). Almost as an afterthought, or perhaps as a bit of theological tidying up, the Council of Nicaea also affirmed the same for the Spirit. Father, Son, and Spirit: all *homoousios*.

Having done that, the council fathers at Nicaea chose the Greek word *hypostasis* to express that which the Father, Son, and Spirit are. Each of that trio is a *hypostasis*, although each is also *homoousios*. The

Greek word *hypostasis* had been used by Aristotle and the Neo-Platonists to distinguish an objective reality from an illusion. However, what confused some in the fourth century was that *hypostasis* and *ousia* (the root word of *homoousios*) had been used almost interchangeably during the second and third centuries.

In one sense, the point probably seems very fine. Yet only an intellectual snob would believe that fourth-century thinkers could not appreciate the problematics of attempting to talk about a mystery as profound as the interrelationship of Father, Son, and Spirit when each is G-O-D. What Nicaea did was to affirm that Father, Son, and Spirit had objective reality (*hypostasis*) yet were also of one substance (*homoousios*) G-O-D. By that affirmation the theophanies, the Johannine Word, and the Pauline Spirit were all confirmed as real encounters between G-O-D and humankind, that is, the likes of you and me. The mystery, however, was not solved. Nor could it have been solved without making something illusory.

We can look backward 16½ centuries and appreciate that the Council of Nicaea chose between an objectively real mystery and a supreme illusion, such as that posited by the Freudian hypothesis. However, it took fourth-century Christianity at least two generations to appreciate and, frankly, to accept what had happened. During the fifty-six years between the first ecumenical council at Nicaea and the second ecumenical council at Constantinople, much of the nitty-gritty conceptual work was done by the three Cappadocians. The two Gregorys and Basil thought long and hard. They wrote extensively, and they corresponded with not only the friends of the Nicaean formula but those who still had both lingering and strong doubts. One of their achievements was to so carefully consider what it could possibly mean to affirm that Father, Son, and Spirit are *hypostases* of but one *ousia* that they satisfied the lingering doubts of most of their contemporaries. The Council of Constantinople in A.D. 381 confirmed Nicaea and, implicitly, ratified the conceptual legwork of the three Cappadocians. The mystery of three *hypostases* in one *ousia* was affirmed and, in time, came to be the orthodox Christian doctrine of G-O-D as Holy Trinity.

V. A Referent from the Sixteenth Century

Approximately fifty years after Johannes Gutenberg published a Bible printed with movable type, and a year before Martin Luther was priested by the Augustinian Hermits of Erfurt, William Lynwood published *Constitutiones,* one of the earliest books printed at the Sign of the Trinity in Saint Paul's Churchyard, London.[28] The title page of this unexceptionable, late medieval survey of canon law bears two symbols of G-O-D as Holy Trinity. First, there is a not uncommon, albeit thoroughly anthropomorphic, three-faced bust. Second, there is a variation of the common Western symbol of the triangle, this one with a central circle connected to each of the triangle's points. It is to that late medieval sign of the Trinity that I want to refer.

The sign of the Trinity almost certainly summarizes a long history of Western Christian Trinitarian thinking that goes back through Thomas Aquinas to Bishop Augustine of Hippo Regius in what is now called Tunesia. The Latin words for Father, Son, and Holy Spirit occupy circles at the three points of the triangle. In the central circle is the Latin word for G-O-D. Along each edge of the triangle are the Latin words *non est* ("is not"). Along three lines connecting the central circle and each of the three points of the triangle is the Latin word *est* ("is"). This sign of the Trinity does not explain the mystery, but it does succinctly summarize that mystery. G-O-D (the central circle) is Father, Son, and Holy Spirit. Yet each is not the other; they are distinguishable one from the other. There are three *hypostases* in one *ousia.*

After something like 1,125 years, the subtle distinctions between *ousia* and *hypostasis* worked out by the three Cappadocians and affirmed by the second ecumenical council were reflected, however crudely, on that title page. Christian orthodoxy was expressed in a complex yet surprisingly simple symbol. The mystery was not, of course, unraveled; but it was symbolized. Creed and doctrine were compressed, compacted into a single sign. Close to one thousand years of theological thought were summarized in what, in all likelihood, both author and printer regarded as an acceptably orthodox symbol. In many ways, it was appropriate that the sign of the Trinity should adorn the first page of a book of canon law, for the two have a fundamental connection: without the sign (and that which it signifies!), canon law is nothing but a simple statement of the rules of this world's authorities.

While there may be ground for a good bit of useful reflection in that idea, what intrigues me is the symbol itself. In contemporary geometrics that symbol can be read as either (1) a body-centered triangle, or (2) a two-dimensional representation of a three-dimensional figure, a tetrahedron. Depending upon our ability to deal with conceptual dimensions, that sixteenth-century sign of the Trinity can be interpreted in rather different ways. If we stay with only two conceptual dimensions, the symbol is little more than a visualization of a mystery that Christian thinkers had probed for over a thousand years. However, if we can tolerate, appropriate, or appreciate a third conceptual dimension, we have a geometric figure that can be remarkably useful, highly suggestive, and much more than a visualized conceptual mystery... although it is that, too.

In these latter days of the twentieth century, the tetrahedron is something quite fundamental. Potentially, a tetrahedral interpretation of that sixteenth-century sign of the Trinity offers a way to "do" theology and, so, be ready for the profundities of childish queries and the very real complexities of adult wonderments. Moreover, it just may be possible to do that without wandering off into one or another of the ancient heresies, a fate that too often infects our attempts to "do" theology with minds working at full capacity in a contemporary idiom.[29]

MODELING A CONTEMPORARY ANSWER

I want to explore a tetrahedron's ability to model what Christian orthodoxy has affirmed for a millennium and a half. However, since language is subject to the vagaries of specialization, I must be explicit about that word *model.* It has several possible and permissible meanings. Thus, it is necessary to make one more clarification before setting out to explore a mystery without (I hope!) so unraveling it that one is left with nothing but a tangled, once-knit skein.

Psychologists speak of *modeling* as what one human can do for another human being; for example, A is a model for B, or B learns to do or know some X by virtue of imitating C's modeling behavior. There is a whole literature about that kind of modeling. Moreover, that kind of modeling can be very useful to anyone attempting the educative task, including parents, who are a child's primary educators. However, I am not interested in that kind of modeling. Actually, I want to appropriate another meaning of the word *model* and the process of modeling. I want to use the meaning that comes out of the discipline of mathematics.

In mathematics, a model is a visualization of a problem which, inherently and inescapably, involves some admittedly gross simplification of a reality. Mathematicians do not expect such a model to prove a theorem or an equation or a function. They are satisfied if the model visualizes the problem in a sufficiently accurate way to make its reality understandable.[30] It is that sense of *model* that I want to use to explore the meaning of some now old, old formulations of what G-O-D is.

A tetrahedron model is apersonal; it is highly abstract (as befits a supreme being); and it is amenable to a dynamic interpretation. Finally, it is a model that is directly connected to both a late medieval symbol and, as well, to a simple exercise for three fingers and a palm. It will not prove anything. But it can explicate a theological problem and, thus, give us humans a way of understanding a fair bit of oft misunderstood, complex doctrinal history.

I. R. Buckminster Fuller's Tetrahedron

In an 876-page contemporary summa, a truly remarkable twentieth-century phenomenon, R. Buckminster Fuller, examines what he chooses to call the *geometry of thinking*. In the 1975 book *Synergetics* and its 1979 companion, *Synergetics Two*, Fuller expounds a way of thinking that is very contemporary and yet very much at the intellectual frontier.[31] For example, he notes that the geometric figure called a tetrahedron functions as unity for a process of the mensuration of polyhedra. He also suggests that the tetrahedron is a fundamental building block of reality, because it can (1) model a completely reversible dynamic physical reaction, (2) serve as a fundament for a goodly number of chemical reactions, and (3) model some basic molecular structures. If we even tentatively consider the possibility that Fuller is correct, the pervasively useful tetrahedron seems to be an attractively contemporary model for G-O-D, the presumed fundament of all reality.

While the sixteenth-century sign of the Trinity on William Lynwood's book of canon law suggests the geometric figure, the conscious use of a tetrahedron forces our thought out of a two-dimensional plane and into a three-dimensional space. In fact, the tetrahedron does even more. For instance, Fuller notes that a tetrahedron can be regarded as a four-dimensional model; it is possible to so erect four perpendiculars from its four faces that they meet in the geometric "center" of the tetrahedron, thus defining that "central point" in four dimensions.[32] A tetrahedron is, then, a three-dimensional figure open to use as a four-dimensional model: it has a surprising and important strangeness about it. If a tetrahedron can model reality, and if we admit the reality of G-O-D, then a tetrahedron seems like an intriguingly "open" model of that being-ful reality we signify by our English trigram G-O-D.

Now, a tetrahedron is composed of four equilateral triangles joined edge to edge. As a result, a tetrahedron has four vertices and six edges. If we translate Lynwood's late medieval sign of the Trinity into a tetrahedron, three of the vertices can be assigned the hypostatic words *Father*, *Son*, and *Spirit*. But what of the fourth, remaining vertex? Of course, we could simply follow out the sign of the Trinity and label that fourth vertex *G-O-D*. On the other hand, if we were willing to be a bit venturesome, we could ask just what God-ness means or, even, meant in that late medieval symbol. If that question be asked and considered seriously, it seems evident that the central circle in the sign of the Trinity affirms the fundamental Western Christian idea of the unity of the Holy Trinity. Thus, we could label the fourth vertex of a tetrahedron model with the word *unity*. If we did that, the result would be a model like that displayed in figure 1.

While we could transfer the *non est* and the *est* from the sign of the

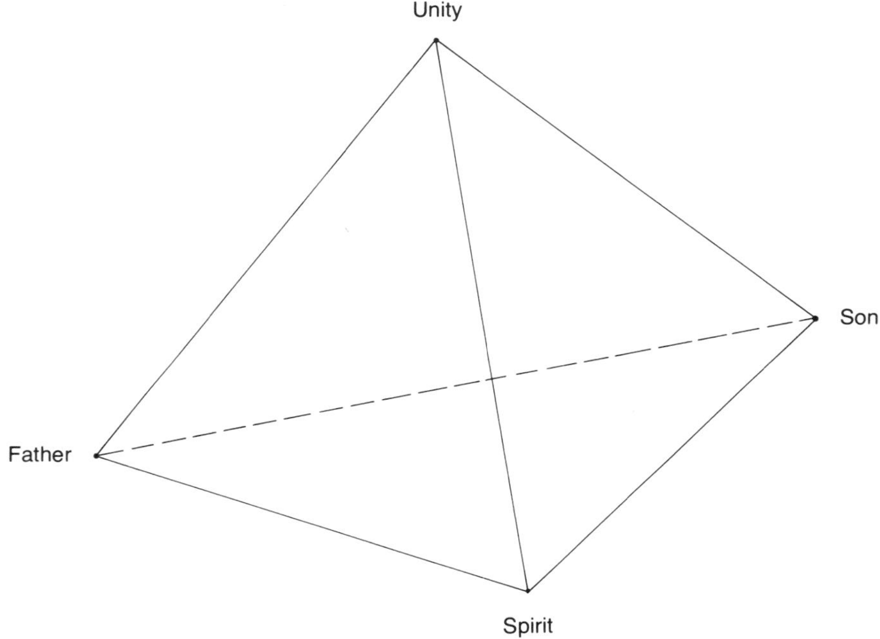

Figure 1. A tetrahedral model of G-O-D.

Trinity to the six edges of a tetrahedron, a far more intriguing possibility is to regard those edges as signs of relationships. We could, then, visualize interhypostatic relationships. An equally intriguing possibility arises from Fuller's thesis that a tetrahedron can be created from only two triangles, so that we have the seemingly strange phenomenon that 1 + 1 = 4.[33] What we can do, it seems, is to unfold a triangle into what Fuller called an "open-end triangular spiral," which can be taken as a model of an event (a combination of an action, a resultant, and a reaction). Thus, by putting two such open-end triangular spirals together we create a tetrahedron model of a reversible event.[34] The tetrahedral model of G-O-D is, in actuality, an *event-model* that is congruent with a quite basic theological affirmation. That is, reversibility implies stability or unchangeableness or, as the psalmist would have it, "You are always the same. . . ."[35] In addition, we should appreciate that reversibility per se involves a form of dynamic stability.

It also seems possible to use the edge pathways of a Fullerian "energy event" to posit something about a tetrahedrally modeled G-O-D that seems to be surprisingly and strangely orthodox. All hypostases (and unity) are involved in any modeled divine action-as-event. The unfolded triangle as an open-ended spiral does, in fact, involve all four vertices of a tetrahedron. For example, we could posit (on the basis of a tetrahedron model of G-O-D) that an action-relationship of the Son toward the Father involves, as a resultant, a relationship of the Father toward the Spirit and, as a reaction, a relationship of the Son toward the unity of the Godhead. While most of us do not think in those terms, the result seems strangely congruent with very orthodox theological affirmations about the interhypostatic relationships within the Holy Trinity.

In addition to whatever benefit we may derive from modeling such interhypostatic events, the tetrahedron itself permits us to conceive of G-O-D in terms of dynamic event, rather than placid state. For example, Fuller notes that it is possible for a tetrahedron to model a quantum composed of electron, proton, antineutrino, neutrino, neutron, and positron. That possibility leads him to posit, "The tetrahedron as a basic vectorial model is the fundamental structural system of the Universe."[36]

Let us not fool ourselves. If that be so, and if we also model G-O-D via the same structure, we are remarkably close to a structuralist statement of what is affirmed of G-O-D in the Johannine Prologue. In addition there is a vast and awesome possibility that the ancient sages were unbelievably right when they wrote in the first chapter of the First Book of Moses that G-O-D decided to create "in our image and likeness."[37] Perhaps *all* things are so created! If that should be even credible, the tetrahedron as a model of G-O-D leads us toward the theological affirmation that (1) if G-O-D is creator of all things, then (2) they all bear the structural sign of their creator. Moreover, if G-O-D be modeled as event by a tetrahedron, then the fundamental theological affirmation that we *are* because of the continual creative *action* of G-O-D implies that only an event-model is appropriate and, if all things bear some sign of their creator, then that sign should also be an event-model. For instance, the wild, awesome dynamism of particle physics may be, in its sheer dynamic eventfulness, a remarkable sign of its creator's nature as continuing event. Certainly the idea that *whatever* one finds in the subatomic realm is not "outside" creation is a theological affirmation that seems to be a clear implication of almost any historic formulation of a Christian doctrine of creation.

But let us remember that a mathematical model does not prove; it only represents. The desire for a proof is our all-too-human need or want or demand. It is our quite normal, seemingly natural question. Yet we have no reason to believe that, at this fundamental level, *our* question will meet with any more success than Moses' query during the burning bush theophany. Still, a model may help us to understand, as far as we can, what is, ultimately, incomprehensible.

II. Some Further Considerations

We were created with binocular vision. One of our basic prejudices is that seeing is believing. If we see a thing, we assume it is, as *we* see it. It has taken us all a fair time to admit that sometimes (1) what we see isn't, or (2) what we see is not all there is to what we can see. In this ninth decade of the twentieth century, we are beginning to acknowledge that reality may be far more complex than our vision suggests. Illusion can simulate reality. In addition, reality is often difficult to discern on "first sight." These are important understandings. But we often tend to confuse them.

We all live in a three-dimensional world. Our binocular vision helps us to understand that world. It helps us to judge distance, and it helps us to take account of those slight variations in height, carriage, or other physical characteristics that identify one of us from another. Moreover, we now know that we learn binocular vision: we see what we have learned to see.[38] If we think about it, we know two paradoxical facts: much of the time our initial prejudice is correct—seeing is believing; yet we must continually expect the unexpected, for seeing does not always show us all there is. We live in a time when those experiential facts are increasingly recognized. It is no wonder that we are sometimes confused.

One of our basic perceptual learnings consists of our ability to locate another object in a purely theoretical plane defined by (1) our present location, (2) an imaginary axis from right to left, and (3) an equally imaginary axis from down to up. That plane itself is geometrically defined by the two imaginary axes. But the distance or the level of that plane, in relation to us, is further defined by our ability to locate ourselves and it.

Now, a tetrahedron model of G-O-D may reasonably be presumed to exist at some other place than that we now occupy. While that is an assumption, if we posit that G-O-D is inevitably other, then it is a necessary assumption. There would seem to be some inevitable conceptual distance between humankind and any model of an active, existent G-O-D. That probably sounds very neutral. It was intended to be so, for I want to explore the perceptuality of our human understanding of G-O-D. In a word, what *do* we see? Even more stringently, what *can* we see and, so seeing, know?

The exploration of that question calls for an extension of the model displayed in figure 1. That extension involves solely our need to introduce humankind into the model. As it stands, the model displayed in figure 1 concerns G-O-D alone: we are not a part of it. But we are a part of the expanded model displayed in figure 2.

The model in figure 2 is either a mirrored image or a doubled tetrahedron. Each may have some usefulness, but I prefer to think of the figure as a doubled tetrahedron which, quite simply, models the perceptual relationship between an epistemic subject (humankind) and G-O-D.[39] For the moment, that will be enough to read into this highly abstract event-model since, in all likelihood, it exists somewhere at the fringes of our cognitive ability.

As it stands, figure 2 suggests that what humankind "sees" of G-O-D is but a part, the "base" turned toward it, or toward which it is oriented. In this figure, by conscious choice, I have modeled a perception of that one-of-four tetrahedral face-planes that contains the hypostatic words *Father*, *Son*, and *Spirit* at its three vertices. Although figure 2 is oriented along an up-down continuum, that is quite arbitrary: the model would say the same whether the presently up-down continuum were rotated 90 degrees to horizontal, or rotated a full 180 degrees so that up is replaced with down and down with up. Earlier it

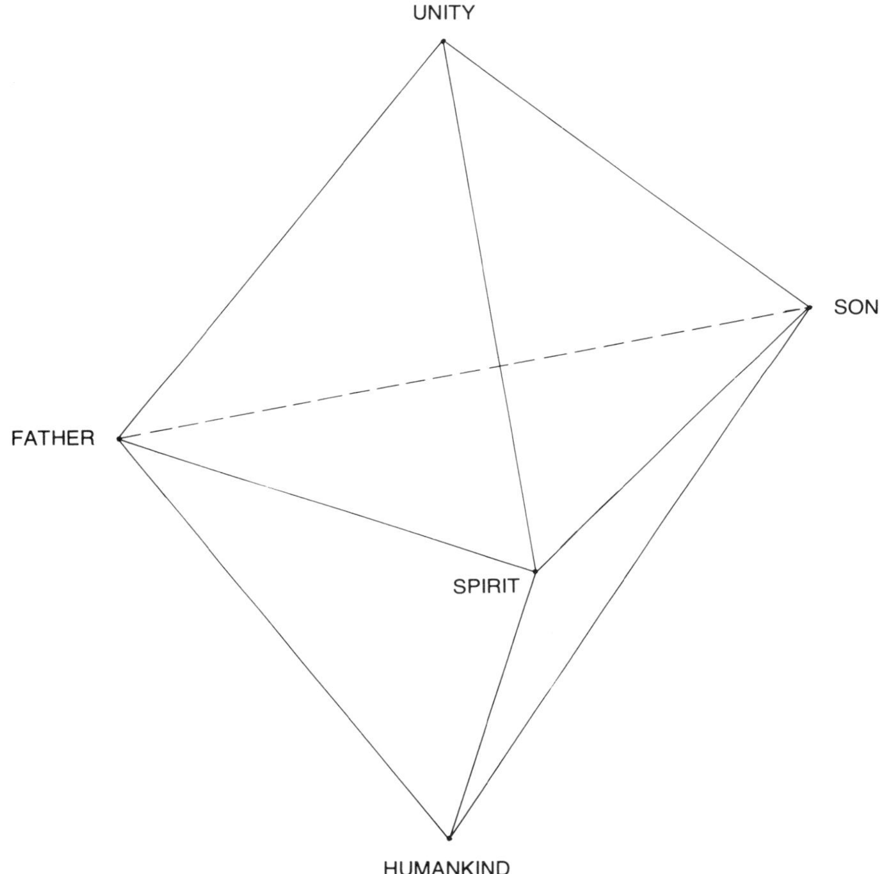

Figure 2. G-O-D and human perception.

was suggested that what humankind has learned of G-O-D through the Judeo-Christian heritage is that God is, and that God is active. The peculiarly Christian contribution was to identify that the event Jesus of Nazareth was an action of that G-O-D, and that there was some continuing human experience of that action which could be termed *Spirit*. What is modeled in figure 2 is a Christian perception of G-O-D, given a tetrahedral model. Somewhat more generally, what is modeled is a *human* perception of G-O-D as active and, through that action, inferentially describable by the three hypostatic words *Father*, *Son*, and *Spirit*. Thus, if we took those three vertices as defining a conceptual plane, this model suggests that (1) the epistemic human subject perceives G-O-D primarily in terms of activity, and (2) that perception is inherently partial. Thus, the thoroughly orthodox affirmation that G-O-D is incomprehensible would seem to be modeled as an inescapable perceptual fact.[40]

Moreover, this model qua model is adaptable to what few of us can ignore: humankind has a diversity of perceptions of G-O-D. That is, the perceived face-plane could be any; one of the four alternatives without denying the fundamental reality of G-O-D. By shifting the face-plane perceived face-plane could be any one of the four alternatives without hypostatic words *Father*, *Son*, and *Spirit* at the vertices to that face plane with hypostatic words *Father*, *Spirit*, and the further word *unity*, we could model another perception of G-O-D. In fact, if we did that, we would achieve a model that seems congruent with a good deal of the "theology" of Judaism.[41]

If we can countenance that possibility, we would also have a model congruent with the practice of some of the earliest European missionaries to the developed cultures in the Indian subcontinent and China. They sought to accept a culture's perception of G-O-D and, then, expand that perception to include the full set of three hypostatic words and all they mean. In some instances, difference of perception may be just that: a difference, *not* the perception of a totally different G-O-D.

Notes and References

1. The reference is to three books: Arnold Gesell and Frances L. Ilg, *Infant and Child in the Culture of Today* (New York: Harper & Brothers, 1943); Arnold Gesell and Frances L. Ilg, *The Child from Five to Ten* (New York: Harper & Brothers, 1946); and Arnold Gesell, *Studies in Child Development* (New York: Harper & Brothers, 1948).

2. It seems quite useful for parental adults to consider their many and multiform experiences as what, here, is called part of their own "continuing Christian religious education." If nothing else, such an idea seems like (a) a reasonable deduction from the thesis that our "religious education" is a

lifelong matter, and (b) an equally reasonable inference from the thesis that nothing in this creation is totally unrelated to the creator.

3. Although it is not specifically directed at the implicit idea that, with age, the "answers" given by adults tend to change from those which children or early adolescents find satisfactory, the report of my analyses of the religious thinking of adults seems to support this idea: John H. Peatling, "Cognitive Development: Religious Thinking in Children, Youth and Adults," *Character Potential: A Record of Research*, vol. 7, no. 2 (August 1977), pp. 100–115, esp. pp. 106–107.

4. My memory of Lewis's point is that he regarded it a fallacy to think too highly or too rigorously of human abilities, since that tended to confuse the human creature with that traditionally nonhuman order of creatures called angels. We are not angels, and it *is* a mistake to permit ourselves to think overly much of ourselves: that is all.

5. In his book *The Life of Greece* (New York: Simon and Schuster, 1939), Will Durant wrote of *hubris* as follows: "throughout Aeschylus and Sophocles the prevailing theme is the nemesis of punishment, by jealous gods or impersonal fate, for insolent presumption and irreverent pride (*hybris*); and the recurring moral is the wisdom of conscience, honor, and a modest moderation (*aidos*)."

The Random House Dictionary of the English Language (New York: Random House, 1967), identifies *hybris* as an alternate spelling of *hubris*, and puts its definition under the spelling I have used in this passage.

6. My phrase "an arrogant excess of self-confidence" is a conflation of the definition found in the *Random House Dictionary*.

7. Clearly I am engaging in the humor of exaggeration here: I do *not* think honesty is retrograde, although it may seem like too simple an answer to some sophisticates.

8. This point is true for mathematicians and scientists, as well as for most of humankind (e.g., the so-called common person).

9. This parental response is a frank and honest answer for parents who may not yet have resolved the question for themselves, but who are willing to share with a child the heritage in which they live.

10. This answer commits parents to an honest acknowledgment of their own belief and, inferentially, puts the full weight of their response upon their own belief. It, too, is a frank and honest reply.

11. Again, this answer commits parents to an honest acknowledgment that their answer is no more than and no less than what they are able to understand. For parents who value understanding, it can be a quite honest reply to a child.

12. This answer is potentially honest and appropriate, if the child is used to such things as grace before meals, prayers at night, and going to church

services at which songs are sung. It is an honest attempt to give a response within the likely range of a young child's experience, without attempting the abstractions which often characterize formulae.

13. This answer could be honest and appropriate for somewhat older but still young children, if they know and can remember their grandparents. Again, it is an example of trying to stay within the range of experience which can be an honest response, as well as a theologically defensible one.

14. Sigmund Freud, *Moses and Monotheism* (New York: Random House, 1939).

15. Gen. 2:3.

16. Unless we recognize an ad hominem argument when we see one, most of us would assent to this rhetorical question. In fact, we would be likely to do so because, at least in part, we are and we do consider ourselves to be a representative sample of homo sapiens.

17. The so-called Johannine Prologue is John 1:1–18.

18. John 1:14.

19. John 1:18.

20. Heb. 1:2.

21. Heb. 1:3.

22. Heb. 4:12–13.

23. J. R. R. Tolkien, "On Fairy-Stories," in *The Tolkien Reader* (New York: Ballantine Books, 1966), pp. 37, 70.

24. 1 John 4:7–12.

25. 1 John 4:12.

26. Gal. 5:13–22; the quotations in this paragraph all come from that passage.

27. Like all attempts at human history, the following section is the result of an interaction between a set of sources which are accepted as having authority, and the mind of a human interpreter who presumedly is searching for truth. The result of such an interaction is always a retelling of some segment of the long, long human story; that is just as true of this section as it is of any other attempt at human history. It is a retelling of a part of that story and, so, is itself a story. This story used the following sources as a set, and they are listed here for the reader's information:

Henry Bettenson, *Documents of the Christian Church* (New York: Oxford University Press, 1943/1947). F. L. Cross, *The Oxford Dictionary of the Christian Church* (London: Oxford University Press, 1957). J. N. D. Kelley, *Early Christian Creeds* (London: Longmans, Green and Co., 1950); idem, *Early Christian Doctrines* (New York: Harper & Brothers, 1958). Walter Lowrie, *Art in the Early Church* (New York: Pantheon Books, 1947). J. Stevenson, A *New Eusebius* (London: S.P.C.K., 1957/1960). F. Van Der Meer and Christine Mohrmann, *Atlas of the Early Christian World* (New York: Thomas Nelson and Sons, 1958).

28. The title page of William Lynwood's *Constitutiones* is reproduced in Arthur De Bles, *How to Distinguish the Saints in Art by Their Costumes, Symbols, and Attributes* (New York: Art Culture Publications, 1925), plate 8, p. 33.

29. While it is inevitably a human hypothesis, it does seem that a reason the attempt to "do" theology in a contemporary idiom so often wanders into one or another ancient heresy is a result of an interaction between (1) an almost imperial sense that some present is simply brighter than any previous past, and (2) an almost enthusiastic desire to deny some past accomplishment, rather than adopt a cautious and conservative agnosticism vis-a-vis those as-yet-unresolved, unstudied paradoxes that often exist when things are looked at from a different standpoint. *Hubris* may come close to the fact.

30. See the entry under *mathematical models* by G. W. Cussons in the *Encyclopaedia Britannica*, 1951.

31. R. Buckminster Fuller, *Synergetics: Explorations in the Geometry of Thinking* (New York: Macmillan Publishing Co., 1975); idem, *Synergetics Two: Explorations in the Geometry of Thinking* (New York: Macmillan Publishing Co., 1979).

32. Fuller, *Synergetics*, paragraph 621.04, p. 335.

33. Ibid., figure 108.01, p. 5.

34. Ibid., figure 511.10, p. 242.

35. Ps. 102:27.

36. Fuller, *Synergetics*, figure 620.06, p. 334.

37. Gen. 1:26.

38. D. O. Hebb, *The Organization of Behavior: A Neuropsychological Theory* (New York: John Wiley & Sons, 1949), esp. pp. 18, 28–35.

39. For the idea of the epistemic subject see Jean Piaget, *Structuralism* (London: Routledge and Kegan Paul, 1971), pp. 68–69.

40. The idea of the incomprehensibility of G-O-D finds expression in the Christian creed known as *Quicunque Vult*, which is sometimes called the Creed of St. Athanasius, where the *hypostases* are termed incomprehensible, while the unity is affirmed by the assertion "there are not three incomprehensibles, nor three uncreateds, but one uncreated, and one incomprehensible."

41. I put the word *theology* within quotation marks because I am aware that contemporary Judaism seems to be hesitant about using that word, not because I have any reason to doubt that Judaism has a theology or does engage in theological reflection.

2

Good God! Action and Response

One of the common experiences of living involves a not-so-simple query and a relatively simple response. The query is: "Why did you *not* do X?" Although we often ask one another why we chose to do something, our real puzzlement often involves why one of us does not do something. Often the response we hear (or give!) is a variation of: "Well, *that* just didn't *look* right to *me*." We learn something about other's perceptions, not their reasons. If we reflect upon that experience, we can appreciate how important perception is to all of our kind. In many ways, perception is a fundamental phenomenon.

TRYING TO GET A FEW THINGS STRAIGHT

If it is correct to affirm that G-O-D is ever active, including a continuing act of creation, and if it is right to assume an inescapable relationship between homo sapiens and G-O-D, then it is important to ask what an involved representative of the genus perceives. Even more precisely, we should wonder what such a representative could possibly perceive.

To ask what a human could possibly perceive of the activity of G-O-D is not (if we are careful) a surrender to the Freudian hypothesis. It need involve no mere projection otherward. It need involve no more than an honest appraisal of our capabilities. We need not be involved in fantasy. Although that possibility is all too real!

The medieval philosophers tended to initiate a speculative argument by identifying some minimal beginning. Their procedure is really not such a bad idea. Thus, let us posit a representative of the genus and ask what such a being can perceive of any action, as near as we know.

If we begin with an infant, we may be close to such a minimal starting point. What can an infant perceive? In part, the answer is simple: "Who knows?" Beyond such a healthy developmental agnosticism, we suspect that the answer is twofold: a lot less than an adult, yet more than we have thought. Certainly since Piaget's observations we have had reason to think that perception initially does not involve a distinction between oneself and all the rest. That distinction is an early and quite fundamental achievement. It is a fundament of our very *human* being. In some way, we learn that there is a real difference between us and all else. Thus, our human tendency to perceive all things as other-than-us is early and fundamental. G-O-D as other is, then, a conclusion that minimally relates to the beginnings of perception.

We do not initially perceive shapes qua shapes; we learn them. However fast that learning, we ignore our experience if we opt for the realist position. We do *not* perceive the thing in itself. Moreover, we begin our existence with a limited interest in motion. While we can note motion early, our interest in it is severally limited. But we do change. We attend to motion more and more. Before long, we discover that we can perceive motion in that undifferentiated "rest" about us, and we can engage in motion ourselves, which is enjoyable! In fact, if the primate studies are applicable, motion may be a fundamental prenatal experience. Yet an infant takes some time before it achieves Piaget's object permanence: that is, out-of-sight may be out-of-mind, but it is not gone for good. The hide-and-seek games infants and tolerant adults play are really an important cycle of learning and discovery. Without such experiences, we might never respond to the G-O-D which acts across centuries, encountering us only now and then in theophanies, yet is continually active on our behalf in ways that call upon us to follow out sequences, and appreciate those complexes we call events.

Ever since Kohler's World War I internment, we have been aware that there is a perceptual phenomenon we can label a *gestalt*. It involves a figure and a ground, and the fundamental contention that a whole may be greater than its parts. A gestalt is a whole perceived pattern that is not explicable by an analysis of the parts. It involves both a perception and a distinction between oneself and that gestalt. With the passage of time that perception develops. At least since the careful studies reported by Piaget in 1961, we have good reason to believe that perception itself undergoes development.

No infant is born with a developed perceptual ability. Neither you nor I nor any other of our species fails to undergo a process of perceptual development. However, what we can now perceive is not limited by that fact. Actually, as "developed" persons we can now perceive as we could not before. New possibilities are open to us, including a perception of an active G-O-D, precisely because we have undergone perceptual development.

G-O-D, HUMANKIND, AND TETRAHEDRONS

A doubled tetrahedron can be used as a model of G-O-D's relationship to humankind. That was the whole point of figure 2 (in chapter 1, p. 27). However, I do not want to focus attention only on the fact that the tetrahedrons are inverted—the one representing humankind is topsy-turvy to the one representing God. Still, if one will play a symbolist's games, it may be a legitimate albeit passing point to note that the upside down-ness of tetrahedrons may model an idea at the heart of all doctrines of original sin: humankind has some persistent problem in understanding G-O-D. Even so, that is a human construction that had best be considered without getting trapped in a dogmatic presumption.

Figure 2 in chapter 1 posited an epistemic subject (humankind) at a vertex of an inverted tetrahedron. It suggested that the subject perceives or, crudely put, looks toward a conceptual plane defined by the hypostatic words *Father*, *Son*, and *Spirit*. If that conceptual plane be the field of G-O-D's action, the model affirms that the epistemic subject can perceive it. But that is all the model qua model suggests. It does not suggest that humankind does normally or always or even often perceive that which it can. (While it is sheer speculation, the early Christian idea that the Word became flesh so that flesh might become divine might be parallel to that distinction between a possibility and a probability.) Thus, let us clearly appreciate the model-ness of figure 2's doubled tetrahedron in chapter 1 and, so, not ask more of a model than it can bear. Still, let us ask what it can bear and, so, learn whatever we can.

Systems analysis has found it almost impossible to do its business without talking about interfaces. My dictionary reminds me that an interface is: (a) a surface regarded as the common boundary of two bodies or spaces, or (b) the facts, problems, consideration, theories, practices, etc. shared by two or more disciplines, procedures, or fields of study. Acquaintance with the presumed science of management leads me to suspect that interfaces are what managers deal with all the time—what they search out, for quite pragmatic reasons. Whether one is trying to approximate a classical PERT (program review and evaluation technique) or work a CPM (critical path method), the interface is both inescapable and important. It is where one thing depends upon another. It is a fundamental event within a total complexity which goes awry if the interface isn't or doesn't work. In a sense, an interface is a necessary, important transition which, in another sense, has little importance except as it facilitates the totality.

I want to appropriate that understanding of an interface. I would like to use it to describe the doubled tetrahedron of figure 2 in chapter 1. Thus, what I want to do is diagramed in this chapter's figure 1, which is merely figure 2 in chapter 1 conceptually separated for purposes of analysis by a space identified as an *interface*. What I want to posit is that it is useful to temporarily conceive of the conceptual plane defined by the hypostatic words *Father*, *Son*, and *Spirit* as a thing with one referent solely G-O-D-ward and another referent solely humankind-ward. What this analytical bifurcation does is to identify that the tetrahedron's hypostatic vertices may be considered from two directions: G-O-D's and humankind's. Therefore, one can address the question of *our* perception of the hypostatic words. In figure 1 in this chapter, the human perceptions are identified as a capital letter with a prime: for example, F = the hypostatic word *Father*; F′ = the epistemic subject's perception of the hypostatic word *Father*.

Unless we are enmeshed in a common-sense realism, we should be able to acknowledge that any F′ is some approximation of F. It is not a complete, full-bodied F. Moreover, since the work of B. F. Skinner and his colleagues, we know that a considerable range of human

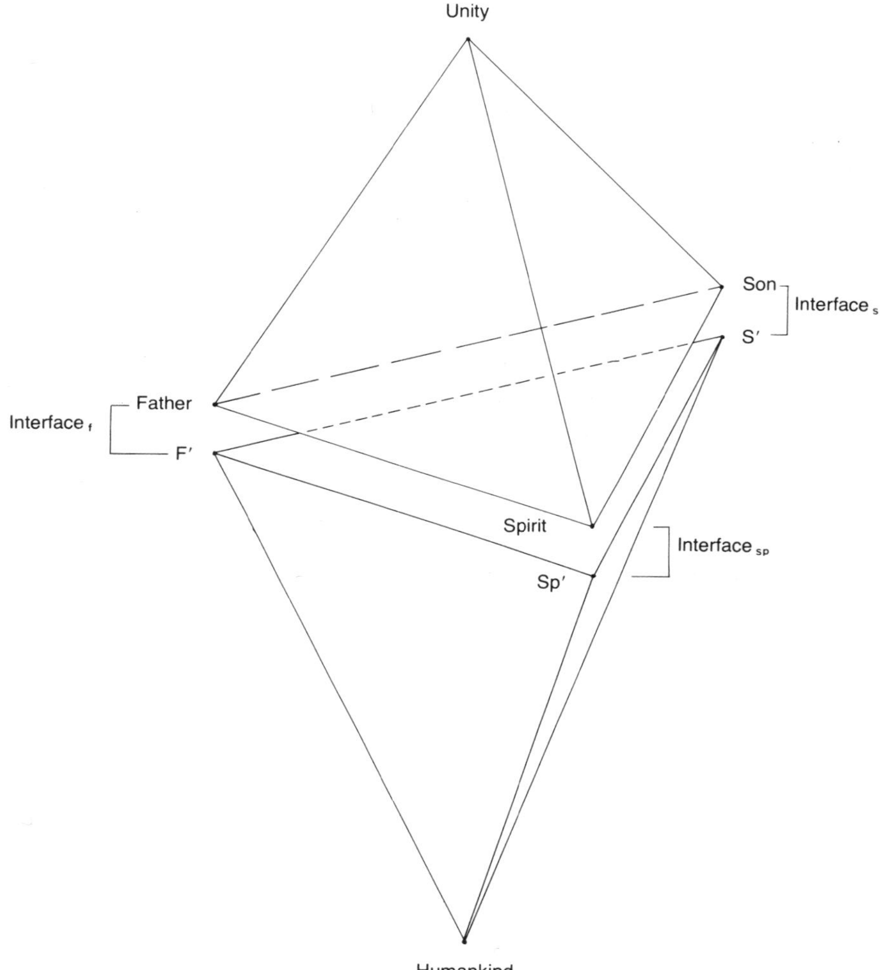

Figure 1. The G-O-D/humankind interface: a conceptualization.

capabilities consist of processes of successive approximation. Thus, to posit F′ as an approximation of F (or S′ as an approximation of S, or Sp′ of Sp) is not to deny truthfulness or reality to the primes. But it is to allow for the possibility of a still fuller insight into the F or the S or the Sp. It is to take our time-boundedness seriously and, thus, to acknowledge that G-O-D is not delimited by our present perception.

That is what orthodox theologians have sought to affirm by maintaining the ultimate incomprehensibility of G-O-D. Probably that is also what the mystics have meant by the Cloud of Unknowing or repeated reference to the ineffability of G-O-D encountered. We do them little honor, and our own rationality even less, when we fail to admit that if they are talking about what they seem to be talking about, human language runs out before one has said much of anything! That is both logical and scientific. In some ways, it is fundamentally scientific: it is an example of the problem that afflicts all attempts to communicate knowledge other than the everyday stuff.

Formally, the same problem exists for anyone who wants to talk about the wildly improbable "world" of subatomic particles, which can be said to be characterized by such things as spin, color, valence, or strangeness, and also have "anti-" doubles. We should be far enough into this century to be able to countenance such a possibility. Thus, we should be able to use our minds to probe what it could possibly mean for humankind to perceive the action of G-O-D.

The plane defined by the hypostatic words *Father*, *Son*, and *Spirit* has been said to be a plane of activity. It is humankind's perception of G-O-D as event. What is it, then, that one can imagine humankind perceiving? That question clearly recognizes a perceptual limitation upon the epistemic subject. But let us ask, even if we are so limited.

Mathematically, a plane can be "filled" with an infinite number of points. The spatial dimension of the diagram is no conceptual limitation. Moreover, suppose that G-O-D acts, and that such an act is describable as a point within that trihypostatically defined plane. The interface. The question of possibility is, then, a question of the match between (a) point-as-action-of-G-O-D and (b) point-as-perceived-by-humankind. In this chapter, figures 2 and 3 isolate the G-O-D tetrahedron and the humankind tetrahedron, albeit both exist within the model posited by figure 2 in chapter 1 and figure 1 in this chapter.

The model of G-O-D as a tetrahedron (i.e., figure 1 in chapter 1) is expanded in figure 2 in this chapter to identify an action-point, A. In addition, a broken line from the vertex labeled *unity* to that point A has been labeled a *theoretical perceptual pathway*. If it is credible that G-O-D is perfect, we might admit that the theoretical perceptual pathway to action-point A is accurate. G-O-D accurately perceives

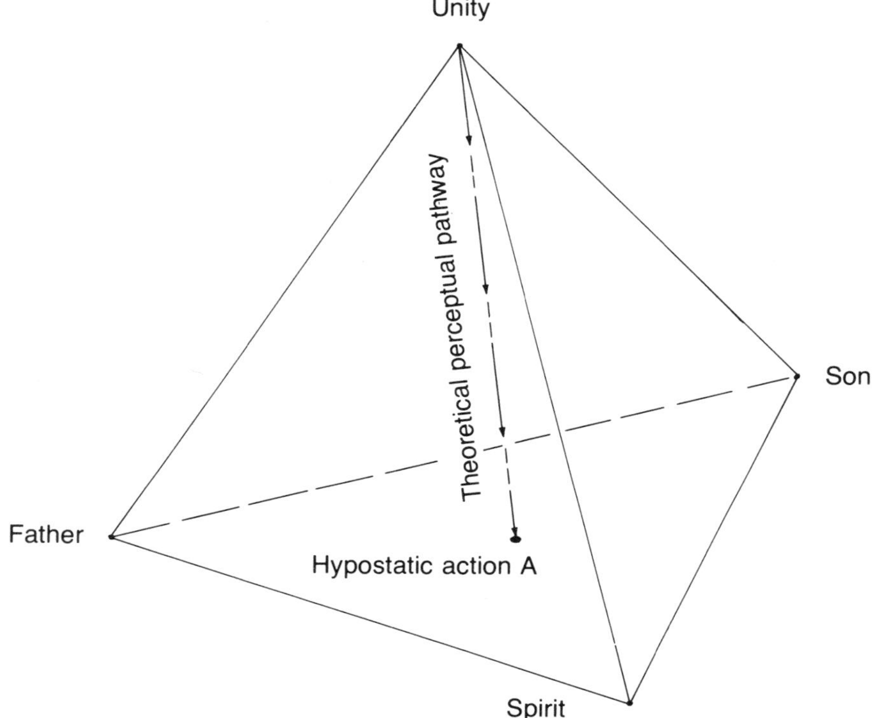

Figure 2. A tetrahedral model of an action of G-O-D as a conceptual point.

action-point A. The question of maximum concern to humans, however, is not G-O-D's perception of action-point A but the possibility of humankind's perception of action-point A.

In figure 3, the inverted tetrahedron modeling humankind's perception of G-O-D is expanded so as to match the action posited in figure 2 in this chapter. However, the action-point has been labeled A′, and a theoretical perceptual pathway has been drawn from the epistemic subject to A′. This model enables us to ask two fundamental questions: (a) Does A′ = A? and (b) Is it credible that humankind's theoretical perceptual pathway to A′ is equivalent to the theoretical pathway from unity to A?

Piety aside, the likelihood of strict equivalence is not too high, given only what we know about perception. We are dealing with a simple

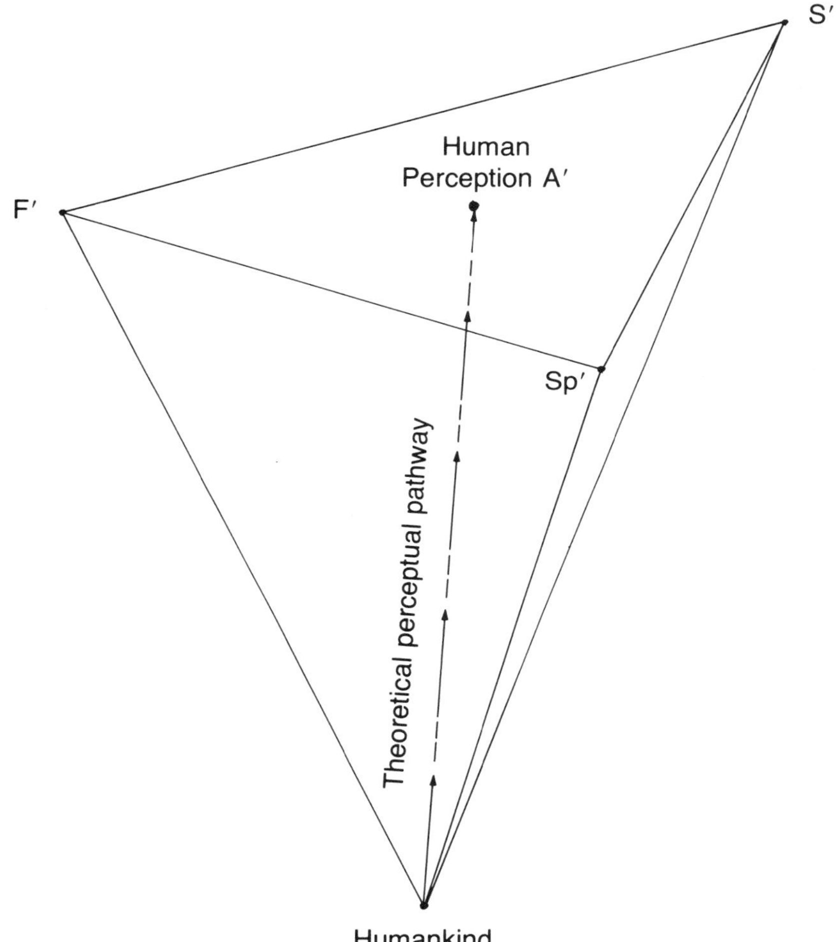

Figure 3. A tetrahedral model of an action of G-O-D as a conceptual point, as perceived by humankind as an epistemic subject capable of perceiving such an action as a conceptual point.

perceptual problem of point recognition. We have not yet encountered a complex pattern, let alone a pattern in motion. Nor have we asked what the perceptual figure is, and what the ground is. But what we have encountered has been enough to give us pause. If we think about that, it probably will be good for us.

In fact, the question of point recognition is twofold. First, do we perceive the point? Second, do we perceive the point accurately? The first of these two queries concerns our ability to perceive a point at all. Far too often we ignore our experience by opting for a satisfying objectivity which suggests that if it is perceivable, it is perceived. A few moments' consideration of that thesis and one's share of human experience should convince almost anyone that what is perceivable is not always perceived. Our attention may be somewhere else. Or following our wont, we blink, sneeze, or close our eyes and, so, miss something. The too-simple suggestion of a kind of objective perceptual inevitability is not to be taken seriously.

Let us be very clear about this matter. It is possible for a conceptual point A to *be*, and for us not to perceive it. If we can countenance that fact, we may recognize that there is no simple answer to the first query. In fact, the real question is not what can be perceived, but the likelihood of actually perceiving. That puts things into a normal context. While we can, we do not always. Thought and experience make that distinction obvious. In fact, we can even estimate a probability for *can*, and for *not always*.

But there is also that second query: If perceived, is the perception accurate? Within the context, that is not merely a question whether we perceive a "something" anywhere in the posited trihypostatic field. The question is much more direct than that. Do we perceive an action-point A within that field accurately? That is, can we "locate" A both within the field and in relation to ourselves? Within the model posited by figure 2 in chapter 1 and by figure 1 in this chapter, and explicated in this chapter in figures 2 and 3, that query concerns the strict equivalence of A and A′.

If we have any reason to even suspect that $A \neq A'$, we have a conceptual problem. In a word, if there is anything in our common human capability that might distort our perception of A as A′, we have a problem of simple perceptual geometrics. One implication of such a problem has been grossly diagramed in figure 4.

In figure 4, one unwarranted assumption by the epistemic subject has been built in. That presumption is that the trihypostatic plane is really at 90 degrees to the epistemic subject's theoretical perceptual pathway to A′. While that is (or may be!) true of action-point A, if A′ is

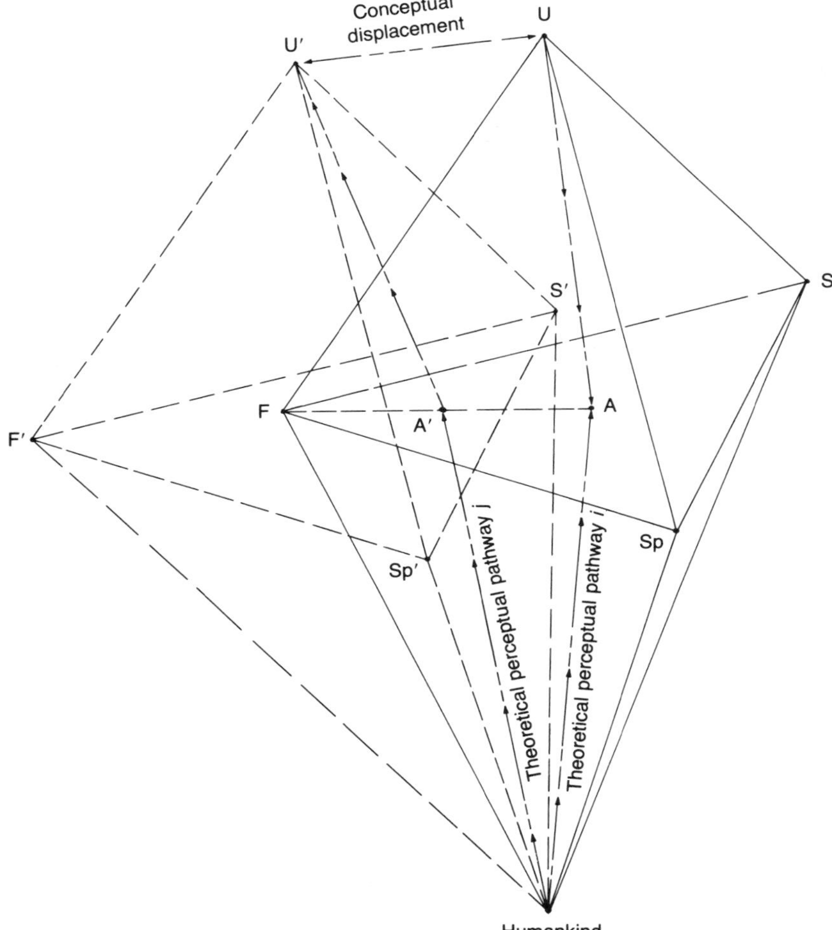

Figure 4. Possible perceptual displacement of a tetrahedral model of G-O-D and humankind in relationship, because of humankind's mistaken view of the action of G-O-D and the interface.

displaced in any way, then we have the situation modeled in figure 4. When A ≠ A′, there is some conceptual "distance" between the two points A and A′. But if humankind presumes that there is not such distance, then the epistemic subject perceives the trihypostatic plane defined by F-S-Sp as a plane defined, instead, by F′-S′-Sp′. As figure 4 indicates, those three are clearly displaced. Of course, it is obvious that no one has a set of units by which to "measure" such a conceptual displacement; but the possibility diagramed can be recognized as both possible and reasonably probable.

One can at least learn from figure 4 to wonder about the likelihood that a nonequivalent perception of A as A′ involves a conceptual displacement of the perceived trihypostatic plane. Thus, the inaccurate perception of *an* action-point (A), coupled with a false assumption, tends toward a misperception of both the plane and the hypostatic words. In terms of figure 4, when A ≠ A′, then F ≠ F′, S ≠ S′, and Sp ≠ Sp′. Moreover, it is our presumption that causes the conceptual displacement and, so, suggests to us that A = A′ when, in fact, they are not strict equivalents. Whether we like it or not, we can conclude that this is normal; but, if we do so, let us remember that the conclusion *is* ours. Let us not blame G-O-D for our exercise of our freedom to choose.

The geometry of figure 4 suggests yet one more idea. Given the initial conceptual displacement of A-to-A′, the displacements of F′, S′, Sp′, and U′ are equal. However, these conceptual displacements are greater than is the displacement A-to-A′. This intriguing geometric fact is not merely an artifact of the model. It seems isomorphic with some of our experiences of reality. For instance, who doesn't recognize that when one begins with a faulty assumption one tends, until that assumption itself is corrected, to move more and more into improbability, unreality, or sheer fantasy? The different conceptual displacements U-U′ and A-A′ in figure 4 may, thus, be quite close to an all-too-common and all-too-human experience.

If that isomorphism be so, then a major part of the problem with an inability to perceive A = A′ is what happens to one's perception of a tetrahedrally modeled G-O-D. U-U′, F-F′, S-S′, and Sp-Sp′ all tend to involve a greater conceptual displacement than is involved in the initial inaccuracy vis-a-vis A-A′. Attempting to work with that thought brings us close to acknowledging an endemic perceptual problem of the epistemic subject vis-a-vis G-O-D. We are also close to acknowledging a fundamental distinction between the epistemic subject and the trihypostatic field as the perceptual object. Without separating those two into mutually inaccessible categories, we are distinguishing them and, clearly, acknowledging a perceptual problem.

Early infant learning may help us to appreciate the distinction as a highly likely part of perceptual development. The real difference, here, is that the distinction has been applied to the epistemic subject's *possible* perception of an action of G-O-D. Naturally, somewhere on beyond our recognition of the problem, there may exist a possibility of a perceptual correction. If so, we might be able to take account of the conceptual displacement A-A′ and so, somehow, lessen the displacement of U-U′. However, any such a correction is bound to require considerable effort. Enough so that, without a clear recognition of the need for the effort, the expenditure is highly improbable. Unfortunately, homo sapiens has no unlearned corrective ability. What homo sapiens does have, most certainly, is an ability to learn a number of complex and difficult tasks. Thus, correction cannot be ruled out as a possibility, even if it cannot presently be affirmed as a normal thing.

The argument may be a bit clumsy, but the problem is sufficiently important to identify it. Let's review. I began with a geometric model. Then I used the possibilities of that model to explicate the problem. It all was quite abstract. In fact, it may not have been everyone's cup of tea. Therefore, I would like to try an entirely different approach to the perceptual problem of what humankind can possibly perceive (or, at least, can expect to perceive) of the action of G-O-D.

A PERCEPTUAL GAME: THE SAME OR DIFFERENT?

One of the findings of perceptual studies is that seeing can fool us. In order to explore that idea without resorting to the wild world of visual puzzles, I have constructed a multi-part target out of nine equilateral triangles. Suppose that each triangle is a conceptual plane defined by the trihypostatic words *Father*, *Son*, and *Spirit*. Moreover, suppose that an action-point exists within each such conceptual plane. Then pose the problem: are all nine action-points the same? or are some (or all of them) different? The nine triangles can be taken to be analogues of nine periodic perceptions. Thus, the answer is an analogue to the question whether G-O-D's action (as it is modeled by a point) is the same across the sample; or is it shifting, changing, creating a pattern?

In order to lessen my natural biases due to handedness, I made use of a table of random numbers. First, I used that collection of randomly ordered numerals to give me a sequence in which to consider the nine triangles for whatever I was going to do next. My copy of Fisher and Yates's *Statistical Tables* gave me a number of ways to enter into a random ordering, and I arbitrarily chose one. I started to read down a column and record the order of the numbers 1 through 9, as they appeared after my entry into the table. Naturally, I avoided (by skipping) duplicates, for I wanted to secure a random order of the numbers from 1 through 9. As a result, I secured the random order 7, 4, 8, 3, 1, 2, 5, 6, 9.

I had already drawn the nine equilateral triangles to be found in figure 5, below, and I had assigned them numbers from left to right across the three rows. What I did with my random order was to decide to let that be a fundamental order of choices vis-a-vis the one-of-three hypostatic word-symbols to be assigned to the vertex opposite the base (the horizontal edge) of each of the nine triangles. I now had a random ordering of choices (in the abstract!); but I had not yet made my choices. To help myself avoid built-in sequential preferences, I went once again to the table of random numbers.

My second use of a table of random numbers involved going to another one of the six pages of such number orders in Fisher and Yates. I picked another arbitrary entry point and started, from that point, to read across a row. This time I was working only with the numbers 1, 2, and 3, to which I had assigned the hypostatic words *Father* (1), *Son* (2), and *Spirit* (3). I wanted a threefold series of 1s, 2s, and 3s. What I got out of this use of the table was the random order 3, 1, 2, 1, 3, 3, 2, 1, 2.

Now I was ready to put my two sequences together. The first one involved triangles in figure 5. The second one involved a choice of one of the three hypostatic words to occupy the vertex opposite the base of a numbered triangle in figure 5. Being systematic, I actually put the two sequences into parallel. My parallel ordering looked very much like the following:

7 4 8 3 1 2 5 6 9	*Triangles*
3 1 2 1 3 3 2 1 2	*Vertex symbols*

When I had this parallel sequence in hand, I had a set of random choices for the placement of hypostatic words at the vertices opposite the base of each of the nine triangles in figure 5. The result was the figure 5 you can see below.

I got to the trouble of explaining almost ad nauseam a simple set of nine equilateral triangles for only one reason. I want a reader to recognize that I tried to keep the "merely me" out of the fundamental describing of what can be taken to be nine analogues of trihypostatically defined conceptual planes. I can share this much with you. But if the set of triangles in figure 5 is to be useful to you, I cannot share with you how the nine action-points were located. In fact, the usefulness of all this recourse to tables of random numbers in order to locate action-points within each of nine triangles centers upon just one problem: Are the triangles in figure 5 the same or different?

Before you start puzzling over that problem, I should explain why I went to all the trouble to "mix up" the order of vertex assignments. I presume that the epistemic subject (humankind) has rotational capabilities. Therefore, at one or another moment of perception, that epistemic subject may be differently oriented toward the trihypostatically defined plane of interface. That is, the conceptual placement of the three hypostatic words will vary from perception to perception, at least in terms of the epistemic subject's natural bilateralness—our tendency to presume that something is either on our right or on our left or, possibly, right in front of us. Such a varying orientation toward the conceptual plane defined by the hypostatic words is a reasonable model of (a) an individual's tendency to be more aware of Father-hood or Son-hood or Spirit-hood at any one moment, and (b) a varying tendency of the epistemic subject (humankind) across its recorded history to be religiously more aware of deity's Father-hood, Son-hood, or

Spirit-hood in any one era. Thus, while the problem posed in figure 5 is admittedly complex, it is a credible modeling of much of the religious history of humankind. So, have at the problem. Are the triangles in figure 5 the same or different, as far as you can tell???

Take your time.

Think about it.

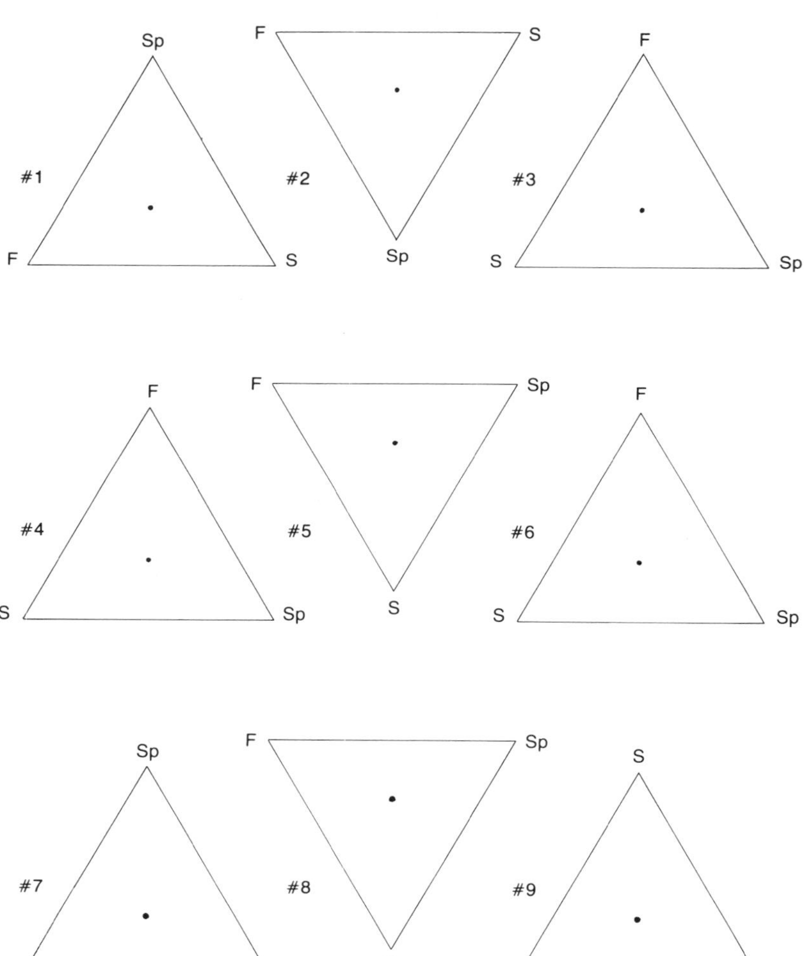

Figure 5. Nine perceptual problems related to an epistemic subject's "view" of a trihypostatically defined plane that may be the field of action for a tetrahedrally modeled G-O-D.

Hopefully, you have thought about the problem posed in figure 5. If you have, you have already considered those nine triangles and come to your own conclusion (whatever it may be). Are they the same? Or are they different? That was the problem posed for you. That is the problem *you* have resolved. Therefore, you are now ready for figure 6. Look at it now.

Figure 6 repeats the statement of the problem, just to keep you on

PROBLEM: How many (if any) of the nine triangles in figure 5 are alike?

Step #1: Circle the answer that seems to you to be correct on the continuum below. If none are alike, circle *None*. If 5 are alike, circle 5.

Step #2: Use the half-matrix to help you do a systematic paired comparison of the nine triangles. If a pairing is IDENTICAL, put an *I* in the column-row intersection representing that particular pairing. If you CAN'T DECIDE, put a *C* there. If they are DIFFERENT, put a *D* there.

Step #1

None	*2*	*3*	*4*	*5*	*6*	*7*	*8*	*All*

Step #2

	1	2	3	4	5	6	7	8	9
1									
2									
3									
4									
5									
6									
7									
8									
9									

CONVENTIONS:

I = Identical

C = Can't decide

D = Different

Number of *I*s = ________
Number of *C*s = ________
Number of *D*s = ________

Figure 6. A perceptual problem and two steps toward a personal resolution.

that problem. But it does more: it also suggests a two-step procedure. First, record your initial resolution of the problem. To do that simply circle your initial conclusion along the topmost continuum. Second, as a way of checking your initial resolution, figure 6 offers you one-half of a balanced nine-by-nine matrix, so that you can do a straightforward paired comparison of all of the logically possible combinations of two triangles. The directions suggest that you write an *I* in a column-row intersection if you think the two triangles are identical. On the other hand, they suggest that you simply bifurcate your decisions of "nonidenticality" and (a) write a C if you just can't decide, or (b) write a *D* if you conclude that a pair of triangles is somehow different. If you are up to this sort of thoroughness, you have exactly 36 such paired comparisons to make. No fewer, but no more, either. Moreover, when you have done that, you know that your decisions of either identity or difference were made as systematically and as completely as possible. Naturally, those decisions *are* yours.

Finally, when you have made all 36 paired comparisons, enter the total number of Is, Cs, and Ds in the spaces provided in the bottom right-hand corner of figure 6. The number of Is, Cs, and Ds should equal exactly 36. If they do not, recheck the count. There simply is no way that you could have entered only an I or a C, or a D into each column-row intersection in that half-matrix and have more than 36 as a total sum. If you should have either more or less than 36, you have miscounted or you have made a double entry. Check your count to be certain the sum is exactly 36.

Now you are ready for figure 7.

At the top of figure 7 there are two continua. The topmost is an equal-interval continuum that runs from 0 through 9. If you have done the 36 paired comparisons in figure 6, then circle the number of Is you found. Also check the number of "alikes" you previously had circled on the continuum at the top of figure 6. Very probably they are much the same, although they may be different. That really barely matters.

What you should now consider is the second continuum at the top of figure 7. It exactly matches the first one. However, it is marked off in what statisticians call *sigma units* (units of one standard deviation of

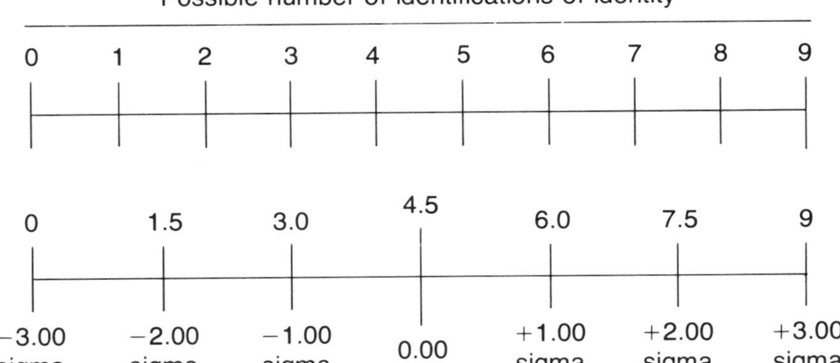

Possible number of identifications of identity of nine figures, under the theoretical assumption of randomness or "sheer chance" choice					
Number:	Sigma Units:	Probability:	Mean:	Sigma Units:	Probability:
0.00	−3.00	0.0013499	0.50	−2.66	c. 0.0034670
1.00	−2.33	0.0099031	1.50	−2.00	0.0227501
2.00	−1.66	0.0484572	2.50	−1.33	0.0885080
3.00	−1.00	0.1586553	3.50	−0.66	0.2546269
4.00	−0.33	0.3707000	4.50	0.00	0.5000000
5.00	+0.33	0.3707000	5.50	+0.66	0.2546269
6.00	+1.00	0.1586553	6.50	+1.33	0.0885080
7.00	+1.66	0.0484572	7.50	+2.00	0.0227501
8.00	+2.33	0.0099031	8.50	+2.66	c. 0.0034670
9.00	+3.00	0.0013499			

Figure 7. Theoretical probabilities under randomness of identifying various numbers of figures as identical, given nine such figures.

the mean). Sigma units and the mean about which they cluster are based (in this instance) on one simple and not-too-uncommon fact: our choices will tend to reflect what we call *chance*. Ever since Galton's studies in the nineteenth century, we have known that a surprising number of things we do and a fair number of our characteristics are distributed in something very like a random distribution. Through what statisticians call the ***binomial distribution***, it is possible to determine the probability (under chance) of identifying any specific number of some finite set of triangles as identical. It is those probabilities that are displayed at the bottom of figure 7.

Locate your number of identities (the number of Is from figure 6) in the left-hand margin. Read across that row. The figure you encounter in the second column is the theoretical number of sigma units your number is from the mean identifiable by assuming many chance choices. If the sigma unit bears a negative sign, your choice was somewhat less than the assumption would forecast. If the sigma unit bears a positive sign, your choice was somewhat more than simple chance would forecast. Clearly, the further away from the chance mean (0.00 sigma units) your choice lies, the easier it is to presume that you made an intentional choice. However, one must be quite careful. A personal choice of either 4 or of 5 was exactly that: it was an intentional choice for the chooser. If it turns out to be forecastable under the assumption of randomness that does not mean, in the actual instance, that it was due to chance. But it does mean inescapably that such a personal choice cannot objectively be distinguished from the chance forecast.

That may be hard to take, but it can be healthy. A large number of choices tend to be indistinguishable from the theoretical operation of simple chance. However, if you thought that only 4 or 5 of the triangles were identical, your experience of choice should help you to understand how important it is to quite clearly distinguish between a theoretical distribution and that personal set of choices that led to your specific choice of a number of identicalities.

On the other hand, your number may be somewhere else on the continuum of possible choices. The figure in the third column is the theoretical probability of making the choice you did make, under the assumption of randomness. For example, under randomness, it is equally improbable to identify either that 2 of the 9 triangles are identical or that 7 of the 9 triangles are identical. If your number of identicalities is close to either 2 or 7, there is a clear reason to presume real intention, a thought-out choice. If you decided, on the other hand, either that none of the triangles or that all 9 of the triangles were identical, look at the probability in the third column for those choices! Under the assumption of randomness, the probability of choosing either 0 or 9 is just over 1 in 1,000. That is an improbable random occurrence. But it is a possible nonrandom, intentional choice. (If that was your choice, you know that to be so for an experiential fact!)

If you have worked your way through figure 6 or, for that matter, however you resolved the problem posed in figure 5, you have immediate experience of both choice and perception. You know the factors that you worked into your choice. Maybe it was experience. Or possibly it was your knowledge of geometry. Or conceivably you had encountered the problem before. Or maybe you have a tendency to look for the "big picture" and ignore the details. In a way, *your* factors are of primary importance to *you*. Just acknowledge them as yours.

I would like now to share with you an item of heretofore unshared information about figure 5. I did do everything I have told you I did. I did use the tables of random numbers in order to avoid simple, personal bias. But I also came to a point in the construction of figure 5 where *I* had to *decide* where to locate the nine action-points. At that moment of choice, I was arbitrary. I did what I wished to do. And what *I* wished to do was to make *all* of the triangles *equal*. They are. The action-point within each of the triangles in figure 5 is equidistant from each of three vertices. Each action-point is in the geometric center of its triangle.

If you guessed that was so, congratulations. If you worked through the paired comparisons of figure 6 and decided it had to be true, you were right. But if you decided that some of the triangles were different, do not feel that you have merely been had. It was no cheap trick. Our perception can and does fool us: perhaps you know that now. Moreover, you are not alone. Some very smart people have looked at those nine triangles and concluded that they were not all alike. A conclusion that some of those triangles are different is not uncommon. Even if it happens that they are all alike.

ACTION AND RESPONSE: A HUMAN PARADIGM

So perceptions are not always accurate. Figure 5's nine-triangle target may have been an immediate experience of that possibility. However, every figure used thus far has presumed that some perception was possible. The doubled tetrahedrons in figure 2 in chapter 1 and in figure 1 in this chapter modeled perception in an abstract, simple, albeit fundamental fashion. In real life our problem is the relative infrequency of such seemingly simple point perceptions.

In real life, action is a complex sequence of diverse stimuli to which, when integrated and interpreted, we respond, usually with an equally complex sequence of diverse stimuli. Consider two humans, A and B. Presume that A acts and that B responds. To keep the interchange simple, let us specify that A's action consists of three relatively common components: a sound, a motion, and a following facial expression. Let the sound be a simple word: "Hello." Let the motion be an extension of the arm, slightly bent at the elbow, with the hand opened—the whole extending toward B at approximately A's waist-level. Let the following facial expression be a certain contraction of the muscles on both sides of A's face: a smile. These three things are a compound action in reasonably normal terms. They constitute for B a set of diverse stimuli.

What can B perceive of that set?

Let's be sure we keep this example simple. There is adequate light: A and B can see one another easily. There is no crowd. B is not distracted by some tragedy, nor lost in thought about something impending. There is no evident difference in the way A and B are dressed. To an observer, it would look like a causal encounter. The question is still a good one: what *can* B perceive of that set of diverse stimuli?

Because B is human and, so, has binocular vision, B perceives A as a three-dimensional figure. B has a relatively accurate perception of the direction of motion and the degree to which A's arm and hand are extended toward B. Moreover, because of binaurality, the sounds constituting "Hello" are heard as, in fact, coming from A. Vision also makes B aware of A's facial expression. All of that is quite objective. But B is more than a passive receiver of stimuli. Certainly, B receives stimuli via the eyes and the ears. But B then proceeds to process those stimuli into information. B's response to a diverse sequence of stimuli emitted by A depends (as near as we know) upon stimuli processed into information. However, B's processing of stimuli into information is what we call covert behavior, or cognitive construction.

Consider what B does to a set of diverse stimuli to make it into the *information* that A has said hello and wants to shake hands: in other words, offers a friendly greeting. First, and most fundamental, B must integrate the set of three stimuli into a connected sequence. B must recognize that they *are* a series of related acts which belong together. In a word, that they are a gestalt. Second, B must hear both a pattern of sound waves and a coherent verbal symbol (i.e., the word "Hello") that is within the range of B's ability to interpret such symbols. In other words, B must accurately hear the word and identify it as part of some set of verbal greetings. That is, B must interpret "Hello" as a greeting. Third, B must recognize the compound motion of A's arm as some common pattern which, in all likelihood, is comparable to patterns B has previously encountered. Then B must conclude that the pattern offered by A belongs, in fact, to that general set of patterns. In other words, B must compare A's arm motion to B's experience and conclude that it really belongs to a set of experiences called shaking hands. Fourth, B must also integrate the visual stimuli provided by A's muscle contractions in the face. This process is possibly quite complex, since both B and A have fine control over the facial muscles (barring accidents of birth or living!). Thus, B must decide the degree of similarity between A's smile and B's set of experiences. B has to determine if A *is* smiling and, if so, whether it is only a faint smile or just a friendly smile or really a warm and hearty smile or, perhaps, is actually something similar but different, a leer. That is, B must decide both whether A is smiling and, if so, what kind of a smile it is.

That's a lot going on. But there is much more, even in this simple interchange between A and B. Fifth, B very probably also engages in a highly complex integration of aural and visual stimuli in order to determine whether A is a stranger, an acquaintance, or a well-known friend. In a word, B determines whether A is to be recognized or not. That process almost certainly involves a series of complex pattern recognition tasks, whereby B compares and contrasts an overall set of visual and aural stimuli (what A looks and sounds like) with some finite series of visual-aural patterns that represent B's friends and acquaintances. If there is a sufficient match between such overall patterns, B probably will determine that A is known. If there isn't a match, B probably will regard A as a stranger. As most of us know quite well, that is a fundamental distinction for B or for any human being. Sixth, B most likely now integrates the prior information with the recognition of A as friend, acquaintance, or stranger. Seventh, B now has a particular bit of information: for example, A is an occasional acquaintance saying "Hello" and offering a handshake as friendly greeting. That is the stimuli transformed into information. But now that information must be processed still further before B makes what we call a *response*.

In all likelihood B has some rules of response that experience or thought have composed. Those rules may be very simple and quite general in their application, or they may be highly structured and complex enough to permit B to make a number of relatively fine distinctions. In the abstract, those rules of response are often called values. Generally, across time, their behavioral expression tend to be called aspects of one's character. That is, B's values and character now impinge upon the processing of B's information about A. Eighth, B probably searches the available rules of response for one that covers the situation posed by A. One way or another, unless B is simply immobilized or autistic, B decides that a particular rule of response seems to cover the situation. Given that decision, B now knows what to do in the situation presented by A's action. Thus, ninth and finally, B responds to A with some set of diverse actions which, in turn, become stimuli for A.

For example, B has among the rules of response that are available one that specifies that occasional acquaintances will be treated like friends. Attached to that "value" B finds a pattern that involves: (a) reflecting the verbal greeting received, with the added word *yourself!*

(b) grasping an offered hand and shaking it vigorously, plus (c) a warm and friendly facial expression somewhere between a grin and a smile. In a word, B's values are so expressed that, across time, B's character is likely to be called *friendly*.

This all-too-simple human interchange has been analyzed in such detail for only one reason. We often talk as if an action-response cycle were something inherently simple and unitary. It isn't. But it is common. The sheer simplicity of the example of A offering to shake hands with B makes that point. In fact, what we often tend to imagine is diagramed in figure 8.

Because the interchange is so familiar, so common, we presume it to be simple. As we have seen, the analogue of information processing helps to free us from that unwarranted assumption. At some quite "high" level of abstraction, this model may be true, but in the actual fact of an A-B interchange, it masks what is going on from us. Moreover, it has taken all of us a long time to recognize that simplicity is not a necessarily legitimate inference from "fast." Our observation certainly tells us that the time between A's action and B's response is normally very little. What we are only now coming to recognize is that we humans can do a remarkable number of things internally very, very fast. This recognition is almost certainly a product of what we tend to

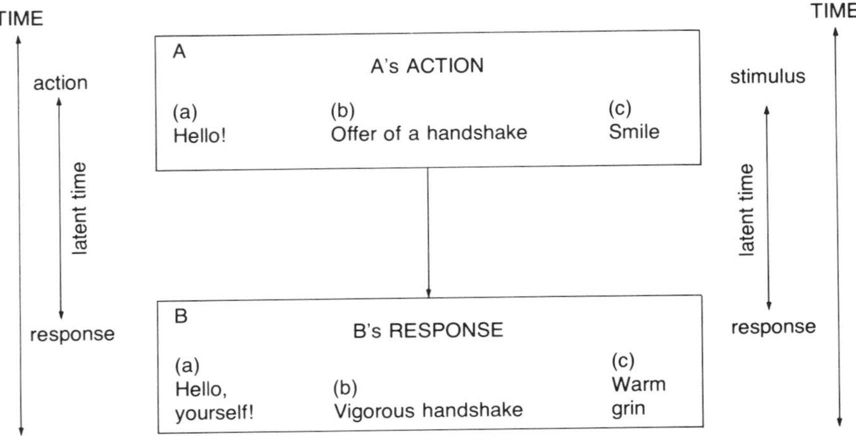

Figure 8. A simple model of an A-B interchange as commonly presumed.

call the computer age and, so, has been available for not much longer than thirty years. But we should not perpetuate what is no more than a now-discarded psychological model (the old stimulus-response model of the early investigators).

When A encounters B and offers a friendly greeting, we have seen that a number of quite complex things probably take place. The interchange involves, of course, a complex whole that consists of both some objective stimuli and a number of subjective decisions which, in turn, involve multiple comparisons, contrasts, matchings, and recognitions. It all occurs very fast. In fact, it probably occurs at a preconscious or semiconscious level. But what we have seen as a nine-step process is simply diagramed in figure 9.

Let us be clear: figure 9 describes covert behaviors intervening between A's action and B's response. The behaviors are all internal to B. But no one can literally observe those processes; one cannot open up another's head for such a purpose. Yet the necessity for such intervening variables has been recognized for at least forty years by the reasonably empirically oriented psychologists of the United States. Presently, much of the psychological argument concerns not the reality of such intervening variables, but how much we do in fact know about them. Skinner's quasi-cybernetic "black box" is a way of recognizing the reality, while avoiding the specification. The computer simulation studies indicate, however, kinds of intervening processes and tend to help us appreciate the remarkable effectiveness of most humans in carrying them out. Figure 9 is, quite literally, no more than an analytical expansion of the simple model found in figure 8. Psychologists use the term *latent time* to identify the period from a stimulus-action to a response-action. While the lines for latent time are different in these two figures, their actual time span is identical. It is just that with analytical care we become aware of so much more that is going on than our simple model (figure 8) would suggest.

Let us be careful. If the information-processing idea diagramed in figure 9 is at all an accurate way of considering a human-to-human response, then we have clear reason to suspect that a human response is inevitably a chosen counteract (i.e., involves some element of a decision of the responder). That *is* what we mean when we say that B's

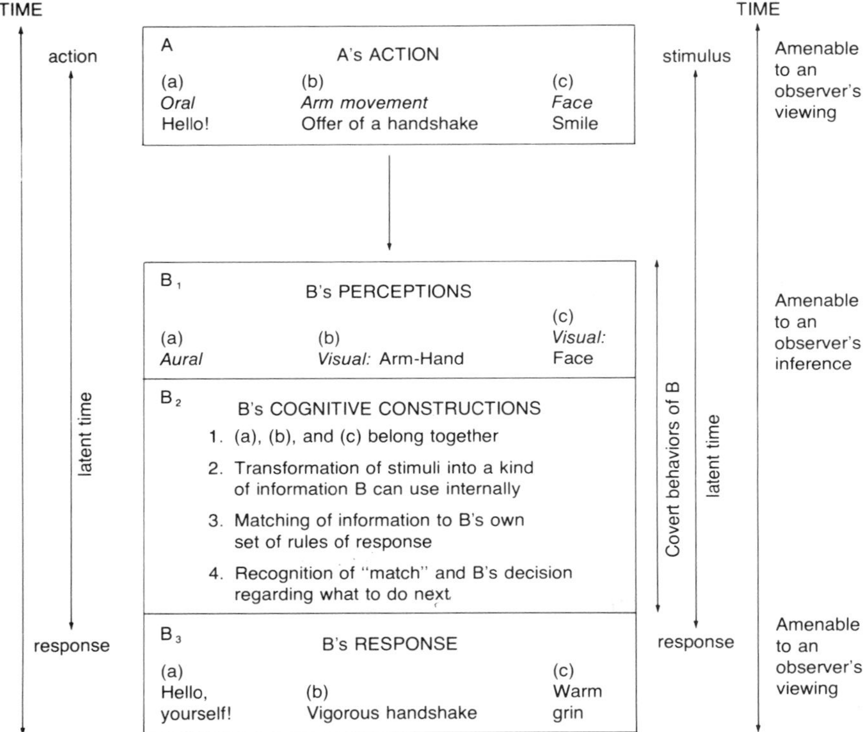

Figure 9. An expansion of a simple model of an A-B interchange as the result of an analysis of B's covert behavior prior to a response.

response to A *is B's response.* Still, let us try and keep our thinking clear. To the perceiver (B), A's action is objective. If it is perceived, to B it is quite clearly objective by any normal standards we may care to use. However, we have seen that such an objective set of stimuli are subjected by the perceiver (B) to a complex processing, in order to transform the raw stimuli into information and, then, to use that information in order to decide upon an appropriate response. Once that is decided upon, B can carry out a response to A's action. Naturally, that response-action by B creates yet another action-response possibility. Human living quite literally consists of myriads of such possibilities.

G-O-D AND THE HUMAN PARADIGM

All of this analysis is rather fundamental when we think about what an epistemic subject (humankind) can possibly perceive of an action of G-O-D. On beyond the sticky matter of whether an action-point A is accurately perceived (i.e., $A = A'$), we can affirm that if A' exists at the interface of G-O-D and the epistemic subject, then A' is "objective" to the perceiving epistemic subject (humankind). However, we can also affirm that any such A' as stimulus is inevitably subjected to a transformation process so that the raw stimulus becomes usable information to the perceiving epistemic subject. Ultimately, then, we can suspect that the epistemic subject's response to any A' will be formally similar to B's response to A's action. That response will involve a remarkably complex procedure prior to a decision which, in turn, tends to determine that counteraction we call a *response*. Yet we also have reason to believe that any such response will be the epistemic subject's *own* response. The response will almost certainly depend upon what can only be called the epistemic subject's cognitive constructions. And those cognitive constructions are well-nigh mathematical functions of the epistemic subject's past experience, as presently assessed during the covert behavior of processing stimuli into information.

While we have seen some reason to be hesitant about affirming any inevitably accurate perception, we have also seen some reason to affirm that whatever a human response may be, it almost certainly will involve a subject's decisions. Please note: we have not denied the possibility of a perception; we have only questioned its inevitable accuracy. We are not in a logician's box yet. Not unless we insist upon affirming that, in this instance of a G-O-D/human action-response cycle, the responder's decisions do *not* make an inevitable contribution.

Unless we posit some quasi-magical "extra" to the interchange between G-O-D and the epistemic subject, an extra which an analysis of a human-level A-B interchange could not identify, we are close to an answer to our initial query: What can an epistemic subject possibly perceive? We are so close to an answer because we have identified in an A-B interchange that B's response depends upon B's interpretation of A's action. We have focused upon humankind and, thereby, discerned an answer in terms of humankind's capabilities or possibilities or probable response. We have left G-O-D's action as quite objectively other: a true perceptual problem for an epistemic subject.

In quite prosaic, common-sense terms we have identified a set of ifs, buts, on-the-other-hands, and probabilities: a set of exceptions to an overly simple generality. However, all of these exceptions are within the epistemic subject. We have certainly found reason to doubt a simple-minded, automatic, quasi-mechanical action-response sequence. Our doubts have been confirmed by an analysis of the epistemic subject as responder. Those doubts, and the subject's inabilities, may have a good deal to do with a "religious" person's sense of unworthiness in the presence of G-O-D. Moreover, they may well relate to that sense of sin that marks much of Christian religiosity. Still, the perceptual analogue for a relation between G-O-D and an epistemic subject has led us to recognize that a cluster of problems reside within that epistemic subject. Without denying G-O-D either action or objective existence, the sheer perception of an epistemic subject has been seen to be iffy enough to cause one, quite minimally, to entertain something very like Aquinas's idea that evil is an accidental result of human choice.

Finally, let us recall that the tetrahedral model is quite achronological. Yet if we introduce time as an orthogonal dimension, that model may suggest something about what it means to posit that G-O-D is good. We may not be just projecting otherward. Not at all. We may well mean a fundamental reference to the inferable persistence of G-O-D in supplying successive action-points, regardless of how the epistemic subject manages to perceive them. If we can tolerate that idea, then to affirm that G-O-D is good is probably much the same thing as to affirm that G-O-D is unchanging, persistent, or ever active. If we can affirm anything like that without merely projecting *our* standards up, out, or otherward, to have focused upon the epistemic subject's relation to G-O-D via the doubled tetrahedron model has certainly been no wasted effort. Quite the contrary.

A Selected Bibliography for Chapter 2

Fisher, Ronald A., and Frank Yates. *Statistical Tables for Biological, Agricultural, and Medical Research;.* 6th ed., rev., enlarged. New York: Hafner Publishing Co., 1963.

Galton, Francis. "Classification of Men according to Their Natural Gifts." In *The World of Mathematics*, vol. 2, edited by James R. Newman, pp. 1173–1188. New York: Simon and Schuster, 1956.

Hays, William L. *Statistics for Psychologists*, esp. pp. 143–156 re. the binomial theorem. New York: Holt, Rinehart and Winston, 1963.

Hebb, D. O. *The Organization of Behavior: A Neuropsychological Theory.* New York: John Wiley & Sons, 1949.

Köhler, Wolfgang. *Dynamics in Psychology.* New York: Washington Square Press, 1940/1965.

Piaget, Jean. *The Mechanisms of Perception.* London: Routledge and Kegan Paul, 1961/1969.

Piaget, Jean. *Structuralism.* London: Routledge and Kegan Paul, 1968/1971.

Piaget, Jean, and Bärbel Inhelder. *The Psychology of the Child.* New York: Basic Books, 1969.

Underhill, Evelyn. *Mysticism*, esp. pp. 347–349 re. *The Cloud of Unknowing.* London: Methuen & Co., 1911/1949.

3

Thank God! Salvation and Such Like

There are times when the obvious is worth noting. It is obvious to many in these years of the late twentieth century that we are what by experience we have become. In a sense, that idea's very obviousness is close to a root cause for a parent's concern with a child's experiences, an educator's concern with something as intangible as a classroom climate, or a libertarian's concern for freedom of expression. Many of us (perhaps most of us!) regard our history as something close to the key to who we are. Among other things, the remarkable popularity of biography across the past decades of seeming change witnesses to just how obvious this idea is, as well as how attracted we are to what we think will be a story that will tell us who someone else really was.

I would like to note that fact, and move on to consider something that is related but not necessarily so easily regarded as all that obvious. I want to consider that there is also an obviousness to the idea that we will be different from what we have been only by virtue of what we hope will yet be. Both Augustine of Hippo, in the long ago, and Charles Sanders Peirce, just about one hundred years ago, observed that the past *was*, the present *is*, and only the future is *yet to be*. Both Augustine and Peirce drew the same conclusion: only the yet-to-be is amenable to the effect of choices made or decisions reached in the ever-fleeting present. Philosophically, logically, that too is remarkably obvious. But that obviousness has yet to work its way into our thinking. At first encounter, the idea is likely to be somewhere between strange and odd; it may even border on the offensive. Yet there is a kind of obviousness to the idea. It hardly matters whether one credits the fifth-century Christian saint or the nineteenth-century American philosopher; the idea has power, the power of the obvious.

One reasonably clear implication of Augustine's discovery and Peirce's reaffirmation is that the stories we tell ourselves and our children are important. Particularly because so many of those stories tell us about a not-present that, perhaps, is really a yet-to-be. Legends, myths, old wives' tales, and fairy stories are readily recognized as such. What is not always so easily recognized is that sacred stories are of the same genre. The Christian's Gospels include such stories, the Epistles imply them, and the Revelation of Saint John *is* such a story. They tell us of a not-yet that lures us on beyond the present and, if we will, challenges us to approximate it in that future over which we have some control through our decisions in the ever-fleeting moments of the passing present. In its own way, that too is obvious and, so, deserves the noting.

Sometime during the academic year 1938–1939, just before Europe was engulfed in World War II, John Ronald Ruel Tolkien journeyed to Scotland's northeastern coast. There on the North Sea coast of Scotland at the University of St. Andrews he delivered the Lang Lectures. His topic was fairy stories. Nineteen years later, in 1947, an expanded version of those lectures was published by the Oxford University Press as one item in *Essays Presented to Charles Williams*; Williams was an Oxford friend of Tolkien's. Presently Tolkien's lectures "On Fairy-Stories" can be found in Ballantine Books' *The Tolkien Reader* (New York, 1966). Although it may seem like a semiesoteric reference, there are few more serious, scholarly, and Christian presentations of the sheer *nature* of myth, legend, and fairy story to be found anywhere.

Tolkien's essay on the world of *faerie* is one of the most perceptive, positive, and realistic statements of just what one is involved in considering when one does consider the Christian *evangelium* that one can read. There are a large number of biblical and theological scholars who, deservedly, have to fall into place behind Tolkien. Without denying their scholarship, what Tolkien does is to go behind, beneath, even before their scholarship to a more fundamental level. His explication of the meaning of myth, for example, makes much biblical scholarship seem slightly shallow. What is remarkable is that Tolkien did not intend to do that, although he did so.

If you are not already familiar with Tolkien's lectures "On Fairy-Stories," do read them. If you can bear the sheer discipline of it all, reread them. You will be amply rewarded. You may also discover why I value them so highly, or why I am shifting to the genre of the fairy story. If the following story partakes of Tolkien's *faerie* world and, so, invites you into it for a moment, my purpose will have been fully achieved. So read, enjoy, and enter into the tale of Old Sailor and the Caretaker.

OLD SAILOR AND THE CARETAKER: A TALE

Up the valley of the Ai, past the first and second shallows, the falls of Tora cascade into the Rasa before its waters join the Ai on their way to the sea. Above the falls of Tora, some distance along the winding Rasa, lies a Community. There Old Sailor sat in the House of the Caretakers, thinking about things from long ago. He was not thinking of his coming to or of his life in the Community. Rather, he was thinking of things from the far reaches of his memory. He was quiet, relaxed, albeit momentarily puzzled by the memory.

Old Sailor was observed by the Caretaker who came to check the house, who noticed the softest signs of puzzlement cross Old Sailor's face. So the Caretaker asked, "Friend, what do you think?"

Without a moment's hesitation Old Sailor replied, "About a time and a place from long ago, far from the mouth of the Ai."

"My friend, you seem puzzled," the Caretaker observed. "Would you share your thinking with me? As you know, I am here to share your thoughts, for sometimes that is a help to us all."

With only a glance at the Caretaker, Old Sailor shared his memory.

"Once, early in my lifetime, I was a million meters (at least!) from the place where the Ai empties into the sea. I was much younger. In fact, I was then Young Sailor, fresh on my way toward today. I had a pass from my ship and, like all of my kind, I walked the streets of the town. Since I was only Young Sailor, I looked at many things, tasted a few, and found (as my kind are wont to do!) that Time's passing is noticeably slow when one is without something to do. In that frame of mind I found a place of refreshment which asked of me nothing but my presence. It was simply furnished, and minimally staffed with Friendly Faces. Their smiles warmed me. I was glad to be there.

"I sat down and looked through the things for reading that were about. I went for something to drink, and found that it was a brew of beans from a place farther than I had yet gotten. I sought nourishment, and found small circular cakes, which tasted good. I was glad to be in a place of quiet, one where I could sit without charge and sup (however slightly) with little cost.

"As I recall it now, I was pleased at my good fortune. Memory tells me that there were symbols discreetly placed about, which reminded me of an earlier time and place, when I was not yet Young Sailor. I was glad to be there. I left and I returned, for it seemed good.

"However, upon my last return, I was approached by a Friendly Face who recognized me as one retreating from the street and its abundant life. The Friendly Face talked with me about the then and the times that stretched backward to my birth. That was good. But somewhere along the path of our talking, the Friendly Face posed an Important Question. I could not answer quickly. Yes and No escaped me. I was not certain what to say. The Friendly Face kept on talking, but my puzzlement would not depart. Finally, I did depart. I did not return."

Old Sailor stopped, looked at the Caretaker, and returned to his thinking of things far away in Time and Place. For his part, the Caretaker seemed to be thinking himself. Finally, he touched Old Sailor's hand and said softly, quietly, calmly, "Friend, do you recall that Important Question from long ago and another place?"

Old Sailor's voice was a low-pitched rumble, but quite distinct. "Yes, friend Caretaker, I can recall the Important Question put by a Friendly Face. I can recall it quite well. But I can no longer clearly see the Friendly Face who asked it."

After but a moment, the Caretaker said, "As I told you, sharing sometimes helps. That is why I am a Caretaker. Would you share with me that Important Question from long ago and far away that puzzled you? Perhaps the sharing will help the puzzlement that, even now, traces your face."

Old Sailor thought about the offer, and finally replied.

"Friend, it was so simple and yet so abstract that its memory often returns. I am certain I know my answer, but there is still a puzzle at the heart of it. The Friendly Face used but three words, yet I have repeatedly wondered what a complete answer might require. Long ago in a place far, far from where the Ai empties into the sea, I heard a Friendly Face query me, '*Are you saved?*'"

The Caretaker nodded, smiled (ever so slightly), and lifted his eyes. Then he asked, as befits a Caretaker, another Important Question: "*Friend, do you* now *know an answer that you did not know then?*"

Time repeatedly passed from the future *not-yet* through the fleeting present *now* toward the all-consuming past *once-was*. And Old Sailor went about his work. Yet life is not all work: he had time to enjoy the signs of Spring along the Rasa. He was grateful for both work to do and a Spring to enjoy. Once again he sat in the House of the Caretakers. He was quiet, relaxed, thinking. Now and again, as memory tossed up its bits and pieces, he recalled another time and a sharing with the Caretaker. He now knew that he had yet another Important Question. That made him smile.

So it was that when the Caretaker came to check the house he found Old Sailor, once again sitting and thinking. But this time there was a trace of pleasure upon his face. The Caretaker took a seat beside Old Sailor and waited for moments and moments and moments. Finally he asked, "Friend, what do you think today?"

Without hesitation, Old Sailor replied, "About how questions lead to answers which, in their turn, carry one on to yet other questions. When last I was here I shared an Important Question from long ago and told you that I now knew an answer. You not only heard me out, you gave me yet another Important Question. I have considered it again and again in those moments within work when the mind ranges free, and as I have watched Spring come to the Rasa. If you are willing, I would talk with you further."

Quietly the Caretaker asked, "Friend, what is your concern? If we are to talk, we must know what we explore, for otherwise we may pass by discoveries like those blinded by the sun, or settle for illusions. Tell me, therefore, what it is that we should talk about."

A smile crossed Old Sailor's face. "I would talk about four things," he replied. "Me, my two Important Questions, and how these three go together. That last is, I suspect, another Important Question. I would talk about these things, for sharing is good, and you have already helped me." He paused, then looked at the Caretaker and asked, "Friend, is that enough to let us talk, discover what we can, and yet avoid illusion?"

Choosing his words carefully, the Caretaker smiled, returned the gaze, and said, "I think so. You know your subject, and I am willing to listen . . . even to learn . . . so let us talk about your four things. But do not be surprised if our talking takes us well into the future."

The pleasure inside Old Sailor surfaced. He almost laughed as he replied, "Friend, I have no desire for instant answers! Long ago I learned how temporary they are! Nor have I any fear of the future. It has brought me treasures that exceeded my hopes. So let us talk. Now and at another time, and at yet other times. I would explore my four things in your company."

The Caretaker shifted into a more comfortable position, smiled, and quietly asked, "How do we start this exploration?"

Old Sailor replied, "Let us *skim* over my first thing and get *quickly* to my Important Question from long ago, *then* let us consider your equally Important Question from not so long ago. *Next*, let us consider what I suspect is their relationship to one another. *Finally*, let us return to my first thing and consider it at more leisure, for it is that with which I am concerned each day. Are you willing to *so* explore with me, friend Caretaker?"

Quickly, confidently, the Caretaker said, "Of course. It was for just this that I was made a Caretaker. Let us explore your as-yet unknown. In such explorations, we *can* discover things more substantial than illusions, albeit they are often things that are fragile. Let us talk."

Old Sailor needed no more assurance.

He began to talk.

"As you know, my work continually involves me in estimating what is possible, calculating probabilities, and reaching informed estimates of that which is likely but has not yet come to pass. I have the opportunity to monitor data, to ask questions of its meaning, and to request yet other data. I live by that which Young Sailor knew ever so slightly as statistics. Inevitably my work affects me and my sense of myself and my approach to Important Questions. The Community is not alone in expecting this of me; I expect it of myself. I am quite comfortable with those expectations.

"Oh, sometimes my apprentices make me uncomfortable when they think that I regard all things as no more than data points. It grieves me when they assume that I am ruled by my probabilities, enslaved by them, a mere creature of them. Minimally, I insist that they acknowledge the assumption as theirs and, so, recognize that it may not be mine. Yet I cannot complain. My work is rewarding, and I am grateful to have it. There is work in the Community I would less like to do. That thought serves me well."

Old Sailor looked quizzically at the Caretaker and asked, "Have you followed me this far?"

Smiling, the Caretaker nodded.

"My apprentices have taught me two things. First, I am; that *is* who I am. Moreover, *I* will be what *I* will *be*. Second, their hopes and their expectations are their *own*; they need not be *mine*. At one time, I was not certain that was so, and I was distressed. But I have come to recognize that my apprentices' vision of me is not as important to me, or to the Community, as my own understanding. Thus, I found *freedom* to do that which I could and, as well, that which was expected of me by the Community.

A grin creased the Caretaker's face as he replied: "Friend, you have discovered a treasure! I think you know that to be so. I only want to confirm it for you. You *are*; that *is* who you are. Given yourself, your being who you are, it is true in the most real sense that, in the not-yet of the future, you *will be* what *you* will be. Your acceptance of that reality is commendable. So, too, is your desire to explore a something else, an other, a place suspected but, as yet, not experienced. Do continue."

Old Sailor nodded his thanks and continued.

"So much for my first thing. Let us now turn to my Important Question from long ago and far, far away.

"Once, long ago, Young Sailor heard a Friendly Face ask, '*Are you saved?'* He could not respond. The memory stayed with him, but I think I understand now what might have been said, had I been who I am now. But that is only a beginning. I am not involved in justifying myself—I have little need of that!—but, rather, I want to consider what the Friendly Face's question could possibly mean."

"Friend, tell me your present answer," the Caretaker interjected.

"Well, I have concluded that an answer should be simply, 'Yes.' As near as I can understand the Friendly Face's query, there is no other response that would fit my condition, then or now."

"Is that enough?" Old Sailor queried.

The Caretaker nodded, smiled, and motioned for him to continue.

"What presently concerns me is the question itself. It is *that* I have thought about. I have considered the obvious dimensions of the query. I have thought about the from and the to and the why and the how. I have returned deep into that which I knew long before Young Sailor was, and I have concluded that the query presupposes four things: (a) a need; (b) a being which can meet the need; (c) an actual meeting of the need, at some point; and, so, (d) the query itself refers to one's appreciation or appropriation of an accomplished fact. That is why I would, now, respond simply, 'Yes.' Thereby I would affirm that (a) is, (b) exists, and (c) has taken place, so that (d) requires (in all honesty!) essentially acknowledgment.

"But I am not satisfied. The objectivity is appealing and almost certainly true. However, I have come to think that the query itself is really a Code. I have tried to think through to discern what that might involve."

"Friend," the Caretaker asked, "what have you discovered, thus far?"

"Since I am who and what I am, I put the hoary Method of Successive Dichotomies to work. I began, as one must with that Method, by identifying my element of unity, which I termed a whole being. Then I concluded that a first dichotomy involved distinguishing between (a) that which was objectively so of such a being, and (b) that which was subjectively so of a *whole* being. That first dichotomy helped, as it always does, but not too much. Next, I concluded that each of those two could be dichotomized. It took me some time to realize that what was *objectively* so of a whole being could be termed its state, while that which was *subjectively* so of a whole being could best be termed its intent. The discerned dichotomies for state and intent, I came to see, were actually grossly distinguished continua. That is, conceptual continua with but two places: a preferred and a dispreferred, or a positive and a negative position.

"At that point, I realized the usefulness (as well as the practical necessity!) of labeling the end-points of my two pairs of continua. I also realized that, by virtue of thinking of continua with simple end-points, I could readily distinguish four combinations of such end-points for both state and intent. I had the ability, I realized, to distinguish four conditions of state and intent. Moreover, I also realized that a pair of such quadrads interact among themselves to make an exhaustive logical set of sixteen combined state-intent conditions."

"Friend," the Caretaker asked, "How do *you* choose to label the end-points of those four continua?"

Old Sailor paused, thought a moment, then replied, "I would label the end-points of the two continua I discern as characterizing a whole being's state as, first, *Ignorance* and *Knowledge* and, second, as *Open* and *Closed*. I would label the end-points of the two continua I discern as characterizing the intent of a whole being as, first, *Delusion* and *Delight* and, second, *Domination* and *Sharing*. I know these words are mine! But I think they serve well for what I have been able to discern, and I think they do relate to my first (and early) Important Question."

"I suspect you are right," the Caretaker said. "If I understand your first Important Question, I am fairly certain that you are correct. However, tell me more."

"Of course. I now understand that the Friendly Face's query posits that our kind can be understood to live in the midst of a process which can be termed *being saved*. That process is. *I* think it is a *result* of that which *has been done* but, while related, it is at least sequentially different. In a way, it seems to *me* that the process is a normal, natural, almost inevitable following-on. Thus at any moment a whole being can be characterized, within that process, by its state and its intent. It is that possibility which my four continua enable me to discern and, more, to model and so consider.

"Moreover, I recognize that my continua express, quite grossly, a set of personal values. For instance: Knowledge seems quite preferable to Ignorance; Openness seems better than Closedness; Delight seems much to be preferred to Delusion; and Sharing seems much better than Domination. My continua can be formally and elegantly expressed as a pair of simple 2 × 2 matrices which, in interaction, create an exhaustive set of sixteen possibilities. To my thought they model a *process of being saved*. That is, they identify a set of possible conditions between a maximum condition of *yet-to-be-saved-ness* and what I can discern as a maximum condition of *saved-ness*. However, since my interest is essentially in the process itself, I will not burden you with my formalities, unless you desire it."

"Thank you," the Caretaker chuckled. Then he added, "Friend, I would like to ask for some information. The answer is obvious to you, but it would help to know how you resolve the from, the to, the why, and the how of the Friendly Face's query."

Old Sailor nodded, smiled, and replied, "Of course. I am one who works from the specifics out to the general, and then seeks examples of that generality in yet other specificities. I have pondered those four dimensions and come to answers that satisfy me. So let me share my answers with you; then you tell me what you think.

"The query presumes that one can be saved *from* something. I have considered alternatives and concluded that the Friendly Face believed one must be saved from some danger, something fearful, such as wrath or retribution. I acknowledge that possibility, but I do not ground my response in it! Rather, I would ground my response in what is equally obvious: the query also presumes that one can be saved *to* something. Obviously, To can be the simple opposite of From or (I am inclined to think!) something akin to peace, joy, or pleasure.

"I am aware, as are all who work as I do, that why is a complex question. I suspect the query presumes some dis-ease, some distress, some need. While I do not doubt that such is often the state of our kind, that is not at the forefront of my thinking. I do acknowledge that a *need* may exist, whether I am aware of it or not. Thus, I conclude that there may be a *need* for one to be saved. However, it is the last dimension that was most challenging, to me.

"I have considered many alternatives. I have even gone back to legends that had almost escaped me. I have come to think that the how of being saved involves a *response*, which is some anticipatory appropriation of a *promise*. Moreover, that promise seems best related to the to, although it does, of course, function also with the from.

"For me, then, the to and the how are more important than either the from or the why. Thus, I find that the Friendly Face's query suggests (or implies!) a great good and, now, I know my response would be simply, '*Yes!*' "

Old Sailor paused, grinned, and asked, "What do you think?"

"Friend," the Caretaker replied, "you have reached a thoughtful, positive resolution of your four dimensions. You have satisfied my curiosity. Do you want to continue, or shall we talk at another time?"

Old Sailor thought a moment, blinked, cleared his throat, and said, "Let us talk further at another time. I will return before Spring turns into the Summer, and then we will talk some more."

As was the custom of the Community, they rose, exchanged the Sign of Acknowledgment, and parted.

It was almost the Memorial of R. A. Fisher before Old Sailor found himself again in the House of the Caretakers. As so often happens, one thing after another had prevented his coming, although the desire to be there had not departed. Spring had come to the winding Rasa, and it was already Midsummer. Old Sailor sat thinking about his last meeting with the Caretaker of this House; a smile settled upon his face as memory brought back their conversational exploration of the meaning of his memory from long, long ago in a place far, far from the place where the Ai joins the great sea.

When the Caretaker came to check the house, he found Old Sailor sitting and smiling. Quietly he seated himself by him and waited. Then he said, "Friend, it has been some time since last we talked, and shared, and explored together. What can we do this day?"

Old Sailor chuckled. Then he replied, "I would explore some more in your company. Are you still willing to do that?"

"Yes, my Friend, I am still willing to explore with you your memories and your meanings. Tell me, where should we begin?"

Old Sailor seemed to be thinking, then he began to talk.

"When we last parted I had told you about my first Important

Question, and we had explored why I *now* think that the only answer *I* could give to the Friendly Face's query from long, long ago would be a simple Yes. Today, I would explore with you what I think about that other Important Question that you gave to me in this very place."

"As I remember it," Old Sailor continued, "you asked me whether I *now* knew an answer that I did not *already* know in that time long, long ago. Is my memory correct, Friend?"

"As near as my memory will tell me," the Caretaker replied, "you are quite correct. Do you *now* know an answer that you simply did *not* know *then?*"

"Thank you for affirming my memory," Old Sailor responded. Then he continued to talk, saying:

"I have thought about your query for several months. I have spent a Spring and a fair portion of a Summer turning it over and over in my mind. I think I have found an answer, Friend Caretaker, to your Important Question.

"In the most objective of senses, I think my answer must be a very simple No. However, I also know that is Old Sailor's answer. At the time of my encounter with the Friendly Face, I was not yet Old Sailor; I was only Young Sailor. So I have considered what, as best as memory will serve me, Young Sailor might have said, had he been able to share with one such as you. I think that even Young Sailor might, with one such as you, have recognized that a Yes was an appropriate answer to the Friendly Face's query. And it is because of this that I find myself content with my No to your Important Question."

"Still, I know that Young Sailor had no one such as you, Friend Caretaker. To him, the Friendly Face's query, 'Are you saved?' was a puzzle. Young Sailor did not know whether a Yes or a No was an appropriate response!

"What I have been able to recognize," Old Sailor said, "was that there is a clue to my present answer in Young Sailor's very hesitation, his sheer uncertainty. That thought has intrigued me. It has led me down heretofore unexamined lines of assumption. As a result, I think I mean by my No that Young Sailor implicitly knew, although he was quite *un*able to *then* bring that knowledge to his conscious use, that the answer to the Friendly Face's query about whether or not he was saved was a simple Yes! I think now that was probably why he hesitated, not certain whether Yes or No or Maybe or, even, I Do Not Know was appropriate.

"Yet, even as I think that about Young Sailor, I find myself wondering why I think that. My present answer is that Young Sailor had heard the tales of things from long, long ago and far, far away in Time and Place which, in their *essence*, speak of the answer to the Friendly Face's query. I think it was that memory, or even its residuals, which accounts for Young Sailor's hesitancy and, I now also think, for my continued recollection of that query and my earlier hesitancy."

The Caretaker smiled. Then he asked, "Are you suggesting to me that the tales from one's childhood are really important to one as a young adult and as an older, more mature adult?"

"Certainly," Old Sailor replied.

Then, grinning, he added:

"My memory of Young Sailor is, of course, a memory of another me. I am the end-product of all that history from Young Sailor to Old Sailor. Yet that history is a tangled tale of my decisions, so I *am* who I *have* chosen to be, just as certainly as *I* will be what *I* choose to be. I am nought else; but I am at least that! In a way, that is so simple. Yet I have traveled far to reach this bend of the Rasa. Far as we measure distance, and far as time itself is counted. For all that travel, I find myself with a simplicity, and not yet a complexity that would challenge my mind. Except that the challenge is *in* the simplicity itself."

Old Sailor stopped talking, glanced at the Caretaker, and seemed to settle into his seat. There was quiet in the House of the Caretakers.

"Friend," the Caretaker quietly said, "You *have* explored a far territory, and you have *discovered* a treasure. Do not forget *that*."

After some moments of silence, during which one could almost hear the wind moving the gentle grasses, rippling them like waves upon the great sea, Old Sailor and the Caretaker arose. They exchanged the Sign of Acknowledgment and parted.

When late Fall came, the leaves were brilliant reds and oranges. The intimation of chill was in the wind that followed the winding Rasa's course toward the falls of Tora. Once again the Caretaker was in the house. So was Old Sailor's coffin. Thinking of sharings and explorations and discoveries made together, the Caretaker began to talk.

"Friends, and my Friend with whom I explored the far reaches of memory and its possible meaning, we are here to bury Old Sailor. He is no longer a part of our Community. Another now does what he did so well. But we are not here to be more than momentarily sad. We are here to recall that one we knew found meaning, before his dying, in his life.

"That meaning was truly his. It completed his life. Thus his dying was the departure of a whole person—one who had discovered his own personal, positive answers to questions that niggle at the far parts of many minds. Let us remember him, then, as one who found what some yet seek and, finding it, was content to be Old Sailor."

As was the custom, Old Sailor's coffin was buried in a plot known as the Yard of the Elders. The spot was marked by a simple tablet with only two words, Old Sailor, and the date of his dying. By the end of Fall the spot was ablaze with the reds, yellows, and burnt oranges of falling leaves. Now and again, on his way to check the house, a Caretaker could be noticed pausing by the bed of leaves, looking down, and then with a smile lifting his eyes. Then, since the wind had now a definite chill to it, he moved on to check the House of the Caretakers, for some other members of the Community might wish to share and explore and, thereby, discover *their* treasure.

Ten Questions for Thinking About "Old Sailor and The Caretaker: A Tale"

Question 1. a. Who do you think Old Sailor might be?
b. Who do you think the Caretaker might be?

Question 2. a. In this tale, how would you describe sharing?
b. Is sharing a "sacramental" act?
c. Why do you think about sharing as you do?

Question 3. What symbols do you think the Friendly Faces might have "discreetly placed about" that Old Sailor would remember?

Question 4. Why do you think the Caretaker asked his Important Question?

Question 5. How do you think Old Sailor answered his third Important Question?

Question 6. a. Is Old Sailor a mature person?
b. Why do you think as you do about Old Sailor?

Question 7. a. Is Old Sailor human?
b. What is it that leads you to think Old Sailor is, or is not, human?

Question 8. a. Was Old Sailor's resolution of the Friendly Face's Important Question satisfactory to you?
b. Why do you think as you do?

Question 9. a. Tolkien wrote, "The Primary world, Reality, of elves and men is the same, if differently valued and perceived." He also wrote that "creative Fantasy is founded upon the hard recognition that things are so in the world as it appears under the sun; on a recognition of fact, but not a slavery to it." Does the tale of Old Sailor and the Caretaker meet Tolkien's criterion?
b. Why do you think as you do?

Question 10. a. How would you answer the Friendly Face's Important Question?
b. How similar to Old Sailor's rationale is your rationale for your answer?

What you think is all-important, for you. Don't hurry. Take your time. But do locate *your* answer. For you, that *is* your answer, at this time. Moreover, knowing your *own* answer is, in some ways, quite important . . . for *you*.

4

O God! Creaturely Reflections on Creation

Once upon a time, long ago and seemingly far away from my present, I sat with a good friend through an afternoon of paper readings. It was only now and then sparkling. During one of several cognitive recesses, we began to doodle out a formula for distinguishing between ideas that might lead to action and ideas that probably would lead only to an abortive effort. We were both researchers, familiar with statistics, so we fell into an attempt to put together things that just might be measured, sometime, although we had little doubt that those things interacted to create one or the other condition. My old notes tell me that it was in late October, 1968, that all this happened, and that we were safely encapsulated in an ecumenical fortress.[1]

What we initially recognized was that our experience suggested that any effort was some function of four very general things. First, we identified that something as general as *ability* had an inescapable place. Then we recognized that in addition there was some part to be played by the first order factor G, or general *intelligence*. Third, we had little trouble adding *experience* to our growing list of variables. Finally, we added a distinction we felt was not covered by our other three variables, something we chose to call *dexterity*. Next, we appropriated Ronald A. Fisher's conceptual model for the analysis of variance and decided to let our four things be related to one another additively. However, we then realized that addition was far too simple to match the reality we knew well; so we enclosed the four things within parentheses and suggested that what actually happened to the sum was that it was raised to a power (being conservative, we merely suggested squaring the resultant sum). Then we realized that what we had was a formula that tended to be quite individualistic. Actions, at least in the context we were considering at that time, tend to be complexes of many individual contributions. Thus we introduced a summation sign (Greek *sigma*) to the left of the parenthesized sum of our things which we had raised to the second power.

We had an intriguing doodle. But we asked ourselves, what (in fact) were we modeling? It may have been inspiration, or something less, but we decided that we had something akin to a measure of the vastness of an idea, in terms of the participants generating it. Alternatively, we thought we might have a conceptual model for the assessment of the quality of planning preceeding any complex action, in terms of both the scope and the rate of the presumed action. Either alternative seemed delightful to us both, as near as I can recall that long-ago moment.

Being slightly addicted to puns, one of us noted that if our formula for vastness of idea were at all accurate, we could readily identify a persistent yet damnable problem by introducing one more relationship: division. So a horizontal line was drawn beneath our formula and the integer two entered as a divisor. This action gave us, we were certain, a formula for a *half*-vast idea—a terrible pun, albeit a phenomenon each of us could affirm we had personally encountered.

Naturally, we were prepared to affirm that it was the function halved that helped one understand why an abortive effort was distinct from an action. We were pleased with ourselves, as punsters usually are, and so happily ended our cognitive recess. We turned our attention back to the papers being read that late October afternoon. But that pun has been a source of recurrent fun and, now and again, of help in discovering a way simply to cope, especially with encountered absurdities.

However, let's be reasonably precise.

The formula for a vast idea and that for its derivative, a merely half-vast idea, are fundamentally conceptual humor. While there may be resonances that remind one of truths suspected or ascertained, no one should think that the social sciences are about to come out with a vastness index. At the very least, *this* social scientist is not about to do so. I leave that to others! Still, I could hardly turn down a well-funded, long-range project to make operational (perhaps through emendation) just such an index. In addition to whatever usefulness it might have, it would be such a delightful thing to try![2]

It has been said that a mark of our humanness is our ability to laugh.

Perhaps so. But if one believes that, and if one can hear those resonances of truth in the idea of a vastness index, perhaps it is not such a bad beginning for a reasonably serious question. That is, what do we think of this creation within which we exist? Is it a truly vast idea? Or is it actually simply a half-vast idea? That question has been asked by many persons across the centuries. It has been answered in both ways, too. In fact, a goodly number of our contemporaries in these later decades of the twentieth century seem to opt for half-vastness.

The distinction is really quite fundamental. It is not merely a simpleminded choice between (a) affirming that "things tend to work out, in the end!" and (b) acknowledging that "life can hand one a pretty raw deal." While the first is often quite true, it is no fundamental statement of the nature of reality. Its appearance in various pious guises is, at best, an expression of hope. Similarly, the second acknowledgment is not really a pessimistic conclusion. Far too often, it is no more than an objective observation of the way things seem to be. To affirm that this creation is actually a truly vast idea is, finally, an act of faith. However, so too is the alternative affirmation that we exist within a merely half-vast idea. It is not a question of faith or fact or anything else. It is a question of which faith affirmation. Recognition of that can be a considerable help, for it reminds us that the distinction is a matter of very human choice. We choose one or the other affirmation. We decide the matter, because we are free to do so. But we should not forget what we have done.

A MOMENTARY DIGRESSION: CHOOSING OR DECIDING?

If one can tolerate the idea that humans not only can but do affirm, by simple creaturely right, one or the other alternative, it can be a help to distinguish between two words: *choose* and *decide*. Admittedly, many of us do not distinguish between *choosing* and *deciding*; we regard them as synonyms. However, my friends Anna L. Miller-Tiedeman and David V. Tiedeman have proposed that these two words represent distinctly different human acts.[3] They suggest that choosing per se is an act that often is primarily impulsive, emotion-laden, essentially prerational or arational. They are not at all concerned with denying the reality of choosing (or choice). It is, as they understand it, essentially a question of the nature of the act. Conversely, they suggest that deciding per se is an act that often is primarily thoughtful, conscious, essentially rational. They are not at all concerned with propagating the absurd idea that humans do decide all things all of the time. But they do observe that less mature humans tend to choose more often than they decide, while more mature humans tend to decide as often as they choose and, frequently, decide more often than they choose. Their thesis tends to be supported by clinical observation of human actions. In fact, most persons beyond thirty-five years of age will at least assent to a very general form of this fundamentally developmental thesis, even if there is a fair-to-abundant clutch of seemingly necessary specific-instance exceptions.

Moreover, if we admit the Miller-Tiedeman/Tiedeman distinction between choosing and deciding, then we have an intriguingly useful conceptual tool for understanding what one could mean by the important word *faith*. In addition, we also have a way of identifying two different meanings to my simple assertion that the alternative affirmations of vastness and half-vastness are, basically, human acts of faith. Actually, the distinction is quite gross. It is not really a fine one at all. It involves no more than recognizing (or is it admitting?) a simple continuum with but a *less* and a *more* position. Truly thoughtful persons can begin adding intermediate positions with surprising ease! Still, it is a useful distinction.

My dictionary tells me that the word *faith* can mean (a) "belief which is not based on proof" or (b) "belief in God or in the doctrines or teachings of religion" or (c) "belief in anything, as a code of ethics, standards of merit, etc. . . ." Those three meanings all speak about belief. However, they are the second, third, and fourth definitions given. The first one is simply, "confidence or trust in a person or thing."[4] I suspect that first definition also defines the sense in which the word *belief* is used in the following three definitional meanings.

Think about it.

Except for a special vocabulary, *faith* means a very human action: belief or confidence or trust in something. Thus, to speak of any conclusion or any affirmation as an *act of faith* is simply to identify it as (a) a human act which (b) arises out of an equally human "confidence or trust." Yet most of us can fairly readily recognize that there is a prior presumed act that lies behind either "confidence or trust." Quite normally, most of us would say that prior presumed act is what we would call a *choice* or a *decision*.

Faith, belief, choice, and decision, then, are not things from completely disparate realms at all. Instead, they belong together within a single process. First, a choice or a decision. Then, as a result, a belief or faith.[5] Without pushing such an argument from common-sense meanings far at all, I merely want to note that the acts of choosing and deciding tend to be unspoken assumptions of an act of faith. Thus, the proposed distinctions between choosing and deciding are relatable to what it normally means to speak of any conclusion as an act of faith.

The alternatives of vastness or half-vastness, when affirmed, are a human conclusion. Thus, they are expressions of a confidence or trust in what we tend to think of as ". . . the way things just are!" Yet such conclusions represent also the end-result, the visible following-out of an invisible, internal, covert action of either choosing or deciding: they are simply an act of faith. It is not only that humans reach such conclusions; such conclusions are a very distinctly human action. In part, because humans are choosers and deciders.

Let us recall that Miller-Tiedeman and Tiedeman proposed that choosing and deciding were distinctly different human acts. One aspect of that difference was their observation that choosing tends to be an early act of a maturing human, while deciding tends to be a later act of a matured human. On a very, very simple developmental continuum, choosing tends to precede deciding. If humankind can accommodate that idea, it can fairly easily also recognize that what one might well term an act of faith could be quite distinctly different depending upon whether choice or decision was its presumed prior. Looking at which human action precedes an act of faith, then, gives us a very general way of considering something like a developmental sequence of such acts of faith.

Let us be very clear about just what I have written. I have suggested that an act of faith is not a unitary thing at all. Rather, it is a whole class of things. Moreover, that class can be so ordered that, depending upon the presumed covert priors to an act of faith (choice or decision), one can meaningfully speak about a quite general continuum from a less mature yet human act of faith (one which presupposes a covert act of choosing) to a more mature yet human act of faith (one which presupposes a covert act of deciding). In terms of the generality *mature*, then, the class of acts of faith can be ordered from a simple *less* to a simple *more*, depending upon the prior preceding act of either choosing or deciding. Thus, via inference, I posited that human acts of faith can be rather grossly distinguished as either less or more mature human acts.[6]

In much the same vein, one really should note that this distinction is not ex post facto (at least, not in any normal sense of that phrase!). It is not the result per se that qualifies a human act of faith for the labels *less mature* or *more mature*. Not at all. It is the Miller-Tiedeman/Tiedeman distinction between the presumed prior action of either choosing or deciding. By inference from their distinctions, then, it is a matter of whether an act of faith is to be credited as the result of impulse or thought, whether it is recognizably arational or rational, whether it is emotion-laden or conscious. The result of the act of faith vis-a-vis the ideas of vastness or half-vastness does not determine the appropriateness of the labels *less mature* and *more mature*.

Let us be reasonably rigorous and tolerably honest.

Such a conclusion is not one that Christians or, for that matter, most "religious" persons take to like the proverbial duck takes to water. The conclusion inherently challenges some of our traditional understandings. Especially our presumption that, of course, our own understanding is quite obvious—to use what I term the Al Capp/Li'l Abner test, "As any FOOL can plainly see!"[7]

Not at all.

However, what such a conclusion preserves is considerably more valuable than any somewhat idiosyncratic assurance of being obviously right. That is, while admitting that a human may decide for half-vastness, we preserve the possibility that a human may also thoughtfully, consciously, and rationally decide for vastness. Either one, if a decision, qualifies as a more mature act of faith. That leaves one with a seeming paradox; but it does get one out of the box of believing untrue things about some human beings who do not agree with one's own act of faith, whatever that may be.

Again, let us try and be reasonably precise. It is a possibility that a human may decide thoughtfully, consciously, rationally for either vastness or half-vastness. That is not to affirm that either of those decisions is, in any objective sense, correct. It is only to acknowledge the very real possibility of a decision either way, given human freedom.

However, if we try to analyze this seeming paradox, we fairly quickly recognize that the paradox rests upon a presumption that either decision is a result of an equally balanced consideration (or weighting) of the *same* facts or presumed facts. Actually, a bit of thought will very likely lead one to the recognition that such a presumption is (minimally) unlikely and (maximally) damn near impossible. Thus, we come to a point of asking quite meaningfully what facts or presumed facts each decision presupposes. That is, we push the query inside the person, rather than leaving the evaluative question to seem objective vis-a-vis the observed conclusion.

Without trying an all-too-early finesse, let us simply note that we have reached a point where *speculation* may be a more precise term for any "on beyond." Still, with that note in mind, let us press forward at least as far as it seems possible to go. Naturally, our motto must be: Tentatively, ever so tentatively!

If it be speculation, then it is. But let us try to move the argument one more step forward. What was said a few sentences back was that the fundamental query concerns the decider, rather than the decision per se. We have a question that, in its more likely or possible form, concerns the difference between the facts (or presumed facts) that decider *i* considers (making a decision for mere half-vastness) and decider *j* considers (making a decision for vastness). If we insist upon concluding that the facts per se are the same, then we are logically bound (or forced) to ask how decider *i* and decider *j* can possibly value the same facts so differently that, from a common factual base, they reach such disparate conclusions. If we push ourselves to that point, the human act of valuing becomes a prime consideration, for that would seem to be *the* explanation of an otherwise paradoxical situation. Yet, on beyond affirming that humans do value things, we are very likely to find ourselves in a conceptual morass.

One reasonably obvious, albeit not ultimately satisfactory, "answer" to the question of why or how humans value anything is simply to affirm that humans value as they have been taught to value. In a word, it is not *a* human who values, but that human's teachers (e.g., parents or community or heritage) who value in and through an existing human. While this answer removes all personal responsibility for either choice or decision from *a* human, it flies full in the face of what many (if not most) humans presume to be their nature, function, or action. Yet, if the why of one's valuing is not simply and solely the product of one's being taught, then there is some contemporary personal contribution to any valuing that *a* human makes.

If one is willing to affirm as much about humans generally, and oneself particularly, then the options for why a human values are reduced somewhat. Aside from what could be called the burp theory of valuing (i.e., a tired body can do nought else!), a why query pushes one back toward something remarkably like a human choice or a human decision. Although that seems like a bit of circular reasoning, it is far more likely a tracing back of what Piaget would call the expanding spiral of human knowledge.[8] Yet, if we are to remain rational about this query, we must recognize that we have (in some way) come full circle. If we are not prepared to buy into the uncontrolled and usually uncontrollable physiology of something like a burp theory of valuing, then we are back thinking about the function of human choice or decision.

Let us admit it: opting for human choice or decision does not answer anywhere near all of our questions.[9] But it does preserve something of quite distinctly human value: what we tend to refer to as our *freedom* and, therefore, our simple, common-sense *responsibility*. Somehow, humans tend to be uneasy if they are not responsible, even though they often go to considerable lengths to ignore that responsibility. Without it, they are apt to feel that they have been *dehumanized*, a peculiarly nasty word in these years of the later decades of the twentieth century.

There is a sense, then, in which we are very close to acknowledging that there is a fundamental mystery about humankind. While we may well choose to label a part of that mystery *choice* or *decision*, we have done very little but label portions of the fundamental mystery. Perhaps that is not only an important insight but, even, an aspect of the truth about humans.

A MOMENTARY REFLECTION UPON AN AUTHORITATIVE SOURCE

The Books of Moses and the prophetic literature, plus the books of the Christian's new covenant, have been acknowledged in an earlier chapter to be an authoritative source. It is interesting and, often, just a bit bewildering to recur to that source in a specific instance. For example, consider my experience in trying to use the biblical scholar's inevitable aide, a concordance. I had readily at hand two older, rather hefty compendiums. First, and earlier in either date of authorship or copyright, was James Strong's *Exhaustive Concordance of the Bible* (New York: Abingdon-Cokesbury Press, 1890; 18th printing, 1948), which is based upon the King James Version of the English Bible. Second, and considerably later, is the production supervised by John W. Ellison, *Nelson's Complete Concordance of the Revised Standard Version Bible* (New York: Thomas Nelson and Sons, 1957), which is based upon the early 1950s North American effort known as the RSV. To each of these seemingly worthy sources I took one reasonably simple question: How often is the idea of choice or decision used in either Testament of a Christian's Bible? The question was a simple one of frequency of use. I was thoroughly prepared to acknowledge varying derivative forms of either key word. Thus, I looked at *choice*, *choicest*, *choose*, *choosest*, *chooseth*, *choosing*, *chose*, and *chosen* in the King James Version vocabulary, and *choice*, *choose*, *chooses*, *choosing*, *chose*, and *chosen* in the Revised Standard Version vocabulary. Similarly, I looked at both *decided* and *decision* in the King James Version vocabulary, and *decide*, *decided*, *decides*, *decision*, and *decisions* in the Revised Standard Version vocabulary.

I carefully counted the recorded uses of these words in both the Christian's Old Testament and the Christian's New Testament. What I came up with was a slightly different picture, depending upon which version of the concordance referenced. These differing results are displayed in figures 1 and 2.

Initially, let us acknowledge that the results displayed in figures 1 and 2 make two fundamental facts obvious. First, two groups of scholars translated some Hebrew and Greek words into English differently, which is not too surprising when one realizes that English is a living, changing language, and when one recognizes that the difference between the dates of the two translations is approximately three hundred years. Second, both figures 1 and 2 suggest that either *choice* words or *decision* words are predominantly words from the Christian's Old Testament. In neither the KJV nor the RSV, does the Christian's New Testament contribute as much as one-quarter of the identified instances of use of either kind of word. These seem to be quite fundamental facts and, whatever we may make of them, we should acknowledge their reality.[10]

However, there is more that may be learned. First of all, if one is willing to trust that the translators of the Revised Standard Version were more in touch with contemporary English usage than their late Elizabethan counterparts, then one might consider the RSV results as currently somewhat more accurate. Second, if that be acknowledged, the simple frequencies can be submitted to an equally simple non-parametric chi-square test, which will permit one to determine the statistical probability of rejecting the hypothesis that the twoTestaments

Key Word:	in the Old Testament:	in the New Testament:	Sums:
Choose	202	38	240
Decide	3	0	3
Column sums:	205	38	243

Figure 1. Frequency of *choice* and *decision* words in two testaments: KJV.

Key Word:	in the Old Testament:	in the New Testament:	Sums:
Choose	202	48	250
Decide	34	14	48
Column sums:	236	62	298

Figure 2. Frequency of *choice* and *decision* words in two testaments: RSV.

are essentially similar in their overall use of either kind of word. That is, one can use chi-square to test what is called a *null hypothesis*. (As some readers may readily recognize, this was a simple, relatively gross, but very common strategy in a variety of forms of social science in the later years of the 1970s.)

In fact, when the frequencies in figure 2 are submitted to such a test, the resulting value for the statistic chi-square is 2.42306 for 1 degree of freedom. Consulting my copy of Fisher and Yates's *Statistical Tables* (6th ed.), I found in table 4 (p. 47) that this value of chi-square *was* statistically significant at 1 degree of freedom with a probability less than 0.20 and more than 0.10.[11] That is not a low enough probability to qualify for the phrase *statistically significant*, if the common criterion of a probability of 0.05 or lower is used. Yet it does mean that difference is likely somewhere between 4-in-5 and 9-in-10 times, a finding that might conceivably be regarded as simply important. Moreover, when the actual cell-by-cell contributions to chi-square are calculated, it is abundantly evident that the largest contributions to the overall value of chi-square are the result of two things: an underrepresentation of *decision* words in the RSV's Old Testament and an overrepresentation of *decision* words in the RSV's New Testament. Conversely, there is a slight overrepresentation of *choice* words in the RSV's Old Testament and a somewhat more noticeable, albeit still small, underrepresentation of *choice* words in the RSV's New Testament.

Admittedly, one must be quite tentative in interpreting this finding. It is not the stuff from which one can build a thesis of great difference between the Christian's biblical Testaments.[12] Still, it is something that may well be considered as a clue to a subtle difference between the writings in the two parts of the Christian's Bible. Moreover, if one acknowledges (as Christians tend to believe!) that there is some form of continuity between the Testaments, then the distinctions in the Hebrew between *choose* and *decide* may be useful in testing the distinction proposed by Miller-Tiedeman and Tiedeman.

Apparently the Hebrew primitive root lying behind the KJV *choose* implies the tentativeness of trying. Similarly, the Hebrew root lying behind the KJV *decision* suggests not a tentative try but a pointed breaking through or division. If one thinks a bit about those two ideas, it seems at least possible to relate the tentative try to impulse, emotionality, or some kind of prerational choice. It also seems possible to relate the pointed division to a thoughtful, conscious, essentially rational decision. While somewhat speculative, not at all improbable.

AN IMPORTANT CAVEAT

The conceivably important clue located in the relative frequencies of *choice* words and *decision* words in the Christian's Old and New Testaments is not to be taken as some subtle rationale for anti-Semitism. While this caveat may seem either (a) a restatement of the obvious or (b) an all-too-time-bound example of contemporary concerns, it is important. The earliest Christian stance vis-a-vis Judaism finds its surest grounding in the agony of a Jewish apostle, Paul of Tarsus. He differed quite fundamentally from most first-century rabbis, political activists, and secularized Jews, but he did not deny that they were still in covenant with G-O-D. He agonized over the disparity between his understanding and that of most of his former compatriots, but he did not give up hope. His solution, it seems, was to leave in the hands of G-O-D the resolution of the seeming paradox. That some of his conceptual heirs have found other resolutions, including force, is their shame, not his, and certainly not Christianity's![13]

Moreover, whatever implication vis-a-vis a presumed developmental continuum along a concept of human maturity we may discern based upon choice or decision as presumedly prior conditions for a human act of faith, let us not forget that it is *our* construction, however true it may be. Thus, let us acknowledge that both biblical Testaments include not only *choice* words but also *decision* words, and let us firmly remind ourselves that the difference is a relative one. There is little in this distinction per se that supports anti-Semitism; there is nothing in it that requires it! No one should wander off from these considerations into some totally idiosyncratic form of late-twentieth-century anti-Semitism. That is neither the intent nor the logical result. It is, quite literally, anathema.[14]

VASTNESS OR HALF-VASTNESS: A HUMAN ACT OF FAITH

The religious term is *creation*. The neutral one may be *universe*.[15] Yet the fundamental query is simply what we think creation or universe to be. Is either a truly vast idea that (after my 1968 analogue) generates a complex of both meaningful and important human action? Or is either simply a truly half-vast idea that (after my 1968 analogue) generates no more than a complex, albeit quite abortive, human effort? However we answer those queries, we engage in what can best be called a human act of faith. We may reach such an act of faith from either a choice or a decision, but it *is* our conclusion, *our* act of faith.

Contemporary cosmology, for instance, really does not provide an answer. There is still an argument between some cosmologists as to whether the universe is continually expanding or is showing signs of slowing down toward an inevitable collapse upon itself to a final singularity. Black holes *are* fascinating subjects of speculation, but we know so little about their actuality, although we suspect a great deal.[16] Yet there is a sense in which these contemporary cosmological questions really are somewhat aside from the fundamental query. At best, they put any answer into some kind of quantitatively vast time frame, one which is of sufficient extent that only via our choice or decision does it (or can it!) have any present effect. The query itself concerns a contemporaneous action of evaluation, an action calling for either human choice or human decision. The query calls for some existential act, which I have called an act of faith. That may not, in fact, be too distant from Kierkegaard's nineteenth-century conclusion.[17]

A much simpler phrasing of the query is to ask of creation (or universe) whether or not it is ultimately meaningful. That form of the query pushes *us* onto the decisional center stage, for it is an inevitably personal query that reduces down to a remarkably simple "what do we think?"

Whatever response we may make, whether we choose or decide for meaning or for nonmeaning, for vastness or half-vastness, is a fundamental action, albeit a very *human* act of faith. It takes only a little knowledge, and a wee bit of wisdom, to recognize that the quality of human living is posited ultimately upon one or the other answer. For example, historians of Christian antiquities noted, long ago, that there was a sign of considerable difference between the funeral art of early Christians and their non-Christian, pagan contemporaries. The difference detected was relatable to how one answered the query of vastness or half-vastness, meaning or nonmeaning. The Christian funeral art, it was held, expressed a kind of confidence in the meaningfulness of creation, even in the face of the death of one who was beloved. The non-Christian, pagan funeral art expressed an opposite view of sharply delimited meaningfulness, which was expressed in terms of seemingly irreconcilable sorrow at the death of a beloved.[18] Inferentially, it would seem that the funeral art of those long-ago persons expressed quite succinctly a different response to the posited fundamental query.

Since those long-ago times, there really has not been much change. The mere form of the query has changed a word or two, but the substance has remained unchanged. Moreover, the possible responses have remained substantially the same. Some opt for meaning. Some for meaninglessness. Our context has changed, of course, but our responses have remained essentially the same. Thus, if we find that similarity to be a clue to an inherent mystery of humankind, we have no reason to believe that mystery to have undergone ought but contextual change.

In an age that has rapidly accepted the idea that the only thing that remains the same is that all is changing, acknowledging anything as stable is a problem. However, it may be possible for even those of us who are most a part of this age to acknowledge that there is a mystery inherent in humankind's way of coming around to ultimate questions of meaning. In fact, we who belong most to this age may be able to understand quite well the attraction of the question of meaning, for sheer change per se is difficult to regard as meaningful. If so, or to the degree that it is so, we may also be peculiarly well prepared to also acknowledge that this discovery of meaning is (minimally!) just that, a discovery. It is not something with which any human is born: it comes, across time and as a result of the experience of living, to humans as their discovery.

If a person can come to a conceptual "place" where such an affirmation seems to be one in which they can place confidence or trust, then a very human belief in meaning-as-a-possibility can arise. Along with that possibility can also come the honest recognition that humans move toward meaning in a strange, remarkable, step-by-step manner which is fundamentally developmental.[19]

Part of the mystery of humankind is, then, that it is developmental. Humans develop not only a physical structure but, as well, a perceptual and a cognitive structure. We are only potentially mature at our birth. It is via a lengthy and meaningful process that we become, in some sense, mature adults. Moreover, it is only as such mature adults that we reach a level of understanding where we can consciously exercise our freedom as responsible creatures within a creation which we can (however vaguely!) recognize as truly vast. Even the recognition of that process itself is something that develops. We are, in a word, thoroughly developmental creatures. That means that in some peculiar way we are involved in a seemingly directional process of actualizing possibilities for ourselves and, thereby, for the genus. We *are* remarkable creatures.

Clearly we are at, or very close to, a three-way intersection between the disciplines of psychology, education, and anthropology. We are affirming something about humans that can function as an answer to the fundamental anthropological query, "What *is* anthropos?" Our human answer to that query tends to determinatively affect how psychology goes about its studies of humankind, and how education goes about its facilitative work with humankind. If we opt for a developmental position, whether as a choice or as a decision, we responsibly turn our attention to the constructions across time of physical, perceptual, and cognitive structures. If we do not so opt, those contructions may seem unreal, unnecessary, or merely improbable. Unfortunately, we humans never quite escape choice or decision. Nor do we more than momentarily escape from the consequences of either of those actions.

* * *

In the following chapters I want to look at what it may mean to opt for a developmental position that presumes humankind to be a complex, continuing construction. I intend to look at a model of a mature human personality, and then ask where religion is to be found within such a model. Next, I intend to look at the human child, adolescent, and adult as a developmental phenomenon, especially attending to the progressive construction of the integrated human. In this way, I hope to cumulatively address that fundamental intersectional query, "What *is* anthropos?" I do not intend to overlook humankind's religious nature, for that is part of the inherent mystery, but I do intend to approach humankind as a continuing developmental construction. If I am successful, or to the extent that I am so, what should begin to come clear will be something very like the architectural principles of human development (or construction).

Notes and References

1. Because of a quite idiosyncratic allegiance to the standards of respect for others and confidentiality, I will *not* specifically identify the date and place, although I am quite able to do so. However, the real cognoscenti will be able to infer both *locale* and, even, *date* of this quite real remembrance. The merely curious will have to take my word for the actuality of the remembered event and the things ascribed to it.

2. Strange as it may seem, I contend that this sentence expresses something absolutely fundamental about the scientific enterprise: it *is* built by humans in the fullness of their humanity, so its *direction* is amenable to something as prosaic as individual interest, or whatever an individual scientifically oriented human might find fun to do. To think less of the scientific

enterprise, or its practioners, is to remove them from the range of normal humans and, if one is not careful, to engage in a quite contemporary form of sheer and simple idolatry. Whatever science may be as a goal, its practitioners—scientists—remain human beings. The scientific discipline really does not do more than define the technology used; the individuals do not escape the choice envisioned in this sentence, nor do they opt in any other way than that implied in it. (While that may well be a most unfortunate thing, it *is* a quite human action. Scientists are not biblical angels and, only now and then, anything like apostles, confessors, or martyrs. One really has to look elsewhere for such models.)

3. My ascription to Anna L. Miller-Tiedeman and David V. Tiedeman is, as near as I know, quite correct. However, I find myself hard put to give an explicit, published reference. That difficulty may arise from either of two possible hypothetical situations: (a) my memory is simply playing tricks on me, or (b) my memory is substantially correct but, in fact, I am synthesizing a number of private conversations, several public papers, and a couple of semi-public contributions to symposia or seminars. The interested reader, however, might well consult the following three sources: Anna Miller-Tiedeman, "Deliberate Decision-Making Education: A Self-Centering Approach," *Character Potential: A Record of Research*, vol. 7, no. 1 (October 1974), pp. 12–21; David V. Tiedeman, "The Self-Constructionist Alternative to Today's Develop or Wither Career Crisis at Mid-Life," and "Discerning 'I' Power in the Developmental Paradigm at Mid-Life," *Character Potential: A Record of Research*, vol. 8, no. 3 (October 1978), pp. 131–139, 148–151. While the words do not quite match my usage, the concept of a distinction between choosing and deciding is inferable.

4. *The Random House Dictionary of the English Language* (New York: Random House, 1967), the word *faith*.

5. Minimally, this process is parallel to that presumed by Christian evangelists and apologists as a human possibility since Simon Peter's explanatory sermon on the day of Pentecost (Acts 2:14–41). Maximally, the process is a simple identity to that which both apologist and evangelist presume to be a human possibility that, also presumably, has saving power, when exercised.

6. I have quite consciously used the four-word phrase, "human acts of faith." I recognize that there is an honorable theological tradition which credits a Christianly important act of faith to the working of God the Holy Spirit. I do not wish to deny that tradition but, *here*, I do not wish to use it either. Maximally, I am concerned with an analogy between a human action and a seemingly similar, albeit different, divine action. Actually, my purpose is quite well served without reference to the somewhat knotty theological affirmation, as long as the reader does not presume that I am trying to say what I am not. I want precision, not gross generality.

7. For what I regard as *the* basic reference to the Al Capp/Li'l Abner test, see the footnote to p. 45, in Al Capp, *The Life and Times of the Shmoo* (New York: Pocket Books, 1948/1949), p. 131. Naturally, readers who remember Capp's comic strip "Li'l Abner" may come up with several alternative references, since the test was repeatedly used.

8. Jean Piaget, *Structuralism* (London: Routledge and Kegan Paul, 1968/1971), pp. 32–35.

9. Without being an alarmist, it seems useful to recognize that answers to a fair number of these unanswered questions would require what most of humankind could recognize as the exercise of sheer magic. Without even trying to deny the reality of magic, one should ponder the age-old distinction between a white magic and a black magic. Reference to the Tolkienian mythology incarnate in *The Lord of the Rings* should make the distinction abundantly evident, as well as put one on notice as to the inherent risks. The curious reader might well consult the entries for Gandalf the Grey and Saruman the White in J. E. A. Tyler, *The Tolkien Companion* (New York: Avon Books, 1976), pp. 192–194, 419–422.

10. This sentence presumes a distinction between data per se and that quite human act of interpretation that transforms data into information. The data per se are real. The interpretation-become-information falls somewhere along a continuum that runs from fantasy toward truth. While this distinction is fundamentally scientific, the biblical scholars' distinction between exegesis and isogesis is quite similar.

11. The blessedly curious reader can locate the formula for the statistic chi-square in Allen L. Edwards, *Statistical Analysis* (New York: Holt, Rinehart and Winston, 1969), p. 153. Once that is located, readers might well calculate the value of chi-square for themselves and then, as a final check, locate table 4 on p. 47 in Ronald A. Fisher and Frank Yates, *Statistical Tables for Biological, Agricultural, and Medical Research*, 6th ed. rev., enl. (New York: Hafner Publishing Co., 1963) and read off the probability level for 1 degree of freedom from the topmost row of the tabled values for chi-square. Thus, such blessedly curious readers might be certain that what I have said is so and, as a result, trust themselves and not just me.

12. It is well to remember that for over eighteen hundred years Christian orthodoxy has rejected the Marcionite thesis that a Christian's Old Testament is solely a statement of superceded law, in contrast to a Christian's New Testament understood as solely a gospel of love. No reader should wander *unaware* into that most ancient of Christian heresies; that is certainly not my intent!

13. In rejecting *any* corporate guilt through association for Christianity, I am remembering two things specifically. First, the intellectual agony of Paul of Tarsus recorded in chapters 9–11 of his Letter to the Romans. Second, the

standard of individual responsibility that was enunciated by the author of Ezek. 18:30—"Therefore, Israelites, says the Lord GOD, I will judge every man of you on his own deeds."

14. The reader may wish to check the meaning of the ancient term *anathema* in F. L. Cross, *The Oxford Dictionary of the Christian Church* (London: Oxford University Press, 1957). I mean every one of the five words in this sentence, in the full sense propounded by Gratian in the twelfth century. Let no reader think anything else!

15. Such a possibly neutral use of the word *universe* may be found in the writing of R. Buckminster Fuller. However, in his later works, the word *universe* takes on a distinctly religious connotation, or so it seems to me. For example, see Fuller's poem entitled, "How Little I Know," in R. Buckminster Fuller, *And It Came to Pass—Not to Stay* (New York: Macmillan Publishing Co., 1976), esp. pp. 44–45.

16. See the feature article, "Black Holes," *Time: The Weekly Newsmagazine*, vol. 112, no. 10 (September 4, 1978), pp. 50 ff., for a recent, uncomplicated review of the contemporary cosmological question.

17. For example, consult *Kierkegaard's "The Concept of Dread,"* trans. W. Lowrie (Princeton, N.J.: Princeton University Press, 1944), p. 123. In this place, Kierkegaard says, "What I am talking about, on the other hand, is something quite simple and plain, that truth exists for the particular individual only as he himself produces it in action."

18. As near as I now know, I first heard this conclusion during a course on Christian art and antiquities that Dr. Eric Dinkler taught during the early 1950s at the Yale University Divinity School in New Haven, Connecticut. The curious reader might also consult Walter Lowrie, *Art in the Early Church* (New York: Pantheon Books, 1947), esp. plates 19–20. Like all historical judgments, this one is quite obviously a matter of interpretation. Nothing can alter that.

19. After some fifteen years of research into the processes of cognitive development, I am struck by how often development seems to be indicated by a step-wise progression of the means, and how rarely it seems to approximate a simple line of linear regression. Naturally, a step-wise progression of means *can* be fit to *some* line of linear regression: no one should think it cannot. However, I have come to believe that such a fitting to a line of linear regression involves an inevitable movement *up* at least one level of conceptual generality from that of the data itself. Thus, development is a particularity, while direction of development is a generality.

5

My God! They Grow Up

Two temporally disparate memories keep interacting in my mind. One memory comes from the earliest months of the life of my first child. On the one hand, it involves a conflict of cognitions and, on the other, a difference of sex roles. I was involved in a course in human development that Hugh Hartshorne taught in the early 1950s at the Yale University Divinity School, and I had a two-to-four-month-old infant at home. Hartshorne was introducing me to the insights of Gesell via readings and classroom visits from his staff, who were housed less than a block from the classroom. At the same time, I was coming home to a wife and an infant who was a beautiful example of so much Gesell described succinctly and accurately. What I discovered was that a harried mother was *not* very impressed with developmental generalities. When she and that infant had had a day, she least needed me to come home full of insights about thrusts forward or plateaus. I learned the practical lesson, but I still remember the awe of seeing my own child exhibit so much of what I had heard and read. That memory has not really left me, although the child is now twenty-eight years old.

The other memory is from my more recent past. It concerns the marriage of my oldest child who, in the long ago, so nicely illustrated Gesell's developmental steps. I recall that I was pleased to act as father of the bride in the rite. I also recall that there was a strange sense that it hardly seemed all that long ago that I chuckled over infant behavior illustrative of developmental generalities. That disparateness remains a part of me, as it may of others who have lived long enough to have had the experience. However, I want to use those memories for something other than a commentary upon the truism that "time *does* pass." Instead, I want to consider the sometimes difficult truth that we are born into a developmental process, live within it all of our infancy and childhood, and quite probably exist in it until the moment of our dying. That is, we are thoroughly developmental creatures.

Philosophers and theologians always want to get definitions clarified, at the very beginning. While that desire can betray a foregone conclusion, defining one's terms is a good thing. Minimally, it tends toward improved communication in the very real present. Thus, I want to look at an extremely knotty definitional question: What is development? What can we mean by development in these early years of the 1980s? What do *we* mean by development?

DEVELOPMENT: WHAT DO WE MEAN?

Everyday language is peculiarly imprecise.[1] One knows reasonably well what A means if he says an adult is a development from an infant. It is tolerably clear what B means if she affirms that adolescence is a developmental stage. It is even comprehensible if C suggests that there are particular developmental tasks associated with the years of midlife. Yet when one asks the fundamental question of exactly what is meant by development, the fuzziness begins to be apparent.

For example, Robert H. Pollack wrote in the late 1960s that his earlier view that "development is simply change in behavior through time, is no longer considered useful because it encompasses too many behaviors shown by analysis to be underlain by different organismic mechanisms."[2] Pollack felt that the concept of development deserved a more precise definition and, so, repudiated his earlier position. He wanted to rid the word *development* of changes in one's behavior that could be regarded as "the result of practice or of deterioration due to organic aging," and he suggested that the reason was that such changes "occur without any concurrent shift in underlying organization."[3]

Yet Drever's *Dictionary of Psychology* defines *development* simply as "progressive change in an organism, continuously directed towards a certain end condition (e.g., the progressive change from the embryo to the adult in any species)."[4] In his far-ranging *Comparative Psychology of Mental Development*, Werner notes that the term *development* could have at least two meanings, and that "although in actual genesis specialization and creation are interlocked, true development itself rests in creation."[5] Somewhat later, he notes that "it does appear that the development of biological forms is expressed in an increasing differentiation of parts and increasing subordination, or hierarchization."[6] Werner adds immediately, "Such a process of hierarchization means for any organic structure the organization of the differentiated parts for a closed totality, an ordering and grouping of parts in terms of the whole organism."[7]

On the other hand, the glossary of Hilgard's *Introduction to Psychology* includes only the phrase *developmental explanation*, defining it as "an explanation of behavior that stresses the historical roots of present activity, focusing on accumulating experience as the individual grows and learns."[8] Moreover, Hebb in *The Organization of Behavior: A Neuropsychological Theory* does not even include an index entry for *development* or any of its derivatives.[9] When Kohler wrote *The Mentality of Apes* in 1924, he did not index *development*.[10] Nor did the great gestalist bother to reference the work of developmentalists such as Buhler or Piaget in *Dynamics in Psychology* or, even later, in *Gestalt Psychology: An Introduction to New Concepts in Modern Psychology*.[11] For Kohler, Hebb, and Hilgard, the concept was clearly aside from the points they wished to make about humankind.

However, Jean Piaget worked for a very long time on development. When Elkind edited *Six Psychological Studies*, he picked works from 1940, 1954, 1956, 1959, 1963, and 1964 to put into a collection of Piaget's then lesser known later works. In the 1964 study, Piaget says, "When we speak of genesis in the field of psychology—and no doubt this is true of other fields also—we must first avoid any definition based on absolute beginnings," and "genesis is always conceived as stemming from an initial state which may also comprise a structure. Consequently, genesis is simply a form of development." Two sentences later, Piaget adds, "We can define genesis as a relatively determined system of transformations comprising a history and leading in a continuous manner from state A to State B, state B being more stable than the initial state and constituting an extension of it."[12]

Later the University of Chicago Press published Piaget's essay on organic regulations and cognitive processes as *Biology and Knowledge*.

There Piaget says, "If we restrict ourselves to the most general characteristics of the notion of development—the temporal transformation of structures in the double sense of differentiation of sub-structures and their integration into totalities—then it is clear that the evolution of organized creatures constitutes a kind of development, just as does the gradual formation of an adult organism from the sperm state."[13] Eleven pages later, Piaget says that "development is a progressive organization implying, on that account, the notion of total structures and a filiation of those structures, so that the structures of stage n are derived from those of stage $n-1$." In addition, he suggests that "this construction of organized structures came to be seen as a sort of progressive equilibration due to an action of autoregulation, first structural (reconstructions of the total structure built up from partial structures) and then functional (activated by feedbacks). Thus, the stages of development have the appearance of graduated steps in a progressive equilibration."[14]

It is reasonably obvious, is it not?

Development can be ignored, or it can become extremely important. One does not need it to be rational about human behavior, yet one can be rational with the concept. One has to *decide* whether or not the idea of development is useful. Unless one simply knuckles under to authority, one must reach some sort of decision. The query, "What do *you* think?" is unavoidable.

Let me be tolerably honest. My decision is to use the concept of development. That does not mean that I cast any aspersions on a Hilgard, a Hebb, or a Kohler for having other interests. It only means that *I* find the concept uncommonly useful in understanding humankind. That is a first decision. However, by itself, that decision does not answer the question of what development is. That I must answer—unless I finesse the issue or simply accept some authority. I have no way to avoid taking *my* stand and, then, exposing it to the reader. Thus, let me explain how I came to a possible meaning for the concept of development.

I began my commitment to the idea of development as the result of watching my daughters in infancy. I suppose that I began with a sense that it was a process with a history that led from one state to another.

That much I learned from Gesell's studies and, later, found again in the work of Piaget. Being theologically trained, I was not bothered by the teleological assumption in Drever's definition, and I may even have found Werner's choice of words intriguing.[15] In my own research, I restricted the notion of development to the twin aspects of a direction and a pattern, at least when I was inferring development from empirical data. However, I am aware that Piaget avoids any a priori assumption of a *telos* and stresses a construction process, rather than any form of preformation.

Before Thanksgiving Day, 1978, I had the good fortune to have sixty hours to devote solely to the question of what development is.[16] It was a period when I could integrate my thinking and my research. It was hard but rewarding conceptual work. At the end of that period, I came to a conclusion that still seems reasonable, one which I want to share. As I understand it, development itself is a stochastic sequence of constructions which integrate the needs for persistence in and adaptation to the environment.

Aside from the fact that those seventeen words are *my* definition of the word *development*, what do they mean? That is a reasonable query, and I want the reader to know why I found myself satisfied with those words, and not some others. Thus, I begin by recognizing that eight out of the seventeen words in my definition require an explanation. Those eight words are *stochastic*, *sequence*, *constructions*, *integrate*, *needs*, *persistence*, *adaptation*, and *environment*. I want to address each of these words and then consider why I think they fit together into an appropriate definition of the concept of development. As I do this, I hope to clarify my assertion that humans are thoroughly developmental creatures.

I. The Word *Stochastic*

The word comes from the world of mathematics and, especially, from the subdiscipline of statistics. In *Introduction to the Theory of Probability and Statistics*, Arley and Buch describe a stochastic process in these words: "One often finds problems in which the distribution of a random variable depends on a non-random variable which is a continuously varying parameter such as time."[17] They also note that "stochastic processes, both discontinuous and continuous, play an ever-increasing role in many practical applications such as physics, engineering (especially telephony), biology, and insurance."[18] Two things seem important in these quotations: first, the association with time; second, the recognition that such processes play an important role in communication (i.e., telephonic engineering) and biology. It seems obvious, albeit sometimes forgotten, that humans are inescapably biological, communicative, and within time.

As C. S. Lewis once noted, it is a fundamental fallacy to consider humans as angels; that is, achronological or nonbiological.[19] Humans are biological, communicating creatures. For good or ill, humans communicate their ideas, their emotions, their desires to other humans who, because they too are communicators, receive and interpret those communications. The "language" can be simple or complex, verbal or nonverbal, but communication is a fundamentally human experience. In fact, when verbal communication is impossible but attempted (e.g., a Tibetan monk addresses me when I do not know Tibetan, or a Navaho directs me to do something although I do not know Navaho), humans tend to reach a basic discrimination between "friend" and "stranger." To most of us, communicators whom we do not understand are strangers. Something deep within us tends to equate strangers with danger and fear, and either flight or fight. Only an ability to abstract ourselves from that tendency enables us to avoid a simple, reflexive response to a communicating stranger.

In addition to being biological, communicating creatures, humans are also within time; we are time-conscious creatures. We are aware, as some creatures appear not to be, or—perhaps more precisely—we are aware of the "passage" of time and, so, of it as an inescapable context of all we are and do. We live in this time and no other, regardless of how we despise it or long for another time. To accept our involvement in time is, therefore, a matter of realism.

Thus, if a stochastic process describes an existence that relates to time, biology, and communication, then *stochastic* is a word applicable to the human state. Since *development* is also a word applicable to the human state, *stochastic* and *development* are related words. One may be useful in defining the other. That is somewhat involved, but reasonably evident. The question is, which does which?

My decision was to use *stochastic* within a definition of *development.* Thereby, I specify a particular general class of processes as *development* and, implicitly, exclude processes not of that class. Definitionally, this means that development is a process, but not necessarily any process. However, the question really is, what do we mean by terming a process *stochastic?*

Felix's *Modern Aspect of Mathematics* contains the following passage.

> As for "stochastic processes," the study of which has been developing for about 20 years, we can understand their object from the following statement of Paul Levy: "The idea of a stochastic process is, at least for a determinist, tied to that of hidden parameters which do not intervene in the description of the apparent present state of the system studied and which nevertheless influences its future evolution. Our ignorance of their value forces us to speak for the future only of a set of possible evolutions, and in certain cases we can define in that set a law of probability incessantly modified by the knowledge of new data."[20]

Felix says that the study of stochastic processes is only about twenty years old, which means that the study per se began about 1940. That is, forty years ago. Yet forty years is barely time for an idea to escape its original discipline and begin to affect humankind's thinking.

We should also note that Felix describes a stochastic process as a surd to the determinist. It is a reality, but it is a reality that pushes a determinist to posit "hidden parameters" which, quite really, "influence" the "future evolution" of a system. If one considers humankind as a system, then a good bit of human experience would seem to be stochastic. Unless one is a thoroughgoing determinist, there is almost no alternative to considering human experience to be a stochastic process.

Another fundamental query is clearly whether *development* and *stochastic* are names for similar processes. If they are, then a stochastic process may well be basic to what one can mean by *development.* But are the processes similar?

In a 1964 work, Jean Piaget says about the implication of a child finding a reversible system, "This is an example of a progressive equilibration and—I must emphasize—of an equilibration which is not preformed. The second or third stages increases in probability as a function of the immediately preceding stage, not as a function of the point of departure. Equilibration," he notes, "is thus a process with sequential probability."[21] If one will but think, it should be evident that Piaget describes a stochastic process, even though he does not use the word. A stochastic process inevitably involves a sequential probability from one state to a yet-next state. Moreover, since Piaget was considering a process of development, the inference that development is stochastic is nearly inescapable.

But what about equilibration? Is it amenable to the conclusion that development is essentially stochastic? Somewhat earlier in the same work, Piaget says that "the third point I should like to emphasize is that equilibrium, thus defined, is not something passive but, on the contrary, something essentially active; the greater the equilibrium, the more activity is required. . . . Equilibrium is synonymous with activity," he concludes.[22] Now, if equilibrium is essentially active, it is either a process or a part of a process. It is not a nonprocess.

Yet, is there more that can be said? I think so. In the same work, Piaget notes that when one asks what psychology means by equilibrium there are three things that need to be said. We have already noted the third of Piaget's trio; let us now consider his first two points.

Piaget suggests, "First, equilibrium is notable for its stability."[23] Since so much of living is marked by stability, this suggests that equilibrium and human experience intersect (e.g., it is possible to consider human experience as the view from the inside of human development). If we can but remember Piaget's third conclusion about equilibrium being active, we can avoid the tempting idea that human experience is too marked by activity to be an instance of equilibrium. Activity is a simple, replicable, clinically verifiable idea that is too clear to be contested. Yet the conclusion that sheer activity denigrates the idea of development is too facile.

The reasonably clear implication of Piaget's observation is that development per se includes what experience knows as moments of stability. Reason pushes, directs, or insists upon something like a Werner *hierarchization* of one's concepts. Perhaps *development* is some supraordinate category which includes *equilibrium* at some differentiated, ordinate level. If that be so, we can also acknowledge Werner's thesis that development per se involves "an increasing differentiation of parts and increasing subordination, or hierarchization."[24] The fact that reason led us to this conclusion can be, in itself, a rationale for the idea that we are quite thoroughly developmental creatures. (Minimally, the idea is worth some consideration before one decides its subjective probability!)

Piaget also suggests, "Secondly, every system is subject to external intrusion which tends to modify it. We shall say that there is equilibrium when this external intrusion is compensated by the actions of the subject."[25] Note carefully. Piaget presumes that every system (e.g., humankind) "is subject to external intrusion which tends to modify it." The generality of the statement must not be allowed to becloud our understanding. This is a statement of one-half of the thesis that all organisms exist in an interactive mode vis-a-vis their environment. The generality *environment* does tend to affect the organism as an "external intrusion which tends to modify it." That is tolerably evident. Moreover, *development* must include such an evident part of human experience, if it is to function as a general, strong description of the specificities of human experience.

Does human experience indicate that such an "external intrusion" tending to modify the existing system is passively received, accepted, and incorporated into the system itself? Although some have thought so, careful consideration of experience tends to make a contrary answer obvious. The human system receives almost nothing passively! Rather, it tends to work upon an "external intrusion" and, in terms of everyday language, make it over into something acceptable. This is exactly what Piaget termed the process of adaptation. It is also exactly what is posited by the statement that such an "external intrusion" into the system is equilibrated when it "is compensated by the actions of the subject."[26] Thus, Piaget's idea of equilibrium clearly seems to describe a process that human experience knows quite well, one that careful, sensitive observation can verify as remarkably common.

It seems that (a) human experience is rationalized when development is posited, and (b) Piaget's idea of development (including his idea of equilibrium) fits human experience remarkably well. Therefore, it seems to me that humankind is thoroughly developmental. If so, and if our experience of development from within is at all trustworthy, then development is also a stochastic process. I see no obvious way to avoid that conclusion, unless one retreats into subjective preference (e.g., rejecting a statistical construct because one dislikes mathematics and distrusts statistics!).

II. The Word *Sequence*

Unlike *stochastic*, the idea of sequence is reasonably familiar. The word refers to a chronological order of events or, more generally, "to the condition or fact of following something else."[27] A sequence is a series. Basically, fundamentally, a sequence is some ordered set of events. Thus, to use the word as part of a definition of development involves the idea that development is a chronological order of events.

For example, in a set of events A, B, C, and D it is possible, if those events form a sequence, to affirm (a) that A precedes B, and (b) that B precedes C, and (c) that C precedes D. C follows B, which follows A, and D presumes a series beginning with A and concluding with C, in which B is the intermediate term. This is so obvious to adults that we often forget that there were months and months early in our lives when none of this was the least bit obvious. The idea of a sequence relates to what Piaget terms seriation, which he found to be something children learn or discover or construct out of a welter of unordered experiences.[28] In a word, a sequence is a developmental accomplishment.

However, let us be precise.

A sequence per se only affirms a history of states behind any existing state. Of itself, it does not specify the nature of those prior historical states, nor does it necessitate that the ordered set A, B, C, and D be ordered in any way except by the time of their appearing. D is not necessarily greater than C, B, or A. C is not necessarily less than D or greater than B or A. A is not less than B, C, or D by any necessity, if one only affirms it as the first in a sequence. Sequence and amount are often related constructs, but they are not inherently so, nor are they in any way identical constructs. Sequence is only ordinal measurement, at best.

All this basic theory is important, for there is an almost overpowering human tendency to ignore the simple fact that sequence is a necessary but not sufficient condition of interval measurement.[29] This tendency is nowhere more bothersome than in what everyday language identifies as *development*. The assumption of a developmental sequence is, then, falsely presumed to imply a relation of "greater than" or "less than," and not a historical "earlier than" and "later than." While that assumption is sometimes true of developmental sequences, it is not the sequence itself that assures its truth. A sequence itself is no more and no less than a time-related ordering of events.

Therefore, to speak of development as involving a sequence is to identify development as an ordered series of events, which are inevitably related to one another historically. By itself, a developmental sequence is not a measure; at best, it is a statement of that which precedes another or, contrariwise, that which follows another. Sequence implies only precedence, nothing else.[30]

III. The Word *Constructions*

As a sequence is solely related to an order of historical precedence, a construction is solely related to a state that can be considered to be ordered in yet another sense. A construction is ordered in the sense that it is a whole consisting of related parts. It is possible to imagine a whole of totally unrelated parts, what a mathematician would call a set of disparate items. However, a construction presumes that there is some quality, a relationship, that makes the various parts belong to a set which makes up the construction.

The late Kurt Lewin proposed that the parts of psychological constructions had a *valence*.[31] He meant by that term a strength, power, or degree. If we can conceive of interrelatedness as manifesting degree, then Lewin's idea of valence may be a very real help. A construction is not a set of disparate parts because it has some minimal valence of interrelatedness. However, that is only a bounding definition: that is, sets below that minimal valence are not constructions, while those at or above it are so.

Inherent in Lewin's idea of valence is the idea of degree. In Lewinian terms, a valence is an analogue to a continuous variable, over some range. Thus, to speak of a construction as a set of parts exhibiting some degree of minimal interrelatedness, as if that were a valence, involves the idea that a construction exhibiting at least that minimal degree of interrelatedness may, as well, exhibit varying degrees of interrelatedness over and above that minimal level.

Admittedly, the argument is complex and, even, a bit esoteric. However, I want to establish that a construction can vary in the degree of interrelatedness of its parts. I want to acknowledge a variety of constructions and, so, conceive that varying valences distinguish one construction from another along a continuum that admits a *more* and a *less* distinction. If interrelatedness can be conceived of as varying, then one can speak of a construction as consisting of parts which may be more or less interrelated. If that is conceivable, then one could assign *strong* to a high degree of interrelatedness and *weak* to a low degree of interrelatedness. Thus, one could speak of a *strong* or a *weak* construction, depending upon the degree to which the constituent parts of that construction were interrelated.

Let us be clear: the words *strong* and *weak* refer solely to a relation existing among the parts. Only our preference for a degree of order would give those words value. Aside from our preference, they are relatively objective descriptions of a state of the construction.

To posit that development involves a construction, in a sequence, is only to posit that development involves the appearance of a whole consisting of some set of minimally interrelated parts. The idea of a sequence affirms nothing more of a construction. In the sometimes picky logic of grammarians, to affirm anything as a construction involves only the affirmation that an item is a whole made up of some set of parts that are, to some minimal degree, interrelated. It does not involve the affirmation that a construction is, in any way or by any criterion, either more or less interrelated than its immediately preceding state. The only thing that can be posited of a state n and its immediately preceding state $n-l$ is that $n-l$ is the immediate predecessor of n. That is, a simple historical statement. The parts of an observed construction may be adjudged to be either more or less interrelated than in their historically given, observed prior state. But there is no inevitability about the *more* or the *less*. (Unless one wishes to posit a comfortingly positive inevitable thrust forward in human development, there seems far too much experience to ignore the reality of periodic regressions, which may not be the denials of a developmental direction that they seem to be, if one can accommodate a hierarchical set of levels of generality.)

Defining *development* as a sequence of constructions is *not* to affirm an inevitable progression. It *is* to permit regressions. It *is* to define a pervasive, clearly evident human phenomenon in terms of that which is observed most often, without falling into the trap of denying the possibility of that which is not explicitly affirmed as a necessity of development per se. To the simple, this is an unnecessary sophistication of the argument. To the wise and the subtle, it is a necessarily useful, positive caveat. To delimit the idea of a construction as I have, is *not* to deny that one can often observe progressions from weak to strong constructions during the processes of human development, but it *is* to reserve such observations to the important and useful category of a special case. Specifically, it is to deny them total, utter, complete generality.

IV. The Word *Integrate*

My dictionary tells me that *integrate* can mean (a) to form into a whole, (b) to incorporate into a larger unit, or (c) to end the segregation of and bring into common and equal membership in society or an organization.[32] Clearly, to *integrate* is some aspect of any construction. To *integrate* is involved in forming some whole, which can, via some perspective, be identified as a construction.

Moreover, there is that second meaning, which implies that *integrate* can apply to a process of hierarchical incorporation of parts into some larger unit, which is marked by sufficient interrelatedness to qualify it as a whole, rather than a set of merely disparate parts and, so, a "larger" unit than any $n-1$ combination of its constituent parts. This second sense of *integrate* is primarily quantitative; it is not qualitative, except by metaphorical extension. It is well to keep that clearly in mind.

Finally, there is that third definition. To *integrate* can mean to bring a set of heretofore disparate parts into "common . . . membership in . . . an organization." If one focuses upon commonness, rather than upon equality, the usefulness of *integration* in a definition of *development* may be evident. It is not an equality of parts that is involved in the complex process humans call *development;* rather, it is an affirmation that, regardless of their uncommonness, the parts belong together in some whole, some construction, which conceptually exists within some generality. The process of integration is a process of inclusion. The qualitative matter of how the included parts relate at varying levels of generality is a secondary question. The primary affirmation of *integrate* is that of inclusion into some whole which is a set of interrelated parts.

Since a *construction* has been identified as an interrelated whole, it is reasonable to suppose that *integration* and *construction* refer to similar, albeit separate, parallel processes. I would like, therefore, to reserve *construction* for the totality which is the end result of these processes themselves. However, I would like to reserve *integration* for those processes themselves. The processes *integrate,* for *integration* is a label for the processes qua processes. If this distinction be granted, then the definitional statement is not redundant; integration is a process which leads to a construction, although it is not the construction itself. The definitional statement is the specification of a relation between a process qua process and a result qua result.

That last sentence could be tricky, unless one shifts upward a level of generality. *Result* and *process* were singular, although the singularity is a generality based upon an observable multiplicity. Processes of integration are many, continuing, and pervasive during the human life span; yet they tend toward a sequence of results, each of which is a construction.

V. The Word *Needs*

I am aware that the history of needs in psychology is both hoary and hairy. Yet I still want to use the term. I want to use *needs* in a sense that is general and yet basic. I do not wish to get involved with the question of whether an organism needs something as complex and general as love or affection or acceptance. I want to use *needs* in the sense of "a condition requiring supply or relief."[33] For that limited sense of *needs*, I want to posit a minimal answer.

The fundamental question is simply what one or two states (or conditions) simply must be supplied or given some relief. Since development is of most interest when it is posited of us, let us ask that question of ourselves.[34] Remember, we are not asking what we would like or what we have become accustomed to having, but what must be supplied unless we are to be in a state requiring relief. My decision involved exactly that kind of a consideration; while it is general, I think it is also fundamental. That decision is, of course, specified in the two words *persistence* and *adaptation*.

VI. The Word *Persistence*

There is an interesting double meaning to the root word *persist*. On the one hand, it can mean to "continue steadily or firmly in some state, purpose, course of action, or the like, especially in spite of opposition, remonstrance, etc."[35] On the other hand, it can mean the ability "to last or to endure."[36] The first meaning presumes a choice or a decision. The second meaning is simply an observation. Without ignoring that first possible meaning, I want to make use of that second, objective sense in a definition of *development*. However, I have used *persistence* to identify one of a minimal pair of needs which are integrated in, through, and by development.

I want to affirm that development is related to an organism's need to endure or last. Another word, *survival*, can be used to emphasize this sense of persistence. I want to keep *development* connected with an organism's ability to survive, endure, or last. Therefore, things which may be unrelated to survival, endurance, or lasting are not developmental. It seems obvious that organisms, especially human organisms which are observed in time, have an inferable need to endure, last, survive. If they did not, one might logically expect that they would not last, would not endure, would not survive. Pushing the logic a bit, they might not be observed in time at all, since even a short-lived organism might be expected to have a need to endure, however short its total life cycle might be. Thus, to push the logic to its limits, if organisms do exist without this need, they are not observable in time, and are non-developmental. Yet human organisms are in time, are observed, and are clearly developmental. Therefore, to posit an organism without a need to endure or last is to posit a nonobservable organism which, in a peculiar way, partakes of a characteristic traditionally allocated to an unseen order of creation, such as angels.[37]

In my definition, I posit that development is related to an organism's need to persist, endure, last, or survive. Thus, what an organism does in order to persist is, fundamentally, an aspect of development. At the level of a biological organism, persistence behavior is developmental. At the level of a human biological organism, we encounter continuously more complexity in the organism as this need for persistence is met, and we observe that the meeting of the need involves increasingly complex actions. We often tend to think that only those increasingly complex actions are development. However, their complexity arises from the needs of an already complex organism to endure or last. For example, when we observe a human adolescent or young adult, an organism of remarkable complexity, we discover a range of actions that are persistence behaviors. In the extreme of a harsh prison camp, as described by a Frankl or a Solzhenitsyn, we see how basic and how complex persistence behaviors can be. In that extreme instance, we are able to identify the need as just that.[38] I cannot ignore that fact of human existence in identifying a basic need.

VII. The Word *Adaptation*

Adaptation is generally understood as simply the act of adapting. My dictionaries define *adapt* as "to make suitable to requirements or conditions; adjust or modify fittingly," or as "to make suitable or fit (as for a new use or for different conditions)." *Adaptation* is a noun form of the verb *adapt*. My large dictionary also notes two biological meanings: "(a) any alteration in the structure or function of any organism or any of its parts that results from natural selection and by which the organism becomes better fitted to survive and multiply in its environment," or "(b) a form or structure modified to fit changed environment."[39] These definitions are, in fact, variations on a single theme: adaptation is an alteration-response to existing conditions, which response involves a modification of the responder adjudged to be either suitable to or fitting in the existing conditions.

In the language of systems analysis, adaptation inevitably involves a form of feed-forward. It is logically clear (if not always obvious) that adaptation per se need not be inevitably successful; yet it is implicit that adaptation was initially presumed to be a possibly successful alteration-response to existing conditions. Only an after-the-fact assessment can identify whether or not an alteration-response was, in fact, successful. However, some tend to avoid that conclusion in the name of some extremely general, theoretically presumed process (e.g., natural selection or evolution).[40]

There is also a technical use of the word *adaptation*. It owes its being to that persistent investigator, Jean Piaget. He used *adaptation* as a supraordinate category for the complementary pair of ordinate category processes of assimilation and accommodation.[41] That is, Piaget identified the pervasive nature of assimilation and accommodation, at least in the cognitive development of a human organism, and he maintained that they were but two aspects of the human organism's continuing relationship with its environment. In addition, he suggested that the mechanism of adaptation is a cycle of assimilation and accommodation. Thus, a pair of ordinate-level concepts define (or thoroughly describe) a supraordinate-level construct. One should not overlook that relationship.

In fact, I want to avail myself of Piaget's thesis that *adaptation* is an appropriate label for the assimilation-accommodation cycle. Thereby, I can affirm the cycle and all it implies about the human organism's response to its environment with a single supraordinate but useful word. Simple observation can convince most humans that we do both assimilate and accommodate our environment. On the one hand, we tend to take into ourselves input from the environment, or what four paragraphs back I termed "existing conditions." That is reasonably clear. In fact, that is what determinists tend to use as a basis for their systems, be they Freudians or strict Calvinists. They presume something "out there" irresistibly determines the organism's response, and posit that something to be its environment. In Piagetian terms, however, assimilation is only one-half of a relationship cycle. That is extraordinarily important to remember!

The other half of a relational cycle involves a limited accommodation by the existing state of an organism to the environmental input. Piaget's identification of this fact enabled him to avoid the determinism of any kind of preformation and, instead, champion the constructive action of an organism. Accommodation inevitably involves an organism's assimilative modification of environmental input into a form amenable to its existing state.[42] Piaget's observations of children are embarrassingly rich in instances of this readily observable action. In fact, careful observation of young children will convince almost anyone of the factuality of the process. It simply occurs, whether our theories account for it or not.

For example, the childish misunderstanding of the words in an evangelical Protestant hymn "Gladly the Cross I'd bear" as "Gladly, the Cross-eyed bear" is an example of a drastically limited assimilation determining accommodation. So, too, is the Catholic child's misunderstanding of the rosary's use of the angelic greeting ("Hail, Mary . . . blessed art thou amongst women") as a surd statement about "monks swimming."[43] Of course, these are *mis*understandings. They are also vividly humorous examples of our tendency to work over environmental input until it becomes something we think we understand, even if the end result is a mysterious surd.

Adults utterly fail to appreciate what is going on when they only focus on the patent misunderstanding. To do only that, and nothing else, is to overlook a thoroughly fundamental half of the adaptation process and, so, only laugh.

I do not want to suggest that the assimilative misunderstandings children generate are not humorous. Instead, I want to suggest that they are signs of our human need to adjust input from the "out there" to that world in which we live, our existing condition. In fact, there are examples of this need that are quite adult. A prime example (at least, for many adults in these years of the late twentieth century) involves an assimilation of the raw fact that sufficient nuclear explosive exists to obliterate humankind from the surface of this planet. We believe it, but then work upon it by a variety of ways that, in fact, change the reality itself. In this instance, we are little different from children. Since we cannot assimilate the reality, we work upon it until it seems less threatening, less awesome, less final, and so accommodate ourselves to that input with which we can deal, since the fact is more than we can deal with in its full range of implications. This is, of course, an extreme example. However, thought will identify others less extreme and more commonplace.

Think for a moment: How do you assimilate existing conditions?

Frankly, I am concerned with preserving both halves of adaptation for the concept of development. Thus, I want to define *development* as an alteration-response to existing conditions, without adding that only those responses which prove to have been successful were actually development. I want to include in development all alteration-responses. A nondevelopmental response, then, involves a static, nonaltering, stereotypically conservative response that affirms only that which is. Put that way, it is clear that a nondevelopmental response is extremely rare, not necessarily age-related, and very often recognized to be pathological. On the whole, humans do not often adopt it. Rather, they make some developmental response.

VIII. The Word *Environment*

In a nation with an Environmental Protection Agency, and in a time when *environmentalist* can be a curse or a blessing, we all know what environment is. Or do we? In its rather odd way, my dictionary says that *environment* is "the aggregate of surrounding things, conditions, or influences, especially as affecting the existence or development of someone or something."[44] An interesting set of words that suggests four ideas:

a. Whatever environment is, it affects both existence and development.

b. Environment's effect involves "someone or something."

c. Environment is an "aggregate" of many things.

d. Environment involves a distinguishing between a thing in itself and all "surrounding things, conditions, or influences."

The experience of environmental consciousness is a good beginning. A recurring experience during the 1970s was the discovery that something in our environment was harmful to human health. As we became more and more careful in our study of the effect of environment upon us, we found things that were harmful and then later found that an alternative was not helpful, either. The frustration with a series of such discoveries could lead us to conclude, "Oh, what the hell!" However, we could also recognize that humans always live with risk. We are never free from the often potentially harmful effect of all "surrounding things, conditions, or influences." If we could be that, we would be close to the idea that each of us exists in a kind of symbiotic relationship with our environment.[45]

However, that idea is either a grand truism (everything is related to everything) or a kind of ultimate contextual wisdom. The truism is useless; it specifies a range of relationships that far exceeds the limited human capacity for either acknowledgment or consideration. Thus, the truism has no specific meaning, or it is a clear invitation to a pathological, free-floating anxiety. On the other hand, the contextual wisdom may provide us a way of recognizing that one should be surprised at very little, once one begins to consider the relationship of almost anything to the human species or, even more specifically, to a single human. The wisdom involves a recognition that within the vast complexity of environment there are only moments of relative certainty. Thus, one can avoid premature claims of finality or completeness or inevitability. Only in the special cases, such as closed and thoroughly investigated systems, is completeness even relatively likely. However, such special cases are poor analogues of the environment, that all-encompassing totality of those "things, conditions, or influences" which affect "the existence or development of someone or something." They are patent invitations to reach questionable conclusions. A pointed way to put this idea is the aphorism that human ignorance still has a vaster range than human knowledge.

Some forty-five years ago, Jean Piaget wrote, "Although we cannot at present fix with any certainty the boundary between the contribution of the mind's structural maturation and that of the child's individual experience or the influences exerted by his physical and social environment, it does nevertheless seem that we should accept both that these two factors are constantly at work and that development is a product of their continuous interaction."[46] Piaget's two interactive factors are (a) the structural maturation of the mind, and (b) the individual experience (or the totality of influences exerted by the physical and social environment). Piaget posits a "continuous interaction," which produces "development." Thus, environment is clearly an aspect of development; the words and concepts belong together.

In the seventeen words I propose as a definition of *development*, environment is an inevitable context within which development takes place. However, environment is not a neutral setting; in interaction with the human organism, via the cyclical process of adaptation, it generates development. The vast complexity which is environment is a stage but, like any stage, one that requires the actors to adapt themselves to itself and its possibilities. We humans are actors, not mere products.[47]

Let us try and be reasonable.

Like the Freudian hypothesis, environment is an all-embracing concept which (a) is pervasively useful, but (b) tends to explain too much. If it isn't us, it is environment. The problem is its sheer inclusiveness—little, if anything, is left out. In the most general of terms, environment is that with which we could interact. No less. However, we are *not* simply counterdependent rebels to make an acknowledgedly arbitrary delimitation, in order to make the concept meaningful in the specifics of our existence. But we should not forget what *we* have done, however necessary such a delimiting may be. If we do forget what we have done, we will find ourselves enmeshed in a conceptual thicket or lost on some conceptual moor.

Still, let us try to be reasonable.

Whatever environment may mean for the genus or for the individual, there are two obvious delimitations. First, there is a historic delimitation: that to which we have interacted. This is always specific, both in the sense of what the environment was and in the sense of how we adapted ourselves to it. But it is irretrievably in our past: a thing once done and not likely to be repeated. Second, there is a perceptual delimitation: that with which we interact or have interacted or will interact with awareness. This introduces human awareness and, functionally, delimits environment to that which we perceive. Obviously, that is a thoroughly subjective delimitation of the environment to a mere subset of that extensive complexity which, objectively, the environment is. Still, we ought to consider such a subjective delimiting seriously. It is useful in any given present. It is, in fact, a functional definition of *environment* in that given present. Therefore, it is useful in any past present or in any not-yet future present. It is a usefully elastic concept across presents, something very like a generality. Thus, I suggest that the idea of development involves, in any specific instance, a recognition of the perceptual environment as that with which the organism interacts and, thereby, generates development.[48]

By focusing upon the varying perceptual environment, we gain a way of acknowledging what seems abundantly evident: A and B may not share the same environment, although they may exist in the same time and place. A's environment may, perceptually, be broader and more extensive than B's, which may be narrower and far more limited. Yet B may have a deeper and more profound grasp upon its limited environment than A has upon its broad one. For example, did Francis of Assisi have as broad an environment as Pope Honorius III? (Almost certainly not.) Did Francis have a deeper and more profound grasp upon his environment than Pope Honorius III? (Almost certainly he did.) Did the patent clerk Albert Einstein or his immediate supervisor have a broader environment? (Almost certainly Einstein had the broader environment.) Which had a more detailed grasp upon the specifics of their environment? (Probably Einstein's supervisor.) The point is that persons have different environments in the same period. That difference in environments is, it seems, best accounted for by recognizing the factor of awareness. Francis was aware of things Honorius III was not, and there was a true vice versa. Einstein was aware of things that his immediate supervisor was not and, quite probably, there was also a true vice versa. Only our after-the-fact assessments say that Francis and

Albert Einstein had a profound awareness of their environment, and we are still learning to integrate their insights.

This may well seem quite obvious. However, I detail the point to remind us that *our* environment is the one to which *we* respond interactively; the one in which *we* seek to persist and adapt successfully. In gross or fine detail, our perceived environment is different from another's. Yet it is that perceived environment to which we respond and, thereby, in which we develop. Individualism of environment is not really a cop-out; the generality that includes us all is the interaction, the response, and the purpose we attempt (persistence and adaptation). We simply must not forget what we have done or are doing or will do. We respond to our environment and, thereby, we develop. But it is always *our* environment to which we respond. Part of human responsibility arises simply from this fact. At times, it may be a pain; but it is also the ground of our human glory, for responsibility and freedom are kissing cousins.

DEVELOPMENT: EIGHT REASONS WHY IT IS USEFUL TO THINK OF IT THIS WAY

Being the person I am, when I finally found my particular ordered set of seventeen words in mid-November, 1978, I was pleased but not quite at ease. I asked myself that useful but not always easy question, why do you think this way? Why do I think development is a stochastic sequence of constructions which integrate the needs for persistence in and adaptation to the environment? As I thought about those seventeen words, and the concept they purport to define, I came to recognize eight reasons why I was persuaded that this was a useful way to think about the concept of development. Those eight reasons were:

1. The definition is applicable across the human life span.
2. The definition is amenable to what seems to be regression, as well as to what is clearly progression.
3. The definition acknowledges the genuineness of changes in one's state that may accompany changes in constructions.

4. The definition affirms that construction is a basic developmental accomplishment.
5. The definition affirms the integrative function of each such construction in a developmental sequence.
6. The definition acknowledges that all developmental entities exist in interaction with an environment.
7. The definition affirms that, within any specific environment, all entities tend to both persist (or survive) and adapt.
8. The definition is applicable to all biological organisms (maximally) and, most assuredly, to all complex organisms that are generally termed *living* (minimally).

Clearly, these eight possible reasons say a good deal about the kind of developmentalist I am. Obviously, I am concerned with considering development as a possibility across the life span, rather than simply as some process of growth that is completed once one is an adult. Moreover, I am also concerned with permitting development to oscillate, so that what seems to be regression is developmental, as well as that which seems clearly progression. In this, I combine a conviction arising from my own research into moral judgment and, admittedly, a suspicion of any theory of inevitable human progress.

In addition, I am concerned with acknowledging the reality of changed states across time so that, while some state *j* may have a history traceable back to some state *i*, state *j* is genuinely different from either state *i* or any prior states of the organism, as well as different from any future state *k*. I want to preserve for *development* an existential sense of the reality of each "now." Partly as a result of that concern, I also want to use the idea of construction as a way of affirming the positive, active participation of the human organism in any developmental sequence. Frankly, my libertarian tendencies suggest to me that successive constructions legitimate that valued thing we call *freedom*.

It seems to me that development through a succession of constructions can be understood as an organism's way of integrating itself and its environment into some totality without, at the same time, defining away the observable fact that some constructions are more functionally adequate than others, while some are patently dysfunctional. I am also concerned with preserving the interactionist thesis that all entities which develop do so via a continuing interchange with their environment. My rationale for avoiding *pre*formation may well be grounded differently from Piaget's but, like him, I prefer the interactionist thesis that development consists of genuine construction.

I think it is simple honesty that leads me to want to include two basic needs of a continuing organism within the concept of development. It seems clear that the human organism has a need to persist (or survive)

A SUMMARY LISTING OF AFFIRMATIONS REGARDING DEVELOPMENT

Development *is not*:	Development *is*:
1. any process	1. a stochastic process
2. thoroughly determined	2. thoroughly probabilistic, since it involves "a law of probability incessantly modified by the knowledge of new data"
3. a passive receipt of input from the environment	3. an active, accommodative receipt of input from the environment
4. equal interval measurement	4 ordinal measurement, at best
5. composed of a set of quite disparate items	5. composed of minimally related items composing a whole
6. inevitably a progression	6. amenable to a regression
7. a special case phenomenon	7. a general phenomenon
8. a matter of equality	8. a matter of commonality
9. a process of exclusion	9. a process of inclusion
10. unrelated to survival or endurance or lastingness	10. related to survival or endurance or lastingness
11. related to things which are unobservable in time	11. related to things which are observed within time
12. suicidal	12. life-preserving
13. a refusal to alter in the face of existing conditions	13. an alteration-response to existing conditions
14. inevitably successful	14. an attempt at success
15. solely either assimilation or accommodation	15. an iterative cycle of both assimilation and accommodation
16. a conservative, static continuation of a present state	16. an active construction of some not-yet future state
17. preformation	17. construction
18. finality, completeness, or inevitability	18. process, incompleteness, or possibility

and a need to adapt itself to that environment in which it exists. These two needs seem quite obvious for all existing entities, even the supposedly inorganic ones. Therefore, I want to include both needs within the meaning of *development*.

Finally, I think development is such a widely pervasive phenomenon that a definition that applies only to a portion of the human experience is but a special case description of the phenomenon itself. Obviously, that is a theoretical consideration but, if it is satisfied, one which can provide strength. As Piaget points out in *Structuralism*, generality is a sign of structural strength, while differentiation into a special case is less structurally strong. This consideration is weighty, and I do not think it should be ignored. That is one reason I think as I do about development.

Notes and References

1. The imprecision of everyday language was a source of much of the linguistic analysis of Ludwig Wittgenstein, and a reading of what is known as *The Blue Book* (1934) will help one recognize that fact. See Ludwig Wittgenstein, *Preliminary Studies for the "Philosophical Investigations" Generally Known as the Blue and Brown Books* (New York: Harper & Row, Publishers, 1958/1965) (Torchbooks TB 1211).

2. Robert H. Pollack, "Some Implications of Ontogenetic Changes in Perception," in David Elkind and John H. Flavell, eds., *Studies in Cognitive Development* (New York: Oxford University Press, 1969), p. 365.

3. Ibid., p. 366.

4. James Drever, *A Dictionary of Psychology* (Baltimore: Penguin Books, 1952/1964), the word *development*.

5. Heinz Werner, *Comparative Psychology of Mental Development* (New York: Science Editions, 1948/1965), pp. 18–19.

6. Ibid., p. 40.

7. Ibid.

8. Ernest R. Hilgard, *Introduction to Psychology*, 3rd ed. (New York: Harcourt, Brace & World, 1962), p. 617.

9. D. O. Hebb, *The Organization of Behavior: A Neuropsychological Theory* (New York: Science Editions, 1949/1961), p. 324.

10. Wolfgang Köhler, *The Mentality of Apes* (New York: Vintage Books, 1924/1956), Index, p. iii.

11. See Wolfgang Köhler, *Dynamics in Psychology* (New York:

Washington Square Press, 1965); idem, *Gestalt Psychology: An Introduction to New Concepts in Modern Psychology* (New York: New American Library, 1947).

12. Jean Piaget, *Six Psychological Studies*, ed. David Elkind (New York: Vintage Books, 1964/1967), p. 144.

13. Jean Piaget, *Biology and Knowledge* (Chicago: University of Chicago Press, 1971), p. 71.

14. Ibid., p. 82.

15. I refer here to Werner's statement that "true development itself rests in creation." That *is* an intriguing assertion.

16. Although a mere sixty hours may seem like a short period of time (as, in fact, it is), during December, 1978, the USA and the USSR devoted only twenty hours of negotiating time to an effort to conclude a second Strategic Arms Limitation Treaty in Geneva, Switzerland. My sixty hours are, in that context, thrice as long as the foreign ministers of two of the most powerful nations could devote to negotiation, after several years of preliminary staff work. Of course, life abounds in such absurdities.

17. Neils Arley and K. Rander Buch, *Introduction to the Theory of Probability and Statistics* (New York: John Wiley & Sons, 1950/1966), p. 48.

18. Ibid., p. 50.

19. C. S. Lewis, *That Hideous Strength* (New York: Macmillan Co., 1946). This third of Lewis's science fiction novels bears the subtitle, "A Modern Fairy-Tale for Grown-Ups," and is an extended comment on the point.

20. Lucienne Felix, *The Modern Aspect of Mathematics* (New York: Science Editions, 1960/1961), pp. 131–132.

21. Piaget, *Six Psychological Studies*, p. 157.

22. Ibid., pp. 150–151.

23. Ibid., p. 150.

24. Werner, *Comparative Psychology*, p. 40.

25. Piaget, *Six Psychological Studies*, p. 151.

26. Ibid.

27. *The New Merriam-Webster Pocket Dictionary* (New York: Pocket Books, 1971/1973).

28. For an extended treatment, see Barbel Inhelder and Jean Piaget, *The Early Growth of Logic in the Child* (New York: W. W. Norton & Co., 1964/1969), pp. 247–268. Also see Piaget, *The Mechanisms of Perception* (London: Routledge and Kegan Paul, 1961/1969), pp. 348–349; Piaget, *Psychology and Epistemology* (New York: Viking Press, 1970/1971), pp. 11–12; Piaget, *Biology and Knowledge*, p. 25.

29. In terms of simple measurement theory, see Sidney Siegel, *Nonparametric Statistics for the Behavioral Sciences* (New York: McGraw-Hill

Book Co., 1956), pp. 23–28. Also see Brian Ellis, *Basic Concepts of Measurement* (Cambridge: Cambridge University Press, 1966).

30. This point is so fundamental that even Siegel's text can be misinterpreted to posit that the *relation* requisite for an *ordinal* scale involves an inevitable quantification. Yet Siegel's statement focuses solely upon a relation, although his illustrations imply some quantitative relation. Here, I am stressing that in a sequence the relation is simply one of precedence; an analogy to Siegel's illustrative relations would be the relation of "is later than" or "is earlier than." (See Siegel, *Nonparametric Statistics*, p. 24.)

31. For Lewin's description of valence, see Kurt Lewin, *A Dynamic Theory of Personality: Selected Papers* (New York: McGraw-Hill Book Co., 1935), pp. 51 ff.

32. *Merriam-Webster Pocket Dictionary*, the word *integrate*.

33. Ibid., the word *need*. Also see Drever, *A Dictionary of Psychology*, the word *need*.

34. Without denying our social need for complexities such as love or affection, I am here trying to get behind that level of thinking to something even more basic and, then, to ask if there is one or (at the most!) two things that the human simply must have.

35. *The Random House Dictionary of the English Language* (New York: Random House, 1967), the word *persist*.

36. Ibid.

37. The reader should be cautious. My argument does not establish the existence of an angelic order of creation, nor was it intended to do so. Instead, it suggests that a need to persist is basic to any observed organism which can legitimately be termed developmental in any sense of that word. Angels are no more than an argumentative contrast, in this place in the text.

38. For Viktor Frankl's and Aleksandr I. Solzhenitsyn's descriptions see such works as Victor Emil Frankl, *Man's Search for Meaning*. (Boston: Beacon Press, 1963) and Aleksandr I. Solzhenitsyn, *The Gulag Archipelago 1918–1956: An Experiment in Literary Investigation*. (New York: Harper & Row, Publishers, Inc., 1973, 1974).

39. *Random House Dictionary*, the words *adapt* and *adaptation*.

40. I am not trying to allude to a creationist-evolutionist controversy, and I do not want to be allied with a simple-minded biblical literalism that takes off after any sign of evolutionary theory! I simply want to stress the logical necessity of an after-the-fact assessment in order to speak clearly about a process of adaptation. For the moment, that is quite enough. Evolution, as theory or fact, must take care of itself.

41. Piaget, *Six Psychological Studies*, p. 8.

42. Jean Piaget and Barbel Inhelder, *The Psychology of the Child* (New York: Basic Books, 1969), p. 6. Also see Piaget, *The Construction of Reality*

in the Child (New York: Ballantine Books, 1954/1971), pp. 395–402. As well, see Piaget, *Six Psychological Studies*, pp. 8, 68–69.

43. My memory tells me that I first heard this particular childish misunderstanding from the liturgical artist Robert Rambusch during some ecumenical meeting in the mid-1960s. As a result, I can only vouch for my memory; Rambusch may, or may not, remember as I do.

44. *Random House Dictionary*, the word *environment*.

45. The idea that an individual and that individual's environment exist within a "symbiotic relationship" is, of course, a metaphor. But it seems an apt one. *Symbiosis* is a biological term that denotes the ability of two actually dissimilar organisms to live together (minimally) and, even, to find that process of living together to be mutually beneficial (maximally). What is often called a "good marriage" is, thus, often a symbiotic relationship.

46. Jean Piaget, *Science of Education and the Psychology of the Child* (New York: Viking Press, 1969/1971), pp. 172–173.

47. See Jean Piaget, *Structuralism* (London: Routledge and Kegan Paul, 1968/1971), p. 59. Here Piaget discusses perception in a way that seems parallel to the point I make here. Also see John H. Peatling and David V. Tiedeman, *Career Development: Designing Self* (Muncie, Ind.: Accelerated Development, 1977), p. 161, where we use Piaget to suggest improvisational drama as a good analogy.

48. This statement does not deny the reality of that complex totality we think of as the objective environment. But it does consciously focus upon that varying subset of that objective environment to which, with awareness, we respond in any attempt to meet the fundamental needs for persistence and adaptation. In prospect, that subset is our environment. Only an after-the-fact assessment of our choices and decisions can identify whether or not they were successful, for in prospect they all were attempts at success.

49. In statistical usage, i, j, and k are used to represent generally any number, item, or variable. Here they serve the same function.

6

My God! Godel and Religious Education

As the month of January, 1978, moved toward its close, the *New York Times* acknowledged the death of Kurt Gödel on a Sunday editorial page. He died in his seventy-first year. The editorialist quoted the accolade from his honorary degree at Harvard University, which described him as the "discoverer of the most significant mathematical truth of this century, incomprehensible to laymen, revolutionary for philosophers and logicians." In an inspired phrase, the writer summed up the problem addressed by Gödel's theorem with the far-from-simple query, "How certain is certain?" He went on to note that for at least a hundred years both mathematicians and logicians had tried to locate a proof that fundamental contradictions in a system (any system) are actually impossibilities. But to no avail. The revolutionary thing that Godel's theorem did, way back in 1931, was to provide a proof that the long-sought-after proof was itself impossible, at least with the tools available.

Gödel's theorem was shocking enough to logicians and mathematicians to generate a fair amount of debate, and a long and lingering rearguard action by those unwilling to conjure with it. Understandably so, too, for the implications were quite literally awesome: the edifices of logic or of that supposedly most pristine of the sciences, mathematics, were not necessarily free of internal contradiction. In a word, what most of us *assume* is no more than that, an assumption, a particular form of a quite human act of faith. The *proof* is simply not to be had, given what we know, the tools available to us! In something approaching sheer poetry, the editorialist for the *New York Times* closed with two memorable sentences: "Edna St. Vincent Millay once wrote that Euclid alone had looked on beauty bare. Gödel's admirers would say that he alone had looked on truth bare and come back with a historic revelation."[1]

Let us admit it, that is pretty heavy stuff.

If one were the least bit simplistic, the conclusion that *nothing* is certain would spring to the forefront of one's mind. If one's mind had been formed by religious belief or grounded in religious faith, that would be something close to an intolerable (albeit quite logical) conclusion. Then, to follow out a very simplistic syllogism, one could *infer* that one's religious formation, the religious "ground," was not provable from within the system it represented and, via further inference, that the system was therefore untrue. While those inferences are attractive, even quite persuasive, only the first is directly related to Gödel's theorem. The other, for a religious person, betrays an extremely shaky, all-too-contemporary vision of what the Christian religion has always known, accepted, and proclaimed. To use an odd mixed metaphor from a profound little book on psychological pathology, Christianity never promised anybody a logician's rose garden![2] It always assaulted our rationality with a claim that meaning arose out of a revelation.[3]

However, that is simple theology. Specifically, it is an affirmation that belongs either to an introductory course in theology or, perhaps, to a survey of the history of Christian attempts to *do* theology. Although my knowledge is limited, I suspect that the affirmation that meaning arises, ultimately, out of the act of deity, G-O-D, in revelation is also a part of Jewish "theology." However, that is a personal, Christian inference and no more. My knowledge of a Jewish "theology" is somewhat limited.

However, before anyone rushes off into a true Hegelian opposite in some kind of dialectical process, let us recall what I wrote a few paragraphs earlier: the first inference has a logical quality to it, the other does not. There is no way, from within a system such as a theological system, to prove the system itself. However, that is far, far different from affirming that the system itself is untrue. Truth is not provable, perhaps, but at its most reasonable, few if any theological systems with which Christians have lived have claimed to be provable via what older theologians would call natural reason. Thomas Aquinas is an almost perfect example of this point.[4] Implicitly, the appeal to a religious "experience" by charismatics of all ages is an affirmation of the need for *some* revelation, theirs. In fact, the history of Christian theology is full of the recognition of the fundamental place of revelation as, in some way, the over-plus to human reason which Aquinas considered it to be. One does not need to be a Christian of the Roman Catholic church to acknowledge as much. Nor does one have to be either a charismatic or a Pentecostalist to recognize as much. All that is necessary is that one know the history of Christian doctrine and theology fairly well, or attend carefully to the scriptures of either Testament of a Christian's Bible. Truth per se is only inferentially a rational quality; one should never forget that when we assume it to be *so*, it is *we* who *assume* that.[5]

Let us not be overly hard on ourselves. We have not sinned, even if we have trapped ourselves into indefensible assumptive positions. We have done no more than make some bad judgments. Yet, from a Christian's perspective, that is little more than an acknowledgment that we are not all that different from most of our forebears within the line of those we can acknowledge as the faithful ones in every generation. Humans do what we may have done, repeatedly. While it may not be commendable or logical, it is not surprising. But *we* did it.

What we all need, some fifty years after Gödel first posited his theorem, is to internalize the thing and recognize its implications for us. Gödel did not "kill off" the deity (G-O-D); that was left for the interpreters of Bishop Robinson to try, and fail.[6] What Kurt Gödel did was to recover a sense that G-O-D (the biblical deity) could not be the utterly abstract, quite uninvolved thing which merely set things going and then retired to see how it all might work out—the deistic vision of the seventeenth and eighteenth centuries.[7] A fascinating witness to exactly this interpretation is Jean Piaget, who has not been noted for any religious interest. In his 1968 work, *Le Structuralisme*, which was published in English as *Structuralism* in 1971, Piaget says, "But God himself has, since Gödel's theorem, ceased to be motionless. He is the living God, more so than heretofore, because he is unceasingly constructing ever 'stronger' systems."[8]

While that assessment is certainly after-the-fact by some forty years for English-language readers, it does identify a quite fundamental value for the Christian who is either religious or theologically alert. Gödel's theorem is not a thoroughly special case; it is a generality of very considerable importance. One we in the 1980s should take into ourselves, precisely because we are religious or religiously inclined or religiously committed. Moreover, we should not be the kind of intellectual prigs who could ignore this insight because it did not come from a cleric, a theologian, or a religious educator.[9]

There is no need to be an intellectual prig in order to be a committed, concerned, or thoroughly religious person in these days. A G-O-D which is credited with creation and (in Christian terms) with the redemptive act of Jesus the Christ is no deists' deity. Such a G-O-D, the biblical deity, is an active agent in human affairs, one which finds voices when and where it chooses. Such a G-O-D seems, according to either the biblical record or the repeated witness of religion, to be quite free of any current religious establishment, any current set of standards by which we humans judge the best instances of what we call religious life. For Christians, at least, this point should be more than abundantly evident in the strange company Jesus of Nazareth chose to keep, the personal histories of those chosen to be disciples and apostles, and the kind of persons Paul of Tarsus found in those first congregations in Europe. Only an intellectual prig could, today, demand a higher and more restrictive standard for religious insight than one normally finds in either Luke's story of the earliest churches or Paul's letters to his missionary congregations.[10] Yet if we today reject Gödel's theorem or Piaget's interpretation of it, because neither was a respected churchman, that is exactly what we risk doing.

Perhaps the point has been made.

When one thinks about G-O-D, strangeness is the expected, not the odd. So is activity. Our expectations are not of necessity the deity's. Thus, thinking persons have almost always known that G-O-D far exceeded their own cognitive grasp, by virtue of what G-O-D is, does, means, or signifies. That recognition is hard only when we let our assumptions control our understanding, and so play out Freud's idea of deity as humankind's ultimate projection. The biblical record can be warped to such a vision, but it does not require it. If *we* will, if *we* decide it, our vision of G-O-D need not be so "contemporary."

However, if we do decide for a G-O-D which is a-Freudian, we are faced with the implication of Gödel's theorem that our present "certainty" is a "not-quite." There is somewhere, somehow, an anticipatable contradiction in whatever system we may find otherwise useful or even truthful. Thus, there must be, for us humans, a clear distinction between our subjective certainty and our ability to know for certain, in some quite objectively verifiable sense. Although we may *feel* certain about a number of things, without necessarily denying the truth of those things, we simply have to be somewhat tentative, holding ourselves back from complete, total certainty. In terms of the biblical story, we are inevitably creatures, even though we be redeemed creatures living in a redeemed creation. We are Christ-bearers, potentially, but we are only metaphorically Christs. The piety of being a Christ-bearer, profound and honorable as it is, must not lead us into thinking we are what we simply are not, Christs in anything like the robust sense of the Johannine Prologue or the Letter to the Hebrews. The pietistic truth, of course, is that we are (or can be) analogues, living metaphors, but that is still *not* being.[11]

Gödel's theorem, via Piaget's interpretation, suggests an active deity. It also suggests that in any given moment there is an act of faith which is very human, and very much a part of our human use of any system. The system may be what we know at the moment as logic or what we call mathematics or what we call theology. To ignore or deny the role of such an act of faith on our part in terms of any system is to presume we are more than creatures, more than what (in fact) we are. Thus, there is an inescapable tentativeness which affects all of our certainties. However, what we should not overlook is that the very bothersome tentativeness comes out of our creatureliness in this creation; it is, fundamentally, a profoundly religious idea. It is not atheism, by a long ways. It is not deism, either. Actually, it is profoundly theological and has many a tie to the highest forms of mystical experience (at least within the Christian tradition). Tentativeness is our rational response to what mystics have persistently termed the ineffable vision of

G-O-D.[12] It is our passing, changing certainties that are our problem, not our present tentativeness.

WHAT MIGHT IT MEAN?

In the same book in which Piaget makes his statement about the activity of a living God, he also has a good deal to say about the general implication of Gödel's theorem for all forms of structuralism. A review of a few of those Piagetian interpretations may help one begin to understand what this remarkably abstract theorem has to do with things as concretely specific as one's approach to living or one's relation to a religion or one's task as a religious educator. As a first human step, such an understanding *is* a prerequisite to anything approximating comprehension, or a fully contemporary rationality. Therefore, it should be useful to think about those possible implications with the Swiss genetic epistemologist as a guide.

In a section entitled "The Limits of Formalization," in the second chapter of *Structuralism*, Piaget says, "The first noteworthy effect . . . was that a notion of greater or lesser 'power' entered into the domain of structures. . . . The hierarchy that was thus introduced . . . soon gave rise to an idea of 'construction,' (and) . . . This idea . . . is incompatible with any simplistic theory of mind or intellectual activity." Piaget continues by pointing out, "Gödel showed that the construction of a demonstrably consistent relatively rich theory requires . . . the construction of the next 'higher' theory!"[13] Given Gödel's theorem, Piaget identifies three intriguing implications. First, that structures (of any sort) may be distinguished from one another along some power continuum. Second, that any such distinction between structures implies some kind of a hierarchy. Third, that such a hierarchy exists, quite generally, within some larger and more extensive hierarchy, so that comprehension of one (the smaller) requires the other (the larger). As Piaget says, "the 'fastening' of any story in the edifice of human knowledge calls for the construction of the next higher story." In addition, he notes that a clear implication is that "rather than envisaging human knowledge as a pyramid or building of some sort, we should think of it as a spiral the radius of whose turns increases as the spiral rises."[14] These metaphors vividly delineate two implications of Gödel's theorem.

Think for a moment about those ideas.

Any story requires a "next higher story" if it is to be entered firmly into Piaget's "edifice of human knowledge." That means that all the stories in such a structure exist in hierarchical relationship to some next higher story, which functions as a fastener for stories that are subordinate to itself. No story, by itself, is really fastened into that edifice. Each one requires an upward reference to a next higher which, by its existence, is a fastening, one that legitimates and is necessarily supraordinate for that story. In a word, not a story in the "edifice of human knowledge" is really self-evident.

Piaget's metaphor of a story may be strange. However, if one will but consider that metaphor, it will suddenly become strangely obvious. This is a reason why we humans consistently find that one thing illustrates another yet more general principle. Or why we humans find that many a simple and quite concrete tale illustrates a particular moral. What educators call a *moralism* is, then, not so much untrue (let alone impossible!) as it is inappropriate. Similarly, specific instances of a general principle *are* because they exist in exactly this kind of hierarchical relation to that principle: for the instance, such principles function as a fastening, next higher story for the subordinate specific instance. But we tend to forget that.

Piaget's image of the rising spiral with a continually increasing radius is, in itself, also a conceptual challenge. On the one hand, it is an image that permits one to acknowledge what only a blindly committed progressivist could ignore: humans tend to recur to the same problems. On the other hand, it also permits us to distinguish one such recurrence from another, for if prior human experience be the radius, each turn of the spiral intersects the same problem sector in three-dimensional conceptual space in a somewhat different way and in a somewhat different manner. Not only is the sector higher but, just as important, a more extensive portion of the sector is traversed by the rising spiral's pathway through that sector. Thus, human progressiveness can be accommodated without denying the human tendency to come back, time after time, to the same problem.

When we put the two metaphors together we have a rather remarkable thing: an extraordinarily general model of much of the history of human thought. The history of human thought, at least as we in this society know it, involves two often antagonistic observations: we do recur to basic problems again and again, and yet we do tend to progress to the recognition of new instances of those same problems across time. It is true that all things change, and that there is nothing new under the sun.[15] The paradox of changeableness and stability continually puzzles us, for we know both to be, yet we continually want to affirm one to the exclusion of the other. However, the Piagetian metaphor of a rising spiral of constantly increasing radius permits us to catch a glimpse of a way in which both human experiences can be acknowledged.

However, Piaget suggests that there is yet more involved in the attempt to come to terms with Gödel's theorem. For example, he notes that "the idea of *structure* as a system of transformations becomes continuous with that of *construction* as continual formation."[16] In addition, he quotes J. Ladriere to the effect that "we cannot survey all the operations open to human thought at one glance": a fascinating use of a simple human perceptual limitation.[17] Moreover, Piaget also leads the reader to recognize that in terms of Gödel's theorem there simply is no such thing as form or content per se. In the hierarchy of that "edifice of human knowledge," any form is bound to be the content for its supraordinate, next higher fastening story, as well as the form for its own subordinate content, for which it functions as a fastening story. Thus, "each element—from sensory-motor acts through operations to theories—is always simultaneously form to the content it subsumes and content for some higher form."[18]

Conceptually, Piaget's interpretation of Gödel's theorem invites one into a world of complex interrelationships, a world of continuing construction, a dynamic world in which the static is no more than a momentary stasis within a larger system. It is not, however, a world in which nothing is known or knowable: it is not an arational world, and it certainly is not an irrational world. But it is a world in which tentativeness of conclusion is both useful and apparently necessary. It is, for many, also a *strange* world.

Still, if we think about it, the world of contemporary knowledge is a strangely dynamic thing with few absolute certainties, but an abundance of reasonably evident interrelationships. The challenge of such a world to any human is real enough. Its challenge to a religious human need be no more than it is to any other human and, quite conceivably, a wee bit less. While many twentieth-century Christians do not recognize the fundamental role played by a doctrine of creation, such a doctrine can be a quite useful referent as one encounters the dynamic, interrelated complex we know as the world of contemporary knowledge. One reason that can be so is that a doctrine of creation can function as a higher fastening story for the world we encounter. In addition, there is that mysteriously hopeful affirmation that the creation is, in some way, basically good.[19] That is right at the heart of any biblically faithful doctrine of creation, regardless of what we may at times be tempted to think.

Let us be reasonably clear about what this all means.

Gödel's theorem *does* destroy our sense of total and complete certainty, replacing it with a final tentativeness. It gives us, however, a way to be rational in the midst of a vast, interrelated complex characterized more by dynamism than by stasis. It helps us understand why we keep discovering principles behind (or beneath) specifics, and helps us recognize why humans keep finding a moral in so many stories. Moreover, it offers us a way of positively acknowledging the paradox of change and stability in human life. We do recur to old, old problems, yet never in exactly the same way. We do progress, even as we also keep encountering our supposedly resolved problems. If we can connect a doctrine of creation (with its affirmation of a continually active, creative G-O-D) and the idea that, since Gödel, all construction is a continual process of formation, and if we can also retain some hold on the recurrent theme from the first chapter of Genesis that this creation is good, we need not be fearful of the world of contemporary knowledge. Moreover, since Gödel, we also need not be enslaved by that world either. It, and we, are in the midst of a vast and remarkable process of continual formation. Our certainties, while held tentatively, require a yet next higher story for their fastening into that edifice we call human knowledge. The religious person, the theologically alert person, can find here one reason for humankind's persistent search for meaning, which often finds itself moving toward deity. That is quite a find; in fact, it is a veritable treasure.

WHAT MIGHT IT MEAN FOR RELIGIOUS EDUCATION?

Far too often religious education is founded firmly on fear. For example, the fear that Freud was right. Or the fear that religion can only be fatally infected by that edifice of contemporary human knowledge. Or the fear that without *our* particular certainty, G-O-D would die. Or even the fear that children's questioning minds will disrupt religion itself, unless we insist upon *our* authoritative system of presumed answers. Or more prosaically the fear that unless *we* do something, our congregation will grow old, exhibit normal mortality, and cease. Unfortunately, fear too often blinds, restricts, inhibits. It is a genuinely faulty foundation.

However, twenty-five years' experience suggests that fear is the unacknowledged rationale for what too often is thought to be religious education. Fearing Freud's thesis of the ultimate projection, religious education ignores human development on the one hand and facilely posits a demonically objectified deity on the other. Fearing the edifice of human knowledge, it too readily retreats into biblical literalism, thinking that only a collection of stenographic transcripts could support faith. Fearing tentativeness itself, it often affirms as certain what many already know to be no more than wisdom. In some ways, the most pathetic of all fears is the fear of children's naturally questioning minds, which can lead to simple denial and the powerful use of simple conditioning to first form and then support one or another presumably authoritative system of "answers" to life's questions. Religious education based on such fears is not only blind, restricted, and inhibited, it tends to infect those who come in contact with it. Like some unconscious carrier, it spreads the disease to those it loves.

The objection to fear as a rationale is value-laden, broad, complex, theological, and experiential. It is not simply pragmatic. Only someone approximating the biblical fool would deny that fear can work wonders. The fear of hell has too long a history and far too vocal a lobby to be ignored. Purists of either the Roman or Protestant affiliation witness to the simple, pragmatic effectiveness of fear. In the secular realm, the code words *balance of power* or *deterrence* or *second-strike capability* witness to the fact that fear is not merely a religious problem. So let no reader think that fear is a useless holdover from less enlightened times; it is a very present fact of a surprising part of living in these times. It is quite a contemporary phenomenon.

Even so, fear is a very poor rationale for religious education. It puts at the heart of the whole effort an intolerable ambiguity: that is, how fear is to be used (in a Christian context) to educate persons toward an appreciation of a message that has inextricably in its core the overcoming of fear.[20] That is a biblically based theological objection. But fear also does more: it feeds on suspicion, feasts on distrust, and, finally, relishes hate. It destroys love. It pits us against one another in blind reenactments of the tale of Cain and Abel.[21] It perverts us, making us less than we could be and were meant to be. It lies at the heart of tyranny, excuses cruelty and torture, and motivates massacres. That is a broad and all-too-experiential objection.

Let us be tolerably honest with ourselves. Fear *is* very pervasive in the human life we know all too well. That life begins with an awesome transition from the womb to the outside. It must be at least tinged with fear's younger cousin fright, for the one undergoing the transition. The infant and child also know fear quite well, the fear that those they depend upon for nourishment, comfort, and protection will not be there when needed. Certainly, with time that fear subsides as the very young child learns that what is needed is, usually, available upon demand. So, too, children only slowly learn to cope with the fearful unknown. Adolescence is also not without fear, and we do not understand either the bravado or the messianism characteristic of the period if we ignore that fear. The years of young and middle adulthood are often far from fearless. From the fear of not finding work or a mate, through the fear of not getting a raise or an advancement, to the fear of not retaining a job, the adult knows fear quite well. Late in adulthood, people often know the fear of losing their job before retirement is really possible and, somewhat later, some fear retirement itself. Older adults begin to and, then, do recognize their own mortality; for many this inescapable recognition is all too tinged with fear. No period of human life is free from fear. However, we are rarely overwhelmed by our fears.

Fear is fundamental. Let us not ignore it. But it is not necessarily controlling. We *do* learn to cope with fear. We even come to a point where we can imagine life without fear. In fact, if we are honest with ourselves, we may even recognize that we need not fear. While that recognition is a very human possibility, there is a strange way in which it is quite often associated with a religious insight or decision. For the Christian, that insight can be associated with the Johannine Christ's declaration that he came to offer humankind a life freed from fear: "I came that they may have life, and have it abundantly."[22] Granted, that is an association most likely to come with maturity. But maturity, in exactly that sense, is a thoroughly legitimate goal of anything any human should recognize as religious education. It is our fault, our own grievous fault, that we all too often have settled for far, far less.

Gödel's theorem is a remarkable generality. Its implications for the whole "edifice of human knowledge" are evident. If we posit that education per se is, quite generally, a process of encounter with knowledge, for the purpose of coping with its present content and, thereby, permitting or even encouraging its future expansion, we are at least capable of understanding the implications of Gödel's theorem for education. The tentativeness that comes out of the theorem, the recognition of the need for a next higher story, the sense of being in the midst of an ongoing process of formation, *are* quite necessary for education to be anything close to education. Without the openness to that which is not yet, coping would be no more than socialization; education would have no function toward the future and would, in fact, be no more than a shaping for the present. But education *is* a strange process of open-ended coping; it cannot ignore the present state of knowledge or the possibility of future expansion.

What we call religious education is a subset of education. There is a legitimately inescapable sense in which religious education is, quite generally, also a process of encounter with knowledge (even if it be only that subset of all knowledge we speak of as religious knowledge), for the purpose of coping with its present content and, thereby, permitting or even encouraging its future expansion. Like education itself, religious education also is a strange process of open-ended coping. It, too, needs the tenativeness that comes from Gödel's theorem, if its open-endedness is to be. Without that tentativeness, the open end is closed, and one has merely socialization to some present. However, as Augustine and Peirce saw so clearly, *any* present is such a fleeting thing that without attention to a future not-yet we are caught by our past.[23] Knowledge is like us, in that respect. Without an open end toward a future not-yet, it is all past. What we call *religious* knowledge is no different; without an open-endedness toward a future not-yet, it is also all past. In fact, then, any program for a socialization to any present is not capable of strict success: inevitably it becomes a program that socializes to some version of a recent past which is never quite any present or any future.

If one will even temporarily consider religious education to be a subset of education, then the implicit tentativeness required by Gödel's theorem may be acknowledged as a necessary generality. Moreover, if one can acknowledge the contribution such tentativeness makes to a process tending toward an open-ended coping, and if one recalls that Christianity has a persistent orientation toward a future not-yet, such tentativeness may even be recognized as fundamental to anything deserving the title "religious education." However, those two *ifs* are often neither simply nor easily acknowledged.

It may well be a strange contemporary fact, but the implications of Gödel's theorem remind us of some easily overlooked dimensions of the very nature of religious education in a Christian context. The inevitable tentativeness about any present certainty reminds us that we live by grace, not by law. The implicit open-endedness of the need for a next higher story as a fastener reminds us that there is an eschatological aspect to the Christian faith. The implicit sense of being in the midst of an ongoing process of formation (construction) reminds us that Christianity involves hope. In fact, if we will but recognize that grace is no less than a sign of active love, and realize that the eschaton is at the heart of what we call faith, we may discover that Gödel's theorem specifies something remarkably similar to the conclusion Paul of Tarsus reached at the end of chapter 13 of his First Letter to the Corinthians: "In a word, there are three things that last for ever: faith, hope, and love; but the greatest of them all is love."[24]

Think about that idea.

It was Paul's conclusion, almost two millennia ago, that faith, hope, and love "last for ever," yet love is "the greatest of them all." It is almost as if Paul posited that love was the next higher story that fastened faith and hope into the edifice of human knowledge; minimally, he recognized some hierarchical relationship between these three "things that last for ever." It was the author of the First Letter of John who, not long after Paul wrote to the Corinthians, concluded, "There is no room for fear in love; perfect love banishes fear."[25] Some in the earliest church had a grasp on the importance of love, and knew that grace was love's act.

In whatever form it may present itself (at least in any Christian context), religious education must facilitate the recognition of Paul's triad and the accomplishment of the principle enunciated in the First Letter of John. Less is simply not religious education. It may be something else, and we may even value that something else. But we should not confuse ourselves or anyone else by calling that something "religious education." It simply isn't.

Now, that *is* a simple, flat assertion. *I* know it, and I *hope* a reader will recognize it for what it is. Also, I hope a reader will recognize at least some reasons why I decided to assert *that*, in a consideration of the implications of Gödel's theorem. If nothing else, I trust that a reader will recognize that both Gödel's theorem and my simple, flat assertion are generalities. Each requires a judgment, at a quite general level. Each can have implications at a much more specific level. It is my contention, at that quite general level, that the assertion and the theorem are (minimally) within the same universe and very probably tolerably well related to one another. Naturally, readers must decide for themselves whether or not they will acknowledge or tolerate as much.

However, let me move on.

I suggested several paragraphs back that there was a simple parallelism between three implications of Gödel's theorem and Paul's

Corinthian triad of faith, hope, and love. I want to look at that parallelism quite specifically, for it is not yet a part of our late-twentieth-century common sense. Thus, consider the following figure. It consists of two columns: one identifies three implications of Gödel's theorem, while the other lists Paul's Corinthian triad.

What Christian theologians call *faith* has a strange similarity to what figure 1 identifies as a parallel implication of Godel's theorem. Each, once operative, makes sense of a great deal of human life. Moreover, each presumes something which is not immediately evident. Finally, each is an inherently hierarchical construct, for each points toward a higher level as that which is necessary to finally come to terms with some present and lower level. The parallel is, of course, odd and a bit surprising. It is a generality, not a specific. But all specificities exist within such generalities.

What Paul of Tarsus meant by *hope* involves a belief that possibilities as yet unseen will be. The parallel implication of Gödel's theorem is a way that kind of possibility could become. Each construct tends toward a kind of optimism, implies a process of dynamic change, and involves a transformation of that which *is* into that which *is not yet*. Granted, the parallel is not what one would call self-evident. But the constructs are, at a general level, oddly parallel.

The *agape* of the New Testament is a strangely rational, strangely unemotional form of love. It is a simple intent for the good of another. It is devoid of our human emotions and, so, is aptly posited of G-O-D and can be commanded of humans. Such a love can afford to be tentative, for it is not amenable to emotion anywhere near as much as it is to the rigor of intending the good of another. In fact, if we will but be honest with ourselves, we will recognize that such a love is possible to humans only as they remain quite tentative about that other for whom they have *agape*.[26] Certainly, the parallel is not so obvious that everyone sees it immediately, but that parallel is strangely real, strangely apropos.

Gödel's theorem is an extraordinarily high-level generality. That is why it can affect either education or its subset religious education. Too often those who call themselves educators expend all of their interest on the specifics of their art, as if any specific were sensible in and of itself. Unfortunately, no specific is inherently sensible. All specifics

Implication of Godel's theorem:[a]	The Pauline triad:[b]
	In a word, there are three things that last for ever:
The construction of any demonstrably consistent, rich theory requires the construction of the yet next higher theory, if that story is to become fastened into the edifice of human knowledge.	*FAITH,*
The idea of structure as some system of transformations is continuous with that of construction as a process of continual formation.	*HOPE,*
Tentativeness, or the fact that there is neither "form" as such nor "content" as such, since any element is always both form to that content which it subsumes and content to some yet next higher form.	and *LOVE*;
	but the greatest of them all is love.

WHERE: [a] = Paraphrases from Jean Piaget, *Structuralism* (London: Routledge and Kegan Paul, 1971), pp. 34–35.
[b] = 1 Cor. 13:13.

Figure 1. A parallel between three implications of Godel's theorem and a Pauline triad from the First Letter to the Corinthians.

become sensible only via some functional relationship to some generality, some reason or goal or objective.[27] The concern with specifics is, of course, very practical: it is a concern with what one will *do*. However, it is also a near-demonic temptation to *avoid* asking the importantly general question: Why are we doing *this?*

Unless that general question be both asked and answered (even temporarily!), the practical concern for specifics becomes nothing more than the idiotic query, "What should I do next?" In the world of the late twentieth century, there is no reason to denigrate the practicality of the question. It is one that, time after time, anyone concerned with instructing a computer must answer in painfully explicit detail. However, while extraordinarily useful when appropriately programmed, computers are and remain humankind's very fast, very accurate, very patient, and very, very useful mechanical idiot savants. Humans who permit a concern for specificities (irrespective of the general *why* question) to control their actions are trying to play computer. That is both sad and stupid. Sad, because it is a surrender of their human capacity. Stupid, because no human is as fast, as accurate, as patient as a machine—unless that human is, quite literally, an idiot savant.[28]

Fortunately, there is more reason to believe that educators (general or religious) are human than there is to believe that they are either machines or true idiot savants. But the temptation to so focus upon specificities *is* quite real. No one should deny that. In fact, we can be grateful to that most abstract of generalities, Gödel's theorem, for reminding us of both the possibilities and the limitations of our humanity.

Although I have taken a quite critical approach to religious education in this chapter, I remain unconvinced that it need fall prey to the temptation to focus upon such machine-like concerns. That is *my* human act of faith.

Notes and References

1. "A Certain Genius," *New York Times*, Jan. 22, 1978. This editorial was reprinted in *Character Potential: A Record of Reserach*, vol. 8, no. 4 (August 1978), p. 161, under the title, "A Note in Passing of More Than Passing Interest."

2. This sentence makes a play upon the title of a remarkable little book by Hannah Green, *I Never Promised You a Rose Garden* (New York: Holt, Rinehart and Winston, 1964).

3. This sentence may best be read against the position Paul of Tarsus took in his letter to the early Christians in Corinth, as we can find that in 1 Cor. 1:18–25.

4. It is instructive to note that this distinction between natural reason and divine revelation is treated by Thomas Aquinas in the first article of question 1 of part 1 of *The Summa Theologica:* that is, at the very beginning of the whole work. See Anton C. Pegis, ed., *Basic Writings of Saint Thomas Aquinas,* vol. 1 (New York: Random House, 1945), p. 5.

5. For this point, see "Appendix 1, Premises of Science," in Michael Polanyi, *Science, Faith, and Society* (Chicago: University of Chicago Press, 1964), pp. 85–90.

6. This sentence has reference to the work of Bishop J. A. T. Robinson, as published in his book *Honest to God* (Philadelphia: Westminster Press, 1963) and to his theological colleagues who, for a period, held center-stage in the theater of contemporary theology. The final comment is *my* retrospective evaluation of the total effort.

7. For a concise statement, see *deism* in F. L. Cross, ed., *The Oxford Dictionary of the Christian Church* (London: Oxford University Press, 1957).

8. Jean Piaget, *Structuralism* (London: Routledge and Kegan Paul, 1968/1971), p. 141.

9. The entry for *prig* in my copy of *The Random House Dictionary of the English Language* (New York: Random House, 1967) reads as follows: "One who displays or demands of others pointlessly precise conformity, fussiness about trivialities, or exaggerated propriety, especially in a self-righteous or irritating manner."

10. My only point here is that Luke's story in the Acts of the Apostles and the Pauline corpus (however one may choose to define it) can reasonably be read to imply that those earliest congregations were populated by a cross section of humans, among whom only a few remarkable persons were deserving of mention for their extraordinary faithfulness. Paul's sometimes sharp words of admonition seem amenable of almost no other interpretation. Piety, more than anything else, may hide this from us.

11. In this passage I refer to a statement credited, as near as I can recall, to Martin Luther. In one of his sermons he is supposed to have indicated that if one would see Christ, right now, one had but to look at the person next to one in the church's nave. This theme, rather than any reference to the older tradition of St. Christopher, lies behind these sentences.

12. See Evelyn Underhill, *Mysticism* (London: Methuen & Co., 1911/1949), pp. 370–371. In these pages, Underhill describes something of the mystic's problem, referencing the experience of Rulman Merswin, Ellina von Crevelsheim, Richard of St. Victor, St. John of the Cross, St. Teresa, and Suso.

13. Piaget, *Structuralism*, pp. 33–34.

14. Ibid., p. 34.

15. For instance, compare and contrast the sense of changeableness inherent in Ps. 102:25–27 with the sense of fundamental stability inherent in

Eccles. 1:9. Apparently this paradox was not unrecognized by those who inhabited what we are likely to consider a biblical world.

16. Piaget, *Structuralism*, p. 34.

17. Ibid., p. 35.

18. Ibid.

19. Gen. 1:3, 10, 12, 18, 21, 25, 30. In these seven places, G-O-D is represented as viewing the stages of creation and, repeatedly, making the evaluation that it is good. If one chooses to regard this initial story of creation as a more philosophical and, therefore, higher story than the story of Adam and Eve, then the divine evaluation echoes throughout this story like a recurrent theme. We should not forget that.

20. This point should be evident to most readers who consider Luke 12:7 and Rom. 8:15, 2 Tim. 1:7, and 1 John 4:18.

21. Gen. 4:1–16.

22. John 10:10b in the Revised Standard Version of the New Testament.

23. See the introduction to chapter 3, "Thank God! Salvation and Such Like."

24. 1 Cor. 13:13.

25. 1 John 4:18.

26. This description of *agape* is the author's slightly expanded version of the words of C. H. Dodd in *Gospel and Law: The Relation of Faith and Ethics in Early Christianity* (New York: Columbia University Press, 1951), p. 42. Specifically, Dodd says the following: "Provisionally, we might say that *agape* (love, or charity) is energetic and beneficent good will which stops at nothing to secure the good of the beloved object. It is not primarily an emotion or an affection; it is primarily an active determination of the will. That is why it can be commanded, as feelings cannot."

In addition to Dodd, two references to this understanding of the New Testament *agape* seem apropos. First, Karl Barth's cômmentary on Rom. 12:9–5, as found in the 6th edition of Hoskyns's translation of *The Epistle to the Romans* (London: Oxford University Press, 1933), esp. pp. 450–454. Second, C. S. Lewis's broadcast talk "Charity," which was first delivered during World War II and may now be found in the little book *Christian Behaviour* (New York: Macmillan Co., 1943/1946), pp. 50–54. Lewis's words anticipate Dodd's by some eight years, but are in general agreement with his.

For example, Lewis says: "Charity means 'Love, in the Christian sense.' But love, in the Christian sense, does not mean an emotion. It is a state not of the feelings, but of the will; that state of the will which we have *naturally* about ourselves, and must *learn* to have about other people. . . . Christian Love, either towards God or towards man, is an affair of the will" (pp. 50, 53).

27. This statement is correct: specifics *become* sensible by virtue of their perceived functional relationship to "some generality, some reason or goal or

objective." However, I am not trying to finesse the hoary means-ends distinction, which is familiar to all those who have encountered at least an introductory course in philosophy or ethics. The point I am most concerned to make evident is that *before* one can value a means inappropriately, there must be some almost overpoweringly attractive end to which it is easily related (e.g., some generality, reason, goal, or objective). The end *is* that which makes any means appear to be sensible. It is our misfortune to know all too well that between seemingly good ends and experienced means, something drastic can often go wrong. Yet it is the end as a generality, reason, goal, or objective which, especially in *those* situations, provides a legitimation for sometimes demonic, inhuman behavior. It *is* a matter of simple pragmatics to insist that means should be clearly and quite unmistakably related to ends, and to also insist that any deviation from that standard is dangerous: human experience teaches that lesson all too well!

28. In a commentary at the end of a conference on the use of computers in the humanities that occurred at the end of January 1965, Robert P. Abelson, then professor of psychology at Yale University, said: "Many things are imaginable for computers but have not yet been anywhere nearly achieved. And in learning what we don't know about how to imitate man, we gain new respect for man, at least in his unstereotyped endeavors. It is mediocrity, not creativity, which is threatened by near-future computer technology. I think that it is salutary to have computers able to produce mediocre products in the arts or as matters of the intellect, because this is simply one more way to expose and laugh at artistic or intellectual sham, at those who follow pat formulas. The computer can follow pat formulas very well indeed." *Computers for the Humanities?* (New Haven: Yale University Press, 1965), p. 154.

7

My God! Piaget and Religious Education

A long, long time ago the desert of Scete harbored a collection of wise persons. It was just over fifteen hundred years ago that the pious searcher for wisdom might there seek out an Arsenius, an Antony, a Theon, a Marcus, or the author Evagrius Ponticus. Approximately a century later, an accomplished Greek scholar living and working in Rome (Pelagius the Deacon) broke off the task of translating into Latin a topically arranged collection of the sayings of these wise persons, because he had been elected to the chair of St. Peter as the bishop of Rome. His work was picked up and brought to completion by another (John the Subdeacon). The work was known by medieval Europeans, who copied and recopied it many times.

Almost at the end of what Latin-reading medieval Europe knew as the *Verba Seniorum*, John the Subdeacon translated this entry:

"A certain philosopher questioned the holy Antony. 'How,' said he, 'dost thou content thyself, Father, who art denied the comfort of books?' He answered, 'My book, philosopher, is the nature of created things, and as often as I have a mind to read the words of God, it is at my hand.' "[1]

Something like fourteen hundred years later, we can recognize that a Swiss by the name of Jean Piaget (1896–1980) expended a scholarly lifetime following out the advice of holy Antony. Certainly, he did not do so consciously. But he did it, nevertheless. He attended to "the nature of created things," most especially homo sapiens as it grows and develops toward adulthood, because he was interested in discovering *how* we know whatever we *do* know. The problem is quite general, of course, but the Swiss was also a philosopher, so he knew that the problem had an appropriate label: *epistemology*. In addition, he was not content to be comforted by the opinions of others, but wanted to read the twentieth-century analogue of holy Antony's book in the original.

Jean Piaget's first book to be translated into English was *The Language and Thought of the Child*, which Harcourt, Brace published in the United States in 1926.[2] In the next six years, five more of Piaget's works were translated and published in English. *Judgment and Reasoning in the Child* appeared in 1928; 1929 saw the publication of *The Child's Conception of the World*. The next year, 1930, saw the publication of *The Child's Conception of Physical Causality*. In 1931 Piaget contributed the article "Children's Philosophies" to the *Handbook of Child Psychology*, which was edited by C. Murchinson and published by Clark University Press. Then, in 1932, Piaget's *Moral Judgment of the Child* appeared in England.[3] It was a remarkable contribution in a short six years. However, it was also a burst of publication that was not to be picked up again for some twenty-eight years, for the next book to be translated into English was *The Psychology of Intelligence* (1950). Flavell's bibliography records some seventeen works in French between 1932 and 1950, so Piaget was not simply resting on a reputation or living the good life off his author's royalties. He was still at work and still publishing. But not in English.[4]

The decade of the 1950s saw seven more books appear in English. Within two years after the appearance of *The Psychology of Intelligence*, a trio of books was published. *Play, Dreams, and Imitation in Childhood*, *The Child's Conception of Number*, and *The Origins of Intelligence in Children* were available by 1952.[5] In October of 1952 Piaget delivered three lectures on the relation of logic to psychology at the University of Manchester in the United Kingdom, and those lectures were published the next year by the Manchester University Press as *Logic and Psychology* (1953).[6] In 1956 Piaget and Barbel Inhelder published *The Child's Conception of Space*. Then in 1958 Inhelder and Piaget published *The Growth of Logical Thinking from Childhood to Adolescence*.[7] In addition, Piaget contributed nine chapters or articles in English to various books and periodicals during the 1950s.[8] The reader of English had available the more recent work and thought of Piaget. Also, it was in 1955 that Piaget established the Centre International d'Epistemologie Genetique at Geneva and, as a result, began to publish the now many volumes of the *Etudes d'epistemologie genetique.*[9]

The 1960s were vintage Piagetian years. The decade began with the publication of *The Child's Conception of Geometry* (1960).[10] Then in 1963 John H. Flavell's encyclopedic *Developmental Psychology of Jean Piaget* appeared. Flavell offered a systematic view of the thought and theory of Piaget up to about 1960 to the reader of English.[11] The following year, Inhelder and Piaget published *The Early Growth of Logic in the Child* (1964).[12] The same year, Ronald Goldman's *Religious Thinking from Childhood to Adolescence* was published in England.[13] That use of Piagetian constructs for research in religious education was followed almost immediately by a second Goldman book, *Readiness for Religion: A Basis for Developmental Religious Education* (1965).[14] In 1966 Millie Almy, Edward Chittenden, and Paula Miller published *Young Children's Thinking,* which reported on North American studies carried out in New York City.[15] The very next year saw David Elkind's collection of lesser-known articles by Piaget, *Six Psychological Studies* (1967).[16] The 1960s came to a close with the publication of five books in one year. Piaget and Inhelder cooperated in writing *The Psychology of the Child* (1969), and Piaget himself published the results of a long series of studies, *The Mechanisms of Perception* (1969).[17] Elkind and Flavell teamed up to edit *Studies in Cognitive Development,* a collection of fourteen essays in honor of Jean Piaget that Oxford University Press published in 1969.[18] That was also the year two introductions to Piaget's work were published. Molly Brearley and Elizabeth Hitchfield published their *Guide to Reading Piaget,* and John L. Phillips, Jr. published *The Origins of Intellect: Piaget's Theory.*[19] By the end of the 1960s not only did the reader have Piaget's own summary of his theory (*The Psychology of the Child*) but a number of helps, guides, and commentaries were on hand and easily available.

The Piagetian publishing explosion begun in 1969 continued on into the 1970s. The decade began with two important little books. Both *Genetic Epistemology* and the two-part *Science of Education and the Psychology of the Child* were published in 1970.[20] The next year saw four more books by Piaget reach publication. *Psychology and Epistemology: Towards a Theory of Knowledge* was published by Grossman in 1971.[21] *Biology and Knowledge* was published by the University of Chicago Press, and readers of English finally had a thorough exposition of Piaget's idea of the relationship between organic regulations and clearly cognitive processes.[22] Piaget's partly biographical *Insights and Illusions of Philosophy* finally became available in English in the same year from the New American Library.[23] The short but important *Structuralism* was also published in an English translation in 1971.[24] Then in 1973 Grossman published two more books, *The Child and Reality* and *To Understand Is to Invent: The Future of Education.*[25] The same year, Harper published a chapter from a 1970 UNESCO publication as *Main Trends in Psychology.*[26] By the next year, 1974, Harper had brought out two more small books based on the same UNESCO publication. *The Place of the Sciences of Man in the System of Sciences*[27] by Piaget made available his introduction to the 1970 UNESCO report *Main Trends of Research in the Social and Human Sciences.* The book *Main Trends in Inter-Disciplinary Research* by Piaget was based upon another chapter of his in that UNESCO volume.[28] The year 1974 also saw the publication of *Learning and the Development of Cognition*, a report by Barbel Inhelder, Hermine Sinclair, and Magali Bovet of some careful cross-cultural research into the effect of training for a next level of cognitive operations.[29] The interest in Piaget's older albeit as yet untranslated work was evident in the 1975 publication of *The Origin of the Idea of Chance in Children*, a book that Inhelder and Piaget had originally published in French in 1951, some twenty-four years earlier.[30]

The reader who has struggled (or staggered) through the previous four paragraphs may be unwilling to believe it, but I cannot claim to have done an exhaustive listing of Piaget's books since 1950, let alone a thorough listing of related and important books. In truth, I have merely organized the things I had readily available. However, I hope the reader will have glimpsed five ideas. First, Piaget's attempt to read the twentieth-century analogue of holy Antony's book in the original *has* led to a truly vast number of publications. Second, all attempts to present Piaget's thought systematically are relatively recent. Third,

Piaget's specific works on a genetic epistemology have become available in English only very recently. Fourth, Jean Piaget tried to address himself to the educational question, although many of us had to wait for the 1970s before we could realize that. Fifth, Piaget for a long time was interested both in the specificities of human development, as those are evident in infants, children, and adolescents, and in what those specificities contribute to a science of humankind. He read the twentieth-century analogue of holy Antony's book line by line, but he also sought the insight that comes only from a literary analysis of any book. Research and theory are both lifelong interests, and they had a most productive interaction in the work of Jean Piaget.

THE BASIC QUESTION: WHAT DOES IT ALL MEAN?

Sometime in the very early 1960s, probably at an annual meeting of the old Professors' and Researchers' Section of the Division of Christian Education of the National Council of Churches in St. Louis, Missouri, I remember Dr. William A. Koppe suggesting, with fervor and force, that religious educators *should* attend to a Swiss named Jean Piaget.[31] I was impressed. I carried the message back to the editors and authors with whom I then worked. As I now remember it, Ms. Agnes M. Hickson, the editor/author of the Seabury Series materials for the early elementary school grades, took my advice: she purchased several books by Piaget then available and started to read them. I didn't hear anything more for about two months, then I did. Ms. Hickson got to me one day and told me in a nicely firm, Southern way that it was very confusing. She asked, as near as I can recall it, the vastly important question: What does it all mean?[32] At the time, I was flustered. Frankly, I did not then know a really good answer to a quite understandably pragmatic query from an educator. Since it was probably the year Flavell's summary was published, I may have directed her to that book. But honesty suggests to me that I really do not know how I "answered" that question, in that long ago. However, the query stayed with me.

Once those of us in the old national Department of Christian Education of the Episcopal church became aware of the use Goldman had made of Piaget in research, we could easily recognize the Swiss as important to us and our work, and we began to ask Hickson's query in earnest. Goldman's books and his visits to our department were stimuli, but the query was really only partially addressed to Piaget-through-Goldman. We sought for our own answer, in terms of Piaget's then available works. What we discovered was a conundrum which, quite frankly, we were not prepared to resolve in those days some fifteen or more years ago. We soon discovered that the Piaget then available in English seemed to suggest that cognition, in which we certainly were interested, was somehow related to the internalization of the actions of a person (e.g., the manipulation of physical objects, as in the classic Piagetian marker tasks with clay, beads, or with liquids). That fact per se didn't constitute the conundrum; we could accept that thesis. What finally became our conundrum was our *search* for those analogues of Piaget's marker actions which could be discerned to be developmentally important to what we then thought religious education (our job!) was all about. We searched, but we could not be satisfied with any of the tentative answers we could discern.

I bother with this extensive memory of a time and place long ago and (for many) long forgotten for only one reason: the reader has no cause to merely retrace our steps. The probability of coming out at our mid-1960s conundrum is simply too great. Unless one pays attention to that later Piaget whom we did not know. In these years of the 1980s, there is no reason to retrace our faltering steps along what was too like the mathematicians' drunkard's walk.[33] Minimally, one can begin with Piaget and Inhelder, *The Psychology of the Child* (1969), which we did not have. A conceptual map is a help in anyone's exploration of the empirically rich and theoretically luxuriant world of Jean Piaget's work.

For some fifteen years I have lived with Ms. Hickson's query. Being the person I am, I have desired a resolution to that important question. I have asked and then re-asked the same question. What *does* it all mean? As time has passed, and as other works have been translated into

English, and as my own research has begun to generate data begging to be interpreted, I have begun to discern a succession of answers. However, they have been *my* answers.

Let me try and be honest. Like Piaget, I have passed no examinations in psychology. Like Piaget, my interest in developmental psychology itself developed across time: it became instrumental to the work upon other more general problems. Like Piaget, I found the interest led me into the work of data gathering, data analysis, and the challenging task of interpreting the gathered and analyzed data.[34] But I am not Piaget, by either training or experience. A parallelism in our experiences (at some level of generality) may exist, but the specificities become quite different. Piaget trained as a philosopher, held teaching positions as a philosopher, and only quite late in his professional life had the support to create a discipline: genetic epistemology. My training has been as a theologian and as a pastor. My professional life has been involved with religious education. My own research has its prima facie meaning in that context. As yet, I do not have the support to create any new discipline, although I can (and do) dream of a scientifically rigorous, experimental religious education. A decade's experience with just-less-than-rigorous, not-quite-really-experimental religious education led *me* right into a paradox.

My paradox consists of two nicely balanced recognitions. On the one hand, I recognize that a fundamental defect in the work we did in the old Department of Christian Education of the Episcopal church during the 1960s was that we were not able to break through to genuinely rigorous, experimental religious education.[35] We always hovered in the just-less-than or the not-quite-really state. After another decade, I do *not* seek a Levitical scapegoat; that is both useless and quite uncalled for. Only hindsight suggests that all of us should have known better; the truth, of course, is that we did not. But that is *our* problem, which (within a Christian context that includes absolution) *each* of us can assimilate. We were who we were, then, and we did what we were able to do, then. To think less of either our effort or of ourselves is, for *us*, to surrender to an obviously pathological floating anxiety which is theologically indefensible and pragmatically stupid.

On the other hand, I recognize that the Episcopal church in the late

1950s and 1960s neither wanted nor was willing to support a genuinely rigorous, experimental religious education. Oh, some may have thought that was what they had from their accursed Department of Christian Education. But that mistaken conclusion is no more than a sign of *this* side of the paradox. As I remember it, there were few if any missives directed toward us that posed such important questions as: (a) What makes you think this is the way to do religious education? or (b) What evidence have you that this is the way to achieve your goals for these pupils? The first of these questions concerns validity, while the second is a matter of reliability. Oh, we responded to our opponents as if they asked those questions, but I do not think they did so.[36] We and they kept talking past one another. As I remember it, now, it seems evident that the message we kept getting was simple and direct: you were not asked to be rigorous or experimental, just "practical." We out here want to feel good about religious education, and we cannot afford to expend much energy on the task; so why do you keep making life difficult for us?

I had an opportunity to work for a decade with bright, intelligent, and creative people, people who could and did argue about many things, albeit we managed to stay within a common dedication to a demanding task, religious education within a particular Christian denomination. In part, I am now convinced, we argued so much and finally failed our client denomination because we never resolved the Hickson query vis-a-vis Piaget and the sheer intractabilities of human development, nor did we successfully resolve our dual allegiance to theology and education. We kept thinking that theology would slay the educational dragon. But it didn't. The worm kept on living; it wouldn't roll over, dead.[37]

There is an all-too-real sense in which the previous three paragraphs are ancient history now in the 1980s. Yet a part of me *is* a historian. I hope that some present can benefit from its not-too-distant past. If those paragraphs cause any readers to wonder or reflect or dig back to find out for themselves what was going on, perhaps my hope will be realized.

But I do not write this chapter as a dirge for long-ago possibilities. I write it because I am who I am, now, and I *still* think that Hickson's query is a vastly important question for religious education. Moreover, without trying to shape a reader's response to Piaget, I think I may be able to offer some guidance toward an appreciation of the research and the theories of Jean Piaget, that remarkable Swiss genetic epistemologist.

SIX CLUES TO WHAT PIAGET MIGHT MEAN

In an earlier chapter I argued that humans must be aware of what they do, the choices they make, the decisions they take, and acknowledge that they did it. I want to do that now. What follows is a record of *my* conclusions. *I* am responsible for them. You may disagree with me but, if you do, acknowledge what *you* do. Be responsible for your own conclusions. That is the way homo sapiens exercises a most valuable attribute, freedom. Moreover, should you decide to simply take my word for what follows, acknowledge what you do. Your acceptance of authority is, naturally, a pleasing thing to me, if I am the authority you accept. But be aware of what you are doing, for your active cognitive freedom is also my desire.

So much for the initial caveats.

As I have read my way into the Piagetian corpus and, especially, as I have sought to use Piagetian constructs to understand my own research, I have come to discern a relatively small number of recurring themes. I have found them extraordinarily useful, which is another way of saying they have been relevant to that reality I have kept encountering as an educator, a researcher, and a priest. Therefore, I want to share them.

The simplest way to do that kind of sharing is simply to set the list before the reader. Commentary can follow; it need not precede the actual listing. In fact, it would only weary the reader and the author. So, here they are: six recurring themes that, for me, constitute *an* answer to what *I* think of as Hickson's query.

1. Cognition (or intelligence) is internalized action.
2. Cognitive structure forms and informs motive.
3. Successive periods of equilibrium constitute a sign of development.

4. Interaction is a third alternative to the nature/nurture debate.
5. Construction is an ongoing, continual process.
6. Wisdom and verifiable knowledge are different, yet necessary.

These six themes *are* generalities. I know it, and no reader should think they are not. Yet they are far less sweeping than Gödel's theorem, which was considered in a previous chapter. In fact, these six themes occupy an intermediate range between the thoroughly general and the thoroughly specific. No one should ignore that. Yet, when one acknowledges as much, one should also acknowledge that each of these six generalities has some clear relation to observable reality (at least within a Piagetian frame of reference). They are generally great ideas, which have some readily observable relation to the reality of human development as we do know it.

No one concerned with religious education should think either less of them or more of them. All too often, religious educators have oscillated between either extreme, as if an intermediate position were demonically inspired. At least in this instance, it isn't. It is no more than what it is, an "in between."

Only presumed value would identify such an intermediate state with a golden mean. I am not prepared, at this point, to push that value. So I hope the reader will acknowledge only what I have explicitly said and avoid presuming something not said.

These six clues occupy an intermediate level of generality between the vastly important and equally vastly general and a level of specificity which is almost painfully limited to any particular instance. Of course, such an intermediate level is extremely useful to us, once one can identify it, for both extreme generality and extreme specificity are too readily limited in their use. Most of us know that to be so from long and sometimes difficult experience.

I. A First Clue: Cognition (or Intelligence) Is Internalized Action

On a Thursday evening in mid-November of 1863, Charles S. Peirce spoke to the Reunion of the Cambridge (Massachusetts) High School Association. It was four months after the conclusion of the Battle of Gettysburg, and an even seven days before Lincoln's Gettysburg Address. Peirce chose to speak on the topic, "The Place of Our Age in the History of Civilization." Toward the end of that address, he spoke these remarkable words:

> The fulcrum has yet to be found that shall enable the lever of love to move the world. . . . Now Lord Bacon, our great master, has said that the *end* of science is the glory of God, and the use of man. If, then, this is so, action is higher than reason, for it is its purpose; and to say that it is not is the essence of selfishness and atheism.[38]

Peirce was a logician and a scientist. His statement that "action is higher than reason" must, therefore, be understood as a statement of logical priority. However, in the work of Jean Piaget, Peirce's position finds a strangely apropos confirmation. For Piaget contends that action is the developmental precursor of reason, cognition, intelligence. While that may seem the very opposite of Peirce's statement, it is not. In fact, it is possible to understand Piaget's thesis vis-a-vis the relation of action and intelligence (or thinking) as a restatement of Peirce's 1863 statement.

In 1958, English language readers finally discovered Inhelder's and Piaget's conclusion that "from the experimental standpoint, *intelligence is first a coordination of acts*—then operations which orient themselves step by step toward certain forms of equilibrium."[39] Eleven years later, in 1969, readers of English found Piaget and Inhelder writing that "although the child's actions seem to reflect a sort of magical belief in causality without any material connection, his use of the same means to try to achieve different ends indicates that he is on the threshold of intelligence."[40] Two years later, in 1971, the Coltman translation of *Psychologie et Pedagogie* (Paris: Editions Denoel, 1969) appeared, a remarkable retrospective commentary on something originally published in 1935, and the reader of English could begin to appreciate Piaget's concern for the processes of education.[41] In the reflection portion of that fascinating work, a later Piaget concludes that there are two "most central truths of the psychology of the cognitive functions." First, that what we would call intellectual operations "proceed from effective action in the fullest sense . . ., since logic is before all else the expression of the general coordination of actions." Second, that such a coordination of actions can be regarded as, of necessity, involving "a social dimension, since the inter-individual coordination of actions and their intra-individual coordination constitute a single and identical process."[42]

In the very next year, Viking Press published the Rosin translation of *Psychologie et Epistemologie* (Paris: Editions Denoel, 1970) as *Psychology and Epistemology: Towards a Theory of Knowledge.* In a chapter entitled "The Myth of the Sensorial Origin of Scientific Knowledge," Piaget considers the relation of intelligence and perception, and says: "Until now we admitted that perception is not alone active in the formation of knowledge, and that, as another necessary source, action and its coordinates are added, which amounts to intelligence." He immediately makes the observation that "by this somewhat vague and rather dangerous word (i.e., intelligence) we mean precisely the functioning of operatory systems emanating from action."[43]

This was no more than another statement of the position Piaget took in his University of Chicago lectures, published as *Biology and Knowledge: An Essay on the Relations between Organic Regulations and Cognitive Processes.*[44] In that work, Piaget notes, "When you come down to it, . . . for the psychologist cognitive functions arise out of organic and motor life . . . (and) for the modern psychologist cognitive functions spring from the organic and motor life of the living creature."[45] Piaget also addresses the question of linguistic priority when he observes that "language is merely one particular instance of the semiotic or symbolic function."[46] He also says that "once language is established as being a particular, although very important, type of semiotic function, it in no way exhausts the operations of intellect, because their origin remains sensorimotor."[47] In a remarkably clear statement, Piaget maintains that "reason itself is not an absolute invariable but is elaborated through a series of creative operational constructions, which introduce new features and are preceded by an uninterrupted series of preoperational constructions. These result," he maintains, "from coordinations of actions and can be traced right back to morphogenetic organization and to biological organization in general."[48]

These references to that later Piaget knowable to readers of English should suggest why a clue to one possible meaning of Piaget concerns his idea of the relationship of cognition (intelligence) and action. They also should suggest why, in this instance, Peirce seems to be an odd, remarkable precursor of Piaget. Intelligence, cognition, reason (choose your term!) and *action* are inextricably related, in an ordered manner. Neither Peirce nor Piaget, of course, say exactly the same thing. That is not too surprising, since they are separated from one another by just over one hundred years. What is surprising and intriguing is that they say something so close to being an exact equivalent. Perhaps they both attended to the available, contemporary analogue of holy Antony's book, "the nature of created things."

II. A Second Clue: Cognitive Structure Forms and Informs Motive

A year after David Elkind edited *Six Psychological Studies* (1967) and a year before Piaget and Inhelder published *The Psychology of the Child* (1969), the Kent University Press cooperated with the Danish publisher Munksgaard to bring to English language readers K. B. Madsen's *Theories of Motivation* (1968).[49] In that fascinating study of twenty theories (and an equally intriguing glance at ten other then more recent theories) Madsen acknowledged that, for his analytic purposes, an initially tentative definition of *motivation* was the gross generality, "all variables which arouse, sustain, and direct behavior." Madsen also referenced James Drever's *Dictionary of Psychology* (1952) to the effect that *motive* means "an affective-conative factor which operates in determining the direction of an individual's behaviour towards an end or goal, consciously apprehended, or unconscious."[50] Madsen and Drever both identify that *motive* or *motivation* are what, in these early years of the 1980s, we might tend to think of as imprecise, basket-type terms. Still, we cannot do without them. All too readily, our experience indicates that they refer to a kind of reality which we do experience.

There is a common, persistent sense that some things influence or tend to determine our recognizable behavior. Those things can be regarded as a set of variables that are either responsible for or, minimally, persistently associated with the arousal or sustenance or direction of behavior. Rather then enumerate that set, we tend to think of them all as motives or motivating things (i.e., variables). The imprecision *is* ours, although analysis quite readily leads us to recognize the multiplicity of things we lump together in the terms *motive* or *motivation*. Once again, we should not ignore what *we* have done. The terms are useful, but only at a relatively gross level of generality.

However, if we think about what a motive or a motivation can mean, we are likely to recognize that we are naming a something that we presume to be an energizing factor lying immediately behind observable behavior. We rarely mean more, even though we may give an evident variety of names to those members of the set of things that we think (presume) explain behavior. If we can but understand what *we* tend to do with ease, then *we* can recognize that behind any and all names there is a sense of energy. We are, then, thinking or talking about the energetics of behavior when we use the constructs motive or motivation. All the rest is instance-specific. The generality across the clear instances of motive is a sense of energy immediately responsible for a behavior.

Although there is a sense in which the construct of motive can be bastardized into an excuse, that is not its inherent meaning. That is a thoroughly secondary use we sometimes make of the construct. By itself, it is no more than and no less than a recognition that some energetics are seemingly inextricably associated with behavior. Moreover, just as behaviors vary, so too do we presume that motives vary. We tend to think of noticeably different behaviors having, by some presumed necessity, different energetics.

If, but only if, we can acknowledge that kind of a tendency, we can begin to appreciate Piaget and Inhelder's statement about motivations in *The Psychology of the Child*. Almos at the end of that book, they say that "affectivity constitutes the energetics of behavior patterns whose cognitive aspect refers to structures alone." They continue, "There is no behavior pattern, however intellectual, which does not involve affective factors as motives; but, reciprocally, there can be no affective states without the intervention of perceptions or comprehensions which constitute their cognitive structure." They immediately conclude, "Behavior is therefore of a piece, even if the structures do not explain its energetics and if, vice versa, its energetics do not account for its structures. The two aspects, affective and cognitive, are at the same time inseparable and irreducible."[51]

Unless one is quite conceptually flexible, that is a challenge, a kind of Pauline "meat" for those of us who may be more familiar with a liquid diet. Piaget and Inhelder implicitly affirm that if we think only of affect as a motivational (i.e., arousing, sustaining, directing) variable responsible for behavior, we ignore a whole class of variables, the cognitive. Their conclusion that the affective and the cognitive are "at the same time inseparable and irreducible" poses a true challenge to us. We keep separating them or reducing one to the other. We also keep ignoring that *that* is what *we* have done.

However, if we admit that behavior is of a piece, which should not be too hard for us to do, then we have hold upon a principle that permits us to acknowledge that the inseparable albeit irreducible are, as best we can think, mutually forming and informing. Suddenly we may be able to gain the insight: it is *our* analytical desire that leads us to want to separate, to aim at a reduction of one to the other. If we can gain that insight, we may be able to genuinely appreciate Piaget and Inhelder's thesis that cognitive structure both forms and informs what we call *motive,* all of those things we tend to think of as providing the energy involved in arousing, sustaining, or directing behavior.

It is interesting that Madsen concludes his analytical survey of the theories of motivation associated with the names of Allport, Hebb, Hull, Lewin, McClelland, McDougal, Murray, Tolman, Tinbergen, and Young with this summary statement: "The main contents . . . of the theory are that *behavior* is *determined by motivation (dynamogenic and cognitive* [directive]) *processes in combination.*"[52] That is not exactly Piaget's and Inhelder's thesis, of course, but it is remarkably close to it. So close, in fact, that it is possible that one can invoke the idea of separate perspectives upon a single human phenomenon. If one can believe that, then Madsen witnesses to the fact that the ten most obviously motivational theories since 1930 acknowledge that motive consists of a duality of (a) arousing and sustaining energies and (b) directing energies. What Madsen did was to uncover this duality and, analytically, identify that *in these ten theories* the posited directing energies were recognizably cognitive contributions to behavior. That is but a very short conceptual step from the position of Piaget and Inhelder in *The Psychology of the Child*.

What Madsen would credit to cognitive factors (the directive function) is very similar to what Piaget and Inhelder credit to the cognitive structures as forming and informing of motive, or affect. That similarity, for our purposes, is close enough to conclude that at a general level the two sources are in an important, fundamental agreement. An agreement which is, for *us*, important because it comes from two disparate positions, each of which considers the same phenomenon in the human being. Thus, we have something very like two independent witnesses.

This involved rationality is worth the effort because it destroys the too-simpleminded dichotomy of cognition and affect, and it specifically undercuts the attractive option that one can make a giant stride forward in education by attending solely to motives or motivation. Religious education has too often put what is called affect over against cognition and, because it wished some quasi-magical over-plus, pitted affective education against something it called cognitively oriented education. But that is to engage in a sheerly semantic battle which is worth neither winning nor losing.

The human reality is not any presumed dichotomy. Reality is a fascinating, complex combination of both sides of the false dichotomy. The Piagetian position, then, offers a genuine alternative: "both and" rather than "either or." Simple but profound. Pervasive in its effect upon thought and action. Therefore, important.

III. A Third Clue: Successive Periods of Equilibrium Constitute a Sign of Development

Piaget and Inhelder are reasonably clear in acknowledging that what we normally think of as development is, in fact, a process of successive construction. They are also clear in acknowledging that, once adopted, such a perspective requires an answer (of some sort) to a central question of any and all constructivism: What is the internal mechanism of the process?

What they posit is a mechanism that "is observable at the time of each partial construction and each transition from one stage to the next."[53] The mechanism is a process of equilibration, which they describe as an equilibrium "not in the sense of a simple balance of forces, as in mechanics, or any increase in entropy, as in thermodynamics, but in the sense—which has now been brought out so clearly by cybernetics—of self-regulation; that is, a series of active compensations on the part of the subject in response to external disturbances and an adjustment that is both retroactive (loop systems or feedbacks) and anticipatory, constituting a permanent system of compensations."[54]

Two pages later, Piaget and Inhelder, after considering the reality of a development of the affective life and of motivations, note that it is impossible to interpret that development "without stressing the all-important role of self-regulations." Equilibrium. They conclude their whole book with a paragraph that begins: "Thus, equilibration by self-regulation constitutes the formative process of the structures we have described."[55] That is, the development of structures (that which constitutes the vast substance of their books) is here credited to "equilibration by self-regulation."

It should take no particularly subtle intellect to conclude that if development is a sign of the operation of equilibrium, then a sign of such an equilibrium is a reason to infer the existence of development. Most persons can and will reach that conclusion, especially if they consider the argument advanced by Piaget and Inhelder in *The Psychology of the Child*. Thus, in any field of human activity, when one can observe a series of successive periods of such equilibrium, there is some reason to regard that activity as a matter of development. Moreover, if it is developmental, Piaget and Inhelder posit that sufficiently acute analysis will discover formative processes that are marked by a cybernetic self-regulation which is both retroactive and anticipatory. In quite simple terms, a temporary condition of apparent or approximate stasis is an inferential result of the operation of a self-regulatory process that adjusts to both the system's past state (retroactivity) and to some possible future state (anticipation). Unfortunately, that simplicity is complicated by an attempt to be analytically precise: from the simple position of an observer, the equilibrium is likely to look like a period of genuine stability (or stasis).

When a growing, developing human is in a period of apparent stability, then, another way of viewing that condition is to posit a period of equilibrium. The advantage of this alternate view is that the apparent stability, when understood as a period of equilibrium, is not presumed to be an end-state. Rather it is understood to be a result of some cybernetic self-regulation, which may be disturbed at some moment, albeit the system will tend to return to a similar state of equilibrium at some chronologically later moment.

What this kind of idea offers to the educator, secular or religious, is two quite important perspectives upon a human student. First, no present state of seeming stability is likely to last forever. Thus, however much one may value any given present state, it is more than likely to change. Second, the human as a cybernetic self-regulating system tends toward stability, regardless of the disturbance it may encounter. Thus, whatever challenge one may provide, stability is the most likely result. In a sense, that is no more than a neutral way of affirming that the human system is remarkably resilient.

There are times when it can be important for an educator to know that, for without recognizing the resiliency of the system, an educator may suffer from either of two grand illusions. On the one hand, the educator may assume a responsibility for the future state of the system, as if any educational input were a process of imprinting. On the other hand, the educator may assume a power to determine a future state of the system, as if any process were bound to change the system in some desired way. The first illusion may lead one into the maze of conscientiousness and, as a result, to little action. The second illusion may lead one full into the temptation to exercise sheer, naked power and, as a result, demand simple conformity. Neither illusion matches the reality of the resilient human system, which tends to be a cybernetic self-regulatory system repeatedly returning to some form of stability.

Naturally, both of these illusions are variations upon a single error: the belief that the system we call a human being is *solely* determined by the action of something exterior to it (e.g., an educator).[56] The thesis of successive periods of equilibrium denies both illusions. The educator's action is exterior to the human learner. Yet that action meets, in the human learner, a system tending toward stability in its own terms. Unless one forces conformity, power is often less than an educator might desire. Yet the learner system's very ability to self-regulate means that an educator's responsibility is less than total.

We are, fortunately, *always* dealing with a resilient human system whenever we engage in the educational venture. Moreover, it is a system that develops through a remarkably numerous series of successive periods of equilibration by self-regulation.[57] The educator's task, therefore, is to attend across time to the series, note its direction, facilitate it if desired, or attempt, if necessary, the far more difficult task of redirecting it.[58] Few things can be done in one move.

IV. A Fourth Clue: Interaction Is a Third Alternative to the Nature/Nurture Debate

For some of us, Arthur R. Jensen's article, "IQ and Scholastic Achievement," in the *Harvard Educational Review*, plus the lengthy series of counterstatements, rebuttals, defenses, etc. it generated are the sure and certain sign that the nature/nurture debate still goes on.[59] In fact, it is at least a tenable hypothesis that North Americans tend to want to believe in the nurture position and, so, to be quite impatient with the nature position. However, I do not want to consider Jensen's admittedly controversial thesis. I only want to use Jensen's experience as a sign that the nature/nurture debate is alive and well.

In the form that the Jensen episode took, the nature side of the debate concerned the relative contribution of heredity to observed ability, while the nurture side of the debate concerned the relative contribution of the person's experience/environment to the same observed ability. Neither side of the debate wished to claim that *only* nature or nurture was responsible for the observed ability, but the two sides differed drastically as to which was responsible for most of the observed ability. Unfortunately, the simpleminded view of a sometimes esoteric statistical argument was that it was a winner-take-all argument between genetics and education. It wasn't. However, Piaget's choice of the phrase *genetic epistemology* might suggest that he had opted for the nature side of the debate. He had *not*. But the implication that he had is powerful.

Regardless of the positions many of us in my generation eventually found ourselves taking, Ernest R. Hilgard's *Introduction to Psychology* has been a touchstone. In his glossary, Hilgard notes that the nature-nurture issue involves the attempt to determine "the relative importance of the hereditary component (nature) and the result of upbringing in the particular environment (nurture) upon mature ability."[60] It was Jensen's impolitic display of what psychologists and geneticists had recognized for many years that, in many ways, caused the remarkably virulent and lengthy brouhaha. Unfortunately, Jensen's article awakened a dozing debate within North American thought and, thereby, affected the understanding of Piaget. Frankly, it is my hypothesis that Jensen's stirring of the nature/nurture debate made it difficult for North Americans to read Piaget as anything other than a complex, perhaps sophisticated proponent of the nature side of the debate. That is a genuine misfortune, to say the least!

A careful reading of Piaget indicates that he has quite consistently sought a middle ground between nature and nurture. Frankly, he has been dissatisfied with *both* nature and nurture as explanatory principles. It is *our* involvement in the North American debate, more than anything else, that has caused us to read him either as favoring nature or as being merely academically ambiguous. He has not been that ambigious at all; in fact, he has been reasonably clear for some time. However, it was not until the 1971 publication of *Structuralism* and *Biology and Knowledge* that his position became quite clear to North Americans.

In those two publications Piaget identifies three positions that have purportedly explained human behavior. One of these corresponds to the nature side of our North American debate. One of them corresponds to the nurture side of that debate. One of them represents an alternative which takes into account both sides, but does not opt for either one. Piaget clearly prefers that alternative and, once that is recognized, one can understand a good deal of the seeming complexity of his earlier works. Piaget is unwilling to settle for a too-simple solution, however attractive it might seem. Perhaps he *had* too carefully read the twentieth-century analogue of holy Antony's book.

One of *our* problems is that Piaget does not use the words *nature* and *nurture* to identify the two sides in the debate. However, what he terms the "nativist" position or in another place calls "innatism," is clearly the nature side of the debate. Piaget identifies that such a position involves some use of the idea of preformation or, even, predestination as an explanatory principle allied with heredity. He also suggests that gestalists can hold to this position by positing simple "emergent totalities" or "wholes" as fundamental elements of human experience. Still, the word *preformation* seems to be the most frequently used term for what he perceives as the essence of the nature position in the debate we in North America know so well.[61]

The other side of our debate, the nurture position, is associated with what Piaget tends to call "socialization" theories which, he suggets, tend to involve a belief in "atomist association" or "structureless genesis" or a kind of "contingent emergence."[62] Piaget is quite clear, however, that this position irreducibly is concerned with growth or development as, fundamentally, a matter of "acquisition from the outside."[63]

In between these two positions, Piaget identifies an alternative. He tends to call it "operational structuralism," and to maintain that its chief mechanism is what he calls "internal equilibration."[64] He speaks of this middle ground as one held by what he terms "constructivist accounts" of human growth and development. Probably he is most obvious in his statements of this alternative when he considers the nature of necessity in human experience. As one in the middle ground, he maintains that the experience of necessity is an outcome of learning, it is not a prior condition of that learning.[65] He contrasts this middle alternative to both of the positions in our debate, suggesting that each (in its own way) presumes that necessity is a prior condition of any act of human learning. The nurture position, for example, seems to presume that necessity comes along with acquisition from the "outside." The nature position, contrariwise, seems to presume that it springs from some innate need.

In *Biology and Knowledge* Piaget identifies the names of Hering and Kant with the nature position.[66] In *The Psychology of the Child* he and Inhelder identify the early psychological empiricists Helmholtz and Lamarck with the nuture position.[67] In both *Structuralism* and *Biology and Knowledge* Piaget clearly identifies himself with the constructivist middle-ground alternative, and he notes that C. H. Waddington seems to have also posited such a process,[68] one almost exactly the same as his alternative. Three words can be used as signs or symbols of the options Piaget discerns: *preformation* (nature), *construction* (the alternative), and *formation* (nurture).

Almost at the conclusion of *Structuralism*, Piaget puts his own thesis in terms that could be a challenge to religious educators. Four paragraphs from the conclusion of that remarkably intriguing work, Piaget says, "The basic epistemological alternatives are predestination or some sort of constructivism." He acknowledges Noam Chomsky's thesis that human reason is essentially innate, and he notes Claude Levi-Strauss's concept that human intellect is permanent, and he rejects both. He maintains that once one considers the available biological facts, neither Chomsky nor Levi-Strauss match those facts (even as we *now* know them).[69] Thus, we are forced back to the identified alternative: predestination or constructivism.

When David V. Tiedeman and I wrote an optimistic book called *Career Development: Designing Self*, we put that quotation from Piaget in the first paragraph of our preface. We said, "Given that alternative, we opt for constructivism or, as we call it, a constructionist position."[70] It took us five years to see our book published, and it has yet to reach the best-seller list. But we were being open and honest about *our* decision in that preface: we considered the alternative, and we made our decision as to where *we* stood. However, I wonder whether the alternative has yet been seriously considered by my colleagues in religious education. (While I may be in obvious error, I tend to doubt that most have seriously thought about the alternative and, then, made their own conscious decision.)

I have no hesitancy in admitting that Tiedeman and I choose constructivism because we value human freedom and the human responsibility that freedom drags along with itself. I cannot speak for my coauthor, but *I* value freedom and human responsibility because of *my* theological understanding. I would affirm that, theologically, it is better to wrestle with the problems implicit in affirming that G-O-D gives freedom and, therefore, holds us responsible for our exercise of that freedom, than it is to "resolve" those problems by affirming anything less than that, which is an open, historic option: predestination.

Clearly, obviously, and acknowledgedly, *my* decision for construction involves a value decision. Being who I am, were I forced to a logical wall, I would have to conclude that the G-O-D posited by strict predestinarians is simply abhorrent to me. I know no way to be faithful to either Scripture or tradition and affirm that kind of a G-O-D. Even so, I do realize that some seem to be able to do what I find myself unable to do. I do not understand how that is possible. But it is. Yet I do not agree with the conclusion. The best I can do is acknowledge the existence of a classic paradox: it shouldn't be, but it is.

As a religious educator, my dis-ease with predestination or preformation leaves me with but two options. Frankly, nurture in its classic sense is not too appealing for two reasons. First, because it presumes that I am too responsible for the imprinting of something on the student. In fact, this presumption seems just too optimistic to be realistic. Second, because nurture is too easy a way to ignore those free exercises of the young that seem to be fundamental to lasting learning. This seems too obvious an aspect of education as the art and science of learning to ignore. Thus, I find myself left with the one option that Piaget identifies as a middle-ground alternative to nature and nurture.

That is almost too prosaic a way to put it. It suggests being driven to an unsatisfactory conclusion, whereas, in fact, the conclusion is really quite satisfactory. The middle-ground alternative does not require one to ignore either the realities of nurture or those of nature. Yet it permits one to also recognize some other realities which, in Piaget's terms, seem to be the result of an interaction between learner and environment. Indeed, it is through such an interactive perspective that freedom seems most likely for both educator and educated. It is in terms of interaction, then, that one is most likely to continually appreciate the fundamental role of the *learner* in education.

While I cannot claim to have resolved anywhere near all my educational dilemmas by this choice, I think I have gained two very important qualities. I have gained a rationale for retaining my realism about myself and the learner. I have also gained both an awesome responsibility as a facilitator of a learner's self-construction and a deep, genuine, and lasting respect for the self under construction.

For *me*, it is relatively easy to translate those qualities into theological terms. Piaget's middle-ground alternative to the nature/nurture debate permits *me* to be realistic about and respectful of learners as creatures within this creation, growing toward freedom and responsibility and, so, constructing ever new dynamic images of G-O-D in themselves. That is a "calling" which, I think, makes meaningful whatever it is that the religious educator does for or with or to a learner of any age.

V. A Fifth Clue: Construction is an Ongoing, Continual Process

More than thirty years ago, in 1949, a me-that-was began, simultaneously, a marriage and a process of training for the ordained professional ministry at the Yale University Divinity School in New Haven, Connecticut. I celebrated my twenty-third birthday three months after arriving in Connecticut from Kalamazoo, Michigan. Legally, I was then an adult. But I was not matured, nor was I through with the processes of growth we humans call *development*.

In four years my wife and our first daughter and I left Connecticut and the Yale community we had known. We returned to Michigan, where I had a job in a parish in northeastern Detroit. The me-that-then-was was subtly different from the me-that-was in the fall of 1949. Four years, two degrees, a child, and a sense of professional identity separated the 1949 me from the 1953 me. I was still me, but I was also a different person. Obviously, as we humans are wont to say, I had grown or developed. Looking back, it is clear that I *had*.

However, that backward glance across the years from now to those years of the mid-1950s identifies an intriguing developmental puzzle. Clearly, I developed between the ages of 22-going-on-23 and 26-going-on-27. Yet the very idea of development is often considered to be terminal: one develops until one is an adult. Perhaps I was simply slow in reaching adulthood; that would be a way to conform my experience and the presumption that one's development is a terminal process.

But it simply won't do.

As I glance backward twenty-five years, I seem to find repeated instances of change, of growth, of development. There are a series of me's-that-were scattered across those years, each one subtly yet really different from one another. That is the intriguing developmental puzzle I can identify as *I* glance backward.

The idea that the construction of structures continues is both an implication I have drawn from Piaget, and a position he took in the works that became available in English during the 1970s. For my part, the idea seems ultimately related to Piaget's use of Gödel's theorem (especially in the little book *Structuralism*, which was first published in English in 1971). However, in a chapter in the 1970 UNESCO volume *Main Trends of Research in the Social and Human Sciences*, which was published in 1973 by Harper and Row as *Main Trends in Psychology* (New York: Harper & Row, Publishers, 1973), Piaget recognizes that development is a matter of sequential constructions and that the process goes on for a long time. For instance, Piaget characterizes both E. Erikson and A. Adler as occupying a special position in the history of psychology, because Erikson "introduced into Freudian psychoanalysis an important notion which was developed in Adler's work... the hypothesis that we continually assimilate the past to the present with a view to adaptations in the prsent."[71] A few sentences later, Piaget observes that in the work of Erikson and Adler, "we are therefore moving towards a real kind of psychological contructivism, with gradual and retroactive integrations as in mental development."[72] Since both Erikson and Adler were as concerned with adults as they were with children or adolescents, Piaget's conclusion implies (but does not state!) that constructivism in Erikson and Adler—"as in mental development"—involves adulthood. Inferentially, then, development is *not* a terminal concept at all.

However, there is more.

After considering the learning theories of Hull, Tolman, and Skinner, as well as the work of Bush and Mosteller, H. Harlow and L. Apostel, Piaget poses a question that has fundamental import: "Is it learning that constitutes the primary phenomenon and explains mental development itself, or does development obey its own laws and does learning, in a certain and clearly defined situation, form only a more or less artificially separated part of it (and that at all ages of life, for in the occupational area, at any rate, development lasts until senility)?"[73] While he acknowledges that what most theories of learning posit is consistent with the first solution within his question, he also notes that such an assumption is "in defiance of the spirit of all contemporary biology. . . ."[74] In addition, he indicates that the second solution within his question seems to be receiving more and more attention, since to presume that development precedes learning "means that learning in any form involves, in addition to the external facts S and the observable reactions R, a set of active co-ordinations, the gradual equilibration of which constitutes a fundamental factor that in fact represents a logic or an algebra."[75]

Moreover, although the parenthetical remark is contained within an overall question, the remark itself is an assertion of the second solution. That is, Piaget clearly states that "at all ages of life . . . development lasts until senility." True, he acknowledges that it is in the "occupational area" that this lifelong development is most evident. But we should not ignore the fact that this means that the idea of development as a terminal concept, a something completed by adulthood, simply is untrue. At best, it is true only of some but not all aspects of development.

Somewhat later, Piaget considers the services psychogenetics could render to psychology. In addition to introducing a structuralism into psychology, there is the idea of a constructivism per se. Piaget notes that the slow, laborious process of development which we can see going on in terms of the "operative structures of intelligence" testify to "a real construction, proceeding by stages, at each of which the results obtained at the preceding stage must first be reconstructed before the process can be broadened and construction resumed."[76] He concludes the paragraph with this quite clear sentence: "In the creative adult, this movement of constant construction continues indefinitely, as shown, among other things, by the forms of technological and scientific thought."[77] Here, at least for the creative adult, the idea of development has lost all semblance of a terminal construct: it "continues indefinitely."

Actually, like the simpler logical paradoxes, my developmental puzzle seems resolved by close attention to definitions. The word *development*, whatever common sense or common usage may be, is *not* a terminal construct. Rather, it is a useful dynamic construct that finds expression in at least the occupational area and in the arenas of scientific and technological thought throughout a lifetime. Thus, my recognition of a need to date any me-that-was is not so much a puzzle as it is an expression of the reality of a continued development. That is what this fifth clue to what Piaget might mean is all about.

In the long ago of the 1960s, my colleagues and I were concerned with what we regarded as an abomination: the tendency to equate confirmation with a kind of Christian education graduation. We knew in our bones that it wasn't so. But people had presumed it was so for long enough to present us with a typically obtuse problem in social change. Actually, I do not think we really ever came close to dissolving the problem; certainly we made some difference, but we did not convince our client denomination (the Episcopal church) that there was no way to "graduate" a Christian at 8 or 10 or 12–13 or at 15 or at 18 or even at 25!

After almost a decade of looking at things from the local level, I am not at all confident that the blasted idea of "doing" one's presumed Christian "development" by 15–16 (at the earliest) or 21–22 (at the latest) is dead. It seems too alive in too many places to permit me to read the Burial Office for that idea. In fact, the recurring problem my colleagues in the field of Christian religious education have with programs for young adults, middle adults, or older adults may well still spring from the idea's failure to die a quiet, natural, or holy death.

Somehow, those of us in religious education have not yet successfully gotten the message through to our clients. Possibly our failure is due to the fundamental fact that *we* simply do *not* believe the message ourselves. We still want to graduate persons into their religious/denominational group at adolescence or, at the least, by the end of late adolescence, sometime in the twenties. But this fifth clue, if we could but assimilate it and then accommodate ourselves to it, is a very different perspective upon our clients and ourselves and the whole of humankind. Construction (or development) *is* an ongoing, continual process. The idea of lifelong religious education is, in fact, no ideal at all: it is the clearest, most obvious fact around, if we would but acknowledge it. It is no ideal; it is reality.

It may be that numerous occasions to read the Order for the Burial of the Dead "opened" me to this Piagetian theme. That is, in the 1928 edition of *The Book of Common Prayer*, which I used for some twenty years, there is a prayer ordered at the end of the service that puts this idea of construction as on ongoing, continual process into what may be its truest perspective. It is in the typical and historic Anglican form of a Collect. Thus, after an ascriptive statement, the petition reads as follows: "grant that, increasing in knowledge and love of thee, *he* may go from strength to strength, in the life of perfect service, in thy heavenly kingdom. . . ."[78]

In his extremely useful *Oxford American Prayer Book Commentary*, Massey H. Shepherd, Jr. notes that this Collect is biblically based upon ideas to be found in Ps. 106:4, Col. 1:10, and Ps. 84:7. He also notes that the Collect is "peculiar to the American book of 1928," that no one is certain of its authorship, and that it is "characteristic of all prayers for the departed introduced by the 1928 revision, in that it views the life of service in the heavenly realm, no less than in the earthly realm, as one of growth and increase in the knowledge and love of God."[79]

It is the idea of "*growth* and *increase* in the knowledge and love of God" that seems to be a clear albeit remarkable parallel to the Piagetian idea that development (or construction) goes on and on. Only in this particular context, that last *on* is out beyond the limits of what we humans initially think of as life.

It is a bit awesome.

Far, far from being terminal, the construct development is, in that Collect, positied as blessedly endless and positive. Who, then, could imagine development to be completed some quarter of the way through a human's biblical fourscore years?[80]

Given that delineation of the problem, few. But that is not too often what we religious educators or our clients have in mind.

In a sense, *we* are all too caught up in a very contemporary idea of what it is we are about. It is, once again, *our* decision, *our* choice, *our* acquiescence in the common way of thinking, that betrays *us* into the foolishness of thinking that a late adolescent has completed development. While it is almost certain that Jean Piaget did not intend to remind us of our folly, this fifth clue can serve to do exactly that.

Construction (or development) *is* an ongoing, continual process!

VI. A Sixth Clue: Wisdom and Verifiable Knowledge Are Different, Yet Necessary

In 1971 Wolfe Mays of the University of Manchester translated from the French what English-language readers know as Piaget's *Insights and Illusions of Philosophy.*[81] This book is a conceptual/intellectual biography which, in many ways, is irreplaceable in any attempt to understand the life, the work, or the thought of Jean Piaget. For instance, until this work was published, readers of English could all too easily fail to appreciate the extent to which Piaget was a philosopher by both training and academic position for much of his life. As Mays points out in a translator's introduction, Piaget admitted that his own thinking "has been deeply affected by his earlier philosophical studies, and this has determined the direction taken by his experimental work." Mays also notes that "one cannot fully grasp its scope and purpose unless this fact is appreciated."[82]

In the author's introduction, Piaget describes the book itself in these words: "Its thesis is simple, and in some circles mundane: *viz.* that philosophy, as its name implies, is a 'wisdom,' which man as a rational being finds essential for coordinating his different activities, but is not knowledge properly so called, possessing safeguards and methods of verification characteristic of what is usually called 'knowledge.'"[83] Piaget suggests that the distinction between a "wisdom" and "knowledge" becomes a problem of something like simple honesty when one fails to identify a limited set of conditions under which one *can* speak of knowledge rather than wisdom. He acknowledges, moreover, that the problems seem to arise at what he calls "the boundary that separates verification from speculation."[84]

North American readers may well find that Piaget's saga involves a whole cluster of European philosophers with which they are only partially familiar. However, the positions are clearly put by Piaget, and a reader cannot lose sight of the distinction between knowledge and a wisdom, at least as Piaget wishes to draw that distinction. Fundamentally, as Piaget puts it, the problem revolves around the question of whether philosophy has access to some kind of suprascientific or parascientific knowledge which is not only other but, as well, *superior* to the scientific knowledge won by careful observation, experimentation, and hypothesis testing.[85]

Let the reader be quite clear: it is not merely otherness that is the problem. It is an otherness plus a claim of superiority that is the problem. The addition of a claim of superiority to the claim of otherness removes the posited knowledge efficiently and effectively from the reach of any process of scientific, normal verification. Careful observation, painstaking experimentation, and clear and apropos hypothesis testing have nothing to do with such knowledge. Thus, the posited suprascientific knowledge is not amenable to normal procedures of verification, either directly or implicitly. Piaget notes that to posit such a knowledge is, in fact, to describe a *belief.*[86]

Interestingly, Piaget does not deny that such a belief-knowledge can exist. Nor does he even suggest that such a belief-knowledge is useless. He clearly acknowledges that while logical positivists might suggest as much, he does not do so. However, he does insist that the failure to distinguish any such belief-knowledge from that knowledge which is verifiable creates a continual problem for "disciplines trying to become scientific," and becomes a strong temptation toward an illusion for philosophers (and others) who relate to those disciplines who are "trying to become scientific." The problem is, of course, that the procedures of observation, experimentation, and hypothesis testing are viewed as unnecessary or, at best, distinctly inferior procedures. The illusion is that a belief-knowledge is truer and, therefore, superior to the knowledge verified by the scientific methods of observation, experimentation, and hypothesis testing.[87]

The problem and the illusion grow from the same root. That is, both posit a hierarchy of knowledge, in which a belief-knowledge is superior. Moreover, being superior, such a belief-knowledge denigrates the other, inferior forms of knowledge and denies their necessity. Once again, it is not simply otherness that is the root of either the problem or the illusion. Rather it is the idea of superiority, added to otherness, that makes for what Piaget calls an illusion. This point is worth making repeatedly, because the idea of superiority is, in fact, the result of a choice or decision that humans make. Thus, Piaget implicitly asks us to acknowledge what *we* have done by spawning the idea.

In his conclusion, Piaget notes that Karl Jaspers, in his *Introduction to Philosophy*, acknowledges the distinction between a wisdom and knowledge.[88] Piaget also quotes Jaspers's contention "Man cannot do without philosophy" with approval. Piaget notes specifically that "the search for scientific truth, which, however, only interests a minority of thinkers, does not at all exhaust the nature of man, even in this minority. Man," Piaget continues, "also lives, takes sides, believes in a multiplicity of values, orders them hierarchically and thus gives meaning to his existence by decisions that constantly go beyond the limits of his actual knowledge."[89] Piaget contends that this giving of meaning via decisions involves a coordination that, in a thinking person, is inescapably rational. That is, he maintains that "in order to produce a synthesis between that which he believes and that which he knows he can only use reflection, either extending his knowledge or examining it critically in an effort to determine its present boundaries and to justify the acceptance of values that go beyond it."[90] It is just such an essentially rational synthesis between one's beliefs and the presently existing "conditions of knowledge" that Piaget calls a "wisdom" and, explicitly, affirms is the clear object of a philosophy.

In the postscript to the second edition, Piaget says, "I have derived from (my philosophical training) nothing else than the general set of problems that has directed my later studies, and this is a considerable debt; only . . . I have only been able to approach the solution of the problems thus stated by abandoning the reflective methods of the philosopher in order to base my work on experiment and more or less formalized deduction."[91] Thus, while philosophy raises problems, it does not solve them, "because reflection does not by itself involve methods of verification."[92] However, Piaget does *not* challenge the reader to decide between wisdom and knowledge, only to distinguish them from one another. As he says, "What is important is the triology reflection x deduction x experiment, the first term representing the heuristic function and the other two cognitive verification, which is alone constitutive of 'truth.'"[93] In addition, Piaget explicitly acknowledges that there "remain problems that science cannot solve either temporarily or in some cases can only solve on a provisional basis, which no doubt will remain final. These problems," he says, "can be of vital importance . . . (although, strictly speaking, they) require equally 'provisional' solutions."[94]

What does this all mean for the religious educator?

I think it means that, to the degree that there is no rigorous experimental religious education, the whole venture falls into Piaget's category of a wisdom. Without such an experimental pedagogy, religious education is a poser of problems, often important problems, yet it is *not* a source of knowledge. What it has, obviously, is an abundance of what I have called belief-knowledge. But that is really no more than a wisdom. At least, it is nothing else until one translates the problem and seeks a verifiable solution, a knowledge.

Certainly, a goodly portion of all education falls into a similar category. The problem per se is not restricted to religious education. However, it also means that the often difficult tasks of educational research are distinctly useful. They are a way, perhaps our most obvious way, of seeking for and determining what knowledge there is available and, so, discerning the important things that must be done because we have only our wisdoms. If this point be considered, it will be clear that Piaget's position that both wisdom and verifiable knowledge are necessary, but different, can only lead to a kind of healthy provisionalism. It certainly should remove the religious educator's hesitancy about research and experimentation, just as it should destroy the unfounded illusion that the religious educator has either a magic to ensure the discipline's goals or a superior knowledge that obviates any need for verification. Religious educators have neither. The sooner we who claim the title realize that, the sooner we will be able to know what it is that we can do and why we are able to do that. That is, the sooner we will be truly able to claim the title of religious *educators*.

Piaget's distinction also offers the religious educator a way out of disciplinary enslavement to that often fickle old pretender to the queenship of the sciences, theology. Theology is inherently, in these terms, a wisdom. It is not a science. It is not a source of verifiable knowledge. However, it is an abundant source of belief-knowledge, not all of which is in agreement with every other part. Thus, theology offers belief-knowledges, or wisdoms.[95]

The distinction between wisdom and verifiable knowledge, plus the clear recognition that both are necessary for human living, should enable religious educators to claim what is possible, equality. For all too long it has been fashionable to acknowledge theology and, worse yet, individual theologians as unchallengeable guides in religious education.[96] It would be far better to grant theology and the theologians a guardianship of a particular wisdom, while claiming for religious education the right and the need to be a translator of important problems into either provisional solutions or verifiable knowledge. The radical transformation of the discipline this suggests probably can only be appreciated by those who have felt the push to be theologians as well as educators, or have recognized long after the pronouncement the damnable difficulty involved in accomplishing a theologian's specified goal.

Please note that it is equality which is suggested here. It is not a simple reversal of roles. Religious education is not superior to theology. Instead, what is suggested is an equality that permits a genuine dialogue, a real cooperation, in place of a director-directed relation more like that of master and slave than anything else. At least in North America, that option has rarely been tried and, even more rarely, been achieved. However, Piaget's distinction between wisdom and verifiable knowledge offers a rationale for the attempt at a sibling relationship, rather than a parental one, between theology and religious education. All things considered, a fascinating idea!

ANOTHER BASIC QUESTION: HOW DOES IT FIT TOGETHER?

These six clues to an answer to Hickson's query may or may not satisfy one. Clearly, they are *my* clues to the vastly important question I heard in the long ago from a colleague. However, a reader must decide whether or not they are satisfactory clues to the meaning of Piaget's work. Moreover, given our human tendency toward simplification, six clues may seem like too large a number or, minimally, more than one would like. After all, six is one more than the number of fingers on most human hands.[97]

The tendency toward simplification is clearly evident, strong, persistent, and pervasive in humankind. No one should think otherwise. In fact, if we stop and think about it in almost any depth, we can recognize that this push toward simplification is inextricably involved in almost anything we humans think of as comprehension. Moreover, with a bit more thought, many of us can recognize and, then, agree with the idea that comprehension is *an* aim of almost anything humans have ever recognized as real education.

While the claim that just about anything is self-evident is an open, obvious invitation to muck around in a conceptual/logical swamp, the idea that the human tendency toward simplification involves some form of level-upon-level hierarchy of constructs is *almost* self-evident. In fact, a good bit of the educational/psychological research on the usefulness of organizing ideas or conceptual maps is no more than a technically precise commentary upon that idea.[98] The important thing to keep firmly in mind as one contemplates the assertions inherent in the last two sentences is that any level-upon-level hierarchy moves upward *from* a specific but manifold number of somethings *toward* a noticeably more limited number of somethings and, then, on beyond *to* a final simplification, which is *a* something. What many of us forget or ignore is that such a hierarchy is built from the specific toward the totally general via a process that technically is called *dedifferentiation*. Such a process is, however, reversible: that which has been identified via dedifferentiation can, technically, be decomposed via differentiation into the initial state![99]

That last sentence is a bit tricky. It identifies a clear, evident, and inescapable implication of a two-way process. That which is built up can, via analysis, also be considered as a totality constituted of, minimally, its parts. Actually, if we will but think about it long enough, that two-way process is so useful, and so often used by us humans, that we can appreciate why Jean Piaget regarded reversibility as a fundamental cognitive achievement.[100] Of course, it is exactly that! Without reversibility, clearly adult thinking would be something else, something less than mature, something we might well call childish.

From a developmental perspective, that observation is no denigration of child-thought, although it is a clear recognition that it is thought-which-is-appropriate essentially at a particular period in a human being's life cycle. Frankly, it is thought-which-is-appropriate in some "now" but not at some developmental "later." (The ability or willingness to make that distinction identifies developmentalists; the inability or an unwillingness to make that distinction identifies those who are either adevelopmentalists or nondevelopmentalists.)

Thus, it seems quite reasonable to recognize that it is a clearly developmental stance to imagine and accept and, so, deal with reversible conceptual hierarchies. Moreover, it is a short extension from a known, present level of discernment toward an as-yet-unknown, future level of discernment to posit the following:

> Developmental "clues" probably exist within some constructural hierarchy which, if discerned, will provide an even further simplification (e.g., supralevel clues to the meaning already clued).

If the reader will even tentatively grant me that last theory, a number of interesting possibilities can be discerned. However, if the reader will not grant me that theory, much of what follows will be odd, to say the least!

I. R. B. Fuller, All-Space-Filling Figures, and Conceptualization

Whatever response one may have to the posited theoretical possibility, clearly the implication of the idea of a hierarchy of levels of constructs is that each level upward is some kind of simplification of that which is to be found immediately below that level. Grossly put, an evident sign of the movement upward is that the sheer number of constructs decreases. Fewer constructs should distinguish levels above that marked by an initial set of *n* constructs. Moreover, if carried to its logical extreme, there should be some level where *a* construct is discerned: that is, presumed simplicity is a peak in any constructural hierarchy. That should be reasonably evident.

In that intriguing summa *Synergetics*, which R. Buckminster Fuller subtitled "Explorations in the Geometry of Thinking," one can read two potentially complementary assertions. Although they occur 150 pages apart, they are potentially complementary to one another (or so it seems to me).

> 1. When we try to fill all space with *regular* tetrahedra, we are frustrated because the tetrahedra will not fill in the voids above the triangular-based grid pattern. But the regular tetrahedron is a complementary space filler with the octahedron. (*Synergetics*, section 621.06)[101]
>
> 2. Synergetics is the geometry of thinking. How we think is epistemology, and epistemology is modelable; which is to say that knowledge organizes itself geometrically, i.e., with models. (*Synergetics*, section 905.01)[102]

The potential complementarity I see in these two assertions involves a bit of reasoning. First, Fuller's idea of filling all space seems translatable to the construct of a conceptual space. Second, Fuller's thesis that thinking or epistemology is modelable suggests that any conceptual space should be modelable. Third, a genuine generalization should involve an all-space-filling model. Fourth, since regular tetrahedra and regular octahedra complementarily fill all space, a genuine generalization probably involves such a complementary combination, if that generalization is to be modeled at all as an all-space-filling geometric in conceptual space.

Obviously, my third and fourth steps *are* mine. I cannot blame Fuller via reference for them; they are my insights or conclusions. But I find them remarkably useful, and I want to indicate how I have used this quasi-Fullerian insight to push my own understanding of Piaget's work a step or two on beyond the six clues identified earlier. Thereby, if I am at all successful, the reader may be enticed into attempting a similar use of an extremely simple yet powerful conceptual device. However, because it is powerful by virtue of its sheer generality, the reader may well be able to find other problems amenable to this device, problems personally more intriguing to the reader than that which I choose to use as an illustration.

II. Answering Hickson's Query via Fuller's Geometry of Thinking

Somewhat earlier, I specified Hickson's query as that vastly important question: What does it all mean? A bit later, I identified what I called six clues to an answer to Hickson's query. Then I proceeded to both expose and expound upon each of those six clues. That is now in the past: I have done it and, presumably, the reader has staggered through all of that to reach this point. Thus, the question at the moment is whether six clues can be so modeled as to fill all of some conceptual space (e.g., that which one might call the meaning of Piaget).

Geometrically, the question reduces to whether, given six somethings, either a tetrahedron or an octahedron is an appropriate model of those six somethings. A tetrahedron has four vertices and six edges. An octahedron has six vertices and twelve edges. Clearly, six somethings can be modeled by either a tetrahedron or an octahedron. However, the models will not be equivalent! In the tetrahedron there are six edges, while in the octahedron there are six vertices. If nothing else, edge and vertex are clearly and obviously different in their geometric function. Thus, using a geometry of thinking quickly leads one into a question of the nature of those six somethings and, then, into the question of whether a vertex or an edge best approximates that discerned function. Without challenging the somethingness of the six somethings to be modeled, the sheer geometrical possibilities lead one into a clarification of the nature of those six somethings.

Within a Fullerian frame of reference, especially as I have used it in earlier chapters, a vertex models a concept or construct (e.g., Son-ness in figure 1 in chapter 1), while an edge models a dynamic relation between a pair of concepts or constructs. If that use be accepted as a principle for the modeling of conceptual space, the question about my six clues is whether they are concepts or relationships. I think it is clear that they are concepts or constructs which, I have suggested, provide clues to the meaning of Piaget's work. Thus, those six clues would seem best modeled by vertices. That is to say, by an octahedron, which is a geometric figure having six vertices.

The octahedron displayed in figure 1 represents the model I created for my own use. As one can readily see from the drawing done in perspective, an octahedron has a quality that forces one into a further, useful clarification of one's thinking: it consists of three pairs of polar-opposite vertices. In a conceptual model, this raises the question of the

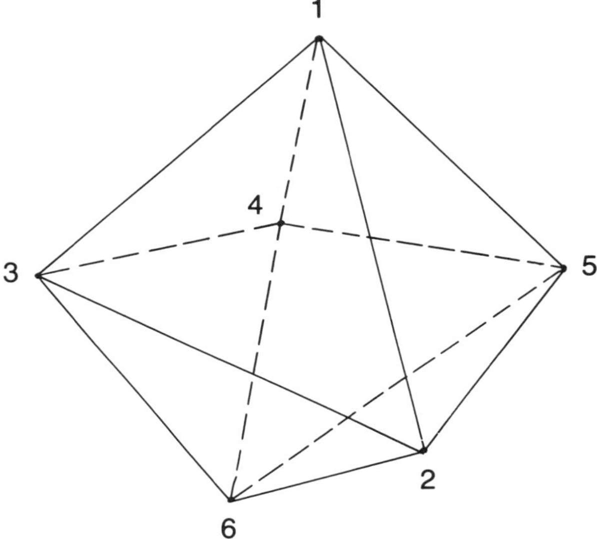

WHERE:
1 = Cognition (or intelligence) is internalized action.
2 = Cognitive structure forms and informs motive.
3 = Successive periods of equilibrium constitute a sign of development.
4 = Interaction is a third alternative to the nature/nurture debate.
5 = Construction is an ongoing, continual process.
6 = Wisdom and verifiable knowledge are different, yet necessary.

Figure 1. Octahedron model of six clues to Piaget's work. Regular octahedron with unit-length edges, in perspective.

interrelationship of the six vertex-concepts. While the figure affirms that all six belong together in what Fuller would call a system, the figure also implicitly affirms that some relationships are closer or stronger than others. In fact, it implies that in any set of six concepts there will be three pairings of minimal closeness or strength. Thus, an octahedral model invites one to (minimally) think about interrelationships that, otherwise, might well be ignored or merely assumed. However, it can do more than that, for the octahedral model (maximally) requires one to make at least three conscious, rational decisions regarding the interrelationships possible within the set of six constructs. Unless one is addicted to sheer intuition, these potentials for thought and decision inherent in an octahedral model are something to be appreciated, a useful conceptual device.

However, being a somewhat cautious theorist, I wanted to check to see what I had done. In a sense, I had engaged in what J. R. R. Tolkien once called an act of subcreation and, as a result, I wanted to see if what I had subcreated could provide an analogue to the conclusion recorded in Gen. 1:31.[103] I first checked the *eight* face-planes defined in my octahedron by three edge-sharing vertex-concepts. Frankly, I used as *my* standard whether the trio of concepts seemed to *me* to have some evident relationship to one another. On the whole, I found that I was pleased with the model-dictated results, even when some of the combinations had not been evident before.

Then, as a second check on my octahedron model, I investigated the pairs of face-planes that connected the model-posited polar-opposite vertex-concepts. Frankly, I once again was looking for what could be called face validity. However, I was also looking now to see if in each such set of four vertices the "middle" pair, while combining with each of the polar opposites, functioned like a pair of conceptual transition-concepts. This was a somewhat more complex requirement and, therefore, a more rigorous test of the octahedron model itself. Again, on the whole I was satisfied with what I found to be the model-dictated sets of interrelationships.

Although I do not want to examine in any detail the four sets of interrelationships identified in table 1, the four slightly different sets in table 2, or the four still different sets in table 3, I do want to comment quite generally on what I have called sequences A, B, and C. Each such sequence is a fourfold set of hypotheses about the meaning of Piaget's work, since the octahedral model is built from my six clues to an answer to Hickson's query. In the three tables, then, there are twelve such hypotheses. As a result, a reader should be able not only to check my sagacity but, as well, to have a variety of hypothetical avenues into the Piagetian corpus itself. Used in that way, the admittedly

Table 1.
Sequence A:
Face-planes of a regular octahedron from one to the other of a pair of opposed vertices.
Conceptual analysis via octahedron model of six clues to Piaget's work.

#1. Cognition (or intelligence) is internalized action. (1)	Cognitive structure forms and informs motive. (2) Successive periods of equilibrium constitute a sign of development. (3)	Wisdom and verifiable knowledge are different, yet necessary. (6)
#2. Cognition (or intelligence) is internalized action. (1)	Successive periods of equilibrium constitute a sign of development. (3) Interaction is a third alternative to the nature/nurture debate. (4)	Wisdom and verifiable knowledge are different, yet necessary. (6)
#3. Cognition (or intelligence) is internalized action. (1)	Interaction is a third alternative to the nature/nurture debate. (4) Construction is an ongoing, continual process. (5)	Wisdom and verifiable knowledge are different, yet necessary. (6)
#4. Cognition (or intelligence) is internalized action. (1)	Construction is an ongoing, continual process. (5) Cognitive structure forms and informs motive. (2)	Wisdom and verifiable knowledge are different, yet necessary. (6)

Table 2.
Sequence B:
Face-planes of a regular octahedron from one to the other of a pair of opposed vertices.
Conceptual analysis via octahedron model of six clues to Piaget's work.

#1.	Cognition (or intelligence) is internalized action. (1)	
Cognitive structure forms and informs motive. (2)		Interaction is a third alternative to the nature/nurture debate. (4)
	Successive periods of equilibrium constitute a sign of development. (3)	
#2.	Successive periods of equilibrium constitute a sign of development. (3)	
Cognitive structure forms and informs motive. (2)		Interaction is a third alternative to the nature/nurture debate. (4)
	Wisdom and verifiable knowledge are different, yet necessary. (6)	
#3.	Wisdom and verifiable knowledge are different, yet necessary. (6)	
Cognitive structure forms and informs motive. (2)		Interaction is a third alternative to the nature/nurture debate. (4)
	Construction is an ongoing, continual process. (5)	
#4.	Construction is an ongoing, continual process. (5)	
Cognitive structure forms and informs motive. (2)		Interaction is a third alternative to the nature/nurture debate. (4)
	Cognition (or intelligence) is internalized action. (1)	

Table 3.
Sequence C:
Face-planes of a regular octahedron from one to the other of a pair of opposed vertices.
Conceptual analysis via octahedron model of six clues to Piaget's work.

#1.	Cognition (or intelligence) is internalized action. (1)	
Successive periods of equilibrium constitute a sign of development. (3)		Construction is an ongoing, continual process. (5)
	Cognitive structure forms and informs motive. (2)	
#2.	Cognitive structure forms and informs motive. (2)	
Successive periods of equilibrium constitute a sign of development. (3)		Construction is an ongoing, continual process. (5)
	Wisdom and verifiable knowledge are different, yet necessary. (6)	
#3.	Wisdom and verifiable knowledge are different, yet necessary. (6)	
Successive periods of equilibrium constitute a sign of development. (3)		Construction is an ongoing, continual process. (5)
	Interaction is a third alternative to the nature/nurture debate. (4)	
#4.	Interaction is a third alternative to the nature/nurture debate. (4)	
Successive periods of equilibrium constitute a sign of development. (3)		Construction is an ongoing, continual process. (5)
	Cognition (or intelligence) is internalized action. (1)	

picky detail of this modeling process might be quite useful. However, that is something readers must determine for themselves.

Let me be both reasonable and honest.

The previous seven paragraphs have been more about geometric conceptual models than some may have expected or desired. At least, I suspect as much. However, there is somewhat more to be done to achieve the initial goal of discerning a Fullerian all-space-filling model. Moreover, there is the distinct possibility that such a model would be somewhat simpler than the octahedral model I have considered thus far. That is why I move ahead yet another step to a consideration of a next possible model, an answer to Hickson's query that has not yet even been considered.

III. Seeking Further Simplification As an Answer to Hickson's Query

Further simplification can begin if we recall that R. B. Fuller notes that "the regular tetrahedron is a complementary space filler with the octahedron." (*Synergetics*, section 621.06)[104] Thus, given an octahedral model, one can ask whether it is complementarily related to some as-yet-undiscerned tetrahedrons in a way that might provide a simple all-space-filling model for the conceptual space occupied by the meaning of Piaget. Fortunately, the answer is simply put: Yes, a complementary relation can be easily discerned.

By adding four regular tetrahedrons to four of the eight face-planes of a regular octahedron, one achieves two things. First, one identifies a geometrically simpler model, the tetrahedron. Second, one identifies a larger all-space-filling model which has exactly twice the volume of the initial octahedron model. Thus, the volume of conceptual space enclosed by the larger tetrahedron is twice that enclosed by the octahedron, which suggests that such a tetrahedral model may be a generalization at some higher level in a conceptual hierarchy. This impression is reinforced by the clear simplification achieved by moving to such a model. However, there is just one problem: the four vertices of this larger tetrahedron are all implicit, as-yet-unknown constructs. All we know are the six vertices of the core octahedron.

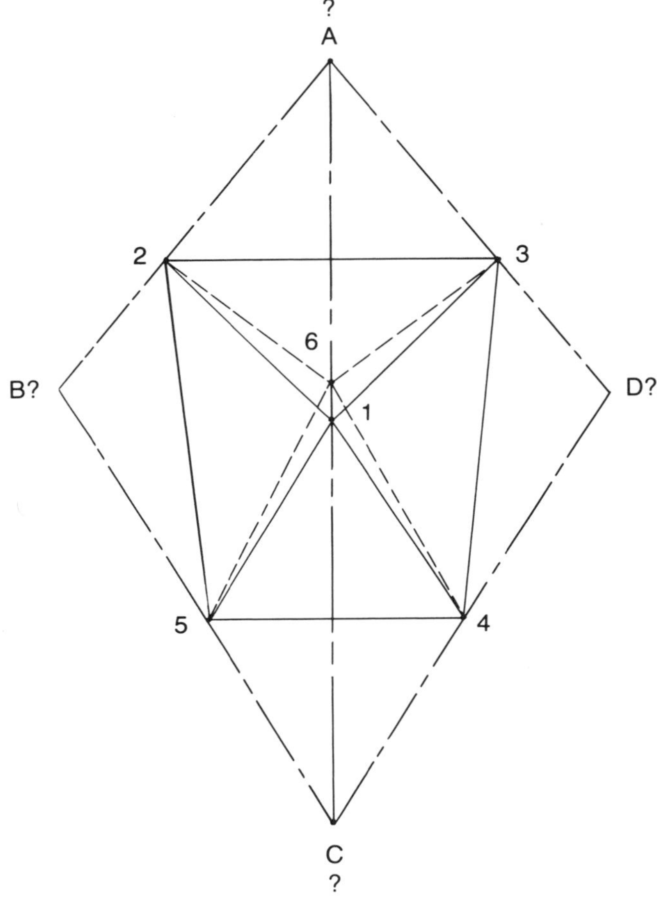

WHERE:
1 = Cognition (or intelligence) is internalized action.
2 = Cognitive structure forms and informs motive.
3 = Successive periods of equilibrium constitute a sign of development.
4 = Interaction is a third alternative to the nature/nurture debate.
5 = Construction is an ongoing, continual process.
6 = Wisdom and verifiable knowledge are different, yet necessary.
A, B, C, and D = Further, unidentified implications of the octahedron model of six clues to Piaget's work.

Figure 2. Octahedron model of six clues to Piaget's work as the center of an all-space-filling implicit tetrahedron with double-unit-length edges.

Actually, the geometrics help the process of discovery. When such a larger tetrahedron is built in this fashion, each of the six vertices of the initial octahedral model fall at the midpoint of one of the six edges of the larger tetrahedron. Thus, if one considers each such edge as a model of the paired relation between vertex-concepts, there is something known about that relationship, even though as yet one does not know the vertex-concepts themselves. That is, one can usefully ask a series of questions, all of which have this general form: What A is relatable to what B in such a way that a midpoint is the specifiable known concept?

I do not intend to lead the reader through the analysis of the various possible combinations, for that would be far too lengthy a thing. However, I do want to indicate very shortly what I did to arrive at the conclusion I will share with the reader. I began my observing that clue 6 was the midpoint of edge B-D. Then, since that clue concerned the relationship of wisdom and verifiable knowledge, I decided that wisdom was either B or D while knowledge was either D or B. Next I considered each of the remaining five edges and asked what general concepts in Piaget's work might fit the posited edge-vertex relationships.

In addition, largely because the sheer geometrics invited me to do so, I also looked at the four face-planes of the larger tetrahedron and found that each was definable in terms of three edge midpoints, each of which was also a specifiable vertex of the initial core octahedral model. The problem, in two of the four instances, was that the midpoints were specifiable and so were two of the three vertices, while in the other two instances the midpoints were specifiable but only one of the three vertices was known even tentatively. As G. Polya pointed out quite some time ago, it was a near-classic instance of a problem to find, rather than a problem to prove.[105] That is, *my* problem was one that mathematicians had recognized for at least some sixteen centuries since Pappus published commentaries on Euclid.[106] My problem was to find two other Piagetian constructs which, in combination with wisdom and knowledge, would seem to function as vertices of this larger tetrahedron.

After a good bit of trial and error, and a fair amount of what was really intuition, I reached a satisfactory conclusion. It seemed to me that action and structure were two such Piagetian constructs. Thus, I had labels for the four vertices: wisdom, knowledge, action, and structure. But I had not yet assigned these four constructs to the specific vertices. That was my next problem to find.

My procedure for solving this new problem to find was to look at each tetrahedron vertex in terms of the three edges which met at that vertex and, then, ask which of the possible Piagetian constructs seemed best to fit in that position. The geometrics helped direct this procedure, although the actual decision was inescapably *my* act. Naturally, I was satisfied with the result of the procedure, but the element of personal decision cannot be ignored without falsifying what was, in fact, done. As Michael Polanyi argues in his book *Science, Faith, and Society*, the place of such processes of personal decision are an aspect of all scientific processes of discovery and, when ignored, tend to pervert our understanding of both science and discovery.[107]

The result of my decisions vis-a-vis the four vertices of the larger tetrahedron displayed in figure 2 was a straightforward set of symbol substitutions. I decided that vertex A represented structure, vertex B represented wisdom, vertex C represented action, and vertex D represented knowledge. To my mind, that seemed like a best possible "fit." However, I did carry out two checks to see whether or not the result seemed valid in slightly different, model-dictated possibilities. As was true earlier, this probably has as much to do with my personal tendency toward caution as anything.

Before I explain my two further checks on the validity of my assignment of Piagetian constructs to the vertices of the larger tetrahedron model, I want to encourage readers to create their own set of geometric figures. The patterns for a regular octahedron with unit length edges, four tetrahedrons with unit length edges, and a larger tetrahedron with double unit length edges found in figures 3, 4, and 5 will permit one to do just that. Since I have found such models almost indispensable, I think they may also help some readers.

The patterns in figure 3 and figure 4 will enable one to create a set of five items—four regular tetrahedrons and one regular octahedron—which can be put together in such a way that the reader will have a three-dimensional model of figure 2. (In my experience, 5-by-8-inch

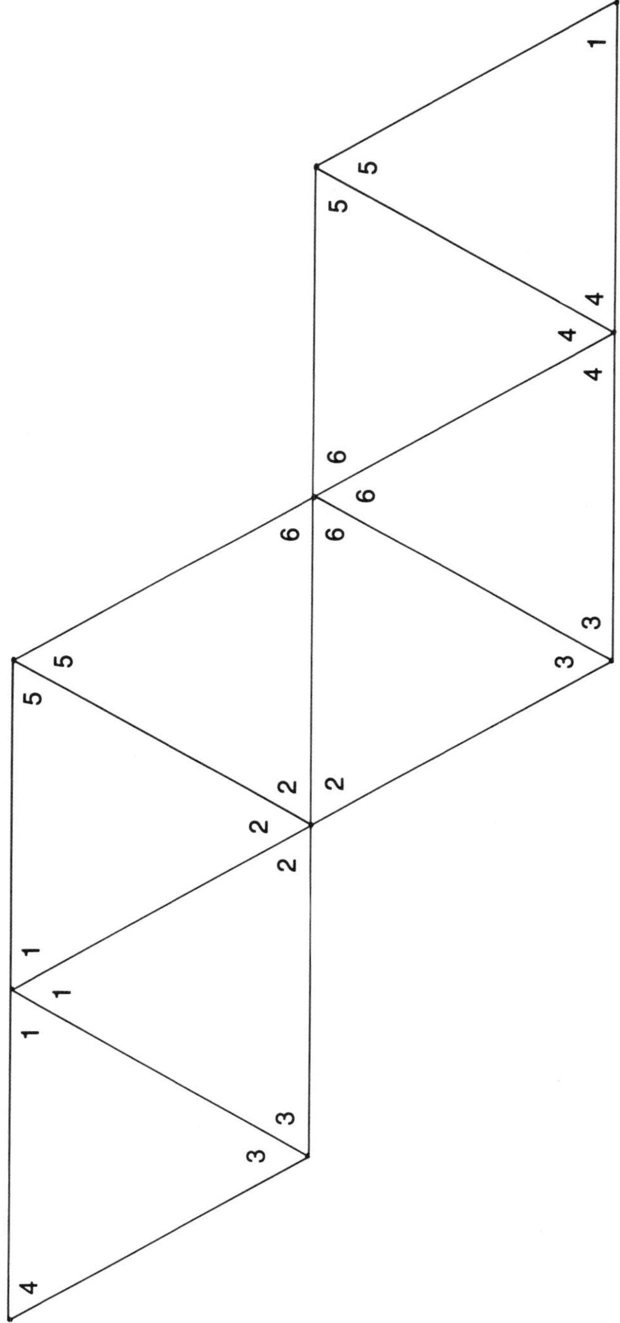

Figure 3. Pattern for a regular octahedron with unit-length-edges (Unit = 2 inches).

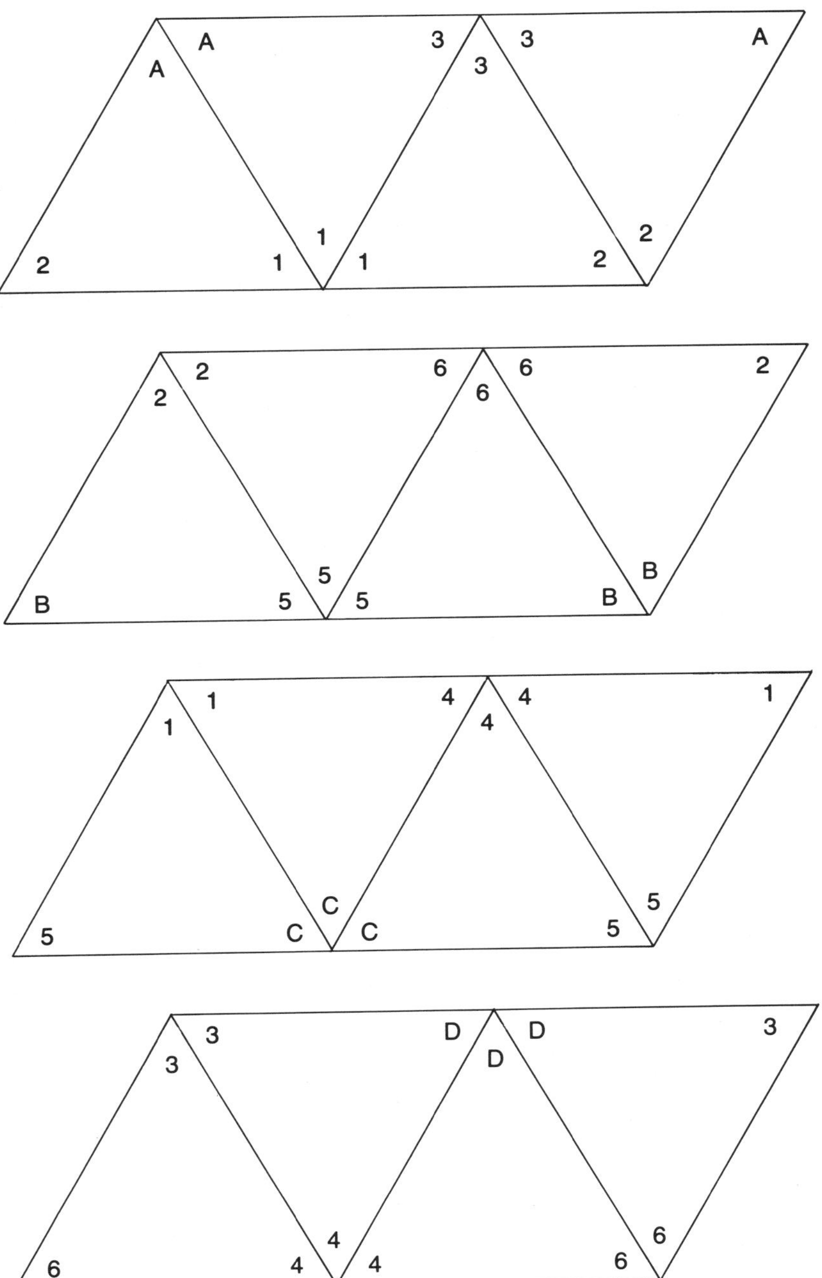

Figure 4. Pattern for four regular tetrahedrons with unit-length-edges. (Unit = 2 inches)

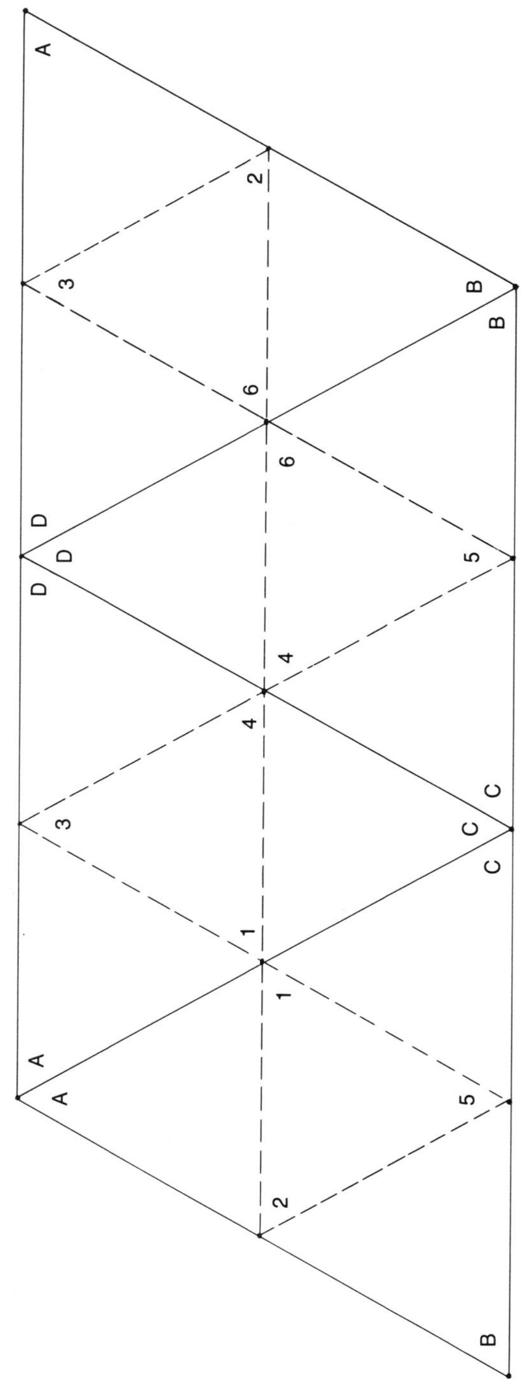

Figure 5. Pattern for a regular tetrahedron with double-unit-length edges. (Unit = 2 inches)

file cards will work quite well; that is, one can use a 2-inch edge as the unit length suggested and get the pattern onto a single card.) The pattern in figure 5 will enable one to create a three-dimensional model of figure 2, as a single all-space-filling geometric figure, with the initial octrahedral model's vertices located as midpoints on the appropriate edges. Naturally, the reader who does not want to be bothered with all this scissors-and-tape cardboard construction can ignore these three patterns. However, the reader who will go to the trouble to use these patterns will have a way of personally visualizing what the two-dimensional form in figure 2 is all about. Thus, the reader may be able to come close to comprehension or even achieve it.

If you are up to this geometric game, stop reading here and get out the scissors and some transparent tape. Transfer the patterns. The 5-by-8-inch file cards will work reasonably well for all three patterns, although the pattern in figure 5 will take a bit of ingenuity (two cards). When you have finished this cut-and-stick project, return to the text.

(Snip, snip! Stick, stick! But take care!)

Now let me share with you my two checks on my conceptualization of the larger tetrahedron (figure 5). My first check was simply to systematically consider the four face-planes specified by this larger model. That is, I considered the meaning of the decided symbol substitutions and, quite frankly, asked myself the reasonable and important question: Does this seem at all possible? Obviously, my generally positive answer to that query had a good deal to do with (a) what I knew of Piaget's work, and (b) how I understood what I knew of Piaget's work. I want to acknowledge that, because it is possible that in some future "other" a reader may decide differently. I cannot, nor do I wish to, deny that possibility. However, I do want to record *my* decision and, thereby, invite readers either to accept it or to disagree and reach their *own* decision. (If readers do that, I would be pleased if, but only if, they acknowledge what *they* have done and, so, take responsibility for their *own* decision: simple counterdependence is just that!)

Quite specifically, I considered the four face-planes of the larger tetrahedron—A-B-C, A-B-D, A-C-D, and B-C-D—and asked myself whether it seemed possible that these four trios could exist together. Using my earlier symbol substitution rule, I decided that it did seem possible. Then, as a part of this check, I also considered the specifiable midpoints along each edge, in a triadic combination, and re-asked myself the same question. Once again, I found myself ready to admit the possibility. In fact, I entertained the idea that what I found was reasonable and, therefore, probable. I was satisfied.

Then, and only then, did I explore a genuinely Fullerian idea: that a tetrahedron could model two energy events (one positive and one negative). I had recourse to figure 511.10 in *Synergetics*,[108] and I systematically investigated what the larger tetrahedron model implied regarding positive energy events, using the four Piagetian constructs already discerned in the modeled conceptual space. That is, using Fuller's models, I considered whether the threefold combination of reaction-action-resultant, in each of the possible combinations within this particular tetrahedron model, seemed to make sense. On the whole, I concluded that the various possible combinations did seem to make sense. Thus, I came to think that this initially theoretical form, an implicit larger tetrahedron, represented a dynamic model of an answer to Hickson's query. Actually, given the interactive nature of Piaget's basic thesis, as well as the importance he placed on action/praxis, this seemed like an extraordinarily apt way to model the meaning of Piaget's work.[109]

Clearly, what I concluded was that the larger tetrahedral model seemed to have face validity and, therefore, that the tripartite analytical division into a reaction, an action, and a resultant offered a series of quite interesting hypotheses. The energy-event analysis displayed in table 4 had best be taken as a set of twelve hypotheses, for then a reader may feel quite free to accept or reject what is suggested there. The only caution I would offer those who immediately want to reject the whole is that it *is* a theoretical projection using a not-exactly-common frame of reference, and that all of us might learn more by attending to the problems of verification than we will by trusting our initial instincts, however well honed those may be!

For example, in table 4 the symbol B is the symbol for the Piagetian concept of wisdom. If one accepts my earlier idea that wisdom is a form of belief-knowledge, and if one posits that religion (or religious education) is concerned with such belief-knowledge, then table 4 suggests a number of quite intriguing hypotheses. To begin with, out of a total of twelve possible conceptual energy events, exactly six arrive at wisdom as either a reaction end-result or a resultant end-result. This is a remarkable thing. Wisdom is a random occurrence, given this modeling, which is to say that it is a quite likely occurrence (given a thoroughly probabilistic perspective). In fact, if one adopts such a probabilistic perspective, wisdom is equiprobable with any chosen other-than-wisdom category! Moreover, the energy-event model suggests that, within such an equiprobable occurrence, there is another equiprobability: wisdom as a reaction or wisdom as a resultant.

It does take a bit of clear thinking to see the difference, but if one can engage in such thought, that difference can be remarkably important for pedagogical practice. Initially, one can begin with the query

Table 4.
Energy-event analysis of a tetrahedron model of the conceptual space constituting the meaning of the work of Jean Piaget.

ID:	*REACTION:*	*ACTION:*	*RESULTANT:*
01	B ← 2 — A	A — 1 → C	C — 4 → D
02	C ← 1 — A	A — 3 → D	D — 6 → B
03	D ← 3 — A	A — 2 → B	B — 5 → C
	(Structure)		
04	D ← 6 — B	B — 5 → C	C — 1 → A
05	A ← 2 — B	B — 6 → D	D — 4 → C
06	C ← 5 — B	B — 2 → A	A — 3 → D
	(Wisdom)		

(*continued*)

Table 4. (continued)

ID:	*REACTION:*		*ACTION:*		*RESULTANT:*
07	B ←——5—— C	---------	C ——4——→ D	---------	D ——3——→ A
08	D ←——4—— C	---------	C ——1——→ A	---------	A ——2——→ B
09	A ←——1—— C	---------	C ——5——→ B	---------	B ——6——→ D
	(Action)				
10	B ←——6—— D	---------	D ——3——→ A	---------	A ——1——→ C
11	C ←——4—— D	---------	D ——6——→ B	---------	B ——2——→ A
12	A ←——3—— D	--------1	D ——4——→ C	---------	C ——5——→ B
	(Knowledge)				

WHERE:
A = Structure
B = Wisdom
C = Action
D = Knowledge
1 = Cognition (or intelligence) is internalized action.
2 = Cognitive structure forms and informs motive.
3 = Successive periods of equilibrium constitute a sign of development.
4 = Interaction is a third alternative to the nature/nurture debate.
5 = Construction is an ongoing, continual process.
6 = Wisdom and verifiable knowledge are different, yet necessary.

AND WHERE: An "energy event" is modeled after figure 511.10 in R. B. Fuller's *Synergetics* (1975), p. 243.

whether one desires wisdom to be the resultant of a pedagogical energy event or a mere reaction to it. While a total, holistic view of education might well lead one to believe that the distinction is ultimately and operationally unimportant, if one thinks that an educational system in any society is "a more or less elaborate social mechanism designed to bring about in the persons submitted to it certain skills and attitudes that are judged to be useful and desirable in the society,"[110] then the distinction between a reaction and a resultant is very important. A resultant is far more likely to be a rationally planned outcome of an educational act than is what, after the fact, we are likely to recognize as a reaction to that act. Thus, it seems educationally more sensible to focus upon the resultant than it does upon the reaction. Pedagogical practice, for instance, intends some resultant. It is only educational research that tends to identify both intended resultant and observed reaction. Pedagogy intends; research describes.[111]

If one will grant that distinction, the energy-event analysis displayed in table 4 suggests that there is only one theoretically most likely way to achieve wisdom as a resultant by beginning with structure or action or knowledge. That is, the random probability of achieving wisdom by starting a pedagogical energy event from any of these three Piagetian conceptual beginnings is 0.3333. Or, in terms of the random distribution of possibilities inherent in the tetrahedral model, the probability of wisdom as a resultant is 3 out of 12, or 0.2500. Only rational decision can affect these probabilities. However, it is exactly such rational decision that is the very stuff of living pedagogical practice. Thus, there is both hope and potential direction in the energy-event analysis for a religious education that intends wisdom as a goal.

Clearly, three energy-event pathways are indicated by the tetrahedral model as maximally rational and efficient. First, the structure-knowledge-wisdom pathway. Second, the action-structure-wisdom pathway. Third, the knowledge-action-wisdom pathway. Alert and knowledgeable educators should have little difficulty recognizing three recurrently attractive educational theses in these three theoretical pathways. What is intriguing, however, is that all three are affirmed as possible, while nine other possibilities are denied.

Frankly, at this point in an admittedly lengthy process of discovery, any denial of possibilities is to be gratefully accepted and even joyously celebrated! It is a sign that the very human desire for simplification may yet be satisfied. Thus, it may well be worth the time to look at those three model-dictated ways to arrive at wisdom. (Whether the reader agrees with this assessment or not, it is the rationale for all that follows.)

First, let me consider the structure-knowledge-wisdom energy-event pathway. The important thing about this theoretical pathway is its middle term: knowledge. Implicitly, as near as I can discern, it is a simple, twofold reminder that what religious educators are apt to recognize as content-oriented education *presumes* that: (a) content/knowledge presentations will lead toward a desired belief-knowledge type of wisdom, which is a conscious goal; and (b) the content/knowledge assumed to lead toward the goal of wisdom is *already* formed, structured, or organized by an often unacknowledged prior action of some structure upon some corpus of knowledge. Grossly put, this is a way of understanding what any denominationally responsible Christian educator begins with as an accepted and acceptable fact. For instance, in the long ago when I worked with the national Department of Christian Education of the Episcopal church, we sought for a denominational consensus on what Episcopalians should believe (as persons of that persuasion) and sought to find ways to reinforce or support or facilitate the development of the several components of such a belief-knowledge complex. We did that because we were responsible educators supported by a client denomination. I have no reason to believe that our colleagues in other denominations did not, then, seek the same goal or, for that matter, that religious educators in analogous positions today do not also seek that goal. It is part of being humanly responsible as an educator.

Probably, in that perspective, the most important thing to recognize is that those of us who, then, were Episcopalians were attempting something similar to but not exactly like what our Presbyterian, Roman, Methodist, or Baptist colleagues were attempting. In a word, our wisdom was not identical to their wisdom. That point is reasonably important. Wisdom, at the level of my illustration, is a plurality: it is really a matter of multiple wisdoms. We knew it in our bones, but our heads kept telling us that there was just one wisdom. I am not aware that we ever found it, although the part some of us played in initiating a Joint Educational Development project was a sure and certain sign that we were prepared to enter upon a search for that Grail!

Second, let me turn to the action-structure-wisdom energy-event pathway. Once again, an important thing about this theoretical pathway is its middle term: structure. As near as I can discern, this pathway is an intriguing reminder that what religious educators might recognize as process-oriented education *presumes* that: (a) the Socratic method of dealing with the stuff of the moment involves a tutor/querier with a firm grasp upon some kind of reasonably relevant structure, as well as an abundant store of question marks; and (b) the process of pragmatic problem solving and discovery involves the use of a conceptual structure frequently enough for it to become either internalized or "second nature." In a sense, this is a way of understanding what the effort to ensure teacher sensitivity is actually all about. The truly sensitive religious educator has both a realism about what is going on at any given moment and a thoroughly known conceptual structure, which can usually be related to that which is going on in some reasonably obvious manner. Grossly put, then, sensitivity to existent process is the imposition of some structure upon some action in such a way that the result is acknowledged as believable. A wisdom.

Third, I want to consider the knowledge-action-wisdom energy-event pathway. Yet again, an important thing about this theoretical pathway is its middle term: action. As best I can discern, this pathway is a fairly clear and almost painfully obvious reminder that what religious educators can easily recognize as experience-oriented education *presumes* that: (a) some determinate level or kind of knowledge can be completed through engaging in some form of seemingly relevant behavior; and (b) learning by doing always involves some prior knowledge as an initial prerequisite for that doing which, hopefully, leads toward or to either a wisdom or, perhaps, an expansion and generalization of that prior, initial knowledge. In a remarkable way, this pathway reminds us of the role of prior knowledge in any and all experiential learning and, as well, warns us that the resultant is most likely belief-knowledge, or wisdom. It is unlikely to generate verifiable knowledge, although it may create what we tend to think of as motivation. Grossly put, experiential education leads only to a wisdom, a belief-knowledge which can quite obviously motivate one to do a very considerable variety of things. Cultists work on this fact, and so do educators of all kinds. However, that is no reason to forswear this energy-event pathway, although it is a reason to use all available means to be certain that one's intention is, in fact, theoretically, socially, and educationally responsible. In addition, one's intention should also be humane.

These three energy-event pathways leading to wisdom as a resultant come from a tetrahedron model of the meaning of the work of Jean Piaget. For the religious educator, they suggest that Piaget's work can have meaning, regardless of which of three educational orientations one may choose. Moreover, the model suggests three theoretical, hypothetical pathways to a belief-knowledge or wisdom; while each is different from the others, all are model-dictated and, therefore, model-affirmed. Arguments between orientations are not arguments about possibilities, the general outcome; they are almost exclusively arguments about one's intentions. While that idea may not stop the arguments, it might clarify the meaning of the battle. Ultimately, it might even suggest to some that there are more productive educational tasks awaiting their energy and their reason.

IV. At Last, Simplification

Let us be tolerably honest: Hickson's query, important as it is, *is* an open-ended query about a vast corpus, Jean Piaget's published work in both English and French. My initial albeit implicit limitation was to focus only on the work published in English. My next but still implicit limitation was to deal only with those works readily available to me. I have emphasized the function of personal decision repeatedly and, therefore, have sought to model the same (quite consciously!) as I have written this text. Thus, this is a personal testament, as well as an attempt to be precise, accurate, and responsible.

After acknowledging the considerable importance of Hickson's query, I identified six possible clues to an answer to that query. Then I modeled those six clues by a regular octahedron, and noted several ways I sought to check my decision that such a geometric figure might be an appropriate model in the conceptual space defined as the meaning of Piaget. Next, I identified (via extension) that it was possible to construct a complementary set of tetrahedrons and an octahedron that, theoretically, offered an all-space-filling model. Then I exposed my reasons for identifying the four vertices of such a larger tetrahedron as the Piagetian concepts of wisdom, knowledge, action, and structure. Finally, I indicated some seeming reasons for thinking that those four concepts were relevant to the concerns (or orientations) of religious educators.

Now, after all of that laborious analysis, let us rejoice in the final simplification that we have reached. The larger tetrahedron of figure 2 can be considered to be several things. It can be considered to be the sum of its parts: four tetrahedrons and one octahedron. It can also be considered to be a thing in itself: an all-space-filling model. Both of these ways of considering that larger tetrahedral model are useful and important in the process of simplification.

The process of simplification reaches a tentatively final equilibrium as it reaches a level where there is *a* something. That level is here modeled by the larger tetrahedron taken as a thing in itself, an all-space-filling model. A level immediately lower in some conceptual hierarchy is modeled by that same larger tetrahedron taken as the complementary sum of four tetrahedrons and an octahedron. Interestingly, a level yet lower in the general-to-specific continuum is modeled by the core octahedron; with that I began my quasi-Fullerian geometric analysis of the conceptual space defined by the general construct of the meaning of the work of Jean Piaget. Thus, after a long and rather painstaking journey, we are in a position to identify a simplification of the initially almost overwhelming complexity involved in responding to Hickson's query.

Let me outline what I now discern.

First, at a most general level, the larger tetrahedron of figure 2, taken as a thing in itself, models the fundamental affirmation that the conceptual space defined by the construct of the meaning of the work of Jean Piaget *can* be modeled by an all-space-filling complementary set of tetrahedrons and an octahedron. While that may well seem an involuted way of saying it, the gross meaning is quite fundamental: the work of Jean Piaget has a meaning that *is* modelable. (If we consider Fuller's thesis that all thinking is modelable, then this kind of a statement is implicit in any affirmation that some construct has meaning.

While we humans often ignore this fact, it is inescapably at the peak of any process of simplification we may attempt.) An even grosser statement of the result is simply that the work of Piaget has a meaning.

Second, at a next lower level of generality, the larger tetrahedron model of figure 2 affirms that the meaning of the work of Jean Piaget can be appreciated in terms of four far-from-simple concepts: wisdom, knowledge, action, and structure. Quite apart from the energy-event analysis of this tetrahedral model, the model qua model affirms that, if one can understand and appreciate Piaget's use of those four terms, a meaning in Piaget's work will be discernible, because it *is* rationally modelable.

All of that is very, very likely true. Unfortunately, it is also quite theoretical. A religious educator might well wonder how one could appreciate those four far-from-simple concepts. So might almost anyone else. Therefore, I want to cycle back to this question very shortly.

Third, at a still lower level of generality, in fact at the very core of that larger tetrahedron model in figure 2, there are those six clues to the meaning of Piaget. Cognitively, conceptually, that was where I began. That is, my reflection upon the work of Piaget, as I knew it, led me to those six clues. I have already expended a good number of paragraphs in the attempt to explicate each of them, and I will not try to rehearse that once again. However, I do want the reader to appreciate that those clues represent a level of generality below that of the four tetrahedron vertex-concepts. If readers do appreciate that fact, then they can also appreciate the way in which I understand this complementary tetrahedral model to be a three-level conceptual hierarchy that peaks in utter, final simplicity.

Between the gross generality that Piaget's work has meaning (because it is modelable as an all-space-filling, simple, regular tetrahedron) and the specificities expounded in my treatment of those six initial clues to an answer to Hickson's query, I have posited four intermediate-level constructs: wisdom, knowledge, action, and structure. Aside from the labels, a reader might well ask, "So, how am *I* to understand those labels?" It is a good question, and I want to attempt a simple answer.

Each of the four vertex-concepts in the larger tetrahedral model of figure 2 can be associated with one or two of Piaget's later works, books neither Ms. Hickson nor I knew about when she formed her important query. Thus, they are not discoveries after the fact of our ignorance, but things we could not have then known. As a result, it is with some pleasure and a good bit of relief that I offer the reader the following listing.

1. A = structure. I know of no better way to understand Piaget's use of the concept of structure than to read his book *Structuralism* (1971).[112]
2. B = wisdom. In the Piagetian corpus available in English, this concept is treated almost exclusively in the book *Insights and Illusions of Philosophy* (1971). Thus, it is both an unavoidable and an irreplaceable source for anyone intent on understanding Piaget and his work.[113]
3. C = action. Two books are necessities, if one wants to understand the way Piaget used this concept. The first and the earliest is his book *Science of Education and the Psychology of the Child* (1970).[114] The second book is his work *The Child and Reality* (1973).[115]
4. D = knowledge. While it is true that almost any of Piaget's books are concerned with this concept, one of the better ways to understand what Piaget means by the term is to read his book *Psychology and Epistemology: Towards a Theory of Knowledge* (1971).[116]

While I obviously cannot guarantee that a reader will discover what I have come to discern as an answer to the vastly important problem posed by Hickson's query, I think I can assure a reader that working through this limited bibliography will give one an understanding of four fundamental Piagetian concepts. Thereby readers *will* have their own answer to the problem posed by Hickson's query, and that will be a very good thing!

Before ending this long and somewhat wearisome expedition into the conceptual continent mapped by the work of Jean Piaget, I want to address the natural question implicit in achieving final simplicity. That is, I want to suggest *one* book as both a summary statement of meaning and an excellent entry point into one's own explorations. That book is *The Psychology of the Child* (1969).[117] This book by Piaget and Inhelder is, to my mind, the best summary statement of the meaning of Piaget's work, and its fewer than two hundred pages should not tax the interest of even the busiest person. Of course, it is not a substitute for reading widely and thinking deeply, but it *will* put all else into a general frame of reference. That can be extraordinarily helpful; especially in this instance, one should not ignore any such help.

Notes and References

1. For this particular interchange from the *Verba Seniorum*, see Helen Waddell, *The Desert Fathers* (Ann Arbor: University of Michigan Press, 1936/1957), pp. 128–129. This is also the first entry in book 21 of the work known as *The Sayings of the Fathers* or *Verba Seniorium*.

2. Jean Piaget, *The Language and Thought of the Child* (New York: Harcourt, Brace, 1926).

3. The five works by Jean Piaget published in English between 1928 and 1932 were: *Judgment and Reasoning in the Child* (New York: Harcourt, Brace, 1928); *The Child's Conception of the World* (New York: Harcourt, Brace, 1929); *The Child's Conception of Physical Causality* (London: Kegan Paul, 1930); "Children's Philosophies," in C. Murchinson, ed., *Handbook of Child Psychology* (Worcester, Mass.: Clark University Press, 1931), pp. 377–391; and *The Moral Judgment of the Child* (London: Kegan Paul, 1932).

4. Jean Piaget, *The Psychology of Intelligence* (New York: Harcourt, Brace, 1950). For references to Piaget's French works, see John H. Flavell, *The Developmental Psychology of Jean Piaget* (Princeton, N.J.: D. Van Nostrand Co., 1963), pp. 454–455.

5. The three works by Jean Piaget published in English during the early 1950s were: *Play, Dreams, and Imitation in Childhood* (New York: Norton, 1951); *The Child's Conception of Number* (New York: Humanities Press, 1952); and *The Origins of Intelligence in Children* (New York: International University Press, 1952).

6. Jean Piaget, *Logic and Psychology* (Manchester, U.K.: Manchester University Press, 1953).

7. For these two references, see the following: Jean Piaget and Bärbel Inhelder, *The Child's Conception of Space* (London: Routledge and Kegan Paul, 1956); Inhelder and Piaget, *The Growth of Logical Thinking from Childhood to Adolescence* (New York: Basic Books, 1958).

8. See Flavell, *Developmental Psychology*, Bibliography, pp. 455–460.

9. Since 1955, the *Etudes d'epistemologie genetique* have been a prime source of "Piagetian" work, although they are (naturally) a basically French-language publication and, so, only differentially available to readers of English.

10. Jean Piaget, Bärbel Inhelder, and A. Szeminska, *The Child's Conception of Geometry* (New York: Basic Books, 1960).

11. Flavell, *Developmental Psychology*. In the final paragraph of a Foreword written by Jean Piaget and dated November 1962, this general assessment of Flavell's coverage is explicitly stated and Piaget entered the caveat that "it cannot be considered the final word" (p. ix).

12. Bärbel Inhelder and Jean Piaget, *The Early Growth of Logic in the Child* (London: Routledge and Kegan Paul, 1964).

13. Ronald Goldman, *Religious Thinking from Childhood to Adolescence* (London: Routledge and Kegan Paul, 1964).

14. Ronald Goldman, *Readiness for Religion: A Basis for Developmental Religious Education* (London: Routledge and Kegan Paul, 1965).

15. Millie Almy, Edward Chittenden, and Paula Miller, *Young Children's Thinking* (New York: Teachers College Press, 1966).

16. Jean Piaget, *Six Psychological Studies*, ed. David Elkind. (New York: Vintage Books/Random House, 1967).

17. For these two Piaget works, first published in English in 1969, see Jean Piaget and Bärbel Inhelder, *The Psychology of the Child* (New York: Basic Books, 1969); and Piaget, *The Mechanisms of Perception* (London: Routledge and Kegan Paul, 1969).

18. David Elkind and John H. Flavell, eds., *Studies in Cognitive Development* (New York: Oxford University Press, 1969).

19. For these two introductions to Piaget's work, see Molly Brearley and Elizabeth Hitchfield, *A Guide to Reading Piaget* (New York: Schocken Books, 1966/1969); and John L. Phillips, Jr., *The Origins of Intellect: Piaget's Theory* (San Francisco: W. H. Freeman and Co., 1969).

20. For these two 1970 publications, see Jean Piaget, *Genetic Epistemology* (New York: Columbia University Press, 1970); idem, *Science of Education and the Psychology of the Child* (New York: Grossman Publishers, 1970).

21. Jean Piaget, *Psychology and Epistemology: Towards a Theory of Knowledge* (New York: Grossman Publishers, 1971).

22. Jean Piaget, *Biology and Knowledge* (Chicago: University of Chicago Press, 1971).

23. Jean Piaget, *Insights and Illusions of Philosophy* (New York: New American Library, 1971).

24. Jean Piaget, *Structuralism* (London: Routledge and Kegan Paul, 1971).

25. For these two 1973 publications of Grossman, see Jean Piaget, *The*

Child and Reality (New York: Grossman Publishers, 1973); idem, *To Understand Is to Invent: The Future of Education* (New York: Grossman Publishers, 1973).

26. Jean Piaget, *Main Trends in Psychology* (New York: Harper & Row, Publishers, 1973).

27. Jean Piaget, *The Place of the Sciences of Man in the System of Sciences* (New York: Harper & Row, Publishers, 1974).

28. Jean Piaget, *Main Trends in Inter-Disciplinary Research* (New York: Harper & Row, Publishers, 1973).

29. Bärbel Inhelder, Hermine Sinclair, and Magali Bovet, *Learning and the Development of Cognition* (Cambridge, Mass.: Harvard University Press, 1974).

30. Jean Piaget and Bärbel Inhelder, *The Origin of the Idea of Chance in Children* (New York: W. W. Norton & Co., 1975).

31. The author's memory has limits, as do all things human, and this attribution to Dr. William A. Koppe is accurate in substance, as near as the author's sometimes fallible memory will permit. He can image the setting, which had to be in St. Louis, Missouri, but he cannot assign a date to that which he images.

32. During the period remembered, Ms. Agnes Hickson was employed by the executive council of the Episcopal church as the editor/author of the Seabury Series materials for the early elementary school grades. Her query, I am reasonably certain, has been rephrased, although the clear and evident substance of it has, I am certain, been retained.

33. What mathematicians refer to as a "drunkard's walk" is an illuminating illustration of the power of chance. It illustrates the fact that if one presumes a drunk begins with a grasp upon a street light upright, and further presumes that each step taken from that spot is randomly chosen (as, presumably, befits a drunk), there is a 1.00 probability that eventually the drunk will wind up *back* at the street light upright from which the walk began. A fictionalization of this basic statistical thesis can be found in Frederik Pohl's little book *Drunkard's Walk* (New York: Ballantine Books, 1960).

34. See Jean Piaget's Foreword in Flavell, *Developmental Psychology* (notes 4 and 11 above), p. vii.

35. Like all after-the-fact evaluations, this one may suffer from the perfect hindsight syndrome. At the time of writing, it seems evident that this was a fact. My colleagues during the 1960s may well think quite differently.

36. While this evaluation *is* based upon my memory, and I affirm it as such, I realize that my colleagues in the former Department of Christian Education of the Episcopal church may well remember the 1960s very, very differently. I acknowledge as much, but still want to make this point.

37. I now regard the expectation described here as literally fond. How-

ever, honesty impels me to acknowledge that I once shared it quite readily. My reason for recalling this foolishness is that, even now, I suspect that *some* of my colleagues in religious education still are bemused by the idea that theology, some theology, will play St. George to the educational dragon. It is my present conclusion that those still holding any such opinion had best meditate upon J. R. R. Tolkien's tale "Farmer Giles of Ham," which can be found in J. R. R. Tolkien, *Smith of Wootton Major and Farmer Giles of Ham* (New York: Ballantine Books, 1969), pp. 61–156.

38. For Peirce's entire address, as well as this quotation, see Philip P. Wiener, ed., *Values in a Universe of Chance* (New York: Doubleday & Co., 1958), pp. 3–14, esp. pp. 12–13.

39. Inhelder and Piaget, *The Growth of Logical Thinking*, p. 270. The emphasis has been added by the author to the original text.

40. Piaget and Inhelder, *Psychology of the Child*, p. 10.

41. Jean Piaget, *Science of Education and the Psychology of the Child* (New York: Viking Press, 1971).

42. Ibid., p. 171.

43. Jean Piaget, *Psychology and Epistemology* (New York: Viking Press, 1972), p. 80.

44. Piaget, *Biology and Knowledge* (note 22 above).

45. Ibid., p. 45.

46. Ibid., p. 46.

47. Ibid., p. 47.

48. Ibid., p. 79.

49. K. B. Madsen, *Theories of Motivation*, 4th ed. (Kent, Ohio: Kent State University Press, 1968).

50. James Drever, A *Dictionary of Psychology* (Baltimore: Penguin Books, 1952/1964), the word *motive*.

51. Piaget and Inhelder, *Psychology of the Child*, p. 158.

52. Madsen, *Theories of Motivation*, p. 350.

53. Piaget and Inhelder, *Psychology of the Child*, p. 157.

54. Ibid.

55. Ibid., p. 159.

56. Although the following argument is clearly this-worldly, psychological and educational, this illusion-spawning error may be peculiarly attractive to religious educators or to religiously committed educators. Without in *any* way denying either the reality or the otherness of G-O-D, it *is* quite clear that one's implicit or de facto theology (which clearly may be at a fair variance from whatever de jure theology one chooses to acknowledge) may (1) stress the otherness of the deity, and (2) involve a sense of G-O-D's continuing action, so that (3) G-O-D, and those through whom G-O-D presently works, are recognized as "exterior" to the learner. The result can be a discomfort with

this argument. Unfortunately, such a discomfort is the result of partial ignorance. Across the centuries G-O-D has been conceived of as immanent or transcendent or both. Faithful Christian believers have held all three relations to be true, and we have no reason to doubt their truth. I strongly suspect that *a* resolution to this theological set of possibilities involves the affirmation that G-O-D is both immanent and transcendent. But if that be so, then the following this-worldly argument should shock few, and its conclusion should be agreeable to most.

57. The author owes this insight into the considerable number of successive periods of equilibrium to his discovery in 1971 in the library of the School of Education of the University of Birmingham (U.K.) of the text of R. W. Rawlinson's unpublished Ph.D. dissertation, "Operational Facility in Relation to Additive Composition and Decomposition" (University of Birmingham, Birmingham, England, 1967). The interested reader will find a concise review of this dissertation on pages 90–93 in the author's own Ph.D. dissertation (New York University, 1973).

58. This sentence *must* be understood to put the decisional responsibility upon the educator, where it belongs, and to avoid putting responsibility anywhere else. The clear and obvious implication is that the decision for either a facilitative mode of operation *or* a remedial mode of operation is, quite clearly and quite rightly, that of the educator most closely associated with the specific case.

59. See the *Harvard Educational Review* reprint series volume, *Environment, Heredity, and Intelligence* (Cambridge, Mass.: Harvard Educational Review, Longfellow Hall, 13 Appian Way, Cambridge, Mass. 02138).

60. Ernest R. Hilgard, *Introduction to Psychology* (New York: Harcourt, Brace & World, 1953/1963), p. 625.

61. See the index entries for *preformation* in Piaget, *Biology and Knowledge*, p. 380, and for *preformationism* in Piaget, *Structuralism*, p. 151.

62. Piaget, *Structuralism* (note 24 above), pp. 8–9.

63. Ibid., p. 90.

64. Ibid., pp. 9, 90.

65. Ibid., pp. 62, 67.

66. Piaget, *Biology and Knowledge* (note 22 above), pp. 244–246.

67. Piaget and Inhelder, *Psychology of the Child*, pp. 114–122.

68. For a description of Waddington's notion of "homeorhesis" see Piaget, *Structuralism*, pp. 49–50. Also, check the entries under "Waddington, C. H." in Piaget, *Biology and Knowledge*, p. 383.

69. Piaget, *Structuralism*, p. 141.

70. John H. Peatling and David V. Tiedeman, *Career Development: Designing Self* (Muncie, Ind.: Accelerated Development, 1977), p. iii.

71. Piaget, *Main Trends in Psychology* (note 26 above), p. 35.

72. Ibid.
73. Ibid., p. 38.
74. Ibid.
75. Ibid.
76. Ibid., p. 47.
77. Ibid.
78. *The Book of Common Prayer* (New York: Church Pension Fund, 1928), p. 332.
79. Massey H. Shepherd, Jr., *The Oxford American Prayer Book Commentary* (New York: Oxford University Press, 1950), pp. 330–332.
80. The idea that human life is fourscore years is found in Ps. 90:10.
81. Piaget, *Insights and Illusions of Philosophy* (note 23 above).
82. Ibid., p. xi.
83. Ibid., p. xiii.
84. Ibid., p. xiv.
85. Ibid., pp. 78–121, esp. pp. 120–121. This reference encompasses the whole of Piaget's third chapter, "The False Ideal of a Suprascientific Knowledge."
86. Ibid., pp. 87–88. Here Piaget uses the specific word *belief* to refer to what he calls "a distinct philosophical mode of knowledge" which is, he maintains, but an aspect of a fairly commonly encountered belief in "a fundamental dualism of knowledge."
87. Ibid., p. xiii.
88. Ibid., p. 210.
89. Ibid., p. 209.
90. Ibid.
91. Ibid., p. 231.
92. Ibid., p. 232.
93. Ibid.
94. Ibid.
95. I do not want to belabor a "straw donkey," but it probably is useful for the theologically trained to stop and reflect and, then, admit that what seems from a theological perspective to be verifiable knowledge involves an important-if-subtle transformation of the definition of *verification*. It probably would be much better to recognize different meanings for that concept than to continue to confuse oneself, and others, by using the same word—*verification*—in distinctly different ways. I am certain that some who acknowledge themselves to be theologians understand this point very well. It is only those who do not that concern me here.
96. The real point here is the improbability of any theologian's being above challenge in guiding religious education or religious educators. A theologian is human and, therefore, fallible. Even if one presumed that there

were such a thing as an infallible theology, it would be partially incarnate in particular theologians. The infallibility of the theology, thus, is always "filtered" through the fallible theologian. This bit of logic (or, perhaps, wisdom) seems part of what one means by positing that all humans are creatures and, at best, faceted reflections of a creator.

97. This particular line of thought is stimulated by the author's memories of a character, J. Wesley Smith, created by the cartoonist Burr Shafer. In the long ago, Shafer's character was pictured meeting Moses as he came down from Sinai and, characteristically, suggesting that ten was too large a number. For example, see Burr Shafer, *Through More History with J. Wesley Smith* (New York: Vanguard Press, 1953).

98. An early and classic statement of this point was David P. Ausubel's 1960 article, "The Use of Advance Organizers in the Learning and Retention of Meaningful Verbal Material," *Journal of Educational Psychology*, 51, pp. 267–272. This article can also be found in Richard E. Ripple, ed., *Learning and Human Abilities: Educational Psychology* (New York: Harper & Row, Publishers, 1964), pp. 420–427.

99. Piaget, *Structuralism* (note 24 above), p. 25. Also see Peatling and Tiedeman, *Career Development: Designing Self* (note 70 above), pp. 126–127, for an instance.

100. Piaget and Inhelder, *Psychology of the Child* (note 17 above), pp. 20–21, 136–140.

101. R. Buckminster Fuller, *Synergetics: Explorations in the Geometry of Thinking* (New York: Macmillan Publishing Co., 1975), p. 337.

102. Ibid., p. 487.

103. See J. R. R. Tolkien, "On Fairy Stories," in *The Tolkien Reader* (New York: Ballantine Books, 1966), p. 37.

104. See note 101 above.

105. G. Polya, *How to Solve It*, 2nd ed. (Garden City, N.Y.: Doubleday & Co., 1945/1957), pp. 154–157.

106. Ibid., pp. 141–148.

107. Michael Polanyi, *Science, Faith, and Society* (Chicago: University of Chicago Press, 1964).

108. Fuller, *Synergetics*, p. 243.

109. Jean Piaget, *The Child and Reality* (New York: Penguin Books, 1972/1976), esp. pp. 63–92.

110. D. J. O'Conner, *An Introduction to the Philosophy of Education* (London: Routledge and Kegan Paul, 1957), p. 7.

111. Like all aphorisms, this one is true only within some limits. Research describes in order to understand and, if possible, identify why what is described occurred.

112. Piaget, *Structuralism* (note 24 above).
113. Piaget, *Insights and Illusions of Philosophy* (note 23 above).
114. Piaget, *Science of Education and the Psychology of the Child* (note 20 above).
115. Piaget, *The Child and Reality* (note 25 above).
116. Piaget, *Psychology and Epistemology* (note 21 above).
117. Piaget and Inhelder, *The Psychology of the Child* (note 17 above).

8

My God! Skinner and Religious Education

In the now-distant year of 1955, I bought a copy of R. M. French's translation of *The Way of a Pilgrim and The Pilgrim Continues His Way.*[1] Thus I came to know the adventures of a simple, nameless Russian Christian: the Pilgrim. I also became aware that this classic combined a profound Christian spirituality with an amazingly pragmatic attitude toward the life we humans know much to most of the time. I was intrigued and fascinated.

The saga of the Pilgrim touched the me-that-then-was and formed, somehow, the me-that-is-now. As I look back, I am intrigued at what is now apparent. The Pilgrim, his friends, and his starets were remarkable persons: they could be honest about humankind as it is and still be firmly yet pragmatically realistic about humankind as it *can* be. Of course, their realism is the stuff of which ideals, dreams, or fantasies are woven.

Still, if one will tolerate the pietistic language and accept the mid-nineteenth-century Russian context, something remarkable becomes evident. Behind, beneath, or through that language system one detects and then recognizes a vision of humankind-as-creature in relation to a G-O-D of remarkable, patient, and loving concern. A G-O-D that hopes, anticipates, and desires the free action of the creature. The fact that the narrative cycles about a hesychast's practice must not obscure the fact that a seemingly impossible thing is, there, seen as a free human decision.[2] However, it is a goal that is reached only by a series of freely accepted disciplines. The way is through training.[3]

A certain *skhimnik* (a monk of the highest level of spirituality) notes that John Chrysostom taught this:

> No one should give the answer that it is impossible for a man occupied with worldly cares, and who is unable to go to church, to pray always. Everywhere, wherever you may find yourself, you can set up an altar to God in your mind by means of prayer. And so it is fitting to pray at your trade, on a journey, standing at the counter or sitting at your handicraft. Everywhere and in every place it is possible to pray, and, indeed, if a man diligently turns his attention upon himself, then everywhere he will find convenient circumstances for prayer.[4]

Strange as it may seem, the words of a late-fourth-century archbishop of Constantinople are peculiarly relevant, apropos, and contemporary in the late twentieth century. Chrysostom's description of busy fourth-century humans is all too true of twentieth-century humans. The fourth-century possibility is what it was sixteen centuries ago: an improbable natural occurrence, but *no* impossibility.

For Chrysostom and the Pilgrim, the key was self-discipline: training. Chrysostom focused upon what could happen "if a man diligently turns his attention upon himself." The implicit idea was that if diligent attention is directed toward the self, then remarkable and otherwise unexpected things become possible. From the vantage point of the late twentieth century, it is a genuinely fascinating idea that the Pilgrim, his spiritual helpers, and the ancient Fathers of the Christian church all were concerned with successively approximating a human possibility.[5] They all were quite clearheaded: it was a possibility to be achieved via a consciously accepted program of training. It was a possibility that, in our terms, might well and honestly be called a program of conditioning.

Although there is no evidence that Burrhus F. Skinner ever knew the Pilgrim's story or Chrysostom's writings on prayer, there is abundant evidence that he explored the possibilities of conditioning extensively enough to come to believe that conditioning opens a vast possibility for humankind. His vision of that possibility is no paraphrase of the vision the Pilgrim and Chrysostom shared, but it is a vision of humankind at peace with itself and its environment. Interestingly enough, B. F. Skinner's program for a society conditioned to be at peace with itself and its environment depends upon humankind's ability to diligently turn its "attention" upon itself. For all its abrasiveness, Skinner's 1971 tract *Beyond Freedom and Dignity* is an extended, if irritating, challenge to exactly such a diligent "attention."[6]

A SMALL CAVEAT

During the mid-1960s I supervised an experimental project for the Department of Christian Education of the Episcopal church on the application of programmed instruction to religious education.[7] With the perfection granted only to hindsight, it is evident that those of us involved in that experiment learned a great deal more than we were ever able to publish. Without being maudlin, I can recall watching our capability dribble away as members of our research team resigned or lost their ability through disuse or got caught up in other important projects. We Episcopalians ventured into that experiment hand-in-hand with the United Presbyterians, but none of us used our experience very well. We all let it fade away.

In the early 1970s I was asked to represent the educational technology of programmed instruction at a regional meeting of the Religious Education Association in Atlantic City, New Jersey.[8] For that meeting, I created an introduction to programmed instruction. I did that because I thought that one ought to experience an idea. Thus, I include it as an Appendix to this chapter for those with a thirst for knowledge.[9] However, I have not tried to program this chapter.

CONDITIONING AND B. F. SKINNER

The Russian Ivan Pavlov won a Nobel Prize for his experiments with dogs, and all of us learned a considerable amount about the process termed *conditioning*. According to B. R. Bugelski, the American psychologists Watson, Gutherie, and Tolman are the real heirs of Pavlov.[10] According to Bugelski, Burrhus F. Skinner is somewhat different, for he is a representative of the general school of E. L.

Thorndike.[11] The basic difference is that Skinner's theory includes, in a way that Pavlov's does not, the function of *anticipation*. Skinner was interested in changing the probability of observed behaviors that seemed to be closely associated with a reasonably large and potentially diffuse category he called *operants*. Unlike Pavlov, who sought to control responses by conditioning them to a variety of preceding stimuli, Skinner was concerned with associating specific, desired, future behaviors or responses with his class of operants.

There is a sense in which it is unfair to maintain that the difference between Pavlov and Skinner is simply a matter of precedence or antecedence. But there is more than a germ of truth in that idea. Skinner consistently focused upon the resulting future state (or behavior). He seemed to care little for the immediately preceding, supposedly internal operations of the organism (e.g., a human). However, he was very caring about what that organism would do in some observable situation when some X-condition existed. As a result of his careful attention to the apparent results of highly specific situation-organism behavior, Skinner came to believe that one could *control* behavior via attention to those X-conditions. His 1948 novel *Walden Two* is a fictionalized, somewhat more specific description of the possible implications of his theory.[12]

Let us be honest.

B. F. Skinner's operant conditioning is not the classical conditioning of Pavlov. However much Skinner may seem to be a conditioning theorist, it is important to recognize that he is also a peculiarly North American pragmatist. He is not a Pavlovian. He is not a brainwasher. By choice and by dream, he is an engineer of humankind. Somewhat like the Pilgrim's starets.

In a number of strangely remarkable ways, Skinner's vision of an engineered humanity is, at the very least, humanitarian. No religious person—certainly no confessed Christian!—should think the less of B. F. Skinner, even if they find that they are in profound disagreement with his vision of humankind. One's disagreement should focus upon genuine differences of belief and value, not upon the notion that B. F. Skinner lacks an ability to feel kindly toward other humans. His 1948 novel *Walden Two* can be dangerously misinterpreted, misunderstood, and misapplied if one thinks Skinner to be so lacking. But that need not be.[13]

In fact, it is a sign of the utterly strange economy of G-O-D that Skinner's tract *Beyond Freedom and Dignity* was prepared with the help of a National Institutes of Mental Health grant.[14] There are times when the secular recognize a humanitarian while the religious are still in a healthy human difference of opinion. Somewhere on beyond jealousy there must be some recognition that the biblical G-O-D does what it wills, quite without attention to our permission.

RELIGIOUS EDUCATION AND SKINNER

In the early 1980s it is all too easy to be critical of Burrhus F. Skinner, especially since he has begun to issue a serialized biography.[15] However, let us not be misled by that fact. Rather, let us focus our attention on Skinner the educator. In a word, let us seek for that which most concerns us as educators, and leave the rest to history or, even, the judgment of G-O-D.

If we adopt such a strategy with the Skinner corpus, then we will find ourselves considering Skinner as the papa of programmed instruction.[16] As those who seek to hold *religious* and *education* together in a description of what we seek to do, such a strategy has much to recommend it. First, it focuses our attention. Second, it permits us to distinguish one thing from another in looking at a long, varied, and highly productive life. Third, it allows us to learn from Skinner the educator, even if we have problems with Skinner the philosopher or Skinner the sage or Skinner the signpost toward some future. Without denying that Skinner has sought such roles, we can seek to understand Skinner the educator (a role we also want to claim).

As the product of an educator, the B. F. Skinner corpus is best approached through his work on programmed instruction. In fact, Skinner the educator may best be understood through his early rationale for programmed instruction.[17] There the North American pragmatic egalitarian is most evident. There he argues from the historical evidence that individual tutoring, as practiced in the oldest English universities, is a maximally effective method of education. However, Skinner was no idealist. He recognized that American schools could not hire enough teachers to provide individual tutoring, even in the mid-1950s.

It was his clear recognition that the societal practicalities made individual tutors impossible for the majority of students, plus a belief that such was a maximally effective educational technique, that lay behind Skinner's adaptation of his operant conditioning to education. Programmed instruction was no less than a North American's attempt to *improve* educational practice, as encountered by most students. Of all persons, religious educators should recognize that fact, rejoice in it, and honor the one who sought an answer.

Apparently, Skinner did what few who claim to be educators want to do: he attended to the process itself, and asked *why* a student had to "fail" so often. His conclusion is still a revolution awaiting its success, at least as far as religious education is concerned. Skinner concluded that there was no reason for pupil failure, except the inadequacy of the teacher.[18] Granted, that is a hard conclusion to accept.[19] But if one stops to think about it, it is a reasonable conclusion, which is not to say that it is an easy thing to remedy. Far from it.[20]

What those of us in the Episcopal church and the United Presbyterian church learned in the mid-1960s was that programmed instruction was grindingly specific, often disappointing, and almost always a challenge to our too-simple assumption that we knew what we needed to know to be effective religious educators. We learned that we still had much to learn; we found that it was difficult to be sufficiently precise to make a program; and we learned that we had to attend to the student. Our theories and then-contemporary theologies did *not* shield us from failure.[21] *That* was a damnably hard lesson!

Above all else, we learned from our successes (such as they were!) that the technology of programmed instruction could work. At a price, a high price. When we managed to do careful analysis, creative writing of very small bits, and then submitted our work to students, who either did or did not learn what we intended, we learned something about the basic process. We also discovered that we had to repeat the cycle until the probability of pupil failure was very, very small. It was mind-squeezing work; a genuine challenge. Perhaps that is why we decided to forget it. The whole process of creating demonstrably effective educational programs was long, wearying, challenging . . . and expensive.

Some future historian may have the insight or the experience to evaluate those efforts and then reach a best possible conclusion. After only a decade and a half, I cannot be that historian. I can still see the vision we never quite reached.[22] I can still feel the anguish at our decision to turn elsewhere. I can still remember the care with which some of us sought out a theological, ethical rationale for even attempting to program religious education. And I can still recall how we satisfied ourselves that what we then tried was ethical, theologically acceptable, and educationally responsible.[23]

As I recall it, some of us involved in that abortive effort to explore the application of programmed instruction to religious education came to recognize a number of often-hidden educational responsibilities. In a way, that was the most awesome thing about the whole venture. We recognized our responsibilities in a clear light that had *not* been our usual way of seeing what we were about. For instance, we recognized that we were not in the business of promulgating one or another educational magic. We recognized that we were not freed by tradition, theology, or the gospel from making human decisions. We also recognized that we were not freed from the existential situation, and that ethical, reasonable, defensible, and describable decisions had to be made if we were to be educators. In a word, we were forced to recognize that we were creatures; that angelic wisdom was not ours; and that we could do only what we acknowledged as our goal, unless we trusted to sheer dumb luck (or, more elegantly put, the wonderfully strange providence of G-O-D)![24]

It was awesome.

History will record that we turned aside from what we saw, felt, or ever-so-vaguely surmised. We could not afford the time or the effort to do what we knew could be done. So we tried other things.

However, let me put the case positively for those who rightly read these paragraphs as sheer history. The question of Skinner and religious education, of programmed instruction's application to religious education, is still a challenge. Past experience is just that: past.

B. F. Skinner the educator identified that the individualized instruction characteristic of a tutorial *was* effective education, perhaps the most effective education. That was a long time ago. But it is very, very probably still true. We religious educators simply have yet to face into the demand it makes upon us. We excuse ourselves by noting that we have classes, groups, congregations to educate. And that is true. Of course we do. But we keep before our eyes a false decision: *all* those potential learners, or just that *few* we could reach with individual care and concern. The falseness of that decision resides in our insistence that we be the tutor, if tutor there is to be. The problem is our insistence on doing the job ourselves. Although that is a classic adolescent stance, it is not an adult one. Someone else might, via some X-method, do not only as well as we do, but even do better than we can do![25]

The promise and the problem are summarized in that idea: someone else can do religious education as well as or better than we can. Once we grant that we simply do not have enough tutors, the problem is full upon us. Frankly and baldly stated, the problem for a religious educator is why *anyone* should settle for *our* second-best, when a good simulation of a better is available.[26] Actually, the economics of programmed instruction are but a distraction, however real they may be. The problem is too pointedly ours to be so resolved. The ethical problem of programming religious education seems more substantive, but it is not irresolvable. For example, we must recognize that entering upon or staying within a demonstrably effective program *can* be a decision; it need not be the socialized action of some biological automation. Neither adult persons nor preadult pupils are such, whatever one may at times think about the peer-oriented.[27]

The theological objections to programmed instruction seem weightier, but all too often that weight is sheer baggage from past deference to that sly old pretender to the queenship of the sciences.[28] An effective program is no more than a statement of an aspect of our creaturely state. Unless we forswear freedom and responsibility as aspects of such a state, an effective program poses for us a remarkably simple decision. Do we use it? Or do we reject it? However, that decision need not be made with any regard to a program's effectiveness. In fact, so far it appears often to be made with a cavalier disregard of that level of specific fact.

Let us be honest with ourselves.

As creatures within this creation, we are always involved in making either analogies or inferences when we try to be theological. While it is reasonably evident that some few creatures have a vision of G-O-D's perfection, as the persistently recurring witness of mystical experience shows, most creatures are involved in the perspectival problem identified in an earlier chapter.[29] However, that is no denigration of the creaturely state. Rather, it is a reasonably objective, verifiable but neutral description of that state.

Inevitably, when we try our hand at being theological, we wind up being creaturely. That is, we make decisions; we accept given values; we are approximately reasonable; but we are always creatures of our time and our place. While that may be what we least desire, unless we are quite unrealistic we know that is what we do, time after time after time. In a word, theology seems always to involve a set of situational, historical, and anthropological presumptions.[30]

However, that is a lengthy aside. The problem of our reactions as religious educators to the use or the disuse of Skinner's educational technology is related to our anthropology and basically, more importantly, and quite powerfully to our value system. It is a question of *what* we value, and of *how* we hold those values. That is, our reactions are an indication of some process of either choice or decision. We choose. We decide. But too often we do not acknowledge what we have done.

That is close to the heart of our problem.

That is why our theology so often seems to prevent us from acknowledging our creaturely limits and, instead, entices us into believing/thinking something about our creaturely selves that is far more appropriate of angelic beings than it is of creatures within *this* creation. That sentence is clearly related to the traditional Christian doctrine of original sin.[31] As creatures, we are unfortunately limited. Reason and honesty ask us to acknowledge as much, for only on beyond that acknowledgment can we use our reason or our logic as a tool in a theology. Prior to that acknowledgment, reason and logic, because they are thoroughly human albeit relatively neutral intellectual inventions, confuse us just about as often as they help us.

If, but only if, we accept something very like Paul of Tarsus's observation, "*Now* we see only puzzling reflections in a mirror," even if we insist upon remembering his immediate affirmation that "but *then* we shall see face to face,"[32] can we have any humanly appropriate confidence in the theology we manage to create. Naturally, in such a posited situation of acceptance, our confidence in *a* theology will be tentative—rather hypothetical, in fact. Yet that is the nature of human, creaturely decisions, including those we decide to call theological.[33] We humans generate hypotheses with relative ease. Our gross disability is that we tend to forget what we have done and then compound our problems with those traces of past serious thought by mistaking them for something like a revelation. But that is really *our* human problem.

Once again, let us try to be honest—with ourselves.

Unless we credit *a* theology as a literal transcript of some specific revelation to humankind (a claim few if any Christian theologies have made), we are left in our creaturely state, with our seemingly inherent perspectival problem vis-a-vis G-O-D. That is, we are left to think hypothetically, using reason or logic as a tool. The fact that we are religious educators does not offer any protection. We are creatures, too. Our theologies *are* always ours.

Now, what has all of this to do with Skinner the educator?

Surprisingly, a good deal. For if we are humanly responsible for our decisions, then our fundamental question about any decision concerns how well it meets a maximum standard of human behavior: is it reasonable, given our present knowledge of who we are and what we can, in fact, do?[34] Past answers are just that: past. Future possibilities are exactly that: alternatives resident in some not-yet. Present options are what must, by a creaturely necessity, concern us.

Once we find that we can reach that recognition, we are in a position to appreciate Skinner the educator. That is, we can appreciate

Skinner as educator precisely because, theologically, we accept our creaturely state. We and Skinner are creatures in this creation in this period and place. Like us, he may sometimes be right, and other times wrong. However, as a creaturely peer, that need neither surprise nor offend us. Therefore, we can learn from him.

Once we are able to accept both Burrhus F. Skinner and ourselves as peers in our creaturehood, we can distinguish Skinner the educator from all the other Skinners. We can acknowledge that his early identification of individualized, tutorial instruction as a most effective educational technique was, in all probability, correct. We can also acknowledge that the technology of programmed instruction was, fundamentally, a remarkably good *simulation* of that most effective technique in a situation where the literal method could *not* be. Moreover, we can also acknowledge that the educational problem Skinner set for himself is remarkably like that which we religious educators know is our problem. There are more students than we can possibly tutor. Yet we cannot be content to give an effective education only to an elite minority. Like Skinner, we too are North Americans, heirs of an egalitarian tradition, and we know in the very structure of our mind that there is no reason to choose second-best when a better is available! Only the damnable intractabilities of some present moment can possibly hide that conclusion from us, once we accept our creaturehood.[35]

SUMMARY AND CONCLUSION

I have spent an inordinate portion of this chapter writing about what it means to be a creature. I have also alluded to several of the works of B. F. Skinner. In addition, I have implied that we religious educators have a very great deal to learn about the specifics of our work, trade, craft, art, discipline, profession, or calling from Skinner's educational technology of programmed instruction, and that we have, as yet, learned only that it is more of a challenge than we care to face. I have done this because I am convinced that until religious educators settle for themselves their place in the theologically fundamental doctrine of creation, religious education will be subject to the whims of current winds and tides, somewhat like a sailing ship with an occasionally true compass and a randomly malfunctioning rudder. 'Tis luck or providence alone that sees such a ship safely into harbor.

I have not intended to present a critique of Skinner the educator, let alone Skinner in any of the other roles he seems to have sought for himself. Rather, I have tried to free readers of some prejudices and, thereby, permit readers to read, mark, learn, and inwardly digest Skinner's work for themselves.[36] If readers will do *that*, they will learn some things of use, discover some things with which they may disagree, and claim their creaturely right to *decide* for themselves. They will be free *and* responsible humans.

The select bibliography attached to the Appendix to this chapter will introduce the reader to Skinner the educator, the papa of programmed instruction. It will also provide the reader with a variety of conceptual grist which, when finely milled by a curious mind, may serve a religious educator remarkably well.

Notes and References

1. R. M. French, trans., *The Way of a Pilgrim and The Pilgrim Continues His Way* (New York: Harper & Brothers, 1952).
2. For a clear definition of *hesychasm*, see F. L. Cross, Ed., *The Oxford Dictionary of the Christian Church* (London: Oxford University Press, 1957).
3. For two descriptions of *training*, see Ernest R. Hilgard, *Introduction to Psychology* (New York: Harcourt, Brace & World, 1953, 1957, 1962), p. 635; and James Drever and Harvey Wallerstein, rev., *A Dictionary of Psychology* (Baltimore: Penguin Books, 1952/1964), p. 302.
4. French, *Pilgrim*, p. 198.
5. James G. Holland and B. F. Skinner, *The Analysis of Behavior* (New York: McGraw-Hill Book Co., 1961), pp. 97–99.
6. B. F. Skinner, *Beyond Freedom and Dignity* (New York: Alfred A. Knopf, 1971). (The author's records indicate he completed reading this book on October 25, 1971. His memory is that he purchased his copy in a bookstore in Middlebury, Vermont, early in September 1971 when he took a daughter to Middlebury College to begin her sophomore year.)
7. I am grateful to the Rev. Dr. David L. Hunter, then director of the Department of Christian Education of the Episcopal church, who appointed me the Episcopalian research team supervisor for this project. For a final

report of the work of that project, as seen by our professional consultants, see J. L. Coffey, R. J. Cress, and C. A. Christner, *Final Report on the Use of Programmed Instruction in Christian Education to Domestic and Foreign Missionary Society of the Protestant Episcopal Church and the Board of Christian Education of the United Presbyterian Church* (Columbus, Ohio: Battelle Memorial Institute, December 31, 1963).

8. The Religious Education Association held an Eastern Regional Conference at the Shelburne-Dennis Hotels on May 12–14, 1974, in Atlantic City, New Jersey, on the basic theme of "Models of Teaching."

9. Those thirsty for knowledge should check the Appendix at the end of these notes.

10. B. R. Bugelski, *The Psychology of Learning Applied to Teaching* (Indianapolis: Bobbs-Merrill Co., 1964), pp. 97–109.

11. Ibid., p. 83.

12. B. F. Skinner, *Walden Two* (New York: Macmillan Publishing Co., 1953).

13. Although it does not quite qualify as an example of misinterpretation, misunderstanding, or misapplication, the introduction and commentary of Daniel B. Stevick to *Walden Two* in the Religious Dimensions in Literature series (New York: Seabury Press, 1968) witnesses to how close a Christian scholar can come to those distortions when he is insufficiently appreciative of Skinner's work as an educator or, perhaps, responds to the several other roles Skinner has attempted to play.

14. See Acknowledgements, Skinner, *Beyond Freedom and Dignity*, p. 227. Here the author acknowledges that he had support from NIMH for the preparation of the manuscript, and identifies the grant as K6-MH-21,775-01.

15. B. F. Skinner's first volume of his autobiography appeared in 1976 and was entitled *Particulars of My Life* (New York: McGraw-Hill Book Co., 1976), 332 pp.

16. For some interesting information on the word *papa*, see *The Oxford Dictionary of the Christian Church*.

17. For the early Skinner rationale for programmed instruction, see B. F. Skinner, "The Science of Learning and the Art of Teaching," *Harvard Educational Review* 24 (1954); idem, "Teaching Machines," *Science* 128 (1958). Also see idem, "Reflections on a Decade of Teaching Machines," in Robert Glaser, ed., *Teaching Machines and Programmed Learning*, vol. 2 (Washington, D.C.: National Education Association of the United States, 1965), pp. 5–20.

18. The conclusion that pupil failure is, in fact, due to an inadequate teacher is obviously based upon a very high view of the role/function of a teacher. Specifically, it presumes that adequate teachers know each student so well that they can and do (a) know what the student *lacks*, (b) what the student

is *capable* of learning, and (c) what, in a specific subject, the student next *needs* to learn. An "adequate" teacher supplies something of what the student next needs to learn that is within the range of what that student is capable of learning and, so, at least partially supplies what that student lacks. This process is very likely to be successful: the student/learner quite probably learns that something supplied, recognizes it as a next learning, and quite probably also recognizes that the lack is decreased thereby.

19. The most apparent reason why any such conclusion is hard to accept has very little to do with any educator's vision of what either educational success or teacher adequacy may mean. It has a very great deal to do with almost any practicing educator's recognition that there is often a vast disparity between the practicalities and the vision. Moreover, it has much to do with a quite human desire to excuse oneself from the middle position of an obvious target. Psychologists sometimes speak of that tendency as a defensive, or self-protective response.

20. What is to be recognized here is that humans repeatedly encounter a situation which, paradoxically, is one thing (via the human invention of logic) and quite something else (via the powerful, personally oriented, emotional response of one who is immediately concerned) at the same time. Frankly, honestly, this situation occurs far too frequently for humans to regard it as anything but anticipatable, or normal. Were we humans the creatures of some *other* order of creation, perhaps we would have reasonable cause to be distressed. But we are not. And we have no such reason for our distress, other than our desire to be what we are not. We would be well advised to remember, in this instance, what *we* have done.

21. After almost seventeen years, I can come closer to an accurate assessment of what this sentence means than I could earlier. I do not think we were peculiarly blind or ignorant religious educators. I do think we were very like most of our colleagues. We thought that our educational theories were correct, and we had sufficient intellectual acumen to have placed our theologies into close relation to those theories. Humanly, we were in a position close to subjective certainty. What we were not, it is now evident, was sufficiently self-critical or pragmatic or experimental. We really did not believe that we had to "try" before we "knew": we had a false sense that right theory or correct theology would ensure our success. The process of attending to student responses, within the technology of programmed instruction, forced us to recognize that neither theory nor theology was a guarantee that the students would *do* what we anticipated. They often would not, and neither theory nor theology could hide our failure from us. As educators, we had to deal with failure. We tried; and we found that we needed to pay much closer attention to the student than we had thought. We learned, thereby, something very practical for any educator to know.

22. That vision, which we never quite reached, involved the mastery of a technology which would enable us to noticeably increase the likelihood of reaching the goals we had. Being optimists, we thought that mastery could be reached by intelligent, knowledgeable persons fairly quickly. That was simply untrue. Mastery took time, money, dedication. We ran out of those things in almost exactly that order: or so I remember the situation. The last thing we lost was dedication to the possibility; however, eventually that went as we found seemingly good reasons to turn attention to other things that, then, clearly needed to be done. Or so we thought.

23. My memory throws up images of explaining why we were into such a project to publishers of programmed texts as often as to colleagues. As I recall the period, those of us involved in the attempt to probe the possible application of programmed instruction to religious education tended to think that *a* possibility within this creation could be useful for religious education, if it was useful for education. We also tended to think that a program was, at its beginnings, a challenge to personal decision: it was an educational device that would, with reasonably high probability, do some specifiable something. If one did not wish that, one could/should opt out. But we, the educators, could describe that something and, so, contribute to the personal decision and the exercise of human responsibility. That seemed both ethical and, in a way, theologically justifiable. We were certainly clear that almost no other educational course, curriculum, or set of exercises could so clearly facilitate the exercise of human decision making and, thereby, the exercise of human responsibility. That is, we knew that an outcome from alternative educational procedures was almost unknown and unknowable, so that prior decision was almost impossible. There was only the students' trust, sheer trust, at the beginning. No decision.

24. In many ways, the recognition of the improbability of success in the venture of religious education, aside from a close to superstitious trust in G-O-D to make all things right, forced some of us to attempt to take the educational technology seriously. But to do that meant we had to be willing to decide, to use whatever help we could garner, and then to set a goal and seek it, with a fair confidence that we could reach it if we were careful enough in building our program. That was humanly possible, or so it seemed. Doing less, it seemed, was to presume on divine remedy.

25. For those who are called to an *educational* ministry, this recognition is a genuinely humbling experience. Unfortunately, one recurringly attractive alternative is implicitly to reject the educational ministry to persons and opt for a ministry to larger social groups in the name of practicality or even "liberation." The unfortunate nature of this alternative, for those called to an educational ministry, is that it involves another ministry. Confusing the two, identifying the one with the other, wreaks havoc with the educational minis-

try, and implicitly presumes that G-O-D can only be as monofocused as we humans, which is a real absurdity!

26. Let us be very careful as we judge this alternative. Unless we take a good bit of care, we find that we are simply arguing for the need for a warm human body in any educational setting. Yet that is to focus solely on the teacher and thereby ignore the student, the learner. If, as educators, we are concerned for the student and the student's learning, we will find that the medium of education is, in some specific situations, better when a simulation of what we might do exists than when a probable/possible human is actually there. In fact, simulation is a possible minimum: an effective program should accomplish a specific goal, not merely simulate a human educator's often-wandering progress toward such a goal. For an exploration of exactly this point, see John H. Peatling and David V. Tiedeman, *Career Development: Designing Self* (Muncie, Ind.: Accelerated Development, 1977), esp. pp. 183–210.

27. Let us at least consider whether the seemingly damnable aspect of those developmental periods when humans seem inordinately well attuned to the behavioral, attitudinal, and emotional standards of their peers is not *basically* the challenge of standards other than *ours*. In Christian terms, such a situation of apparent allegiance to differing standards calls for all of the subtlety of apologia, not for the attempt to use whatever equivalent to Diocletian authority we may have available to us. Certainly, the damnableness of the situation is that we are faced with once-dependent creatures who, now, are either counterdependent or trying out independence. Historically, our problem is a close analogue to that of the Roman Empire at the very beginning of the fourth century A.D. But neither counterdependence nor independence are, of themselves, signs of sheer, simple socialization to the level of automatons! We must take care.

28. Please read this sentence carefully. I am not denigrating theology per se, only questioning its pretenses. For example, I am glad to have had a theological education. I am also convinced that theology has a "word" for each and every situation, period, decade, or age. What I am not willing to grant is that *a* theology constitutes, by itself, an unchallengeable court of last resort. On beyond any theology, because of our creaturely perspectival problem, there has to be, at any given time, an appeal to raw, bald human experience (or its formalization via logic or reason). Like any theory, *a* theology helps us interpret the data we know; but we simply must understand that we may encounter surd data at any moment, data which shows, by its existence, that our theory/theology is not an all-sufficient, exhaustive thesaurus of human possibilities or potentialities. This sentence is, therefore, no more than a "taking seriously" of our limitations as creatures within this particular creation.

29. See chapter 2 for "the perspectival problem." For an extensive compendium of that reasonable evidence that some few creatures seem to have a vision of G-O-D's perfection, see Evelyn Underhill's classic *Mysticism* (London: Methuen & Co., 1911), esp. pp. 3–164.

30. Probably the greatest disservice anyone can do to theology per se is to equate theology with revelation. While the Judeo-Christian religious heritage is, certainly, fundamentally committed to the possibility and the reality of revelation, it is not at all committed to the proposition that each and every theology *is* a revelation. Anyone ever exposed to the history of at least Christian doctrine should be aware that theology (a) has a history, and (b) has existed as a plural in most periods. It is too obviously a high but human exercise to be granted, now, the old medieval pretense that it is the queen of the sciences. It is not. But neither is it the servant of the sciences! It is the interlocutor of the sciences, as it has always been, and in that role it is both a human act and a necessity. But theology per se is not revelation. We humans have no such nice "out." We must still decide and accept our responsibility; theology will not and cannot relieve us of those aspects of our creaturehood, our humanity. To think otherwise is to seek to be other than creatures of *this* creation.

31. Quite aside from the specific mechanism for transmittal, the Christian doctrine of original sin generally posits that humans are repeatedly caught in the Pauline experience of doing what we know is less than we would wish to do (Rom. 7:13–24, RSV). We have a disability: it is as simple as that. While we can imagine, even image, a "better," we are far too often involved in a "worse." The condition is persistent, inescapable, seemingly just a part of our humanity. Thus we speak of it as *congenital* (although we sometimes forget that a dictionary tells us that the word *congenital* means "existing at or dating from birth but usually not hereditary"). If we mean that we can no longer remember a time when, for us, it was not a present, known reality, we may be right. If we wander off into speculations about how that experience might be so persistent, generation after generation, we had best acknowledge our wandering, and our speculation, as exactly that: the action of a quite curious creature, one which seeks satisfactory explanations.

32. 1 Cor. 13:12 in *The New English Bible* (New York: Oxford University Press & Cambridge University Press, 1961).

33. Let the reader take care: this sentence posits only that human decisions are fundamentally hypotheses and, therefore, tentative (e.g., they may be changed or "un-decided" at some posterior time). The challenge in the sentence, if such it is, may be the author's inclusion of theology in the general category of human decisions. Clearly, he considers it such. Readers must, therefore, decide whether or not they agree.

34. The author has no intention of positing that reason is some Platonic

archetype accessible to humankind. This sentence does not say that. Rather, it suggests that reason is a covariate to "our present knowledge of who we are and what we can, in fact, do." Moreover, the sentence posits only that such reason is "a maximum standard of human behavior." To this degree, the author is a rationalist. But he hopes that a reader will understand what he has written and not, as humans often do, read into this sentence things which are no more than the reader's own assumptions about reason, rationality, or those who try to be reasonable, even about theology.

35. This paragraph presumes that creatures in this creation know that they are limited, in one way or another, not only by virtue of their specific experiential repertoire but, unavoidably, by virtue of their creaturehood. It also presumes that, within or (even) on beyond that knowledge, creatures do tend to prefer a recognized and known "better." Thus, when situationally intractable conditions preclude such a better, creatures tend to look for and accept some recognizably close "next-better." It is in that specific situation of looking for a next-better that a simulation of the better can be recognized both for what it is and as an acceptable alternative. If and when the intractabilities of any given moment (such as the present) make the better impossible, a simulation *is* (then!) a clearly preferable option. The author's argument in this paragraph is no more than an application of those presumptions vis-a-vis creaturehood to the question of a religious educator's reaction to B. F. Skinner the educator.

36. The phrase, "read, mark, learn, and inwardly digest," comes from a Collect currently appointed for the Sunday closest to November 16, where it clearly refers to a Christian's approach to Scripture. The author's use of this particular phrase, in this place, does *not* suggest that he regards the works of B. F. Skinner as "scripture" for a contemporary Christian; rather, it is meant to suggest an approach to a text, any text, as a potential teacher of that which is worthy of serious attention. It is used, quite strictly, in an analogical sense. However, granted these caveats, the author does want to press the point that the analogy is worth human attention. See *The Book of Common Prayer* (1979), pp. 184, 236.

Appendix to Chapter 8

These materials on programmed instruction were prepared by myself for a regional meeting of the Religious Education Association, May 12–14, 1974, in Atlantic City, New Jersey. They include an outline of the conference, an outline of sessions on programmed instruction, and materials I presented:

I. "Voices from the Past: An Experiential Approach to Programmed Instruction"
II. "Perspectives on Programmed Instruction: An Even Dozen Perspectival Positions"
III. A Select Bibliography for Programmed Instruction

OUTLINE OF THE CONFERENCE

The theme was "Models of Teaching." The basic resource for the planning of the conference was the book *Models of Teaching*, by Bruce Joyce and Marsha Weil (Englewood Cliffs, N.J.: Prentice-Hall, 1972). Described in the book are some sixteen models or modes of teaching organized in four families. Eight of these models of teaching were presented at the conference, and each participant was encouraged to choose three (each from a different family) for the three major periods of time on Monday, May 13. These are the eight models of teaching organized by family, and the names of the conference leaders:

I. Information processing
   A. Cognitive-inductive-inquiry-concept attainment (Bruner, Taba, Kohlberg, etc.); Charles F. Melchert, conference leader

B. Developmental (Piaget, Kohlberg, etc.); Brother John F. Emling, leader

II. Social interaction

A. Laboratory method (NTL—Benne, et al.); Portia Bowers, leader

B. Social science (Dewey, Lee, etc.); James Michael Lee, leader

III. Personal sources

A. Nondirective, student-centered (Carl Rogers, etc.); Jay Pichenor, leader

B. Confluent-affective-values (George Brown, William Cutter, etc.); Bert S. Gerard, Audrey Miller, leaders

C. Synectics-transactional awareness (William Gordon); J. Allyn Bradford, leader

IV. Behavior modification: programmed instruction (B. F. Skinner); John Peatling, leader

OUTLINE OF SESSIONS ON PROGRAMMED INSTRUCTION

I. Initial gathering of the group

II. Introduction to the subject

III. Reading of "Voices from the Past: An Experiential Approach to Programmed Instruction"

IV. Group discussion

A. Questions posed by individualized instruction

B. Programmed instruction as a model of teaching

V. Reading of "Perspectives on Programmed Instruction: An Even Dozen Perspectival Positions"

VI. Group discussion

A. Considered responses to the teaching model

B. Identification of possibilities: long/short range

C. Presently discernible problems

D. Theoretical/practical implications of the model

VII. Leader's concluding remarks on the programmed instruction model of teaching and the practice of religious education

VOICES FROM THE PAST: AN EXPERIENTIAL APPROACH TO PROGRAMMED INSTRUCTION

In this material, which is presented to participants as a preliminary, individual experience of the teaching method of Progammed Instruction, there are four parts:

I. An overview of programmed instruction (what to expect)
II. An experience of programmed instruction (what it is like)
 A. A program, "What Programming Is All About"
 B. A set of three questions to consider
III. A listing of problems discerned as a result of experimentation
IV. A presentation of research data resulting from experimentation

I. A Voice from the Past: What to Expect from Programmed Instruction

	Programmed instruction will NOT . . .	*BUT*		*Programmed instruction WILL . . .*
(1)	Take the place of group discussion, or the life together the members of a group may develop	*but*	(1)	Give background *facts* that can be a contribution to a group discussion.
(2)	Take the place of the teacher in the classroom	*but*	(2)	Give the teacher in the classroom *more* time for class discussion and other creative activities.
(3)	Solve *all* of a teacher's problems	*but*	(3)	Solve *some* of a teacher's problems and, like any other teaching method, create some other problems for a teacher.
(4)	Deal exhaustively with a particular subject, so that there is nothing else to do in the classroom	*but*	(4)	Provide a common, working base of information upon which students and teacher can build classroom work.
(5)	Hold the interest of every student	*but*	(5)	Interest many but not all students, just like any piece of educational material.

(6)	Provide a student with a thrilling literary document	*but*	(6)	Supply information in a clear, orderly, and logical fashion to a student.
(7)	Let a student daydream as his eyes wander from page to page	*but*	(7)	Require a student to respond definitely to each of many steps along the way.
(8)	Allow a student to make numerous mistakes as he learns new material	*but*	(8)	Help a student to come up with a correct response and be aware of mistakes as they are made.
(9)	Make a student confused or discouraged because a class goes too fast or slow	*but*	(9)	Allow a student to progress toward the program goal at his own speed.
(10)	Inspire a student with a general sense of uplift	*but*	(10)	Present either facts or a point of view to a student and, so, lead him to consider new ideas and gain new knowledge.

(Based on "What about Programmed Instruction?" dated ERT-1-26-'65.)

II. An Experience of Programmed Instruction
   A. A Sample: What Programming Is All About
   (by Elizabeth Rooney and Harold Bassage)

The sample program's frames:	Intended responses:
1. This is a sample of programmed instruction. It's called a *program*, for short. A program like this one consists of a numbered series of instructional fragments called *frames*.	
2. A program helps you learn by making you respond to its teaching. In a program like this one you respond by filling in blanks. When you come to a blank in this program, please __________ it in.	fill

3. After you fill in a blank, check your response against the one printed at the right side of the paragraph in each frame. A program teaches by telling you immediately whether your answer is ________ or wrong.	right
4. To avoid seeing the correct, printed *response*, always use a piece of paper or cardboard to cover the right side of the frame you are reading, until after you have written your own ________.	response (or equivalent)
5. Now you know how to work this thing. The next question is: Why is the church interested in p________ i________?	(p)rogrammed (i)nstruction
6. The church is in the *teaching* business. Programmed instruction is a new method of ________.	teaching
7. The church (any denomination) has a large investment in education. Personnel, materials, building space, money—all are used to ________ the Christian faith.	teach
8. Consequently, leaders in Christian education are interested in all methods that will make Christian ________ more effective.	education
9. An effective program is so written that students will ________ what the program is designed to ________.	learn teach
10. Programmed instruction (sometimes called programmed *learning*) makes use of psychologists' discoveries about several principles of ________.	learning

11.	The guidelines for creating programmed instruction are four experimentally derived principles of __________.	learning
12.	The first principle of learning used in programmed instruction is the principle of *small steps*. A program presents the material to be learned in __________ amounts.	small
13.	To prevent discouragement and to ensure thorough learning, a program introduces new material in __________ steps.	small
14.	When material in a program is carefully organized, slow learners are helped by the principle of __________ __________.	small steps
15.	A second characteristic of programmed instruction is based on the principle of *active responding*. This principle is in line with the old adage that we learn by __________.	doing (or equivalent)
16.	In doing this program, you are asked to write in your responses so that your learning will be increased by your active __________ing.	respond(ing)
17.	A student in a class may respond only occasionally; a student taking a program responds __________.	frequently (or equivalent)
18.	Psychologists believe that in the process of learning, the more a student responds, the more he __________.	learns
19.	A student may or may not learn from a teacher who calls for no response from him. He is more likely to learn when he is required to __________ actively.	respond

20.	Two characteristics of programmed instruction are: a) Presenting material in ________ ________ b) Making students ________ actively.	small steps respond
21.	A third characteristic of programmed instruction is based on the principle of *immediate reinforcement*, or feed-back. The correct response printed at the right side of each frame tells you immediately whether your response is ________ or wrong.	right
22.	Experiments indicate that people learn faster when they find out ________ whether or not they are moving toward the teacher's goal.	immediately (or equivalent)
23.	The fewer mistakes people make, the faster they ________.	learn
24.	By immediate reinforcement (or feedback) a student learns at once when he makes a mistake; this helps him avoid ________ the same mistake in successive frames.	repeating (or equivalent)
25.	When a student completes a frame successfully, he is "rewarded" by being shown immediately that the response he made was ________.	correct (right)
26.	Immediate reinforcement prevents repeated ________ and rewards ________ responses.	mistakes correct (or right)
27.	Reducing mistakes and rewarding achievements will (increase *or* decrease) learning. (Write your response) ________.	increase
28.	Reinforcement is more effective when it is ________ than when it is provided later.	immediate

29. The learning process is improved when __________ is immediate.	reinforcement
30. The third characteristic of programmed instruction, then, is __________ __________.	immediate reinforcement (prompt feedback)
31. Psychologists have found three prerequisites for learning. They are the principles of: a) __________ steps, b) Active __________, c) __________ reinforcement.	 Small (steps) (Active) responding Immediate (reinforcement)
32. Students' progress is increased when they learn by: a) Small __________, b) __________ responding, c) Immediate __________.	 (Small) steps Active (responding) (Immediate) reinforcement
33. Programmed instruction is also guided by the principle of self-pacing. Because each student does a program by himself, he can spend as much time on it as he needs to, working at his own __________.	speed
34. When students work at their own rates of speed, fast learners may go as __________ as they like and slow learners may go as __________ as they like.	fast slowly (or equivalent)
35. Self-pacing keeps __________ learners from getting bored and keeps __________ learners from having to move ahead without enough time to do their work thoroughly.	fast slow
36. Programmed instruction flexibly meets the needs of students who work at different speeds because it is __________-pacing.	self(-pacing)
37. The fourth characteristic of programmed instruction is based on the principle of __________-__________.	self-pacing.

38. In a well-designed program, the student: a) Learns in ________ ________, b) ________ actively and frequently, c) Receives immediate ________, d) Sets his own rate of ________.	 small steps Responds reinforcement (feedback) speed
39. So, a program is a device that is designed to ________.	teach
40. Programs are designed to help students ________ quickly and effectively.	learn
41. Programmed learning (or instruction) makes use of four tested principles of ________.	learning
42. These four principles of learning are the principles of: a) ________ ________; b) Active ________; c) Immediate ________; d) Self-________.	 Small steps (Active) responding (Immediate) reinforcement (Self-)pacing
43. To the extent that these principles are valid and that a given program conforms to them, programmed instruction can ________.	teach
44. Does programmed instruction have any limitations? (Yes/No) ________	Yes
45. Because programmed instruction calls for specific responses, it is most suitable for subjects in which right and ________ answers can be stated precisely.	wrong
46. A program can teach facts, data, specifics; it is (more/less) adaptable to teaching subjects in which there are no unquestionably right answers. (Please write your response.) ________	less (not yet, anyhow)

47.	The content of a program like this one cannot be varied to suit the needs and interests of ________ students.	different (individual) (or equivalent)
48.	Programs can teach only those students who are willing to do the program. This kind of program is not very useful if a student merely reads it quickly; it is effective only when a student actively makes the ________ that are called for in the program.	responses
49.	Programmers hope their programs will be so irresistible that students will want to do them thoroughly. You (can/cannot) be sure that a student will want to do a program thoroughly. (Please write your response.) ________	cannot
50.	In fact, because of the problem of monotony, students may be unwilling to complete a program when it seems ________ to them.	boring (or equivalent)
51.	A program can present many different opinions, and it can even evaluate them. But a program cannot discuss something with a ________.	student
52.	After a group of students learn some facts from a program, they and their teacher (by engaging in discussion) can relate those ________ to the personal concerns of the group.	facts
53.	Because a teacher can accomplish many things that a program cannot, programmed instruction will never replace ________.	teachers
54.	Despite its limitations, programmed instruction can be valuable for both ________ and ________.	students (and) teachers (either order will do)

55. You have just finished an introductory program on programmed instruction that was originally prepared in 1964 by Mrs. Elizabeth Rooney and by Dr. Harold Bassage, Ph.D. Most of what they had to say, then, still seems to be true. The vantage point of the present might qualify a few statements in their program, but the program would probably read remarkably like what you have just finished if it were to be written today. (No response required)

B. A Set of Three Questions to Consider

Why do you think a new program would be so similar to this one? (Use the space below to record your thoughts, if you wish.)

How do you think programmed instruction may, eventually, fit into the future shape of religious education? (Use the space below to record your thoughts, if you wish.)

What similarities can you detect between programmed instruction and what is known as behavior modification? (Use the space below to record your thoughts, if you wish.)

III. A Voice from the Past: Problems Discerned vis-a-vis Programmed Instruction

Initial reservations about the process of programming have tended to fade as the members of the Research Team[1] became familiar with this technology of programmed instruction. However, at this point (May, 1964) it is possible to enumerate several real and several potential problems in the use of programmed instruction for the Christian education of children, youth, and adults in the Episcopal church. The problems that can be discerned:

1. *Cost.* To develop an item of programmed instruction is a costly procedure, since it requires time, personnel, and money. It will be necessary to consider whether the cost of programming can be amortized over a sufficiently long period to make it the most appropriate procedure in any given instance.
2. *The form of programming to be used.* It is possible that the near-classic linear programs of B. F. Skinner may not be the most appropriate form of programming for Christian education. If this should prove to be so, then more novel forms, more eclectic approaches to programming would need to be tried, tested, and evaluated by qualified persons in the field of research.
3. *The statement of objectives.* Since programmed instruction calls for the statement of the objectives of a given program in the form of observable behaviors, programming will necessitate a continuing dialogue with the overall purpose of Christian education. This dialogue should lead to a clarification of the meaning of the purpose of Christian education and, as well, to a delimitation of the possible objectives of a program.
4. *The need for social responsibility.* Since the technology of programmed instruction is a powerful tool for the shaping of behavior, there will need to be a continuing concern for the exercise of social responsibility by Christian educators. This concern will be served by the dialogue between objectives, which has been referred to above (in item 3).
5. *Acceptance of programming.* Since the success of a program is probably directly related to the degree of acceptance of the program and its inherent demands by the user, an educational effort should precede the introduction of programmed instruction into a set of curriculum materials in Christian education.
6. *Motivation.* Since motivation seems closely related to the degree of acceptance with which a program is met, some way of motivating the user of a program may need to be built into the plan of use of items of programmed instruction. Perhaps making completion of a program prerequisite to some further step in the process of Christian education would be a way of making the user's motivation sufficiently high to engage in the continuing interaction with a program that is so much a part of this technology.
7. *Restriction of programmed instruction.* Since it seems quite evident from the use of programmed instruction in other disciplines that programming can present factual material effectively and efficiently, there may be a tendency to limit programming in Christian education to just the presentation of factual materials. While this use is certainly valuable and valid, any tendency to restrict programming so sharply should be avoided. Instead of restriction, various other ways of using programmed instruction at all levels of Christian education should be investigated, before it is assumed that programming per se can make no other contribution to Christian education than the presentation of factual materials.
8. *The role of the teacher.* The use of programmed instruction in Christian education would seem to call for a reexamination of the role of the teacher.

This technology may offer a standardized mode of presentation for factual material. If so, it may eliminate much of the pressure on teachers to be, themselves, the presenters of such (factual) material. If this were to happen, then the role of the teacher might well become, of necessity, much more that of a relater-to-life, instead of a presenter-of-information. To the degree that this (possible) change in role runs counter to the present expectations of teachers, programmed instruction may well be understood as a threat to the teacher's role in the classroom. Conversely, to the degree that teachers understand their role to be that of relaters-to-life, programmed instruction will be understood as a potentially valuable ally.

9. *Preservation of programming capability.* While the Research Team's work so far can be adequately justified as insurance (i.e., an attempt to ensure an experience-informed decision vis-a-vis programmed instruction and the place it might play in this department's work), such a view is essentially negative. That is, it does not come to terms with the positive potential within the department that now (in May of 1964) exists as a result of the work of the Research Team: there are three program writers on the staff who have experience in writing, one project manager, and two contract programmers who are related to this department. This potential to produce a program or to field test programs now exists. However, unless this skill and knowledge is used in other projects, the present capability of this department to produce items of programmed instruction may well fade away, due to the extinguishing action of a lack of use of skills once gained, and the powerful force of simply forgetting. This problem is worth serious consideration, since the Research Team can point to the past eighteen months as the cost (e.g., in time, money, and personnel) of tooling up to produce programmed instruction items from within this department.

Reference

John H. Peatling, *A Progress Report on an Experimental Project on the Application of Programmed Instruction to Religious Education* (New York: Department of Christian Education, the Episcopal church, May 1964), 8 pp., dittoed. Esp. pp. 5–6.

Note

The members of the Research Team of the Department of Christian Education of the Episcopal church during the lifetime of the experimental project on the application of programmed instruction to religious education (i.e., 1963–1964) were as follows: Miss Elinor Eccles, then editor of junior materials (PI-6, Jesus and the Pharisees); Mrs. Elizabeth Rooney, program writer under contract (PI-8, David); Miss Deborah Vaill, then editor of preschool and kindergarten materials (PI-10, How God Acts); Dr. Harold Bassage, Ph.D., then editor of adult materials (PI-GA, The Witnessing Community); The Rev. William S. Brown, program writer under contract (PI-SA, Learning to Work in Groups); The Rev. John H. Peatling, then associate secretary, curriculum development (project manager); Mr. John L. Coffey, the project engineer (Psychological Sciences Group, Battelle Memorial Institute, Columbus, Ohio) assigned under contract to the Research Team.

Historical Note May 7, 1974

Two of the five experimental programs written during the lifetime of the Research Team were, eventually, published by the Seabury Press as pupil materials to accompany courses in the Seabury Series of Christian education materials. These two programs were the eighth grade experimental program on the story of David (PI-8, David) and the tenth grade experimental program on the so-called dramatic analogy of the Bible (P-10, How God Acts). The other three experimental programs were written and used solely in the research on the possible application of programmed instruction to religious education.

—John H. Peatling, Ph.D.

IV. Statistical Results of an Experimental Set of Five Programs

Grade-level or age-level:	Program titles:	N: (E/C)	t:	P:	Omega²:
Sixth grade	*PI-6, Jesus and the Pharisees*	15	7.88177	.001	0.67077
Eighth grade	*PI-8, David*	11	6.63707	.001	0.66180
Tenth grade	*PI-10, How God Acts*	06	6.15088	.001	0.75426
General adult (adult laity)	*PI-GA, The Witnessing Community* (Chapters 3 through 7)	08	5.98285	.001	0.68500
Special adult (clergy and lay DCEs in training laboratory)	*PI-SA, Learning to Work in Groups:*				
	a) Criterion Test, Part 1 (42-question cognitive test)	11/13	3.15037	.005	0.27106
	b) Criterion Test, Part 2 (36-keyword vocabulary test)	11/12	4.19148	.001	0.41872

References

William L. Hays, *Statistics for Psychologists* (New York: Holt, Rinehart and Winston, 1963).

a) P. 674, table 2, "Upper Percentage Points of the *t* Distribution."

b) Pp. 323–329, re. the statistic omega squared (proportion of variance in Y accounted for by X)

John H. Peatling, *A Report on the Field Testing of Five Items of Programmed Instruction in an Experimental Project on the Application of Programmed Instruction to Religious Education* (Department of Christian Education, the Episcopal church, December 2, 1964), 24 pp., dittoed.

(E/C) = No. in experimental group (programmed)/No. in control group (prose)
N.B.: For programs PI-6, PI-8, PI-10, and PI-GA, the statistic *t* figured on differences observed between pretest and posttest scores for persons exposed to an experimental program.

PERSPECTIVES ON PROGRAMMED INSTRUCTION: An Even Dozen Perspectival Positions

The following are the articles or books from which the twelve perspectives come, and the authors:

1. "Shaping Behavioral Change" (Dr. John Hough)
2. "Shaping Behavioral Change" (Dr. John Hough)
3. *Science of Education and the Psychology of the Child* (Jean Piaget)
4. *Science of Education and the Psychology of the Child* (Jean Piaget)
5. "The Nature, Purposes, and General Methods of Measurements of Educational Products" (E. L. Thorndike)
6. *Experience and Education* (John Dewey)
7. *Experience and Education* (John Dewey)
8. *Walden Two* (B. F. Skinner)
9. *Science and Human Behavior* (B. F. Skinner)
10. "The Teacher's Vocation" (Evelyn Underhill)
11. *The Psychology of Learning Applied to Teaching* (B. R. Bugelski)
12. *Grooks*, *Grooks 4*, and *Grooks 5* (Piet Hein)

Whatever order one may choose for the reading of these perspectival positions, the reason for them remains one. That reason is a full, multidimensional view of the subject of programmed instruction as a model of teaching. Such a view partakes of something of the nature of a gestalt figure-ground phenomenon. The reader brings his experience and her knowledge to the exercise: these dozen positions suggest ways to discern order and some pattern in the teaching method, but individuals must "see" that order or pattern for themselves. No one can do it for another person.

First Perspective on Programmed Instruction

Unless programmed instruction can teach basic knowledge and skill in a context of understanding which is useful to students as they strive to discover themselves and personal meanings in these understandings, it will fail to be a significant educational breakthrough. It will simply prove to be another means, and a good one, of perhaps more efficiently and effectively doing the same old thing we have been doing in secular education and religious education for many years. Unless instructional programs can be written so as to change behavior or produce the structure of skill and understanding for significant behavioral change, this new method will never really become the important innovation that we have talked about.

Fortunately, there is evidence that programmed instruction can be used effectively to change human behavior. That in fact it has not been done in many places, in no way negates this principle. Knowledge affects behavior only when it exists in a context of understanding and personal meaning. Instructional programs can be written to teach understandings and basic generalizable concepts. Human teachers working with students who are armed with such knowledge, can help these students to find personal meaning in such knowledge. It should be obvious, therefore, that programmed instruction is not designed to do away with teachers; rather, in fact, if adequately used, it is designed to free teachers from much of the information giving and skill building that they have had to use most of their time for in the past. This frees them for encounter with students in which students may find personal meaning from what they are learning.

. . . the extensive use of programmed instruction in religious education is not something which is going to come overnight. But I can visualize—if you will allow me to dream for a moment—a day when experts in the field of Christian education will be writing instructional programs which, in addition to teaching the facts and skills of our Christian heritage, will weave these facts and skills into a meaningful fabric of conceptual understanding. I can picture students who, after learning these facts and skills in a context of understanding, will work with church school teachers and clergymen, whose primary responsibility will now become that of helping students to find personal meaning in these new understandings. It is in such an educational program that significant behavioral changes, I believe, may be effective. Programed instruction will have a role to play in this important work, but before it can play this role, much needs to be learned about how to program for Christian behavior.

Dr. John Hough, "Shaping Behavioral Change," in *The Consultation on Programmed Instruction (A Report)* (New York: Commission on General Christian Education, National Council of Churches of Christ, 1965), pp. 7–8. (Consultation held January 13–17, 1964, in Atlantic City, New Jersey, at the Deauville Hotel.)

Second Perspective on Programmed Instruction

"But *can* programmed instruction be of use to Christian educators whose job differs so significantly from that of the public school teacher or the industrial trainer?" This is a question which has, with varying degrees of seriousness, been asked by many religious educators in the last couple of years. . . . Judging from the interest in programmed instruction which is beginning to develop in various church circles, it would seem that at least some religious educators have already answered this question (tentatively at least) in the affirmative. These churchmen are now proceeding with experimentation and study to find answers to the next question, "How *shall* we use programmed instruction in Christian education?"

I should like to suggest that although the second question concerning *how* to use programmed instruction may, in fact, follow logically from the first (i.e., "Should it be used at all?"), *neither* question holds a position of primary importance. The more relevant first question is: "What specific behaviors do we want to teach as a result of Christian education?"

By this (question of specific behaviors) I do *not* mean vague, general statements of objectives that are difficult, if not impossible, to measure. Nor do I mean isolated facts or abstract understanding which, except in the minds of people who write programs, are unrelated to Christian living. What I *am* referring to, rather, are *precise* statements of Christian behavior which will bring into focus the *understandings and skills and attitudes* which are the *necessary* basis for such Christian living.

When, and *only* when, we have done this, will the question of how to use programmed instruction be a really relevant one.

Hough, "Shaping Behavioral Change," p. 7.

Third Perspective on Programmed Instruction

In more or less close connection with the Pavlovian school of Soviet reflexology . . . , American psychology has evolved a certain number of theories of learning based on the stimulus-response view (or S-R). First Hull then Tolman developed detailed theories depending upon the effects of habit formation, then of "hierarchies of habits," the use of indices of significance, etc. . . .

The most recent of the great American learning theorists, Skinner, the author of some remarkable experiments with pigeons . . . adopted a more resolutely positive attitude. Convinced of the inaccessible nature of the intermediate variables and of the excessively rudimentary state of our neurological knowledge, he decided to confine his attention to stimuli, or *inputs*, that could be varied at will and to observable responses, or *outputs*, and then to take account only of the direct relationships between them, ignoring the internal connections. This "empty box" conception of the organism . . . thus deliberately thumbs its nose at all kinds of mental life, human or animal, and confines itself solely to behavior in its most material aspects, ignoring any possible search for explanations in order to concentrate exclusively on the broad laws revealed by scrupulously detailed experimentation.

. . . since the empty-box conception of the organism renders so many preliminary considerations of the internal factors of human learning unnecessary, it was sufficient to be familiar with the general laws of learning and with the subject matter of the branches of knowledge to be taught, in order to construct programs at least equal in content to the body of knowledge commonly required.

The experiment was tried and proved a total success. And it goes without saying, if we confine ourselves to the usual methods of teaching by means of verbal transmission and receptive processes, that it could not fail to succeed. The sentimental and the natural worriers have been saddened by the fact that schoolmasters can be replaced by machines. In my view, on the other hand, these machines have performed at least one great service for us, which is to demonstrate beyond all possible doubt the mechanical character of the schoolmaster's function as it is conceived by traditional teaching methods: if the ideal of that method is merely to elicit correct repetition of what has been correctly transmitted, then it goes without saying that a machine can fulfill those conditions correctly.

Jean Piaget, *Science of Education and the Psychology of the Child* (New York: Viking Press, 1969, 1970), pp. 75–77.

Fourth Perspective on Programmed Instruction

It has also been objected that the machine eliminates all affective factors, but this is not true, and Skinner justly claims that it is often possible to achieve a greater intensity of "motivation" (needs and interests) with machines than is found in many traditional "lessons." The question is, in fact, to establish whether the teacher's affectivity always performs a desirable function. Claparede had already expressed the opinion, in his day, that a sufficient period in a teacher's training should always be given over to practice in animal training, since when that training fails the experimenter is bound to accept that it is his own fault, whereas in the education of children failures are always attributed to the pupil. And in this respect, it should be noted, Skinner's machines provide evidence of good psychology in that they make use exclusively of positive reinforcements and dispense totally with negative sanctions or punishments.

As for the intrinsic value of such a teaching method, that naturally depends upon the aims that are assigned to it in any particular field. In cases where it is a matter of acquiring a set body of learning... the machine does seem to be accepted as of undeniable service.... In cases where the ideal is to reinvent a sequence of reasoning, however, ... though the machine does not exclude either comprehension or reasoning itself on the student's part, it does channel them in an unfortunate way and excludes the possibility of initiative....

Generally speaking, since every discipline must include a certain body of acquired facts as well as the possibility of giving rise to numerous research activities and activities of rediscovery, it is possible to envisage a balance being struck, varying from subject to subject, between the different parts to be played by memorizing and free activity. In which case, it is possible that the use of teaching machines will save time that would have been needlessly wasted by more traditional methods and therefore augment the number of hours available for active work.

... if the periods of active work include team work, with all such work entails in the way of mutual incentives and checks, while the machine presupposes an essentially individualized kind of work, then this balance would at the same time be realizing yet another necessary kind of balance: that between the collective and individual aspects of intellectual effort, both so essential to a harmonious school life.

... this is a question, like all pedagogical questions, that cannot be resolved by any amount of abstract or notional discussion, but solely by accumulating the requisite amount of facts and controlled tests.

Piaget, *Science of Education and the Psychology of the Child,* pp. 77–79.

Fifth Perspective on Programmed Instruction

Whatever exists at all exists in some amount. To know it thoroughly involves knowing its quantity as well as its quality. Education is concerned with changes in human beings; a change is a difference between two conditions; each of these conditions is known to us only by the products produced by it—things made, words spoken, acts performed, and the like. To measure any of these products means to define its amount in some way so that competent persons will know how large it is, better than they would without measurement. To measure a product well means so to define its amount that competent persons will know how large it is, with some precision, and that this may be conveniently recorded and used. This is the general *Credo* of those who, in the last decade, have been busy trying to extend and improve measurements of educational products. . . .

The purpose of measurements of educational products is in general to provide somebody with the knowledge that he needs of the amount of some thing, difference or relation. The "somebody" may be a scientific worker, a superintendent of schools, a teacher, a parent or a pupil. He may need a very precise or only an approximate measure, according to the magnitude of the difference which he has to determine. He may need it for guidance in many different sorts of decisions and actions. . . .

There is, however, a real danger in sacrificing soundness and principle and precision of result to the demand that we measure matters of importance and measure them without requiring elaborate technique or much time of the measurer. The danger is that the attention of investigators will be distracted from the problems of pure measurement for measurement's sake, which are a chief source of progress in measuring anything. Perhaps not even one person in a million need feel this passion, but for that one to cherish it and serve it is far more important than for him to devise a test which thousands of teachers will employ. . . .

An intelligent student of education could probably in a single day note a score of sure ways of improving the scales and tests which we now use. That is really child's play. The hard thing is the actual expert work of remedying the imperfection, for this involves hundreds of hours of detailed expert planning, experimenting and computing.

Edward L. Thorndike, "The Nature, Purposes, and General Methods of Measurements of Educational Products," in *The Measurement of Educational Products*, 17th yearbook of the National Society for the Study of Education, part 2 (Bloomington, Ill.: Public School Publishing Company, 1918). In Geraldine M. Joncich, ed., *Psychology and the Science of Education* (New York: Bureau of Publications, Columbia University, 1962).

Sixth Perspective on Programmed Instruction

A genuine community life has its ground in this natural sociability. But community life does not organize itself in an enduring way purely spontaneously. It requires thought and planning ahead. The educator is responsible for a knowledge of individuals and for a knowledge of subject-matter that will enable activities to be selected which lend themselves to social organization, and organization in which all individuals have an opportunity to contribute something, and in which the activities in which all participate are the chief carrier of control.

The principle that development of experience comes about through interaction means that education is essentially a social process. This quality is realized in the degree in which individuals form a community group. It is absurd to exclude the teacher from membership in the group. . . . That children are individuals whose freedom should be respected while the more mature persons should have no freedom as an individual is an idea too absurd to require refutation. . . .

The only freedom that is of enduring importance is freedom of intelligence, that is to say, freedom of observation and of judgment exercised in behalf of purposes that are intrinsically worth while. The commonest mistake made about freedom is, I think, to identify it with freedom of movement, or with the external or physical side of activity. . . . For freedom from restriction, the negative side, is to be prized only as a means to a freedom which is power: power to frame purposes, to judge wisely, to evaluate desires by the consequences which will result from acting upon them; power to select and order means to carry chosen ends into operation.

The ideal aim of education is creation of power of self-control. . . . Impulses and desires that are not ordered by intelligence are under the control of accidental circumstances. It may be a loss rather than a gain to escape from the control of another person only to find one's conduct dictated by immediate whim and caprice; that is, at the mercy of impulses into whose formation intelligent judgment has not entered. A person whose conduct is controlled in this way has at most only the illusion of freedom. Actually he is directed by forces over which he has no command.

The educator by the very nature of his work is obliged to see his present work in terms of what it accomplishes, or fails to accomplish, for a future whose objects are linked with those of the present. . . . the sound principle that the objectives of learning are in the future and its immediate materials are in present experience can be carried into effect only in the degree that present experience is stretched, as it were, backward. It can extend into the future only as it is also enlarged to take in the past. . . . The nature of the issues cannot be understood save as we know how they came about.

John Dewey, *Experience and Education* (New York: Collier Books, 1938, 1963), pp. 56, 58, 61, 64–65, 76–77.

Seventh Perspective on Programmed Instruction

Failure to give constant attention to development of the intellectual content of experiences and to obtain ever-increasing organization of facts and ideas may in the end merely strengthen the tendency toward a reactionary return to intellectual and moral authoritarianism. The present is not the time nor place for a disquisition upon scientific method. But certain features of it are so closely connected with any educational scheme based upon experience that they should be noted.

In the first place, the experimental method of science attaches more importance, not less, to ideas as ideas than do other methods. There is no such thing as experiment in the scientific sense unless action is directed by some leading idea. . . .

In the second place, ideas or hypotheses are tested by the consequences which they produce when they are acted upon. This fact means that the consequences of action must be carefully and discriminatingly observed. Activity that is not checked by observation of what follows from it may be temporarily enjoyed. But intellectually it leads nowhere. . . .

In the third place, the method of intelligence manifested in the experimental method demands keeping track of ideas, activities, and observed consequences. Keeping track is a matter of reflective review and summarizing, in which there is both discrimination and record of the significant features of a developing experience. To reflect is to look back over what has been done so as to extract the net meanings which are the capital stock for intelligent dealing with further experiences. It is the heart of intellectual organization and of the disciplined mind.

. . . I have taken for granted the soundness of the principle that education in order to accomplish its ends both for the individual learner and for society must be based upon experience—which is always the actual life-experience of some individual. . . . The greatest danger that attends its future is, I believe, the idea that it is an easy way to follow, so easy that its course may be improvised, if not in an impromptu fashion, at least almost from day to day or from week to week.

I do not wish to close, however, without recording my firm belief that the fundamental issue is not of new versus old education nor of progressive against traditional education but a question of what anything whatever must be to be worthy of the name *education*. . . . The basic question concerns the nature of education with no qualifying adjectives prefixed. What we want and need is education pure and simple, and we shall make surer and faster progress when we devote ourselves to finding out just what education is and what conditions have to be satisfied in order that education may be a reality and not a name or a slogan.

Dewey, *Experience and Education*, pp. 86–87, 89–90, 90–91.

Eighth Perspective on Programmed Instruction

As a teacher I had given little thought to the "philosophy of education." Teaching was a job to be done without benefit of perspective or program. I knew, as all teachers know, that education was inadequately supported. That was perhaps not its own fault, but its outmoded techniques certainly were. Furthermore, education was completely bewildered as to its place in the world of the future. It could inspire no sense of belonging to a movement, no *esprit de corps*. I could get no satisfaction from atavistic or nostalgic attempts to reconstruct a happier era, and so I contented myself with doing the day's work.

Now, fresh from my experience at Walden Two, I saw that this could not go on. But I also saw that educators themselves could not save the situation. The causes were too deep, too remote. They involved the whole structure of society. What was needed was a new conception of man, compatible with our scientific knowledge, which would lead to a philosophy of education bearing some relation to educational practices. But to achieve this, education would have to abandon the technical limitations which it had imposed upon itself and step forth into a broader sphere of human engineering. Nothing short of the complete revision of a culture would suffice.

B. F. Skinner, "Reflections of Professor Burris after Leaving Walden Two: Seated on a Park Bench," in *Walden Two* (New York: Macmillan Company, 1948), p. 312.

The president of my university had been in the city, making his most recent version of a standard speech. The article was rewritten from a press release and badly handled, but it would have been difficult to do serious damage to so distinguished an assemblage of cliches. The theme was the "Task of Education in the Postwar World," and phrases like "encouraging individual initiative," "ministering to the whole man," "stimulating a spirit of inquiry," "fostering an open mind," and "restoring the dignity of the human soul," were packed tightly together. As usual, I was not sure what any of these utterances meant, though I experienced a nebulous sense of agreement. Insofar as they had meaning at all, they seemed to refer to worth-while goals. But on one point my reaction was definite: it was obvious that no one, least of all the speaker, had any notion of how to set to work to attain them.

Skinner, "Reflections of Professor Burris after Leaving Walden Two: Reactions to a Newspaper's Headline, 'Dignity of Man Baccalaureate Address Theme," in *Walden Two*, pp. 311–312.

Ninth Perspective on Programmed Instruction

The application of science to human behavior is not so simple as it seems. Most of those who advocate it are simply looking for "the facts." To them science is little more than careful observation. They want to evaluate human behavior as it really is rather than as it appears to be through ignorance or prejudice, and then to make effective decisions and move on rapidly to a happier world. But the way in which science has been applied in other fields shows that something more is involved. Science is not concerned just with "getting the facts," after which one may act with greater wisdom in an unscientific fashion. Science supplies its own wisdom. It leads to a new conception of a subject matter, a new way of thinking about that part of the world to which it has addressed itself. If we are to enjoy the advantages of science in the field of human affairs, we must be prepared to adopt the working model of behavior to which a science will inevitably lead.

Science is first of all a set of attitudes. It is a disposition to deal with the facts rather than what someone has said about them. . . .

Science is a willingness to accept facts even when they are opposed to wishes. . . . The opposite of wishful thinking is intellectual honesty—an extremely important possession of the successful scientist. . . . It is characteristic of science that any lack of honesty quickly brings disaster. . . . The same practical consequences have created the scientific atmosphere in which statements are constantly submitted to check, where nothing is put above a precise description of the facts, and where facts are accepted no matter how distasteful their momentary consequences.

Scientists have also discovered the value of remaining without an answer until a satisfactory one can be found. . . . It takes considerable training to avoid premature conclusions, to refrain from making statements on insufficient evidence, and to avoid explanations which are pure invention.

Science is . . . (also) a search for order, for uniformities, for lawful relations among events in nature. It begins, as we all begin, by observing single episodes, but it quickly passes on to the general rule, to scientific law. . . . In a later stage science advances from the collection of rules or laws to larger systematic arrangements. . . . It sets up a "model" of its subject matter, which helps to generate new rules very much as the rules themselves generate new practices in dealing with single cases.

The scientific "system," like the law, is designed to enable us to handle a subject matter more efficiently. . . . When we have discovered the laws which govern a part of the world about us, and when we have organized these laws into a system, we are then ready to deal effectively with that part of the world.

B. F. Skinner, *Science and Human Behavior* (New York: Free Press, 1953), pp. 6, 12–14.

Tenth Perspective on Programmed Instruction

If, then, from one point of view, your work means taking your place by the side of the shepherd and sharing as nearly as you can his outlook on the sheep; from another, it means taking your place by the side of each of those different sheep, trying to share and understand their limited outlook, and thus humbly learning the way in which you can help them best. While on the one hand you want to lead them deeper and deeper into the wonderful joy and interestingness of religion, make their lives as full and rich as ever you can; on the other hand you have got to teach and encourage them to find spiritual food where they are—in the paths of common life, where most of their time is going to be spent. I think it is because young people are not taught more to find God here, recognize Him in ordinary life, that many fail to find Him at all. Therefore you must teach your little flock to find the food of their souls as they go along the highroad. You must first find it there yourself, and then teach them to take it. If you ever let yourself think that the religious turnips and things which you chop up and administer in the Sunday school or class are the only spiritual food of the flock, and God only feeds them in that particular way; then, under the exacting and largely irreligious conditions of modern life, you are going to make a very bad job of their training and nourishment, and must not be surprised if a lot of them wander away and look elsewhere for food. They ought to learn from you to get as much of the heavenly food of Eternal Life from nibbling the ordinary grass on the edge of the road, as they do from the special feeding of the Church. You want them to find there the savor and presence of God; because you know as a matter of fact that He is in those daily events, joys and pains of their lives. Therefore you should make it your business to turn those ordinary things of life into spiritual food for the souls you teach.

Most of the children who are committed to you will grow up to busy, driven lives. . . . Hence it is very important to make them realize now that the Christian communion with God takes many different forms; there is no outward act, no kind of work, no drudgery, joy, suffering, which cannot be turned into a means of intercourse, a virtual prayer, provided it is accepted from the hand of God in a spirit of love; that He can and will come to them incessantly in the tram and the office, the shop, the factory, the home; perpetually offering something which, faithfully accepted, will become real food for their souls. It is your greatest privilege to teach your children to recognize this.

Evelyn Underhill, "The Teacher's Vocation: An Address to Teachers of Religion," in Lucy Menzies, ed., *Collected Papers of Evelyn Underhill* (London: Longmans, Green and Co., 1946), pp. 169–170. (An address originally given in 1927.)

Eleventh Perspective on Programmed Instruction

As long ago as the days of Socrates this principle of logical sequences was appreciated by teachers. The Socratic method is famous for its logical progress from simple beginnings to more complex outcomes. In Socrates' days there were no learning theorists, but his work often has been cited by programmers as examples of what they are about. In the *Meno* of Plato, for example, Socrates attempts to establish the notion of "innate ideas." He undertakes to prove that a slave boy with no education already possesses rather complex mathematical ideas as part of his inborn reasoning capacity. It is interesting to watch Socrates at work and to compare his operation with what a modern programmer would do with the same problem. Dr. Ira Cohen (1962) has prepared just such a comparison. . . .

When university students were asked to follow along with Socrates, only 17 out of 32 were able to state the theorem with which Socrates ended his lesson. Let me note here that we have no proof that the slave boy was any brighter than modern college students. He was not asked to state the theorem—*only to agree to it;* this is very different from what modern programmers want from their subjects. This he could do, just to please the teacher. There is no proof, then, that the Socratic program has any merit, only presumption. Because Dr. Cohen has given his modern-dress version to many students, he has been able to check their answers and discover where the program was faulty. He found that, in general, Socrates had presented a reasonably good version of a proper modern program. Some of his steps were a little too large and needed additional help; some of his steps were not in the best order. By revising Socrates' program, Dr. Cohen was able to get 27 out of 33 college students to state the theorem involved when they had completed his program, a marked improvement over the results mentioned above.

Cohen's work demonstrates one immediate advantage of the modern programmer's operations. When records of errors are kept, it is possible to make changes in suitable places in the program to prevent these errors in future editions and to strengthen the appropriate behavior. In short, the basic advance in teaching in 2,500 years may have been the development of *evaluative* methods. . . . But the real contribution to teaching was still that of Socrates. He taught us that a *logical presentation of material can be effective.*

B. R. Bugelski, *The Psychology of Learning Applied to Teaching* (Indianapolis: Bobbs-Merrill Co., 1964), pp. 223, 226, 227.

Twelfth Perspective on Programmed Instruction

PROBLEMS

Problems worthy
of attack
prove their worth
by hitting back.

ON PROBLEMS

Our choicest plans
have fallen through,
our airiest castles
tumbled over,

because of lines
  we neatly drew
and later neatly
  stumbled over.

EXPERTS	Experts have their expert fun ex cathedra telling one just how nothing can be done.

TECHNIQUE	The height of
	  technical felicity
	is to combine
	  sublime simplicity
	with just sufficient
	  ingenuities
	to show how difficult
	  to do it is.

HIDE NOTHING!	If your thoughts are rubbish merely don't express yourself too clearly.

Piet Hein, *Grooks* (Cambridge, Mass.: M.I.T. Press, 1966), pp. 2, 17, 23.

Piet Hein, *Grooks 4* (Garden City, N.Y.: Doubleday & Co., 1972), p. 47.

Piet Hein, *Grooks 5* (Garden City, N.Y.: Doubleday & Co., 1972), p. 42.

A SELECT BIBLIOGRAPHY FOR PROGRAMMED INSTRUCTION

I. For basic orientation to the field

Deterline, William. *An Introduction to Programmed Instruction.* Englewood Cliffs, N.J.: Prentice-Hall, 1962, 131 pp.

Lumsdaine and Glaser. *Teaching Machines and Programmed Learning: A Source Book.* Dept. of A-V Instruction, National Education Association, 1960, 724 pp.

Markle, Eigen, and Komoski. *A Programmed Primer on Programming.* 2nd ed. Vol. 1, Principles;Vol. 2, Practical Problems in Writing a Program. The Center for Programmed Instruction, 1961.

Mager, Robert. *Preparing Objectives for Programmed Instruction.* Fearon Publishers, 1962, 62 pp.

II. For the classical Skinnerian position

Skinner, B. F. *Science and Human Behavior.* New York: Free Press, 1953, 461 pp.

Skinner, B. F., and James G. Holland. *The Analysis of Behavior.* New York: McGraw-Hill Book Co., 1961, 337 pp.

III. For fictionalized projections of programmed futures

Alban, A. *Catharsis Central.* New York: Berkley Publishing Corp., 1969.

Clarke, A. C. *Against the Fall of Night.* New York: Pyramid Publications, 1953, 1960.

Clarke, A. C. *The City and the Stars.* New York: Harcourt, Brace & World, 1953, 1956.

Skinner, B. F. *Walden Two.* New York: Macmillan Publishing Co., 1948.

IV. For a variety of perspectives on programmed instruction

Bugelski, B. R. *The Psychology of Learning Applied to Teaching.*

Indianapolis: Bobbs-Merrill Co., 1964, esp. chapter 10, "Programmed Learning," pp. 207–233.

Dewey, John. *Experience and Education*. New York: Collier Books, 1938, 1963, 91 pp.

Hein, Piet. *Grooks*. Cambridge, Mass.: M.I.T. Press, 1966, 61 pp.

Hein, Piet. *Grooks 4*. Garden City, N.Y.: Doubleday & Company, Inc., 1972, 57 pp.

Hein, Piet. *Grooks 5*. Garden City, N.Y.: Doubleday & Company, Inc., 1972, 57 pp.

Joncich, G. M., ed. *Psychology and the Science of Education*. New York: Bureau of Publications, Teachers College, Columbia University, 1962, esp. pp. 151–158.

Piaget, Jean. *Science of Education and the Psychology of the Child*. New York: Viking Press, 1969, 1970, 186 pp.

Underhill, Evelyn. "The Teacher's Vocation." In Lucy Menzies, ed., *Collected Papers of Evelyn Underhill*. London: Longmans, Green and Co., 1946, pp. 157–171.

V. For taxonomies of educational objectives

Bloom, B. S., ed. *Taxonomy of Educational Objectives: The Classification of Educational Goals. Handbook I: Cognitive Domain*. New York: David McKay, 1956.

Harrow, A. J. *A Taxonomy of the Psychomotor Domain: A Guide for Developing Behavioral Objectives*. New York: David McKay Co., 1972.

Krathwohl, D. R., B. S. Bloom, and B. B. Masia. *Taxonomy of Educational Objectives: The Classification of Educational Goals. Handbook II: Affective Domain*. New York: David McKay Co., 1964.

VI. For the sheer fun of it all

Baker, Robert A., ed. *The Stress Analysis of a Strapless Evening Gown*. Garden City, N.Y.: Doubleday & Co., 1963, 1969, 212 pp.

9

O God! Attending to the Present Realities

INTRODUCTION

The Christians' year 1979 was memorable for many things. There were crises of confidence, energy, national will, and international terror. Chances are that all too few recognized 1979 as the year of the seventy-fifth birthday of Theodore Seuss Geisel. Although T. S. Geisel was a well published, thoroughly successful author and illustrator, far too few of us living then knew him by that name. For purposes best known to Geisel himself, almost all of his published books were credited to another, a Dr. Seuss.

Even in A.D. 1979 parents could recognize the pen name of Dr. Seuss. One or another of his intriguing, delightful works were likely to be old and all-too-familiar friends. Children still seemed to resonate to the simple, short stories and the remarkably ingenious, imaginative illustrations that Dr. Seuss provided as a visual accompaniment to a short, simple story line. The combination captured children's attention and, quite often, captivated, intrigued, and puzzled parental adults. By 1979, the television animation of Dr. Seuss's tale *How the Grinch Stole Christmas* was a delightful memory of repeated viewings, although few of us realized that Random House first published that particular tale way back in 1957.[1]

My memories of raising three daughters are quite mixed up with my memories of reading and then rereading one or another of the tales of Dr. Seuss. One of those tales, *Horton Hears a Who,* had a theme that as a sometime parent and full-time person I cannot forget.[2] That theme was a simple Seussian tag: A person's a person, no matter how small! The tale was built around that tag, and no one who has ever read that story to children can quite forget the tag or want to deny its obvious moral.

Although Horton's Seussian tag has profound moral dimensions, I want to use my sometime parental memories of it for only one present point. I want to recall that Seuss's Horton, because he explicitly and quite literally took the tag at its face value, was able to do what few of his contemporaries could do: Horton accepted a really general idea and then put *that* generalization to work in his specific, idiosyncratic existence. Thus, he recognized a unique-but-present reality. Horton heard a Who, although none of his contemporaries did, and he went to great lengths to protect and to preserve the Who-person he heard. In a word, Horton was able to attend to his present reality, even when it meant being considered odd, strange, or crazy by his contemporaries, who were caught up in their own presumptions and so thought Horton's reality impossible!

Let us be both careful and honest.

I do not want to suggest that the wildly improbable is, via some sort of conceptual inversion, actually the probable and real. Not at all. But I do want to use the Seussian tale to make the point that a very great deal can be won or lost by our ability and willingness to attend to present realities. Moreover, I want to acknowledge that Horton's story reminds us that whenever we do manage to attend to present realities, we risk being different. For more of our time than we may wish to acknowledge, we humans are far more like Horton's contemporaries than we are like Horton himself. That is the wonderfully sharp point of this Seussian tale.

Even in the sometimes improbable worlds of Dr. Seuss, J. R. R. Tolkien's thesis that "the Primary World, Reality, of elves and men is the same, if differently valued and perceived" is simply true.[3] Tolkien's somewhat later observation that "creative Fantasy is founded upon the hard recognition that things are so in the world as it appears under the sun" is also true of the Seussian worlds.[4] What Seuss did was to remind us that our presumptions all too often are like very dark and quite ineptly ground glasses which, because we wear them, prevent us from knowing "the world as it appears under the sun." In a word, we are self-disabled. But we do not know it!

Perhaps the point is evident.

We humans tend to ignore the bald, clear facts of "the world as it appears under the sun." We do so because our presumptions so filter that world that we mistake it for what it is not. We do *not* do so because we are really Tolkien's elves, who very well may look at this world and differently value and perceive it! At least, that is *not* the state of most of us. We value and perceive our world through the dark, faulty glasses of our presumptions. Thus, we can neither understand the valued and perceived world of Tolkien's elves nor, quite, that "Primary World, Reality, . . . (which) is the same" for elf and human and any other creature in *this* world. Yet all is not lost.

Repeatedly if occasionally we have intimations that things are not as our dark, faulty glasses suggest. We are not left without reminders that a different perception, a different valuing could be. Really the threshold of our awareness is relatively low. Seuss or Tolkien often will do quite well.[5] So will a careful exegesis of Paul or Matthew, Mark, Luke, or John.[6] We can and do cross that threshold. In a word, we are actually fortunate. Our presumptions can fairly readily and quite easily be brought into question.[7]

Perhaps we *are*, after all, objects of grace.

A CREEDAL CAVEAT

There are an interesting pair of ideas about G-O-D enshrined in the liturgical text of the Nicene Creed. The International Consultation on English Texts visualized and auralized the essential Trinitarian nature of that creed by the threefold repetition of the phrase, "We believe in. . . ." The third such occurrence concerns "the Holy Spirit, the Lord," who is identified as both "the giver of life" and the one who has "spoken through the Prophets."[8] These two creedal ascriptions are worth our consideration, especially if we think we are in any way religious, or religiously committed Christians.

The first of these two ascriptions posits that it *is* the Holy Spirit who is "the giver of life." Unless one limits creation to a long-past act of deity, or considers G-O-D to be that distant, uninvolved but observant supreme being of the deists, the creedal statement suggests that life per se is the result of an act of G-O-D. Interestingly, the Nicene Creed does not specify any particular mechanism, procedure, or process, only that life and G-O-D are inextricably related as gift and giver.[9] Thus, it is possible to imagine that life itself is a sign of continual giving, continual action by G-O-D as Holy Spirit. The inference, then, is attractive that no living being is ever without a sign of the present action of G-O-D: minimally, all that is required to see, know, experience that action is to consider one's own particular liveliness. Although this inference certainly leaves much to our curiosity, speculation, and discovery, it also affirms something of quite clear worth. By virtue of our very life, we are signs to ourselves and others of an action of G-O-D that is positively fundamental.[10] Moreover, if we are also educators, life-as-a-sign gives our efforts a meaning they might not otherwise have.[11]

The second creedal ascription posits that it is the Holy Spirit which "has spoken through the Prophets." That does more than confer canonical stature on those writings. It asks us to consider the biblical prophets, whoever they may in fact have been, and their message to their own time and place as what they claimed, a word "spoken through" them.[12] Inferentially, that very idea suggests that the popular Protestant idea of a prophetic ministry may be more of an ideal than it is a reality, especially when one contrasts the biblical and the contemporary and, frankly, recognizes the mediocrity of all too much such prophecy. However, the inference need not deny the possibility of a contemporary prophecy; it merely raises the standard quite a bit, and tends to reduce the number of candidates rather drastically. In a word, that inference saves us from the ephemerally popular and pushes us toward the persistently recurring concerns of humankind.[13] Actually, that is almost no loss and, in all likelihood, a very considerable gain!

But there is more.

The creedal identification also helps us to appreciate the prophets as quite human types indicative of a concern positable of G-O-D. If one will but grant that prophetic claim to record a word of G-O-D to their contemporaries, then the substance of such prophetic words may represent a clue to the concern of deity with humankind and its history.[14]

That is, while it is true that the prophets inveigh against injustice, what is even more intriguing is the idea that the prophetic words of G-O-D were addressed to the specificities of human living in particular times and places. Prophetic words were rarely generalities about abstractions; far more often they were applications of generalities to quite local, quite time-bound situations. Thus, a generality that we may discern in the canonical prophets is that the G-O-D which addresses humans through a prophet is concerned, above all else, with the way things actually are. In all likelihood, it as a result of such a concern that what we think of as prophetic utterances tend to be so specifically evaluative. Thus, we may from the creedal affirmation draw the conclusion that G-O-D is concerned with what simply *is*.

AN ETHICAL CAVEAT

Let us be quite careful.

To affirm that it can be concluded from the third paragraph of the liturgical text of the Nicene Creed that G-O-D is concerned with what simply is, does not involve the ethicist's naturalistic fallacy, nor does it involve that Leibnizian conclusion so effectively satirized by Voltaire's *Candide* (1759). The conclusion does not of itself affirm that what *is* should be: the naturalistic fallacy. Neither does the conclusion suggest, by itself and without our inferential act, that what *is* can be considered Leibniz's best of all possible worlds.[15] Not at all. But what the conclusion does affirm is that G-O-D is concerned *with*, interested *in*, and so, periodically addresses a word *to* the way things simply are in some specific time and place—through a prophet. The conclusion asks us to take seriously the recorded prophetic word to *a* time and place. Implicitly, it asks us to be careful, very careful, about generalizing such a word and, so, transforming it into an abstraction usable in any time or place.[16]

There is a strange, almost wild sense in which the conclusion asks us to consider the creedal prophet as the initial, original, and archetypal situational ethicist.[17] That is one way of putting the conclusion into our terms. However, if one can tolerate the idea, it is also a way of raising the standard for what can be acknowledged as a genuine situational ethic; it must, someway, partake of the quality of prophecy in rather strictly biblical terms. If it does not, while it may well seem situationally apropos, it is more than likely to fall into that category of prophecy which paralleled and often denied what word the canonical prophet had to deliver.[18]

The problem of acknowledging each and every situational ethicist as a prophetic voice is awesome. It is also, for many, close to an absurdity. But that is not to deny the possibility of such a contemporary prophetic word in this time and place. Yet it is to enjoin a certain caution, a certain tentativeness, a certain care in ascribing to another human the role and function of a creedal prophet.[19]

Notice what has happened.

The suggested conclusion from the third paragraph of the liturgical text of the Nicene Creed has been seen to affirm that G-O-D is concerned with the way things are, without also affirming that is the way they should be, and biblical prophecy has been interpreted as an example of exactly that concern. That does not involve one in committing the naturalistic fallacy and, then, thinking one has gotten away with it.[20] Nor does it involve one in being blind to Voltaire's biting, sarcastic commentary in *Candide* on Leibniz's thesis that this world we know is the best of all possible worlds. It is only our all-too-human presumptions which have been denied.

Now, notice what is possible.

If we think about what it means to posit that G-O-D is concerned with, interested in, and so periodically addresses a word to a particular time and place, we begin to catch a vision. It is the situational particularity that concerns, interests G-O-D, not the vast abstract generalities we humans so often think are G-O-D's prime interest. Or, perhaps a bit more precisely, it is the situationally particular instances of those vast abstract generalities which concern G-O-D. That is the stuff of a vision of G-O-D as, for all we humans can know, quite interested in the prosaic, the common, the ordinary—that which simply is. Thus, strange as it may seem, by attending to such simple things we manage to attend to that which a biblical, creedal G-O-D may well find of most interest, now.

Let us be both careful and venturesome.

A biblical, creedal G-O-D interested in that which we accept as the prosaic, the common, the ordinary *is* positably interested in a good deal that we humans forget, overlook, or persistently ignore. In part, we do so because we cannot tolerate that to which, otherwise, we would have to attend. For instance, I reached a place in Aleksandr I. Solzhenitsyn's *Gulag Archipelago* where I simply was unprepared to read any further: the prosaic, common, ordinary events of the life he was reporting were so disturbing, so demonic, that I stopped reading![21] Now, it was my decision. It was a decision based quite simply upon my then-present level of tolerance. It was not a decision that involved my judgment that Solzhenitsyn's record was either untrue or impossible. It was a personal decision: I was unprepared to "take it" any longer. It was as simple as that, and I know that for a fact.

My encounter with the intolerable horrors so faithfully recorded by a Solzhenitsyn is, I think, but an example of a reasonably common human tendency to ignore, overlook, or forget a good bit of the common, ordinary, prosaic present reality of this world. While I do not want to excuse my action, I do want to suggest that it is but an example of an all-too-common human tendency. I want to contrast what I did regarding such prosaic, ordinary, common stuff with what we have glimpsed as a positable interest of G-O-D. Clearly and specifically, what I could not then tolerate, even in a book, is and was of interest to a biblical, creedal G-O-D.

However, that is an extreme argument, to make a point!

The point to be made, I suspect, is that the range of things that are—the prosaic, common, and ordinary—is far greater than many of us are prepared to admit initially. Naturally, this point also equally clearly implies that the seemingly minor events of normal, ordinary existence are of interest to such a G-O-D. What one says or doesn't say to children and spouse are well within the range. So are the kindnesses done or left undone. And so are the sacrifices of existence, the things consciously given up or forgone, whether they be of seemingly great import or not.

In very old, quite traditional language, what has been described is something akin to what older theologians very probably meant when they spoke about the omniscience of G-O-D.[22] Personally, but only personally, I think my line of thought is most like that of Whitehead or Charles Hartshorne. However, the theological antecedents should be a relatively minor concern for a contemporary person: the real question is what we now can or do think. The views of theologians, previous or contemporary, are views. No more. They may or may not help *us*; but, if they do, let us at least acknowledge *our* acceptance of *their* view.

Actually, the argument of this caveat is quite complete if one can but tolerate the idea that a biblical, creedal G-O-D is concerned for that prosaic, common, ordinary stuff of daily living that we tend to overlook. Of course, if we can also tolerate the idea that our presumptions are too like dark, faulty glasses, we can imagine that Tolkien's elves and G-O-D, for that matter, may see "the world as it appears under the sun" and yet differently value and perceive that "Primary World, Reality." That may well be a reason why it is an attractive inference that G-O-D is concerned with what is.

A SELECT LOOK AT PROSAIC, COMMON, ORDINARY THINGS

The trouble with the prosaic, the common, or the ordinary things of life is, of course, that they are just that. By our evaluation, they are merely prosaic, common, and ordinary. They are, even so, the very stuff of daily living. They are the things we accept as such, because we want to attend to those things which are witty, uncommon, or extraordinary—if and when they occur in *our* life. In a word, we are habituated to the prosaic, the common, and the ordinary.

Let us be honest with ourselves.

We are habituated to the ordinary, common, prosaic things of life as a part of our nature as creatures in, on, and of this world. Positively put, we need and depend upon that habit. Yet we can also recognize both the need and our nature and, at least in that sense, transcend ourselves. We can list and note those things which, for us, are prosaic or common or quite ordinary. We can acknowledge those things as the stuff of normal daily living and acting. Thus, we can, if we wish, attend to those things. However, most of the time we do not do so. We are strange creatures: habituated yet capable of looking at our habituations. Now and then, we can transcend ourselves, look at our life and actions, and see things going on we normally merely accept as a matter of course. Perhaps that capability is what the psalmists had in mind when they sang of humankind that it was but "little lower than the angels."[23]

Our problem is that we can attend to the prosaic, the ordinary, and the common, if we wish to do so. But most of time we do not so wish. We tend to prefer our habituation and, so, filter the ordinary, common, prosaic stuff of living and acting through our habit-supported presumptions. In a way, here is a reason for the ineptly ground, dark glasses that shield us so much of the time from Tolkien's "Primary World, Reality, of elves and men," that within which we can reach "the hard recognition that things are so in the world as it appears under the sun."[24]

However, contemporary persons do have an option. It comes to us from our own world, asking only that we avail ourselves of it, explore its potential, discover its limits, but appreciate its strange ability to be semi-self-correcting and, so, useful across whole sets of quite different historical presumptions. That option is what we call *research*.

Research is a part of our contemporary world. It has exhibited a great potential across the past one hundred years for benefiting humankind. It has, we may well suspect, limits, although we probably are too prone to speculate on where or what they may be. Moreover, it has a strange ability to be semi-self-correcting across time. Sooner or later, research identifies the discoverable incongruities in a set of presumptions (e.g., a theory), and then stimulates humankind to develop an alternative set of presumptions. Research, as we know it, owes much to its persistent historical concern for the specific, the common, the ordinary, the prosaic. It also owes much to an early Franciscan friar.

Sometime in the middle of the thirteenth century, the English scholar who was one of the first to lecture on Aristotle at the medieval university at Paris returned to Oxford. By the time Roger Bacon arrived in Oxford from Paris, he already had devoted approximately four years to experimentation and the science of his day. There, sometime around A.D. 1251, Bacon joined the Franciscan order, which was then but forty-one years past Francis of Assisi's first rule and only some thirty-four years beyond the Pentecost Chapter at Assisi, which organized the order into provinces.[25] Although it may be difficult to assess Roger Bacon's contribution to science or philosophy from our distant perspective, it is well to recall that later medieval scholars gave him the title "Doctor Mirabilis." It is also worth noting that Bacon was a writer of real originality, a man of independent views, and a critic of many then-contemporary presumptions. It seems likely that he also invented a thermometer, gunpowder, and a rudimentary telescope, some three hundred years before Galileo Galilei used the telescope to discover four of Jupiter's satellites. Bacon the Franciscan died in A.D. 1292. He could not know it, but he had stimulated a lasting interest in the building of knowledge from experimentation and, so, is an apt father of research.

Naturally, the research we know in these last decades of the twentieth century is different from Bacon's early work. Almost seven hundred years have passed since his death, and humankind has learned a good deal about research in that time, and our world is not Roger Bacon's world. But the effort is still quite basically the same. We seek to learn from careful attention to what all too easily we regard as the prosaic, common, and ordinary how the things of this world work together. Perhaps now we are more interested in how persons in this world work together than earlier ages, but it is still research that we use to help us discover answers to today's questions.

I. What Do We Mean by Research?

My dictionary defines *research* as "studious and critical inquiry and examination aimed at the discovery and interpretation of new knowledge."[26] Without attempting a thorough exegesis of that definition, it is clear that research involves an "inquiry and examination" directed toward both a "discovery" and an "interpretation" of the discovered. Unless we are rather careful, the idea of "new knowledge" can mislead us. The most likely way that phrase can mislead us is by focusing our attention upon the question of whether the discovered knowledge is, as we are wont to say, really new. We are less likely to be misled if, instead, we focus upon the question of for whom the discovered knowledge is new. If we do that, we are able to appreciate that "discovery learning" is an example of research, just as is comparison shopping. In these instances, knowledge is new for the discoverer, who may be of almost any age and, most assuredly, can be of either sex! Also, in these instances, instead of wondering about levels of newness or the criterion of the really new, we can appreciate that research is a way of attending to present realities and via inquiry and examination coming to interpretable discoveries that, for us, are new. In a word, research is a large part of what, from another perspective, we call learning. From yet another perspective, research is *a* (or, perhaps, *the*) method of education.

If we will think about it, research as either *a* method or, even, *the* method of education suggests why it is a tautology to speak of education as learning. Research is a way, method, or procedure for learning, which is a basic aim of anything we can recognize as education. Thus, the method of research is no more and no less than a way to learn via the processes of inquiry and examination.

II. What Might We Learn by Research?

Research-as-a-method does not tell us where to direct our inquiry, nor does it specify what can be examined. As a method, it certainly does not tell us that any here or some there is to be avoided. As a method, it also does not forecast what we may discover, nor does it by itself instruct us in how we should interpret what may be discovered. Research-as-a-method requires a human decision to be used, and then involves us in a series of decisions as we use the method, and finally requires decision when we come to the point of interpreting our discovery. In this sense, research is basically a method that requires the continual exercise of human freedom and the repeated acceptance of human responsibility.

Across the seven hundred years since Roger Bacon's lifetime, research-as-a-method has helped humans discover and interpret numerous new aspects of the world they inhabit. In the so-called physical sciences, especially, research has had both a long and an obviously productive, potentially human-benefiting history. Moreover, it has changed the way humans look at their world quite markedly: enough so that a Roger Bacon might be quite as confused to encounter us as we to encounter him. Thus, without suggesting that the physical science model of research is the only one, it will pay to attend to that present reality.

One of the most obvious aspects of contemporary physical science is that it has developed a goodly set of often highly specialized tools. Some of those tools are instruments—devices to let us see more or measure ever more precisely or store, combine, contrast, or compare our records of that which we have seen and measured. However, some of those tools are conceptual inventions—theories that seem to account for what we see or measure, procedures for calculating the relationships between our observations, symbol systems that permit us to consider things both very small and very large. Thus, aside from following the directions so that the tools are not misused, research itself remains very much a matter of basic critical inquiry and examination for the purpose of finding out, discovering, something new and then seeking an interpretation. The model of the physical sciences' research methodology actually alerts us to but two possibilities: the usefulness both of instruments and of what are best regarded as conceptual inventions.

If the reader will even tentatively acknowledge the result of this quite broad brush summary, then it is possible to conclude that research-as-a-method is a relatively neutral way of using the tools available in any given time or place for purposes which depend, finally, upon a quite human decision. In a word, *we* decide how research will be used. It is our decision that controls what research focuses upon. Which is not to maintain that the tools—instruments and conceptual inventions—appropriate for that research are available.[27] But the neutral method is potentially pervasively general. No subject is, by itself, out of bounds. Yet research-as-a-method has no way, by itself, of ensuring that it will discover aught but that the presently available tools are inadequate to the problem and, so, requiring one more interpretation of a discovered boundary between human knowledge and human ignorance. In this sense, while research has great positive promise, it also has fantastic potential for helping us discover the present limits of that reality we can apprehend. Thus, research-as-a-method is a way for us to approximate that wisdom which, in other times, was credited to those who discovered the boundary between the presently knowable and the presently unknowable.

When we turn our attention to the present reality of the social sciences, we discover much the same thing. Research-as-a-method is just as involved in the tool use of instruments and conceptual inventions in the social as in the physical sciences. As in the physical sciences, the importance of our decision is just as great. We decide the purpose of research and, so, how research will be used, what will be its focus, and what is an appropriate interpretation of whatever we may discover. In the social sciences the primary difference in the use of research-as-a-method is that we are ourselves the focus, as well as the tool users, and the ones who make the important controlling decisions. In addition, the set of available instruments is more general and less specialized than is the case in the physical sciences. In a word, hardware is less obviously a part of the social sciences. Moreover, the set of conceptual inventions is also less well developed, although that is not to suggest that theories, procedures, and symbol systems are lacking.

Let us try and be clearheaded.

Being both the focus of research-as-a-method and the ones whose decisions control the relatively neutral method is a real difference. There is an inescapable sense in which the social sciences involve humans in something close to an act of reflection. Unlike the physical sciences, in which a sense of being personally involved as the subject of research is relatively absent, the social sciences repeatedly involve us in the recognition that we are the subject of our use of research-as-a-method. That is both a real and an important difference. In fact, it calls for a decision that is most unlikely in the physical sciences.

While the decision of a focus is formally similar in any use of research-as-a-method, in the social sciences we are intimately, personally involved in the decision and the results of that decision in multiple ways. Unless we sharply delimit the social sciences to seeking new knowledge about the odd, the strange, the uncommon events of human existence, the decision of focus is likely to involve us in using research-as-a-method upon things we consider the prosaic, the common, or the ordinary. In a word, the social sciences invite us to focus on that to which we are most habituated, that which may account for those ineptly ground dark glasses that distort our perception of Tolkien's "Primary World, Reality, of elves and men."

In addition to our habituation with much that the social sciences wish to focus upon, there is another complication. It is the remarkable similarity between the social sciences' use of research-as-a-method and the old, old act of human reflection. In both reflection and the social science use of research-as-a-method there is a search for new knowledge. In both the effort is to probe the area of the known and, perhaps, identify where the boundary of the presently unknown lies. In both, humankind is often the subject of concern. However, reflection is much older, much more familiar to humans, and often seems easier. Probably age, familiarity, and seeming ease account for the fact that humans often prefer reflection or, perhaps, mistake reflection for research. That is unfortunate; for, while the two are not necessarily unrelated, they are different in the way they encourage us to attend to our present realities.

The act of human reflection fundamentally presumes that we can perceive Tolkien's "Primary World, Reality, of elves and men" simply and directly: there are no glasses, let alone ineptly ground and darkened ones. Moreover, the act of human reflection is essentially a cognitive act, an act of thought, what we rightly call an internal act of a person. Its primary instruments are a biologically matured brain, a mind well stocked with current knowledge, and undistracted time to think things through. Often the primary conceptual invention it uses is human logic. Its limits are, quite literally, those of human imagination. Its often-fatal flaw is its presumption that humans have simple, direct perception of "the Primary World, Reality." Thus, it too often is less than interested in confirming its results through observation, that act of attending carefully to the present realities.[28]

There is a distinction worth noting!

Research-as-a-method *is* a way of observing or carefully attending to the present realities. Often-to-almost-always it factors into the decision to focus some result of thought. But it does so for the purpose of confirming or disconfirming what thought suggests should be the state of those present realities. The new knowledge that can be so discovered can, then, be distinguished from imagination. Or we can discover that our as-yet-available tools do not permit us to observe such a state. Either to confirm our thought or to know that as yet we cannot do so, is a form of new knowledge of great value! Especially when the focus has been upon that prosaic, common, ordinary stuff of daily living to which we are so habituated. Then we have managed to perceive a part of "the Primary World, Reality, of elves and men" with some clarity, and our presumptions can be changed to accommodate such new knowledge.

What has just been described as a result of the use of research-as-a-method is more than simply a formalization of skepticism: it is a dialogue between thought and reality; it is a cycle in which research contributes to theory as well as tests theory. As Tiedeman and I suggested a few years ago, it is what is involved in being fundamentally scientific about human possibilities.[29] It is also similar to if not identical to Piaget's analysis of the adaptation process as a cycle composed of assimilation and accommodation.[30] It is what the social sciences are all about; and it is a reason why their potential for human benefit is both so great and, sometimes, so disturbing to our habits.

III. Why Should We Bother with Research?

Let us, once again, be honest with ourselves.

To use research-as-a-method in the social sciences involves us humans in a complex decisional situation. In addition, if focuses upon those very things to which we are likely to be most habituated. Moreover, we are so habituated to the ordinary, prosaic, and common things of living for a very good reason: we simply cannot attend to all things at one time.[31] It is understandable that humans tend to prefer the seemingly easier way of reflection to the seemingly more difficult way of research. Therefore, a good and powerful reason for deciding to use research-as-a-method must be had before any human will accept the responsibility for that decision.

If we consider ourselves to be religious persons, a religious reason might be good enough and powerful enough for us to decide responsibly to avail ourselves of research-as-a-method. Such a reason might even make that decision a religious obligation. That would be, of course, something that early Franciscan Roger Bacon might well understand.

Somewhat earlier in this chapter it was suggested that the third paragraph of the Christians' Nicene Creed encourages us to posit two things of G-O-D: human life is a gift from G-O-D the giver, and the biblical prophet is a sign of G-O-D's concern for, interest in, the specifics of time and place in life. If we can accept those two things as positable of G-O-D, and if we consider that we normally mean by G-O-D a supreme being, or the ultimate reality, we have the stuff for an intriguing inference. G-O-D, the ultimate reality, is concerned with human life in its specificity, which is but another way of saying the prosaic, common, and ordinary things of human living. G-O-D is interested in that which we ignore, because we are habituated to it. While we may well believe that a supreme being knows that we cannot attend to all things at any one time, and that we need our habituation, that belief need not cause us to deny the inference. In all likelihood, that is a clearly noticeable difference between us humans and G-O-D: we ignore much of the time that which simply is, while G-O-D is concerned with exactly that which we tend to ignore.

If research-as-a-method can be understood as a way to attend to the present realities of human life, including that prosaic, ordinary, and quite common stuff we accept by habit, then to decide to use that method and to focus upon such aspects of our life is a way of attending to what simply is, with which G-O-D is positably concerned. Certainly, attending to that with which we have reason to believe G-O-D is concerned is not to probe the mind of G-O-D. But it is at least to attend to the same things. In a way, it is to prepare ourselves for any contemporary prophetic word that may be given. It is also a way of understanding human living in terms of those things about our life that G-O-D is quite likely to find of interest. In a word, it is to match our concerns to those of the deity.

The idea of matching human concerns to those of G-O-D lies at the heart of that old, traditional Christian idea of sanctification. It is what mystics and the faithful across the centuries have recognized as a goal, even a reason for the gift of life itself. Therefore, while it may seem a strangely surprising conclusion, a religious reason for deciding to use research-as-a-method may be that it is a presently available avenue for our sanctification. If that conclusion should be acceptable or even tolerable, then a religious person can responsibly decide to attend to present realities, that which simply is, by using research-as-a-method. In fact, such a decision may, in this time and place, be close to a religious obligation.

Let me try and be precise.

The suggestion that research-as-a-method may, in this time and place, be an avenue for our sanctification and, therefore, close to an obligation for a religious person *is* a potential rationale for a possible human decision. It is, quite consciously, couched in religious terms. It is offered as *a* rationale for religious persons, not as a generality for all of humankind. It may be intolerable for some humans, or simply unacceptable. If so, their decision to use research-as-a-method will have another rationale. Granted. But my concern here is with the religious person who, without too much thought, is tempted to consider research-as-a-method as either areligious or, even, antireligious. It need not be so considered: that is the argument of this chapter. Moreover, it is an implication of that argument that for the religious person to persist in avoiding research is more like an instance of original sin than it is like an example of faithfulness.

While research-as-a-method may not permit us to probe the mind of G-O-D, it may at least conform our concerns to that concern we have seen some reason to believe is G-O-D's. For the religious person, then, it can be a way of building toward an even firmer faith in One concerned for life-bearers such as we humans. Still, much depends on our quite human decision.

Notes and References

1. Dr. Seuss, *How the Grinch Stole Christmas* (New York: Random House, 1957).

2. Dr. Seuss, *Horton Hears a Who* (New York: Random House, 1954).

3. J. R. R. Tolkien, "On Fairy-Stories," in *The Tolkien Reader* (New York: Ballantine Books, 1966), p. 52.

4. Ibid., p. 55.

5. The point here is simply that the work of either a Dr. Seuss or of a J. R. R. Tolkien can not only expose us to a different perception or a different valuing but, in addition, can carry us on to recognize that what we encounter is a possibility. Thus, our presumption of the way things simply are is challenged, and the challenge is also recognized for what it is: we become aware of an alternative.

6. The point of referencing the writings credited to Paul, Matthew, Mark, Luke, or John is simply to remind us that the Christian's New Testament clearly recognizes that the Good News is, for some, a scandal or stumbling stone. This idea seems clearly related to one way in which Christianity persistently tends to remind us that a different perception, a different valuing, is both possible and preferable to our habituated way of perceiving and valuing. The Greek word σκανδαλον lies immediately behind this particular idea.

7. While the ability to bring our normal presumptions into question may be, as I suggest here, fairly readily and quite easily actualized, this bringing into question does *not* per se lead humans to decide for an alternative set of presumptions. It may be a necessary prelude to such a decision, but there seems to be something more required to make the decision. The long history of Christianity may be taken as a witness to this distinction. Still, the opportunity is repeatedly ours.

8. For the liturgical text of the Nicene Creed agreed upon by the International Consultation on English Texts, see *The Book of Common Prayer* (New York: Church Hymnal Corporation and Seabury Press, 1979), pp. 358–359.

9. Although the Nicene Creed does not specify any mechanism, procedure, or process whereby G-O-D gives the gift of life, the long history of at least Christian theology is scattered with a variety of speculative answers. However, by itself, the text of the Creed simply affirms a relationship without specifying *any* when or how. It is our inference that supplies one or another answer, and we should acknowledge that we are responsible for those answers which presently satisfy us.

10. The point here is simply that life is the unspoken and often unacknowledged presupposition of human existence. Thus, the presence of life is a fundamental fact and, here, a sign of the action of G-O-D.

11. To see in life itself a sign of an action of G-O-D as giver means that educator and student have always one fundamental common gift. If one goes on to value that gift, then education cannot be equated with a merely mechanical series of actions; it must be, in some way, a meeting of gifts, a giving of gifts, an acceptance of gifts, because both the learner and the educator are, themselves, signs of a gift and a giver. To so value life as a sign,

can alter the relationship of educator and learner that is both fundamental and persistent to education.

12. See chapter 1, p. 21, where this aspect of biblical prophecy is considered. It is also instructive to think about the range of meaning that can be given to the creedal word *through*. In itself, it does not suggest that a prophet was other than a human, or that the prophets contributed nothing of their nature to the word spoken through them. This is not the conceptual peg upon which to hang any doctrine of inerrancy.

13. At this point, the suggestion is that the way things simply *are* is more likely to be located in those persistently recurring concerns of humankind than in the ephemerally popular. Popularity seems most likely to be but an instance of the perceptions credited earlier to dark and ineptly ground glasses than to an accurate perception of Tolkien's primary world, reality.

14. See chapter 1, p. 21. The substance of prophetic words is, here, used as a synonym for that concern of G-O-D with situational specifics, such as the common, ordinary, prosaic things of living in any given time and place.

15. Gottfried Wilhelm Leibniz (1646–1716) was a student of the law, mathematics, and philosophy. His *Essais de theodicee sur la bonte de Dieu, la liberte de l'homme et l'origine du mal* of 1710 was written when Leibniz was in his mid-sixties and, according to older scholars, made a wide and deep impression on the eighteenth century. In this book he developed the idea that this world is the best world which could possibly exist.

16. For a consideration of why we need to be careful about generalizing via abstraction, see Paul Tillich, *Systematic Theology*, vol. 1 (Chicago: University of Chicago Press, 1951), pp. 16–17.

17. The phrase "situational ethicist" is a clear reference to Joseph Fletcher's book *Situation Ethics: The New Morality* (Philadelphia: Westminster Press, 1966). Whatever one may think of that book, a much earlier instance of a situational ethic can be found in 1 Cor. 7:17–38. The contemporary Christian need not "buy into" the Fletcher thesis to understand or appreciate situational ethics.

18. See chapter 1, p. 22, for the author's speculation about such false prophets and their relationship to the canonical prophet.

19. The need for tentativeness and caution in ascribing to another human the prophetic role was indicated by the discovery of November 1978 of the pathos of a mass suicide/murder at Jonestown in the jungle of Guiana. While an extreme example, perhaps it can help make the point.

20. This sentence involves an obvious play upon the title of Lawrence Kohlberg's article, "From Is to Ought: How to Commit the Naturalistic Fallacy and Get Away with It in the Study of Moral Development," in T. Mischel, ed., *Cognitive Development and Epistemology* (New York: Academic Press, 1971), pp. 135 ff.

21. Aleksandr I. Solzhenitsyn, *The Gulag Archipelago* (New York: Harper & Row, Publishers, 1973, 1974).

22. For instance, see the entry for *omniscience* in Van A. Harvey, *Handbook of Theological Terms* (New York: Macmillan Co., 1964).

23. Ps. 8:6.

24. Tolkien, "On Fairy-Stories," pp. 52, 55.

25. For more information on Roger Bacon, see the entry in F. L. Cross, ed., *The Oxford Dictionary of the Christian Church* (London: Oxford University Press, 1957).

26. *The New Merriam-Webster Pocket Dictionary* (New York: Simon and Schuster, 1971), the word *research*.

27. This is a useful and not-always-recognized distinction. To maintain that research-as-a-method can be focused upon any topic is not the same as to maintain that any topic will prove amenable to research-as-a-method. It is a legitimate and an important discovery when we find that the available tools are simply inadequate to the method-topic combination. Far too often we make an a priori judgment that the tools are inadequate and then think we have identified a topic for which research-as-a-method is illegitimate. We have not done so, if our judgment is actually a priori. Minimally, we should recognize what we have done and why we have done that.

28. This distinction between research-as-a-method and reflection is similar to the position taken by Jean Piaget in *Insights and Illusions of Philosophy* (New York: New American Library, 1971). The interested reader might benefit from considering chapter 2, "Science and Philosophy," pp. 39–77.

29. John H. Peatling and David V. Tiedeman, *Career Development: Designing Self* (Muncie, Ind.: Accelerated Development, 1977), p. 50.

30. For a full and reasonably precise discussion of adaptation, see Jean Piaget, *Biology and Knowledge* (Chicago: University of Chicago Press, 1971), pp. 171–185, esp. pp. 172–174.

31. This point was expressed by J. Ladriere in the journal *Dialectica*, vol. 14, p. 321, in 1960 in these words: "We cannot survey all the operations open to human thought at one glance." Jean Piaget, for one, quotes this sentence in a consideration of logical structures in his book *Structuralism* (London: Routledge and Kegan Paul, 1968/1971), p. 35.

10

Thank God! There Is a Way

INTRODUCTION

The year 1980 began with an awesomely wonderful idea. A five-word headline in the January 4, 1980, issue of *Science* announced, "Psychotherapy Faces Test of Worth."[1] The story reported an effort by the United States Senate Finance Committee's health subcommittee to determine whether to permit direct federal reimbursement for mental health treatment via psychotherapy under the existing Medicare program. The specific decision involved clinical psychologists' right to bill the government directly, as psychiatrists already were allowed to do. Permitting psychologists to do that would, it was feared, set a precedent that would encourage social workers, nurses, and other health-related professions to request the same right. Therefore, the subcommittee staff was "asking for hard data on various types of psychotherapy showing that they are (i) safe and (ii) genuinely efficacious."[2]

As one might expect, that request was less than enthusiastically received by the professional organizations representing the various types of psychotherapy. The president of the American Psychological Association, Nicholas Cummings, suggested that even with government financing it would take at least ten years to test for safety, and a subsequent ten years to test for efficacy. Quite possibly he was right. But that meant a twenty-year program of research before any whole answer would even be in sight. Both the request and Cummings's response were part of an awesomely wonderful idea: safety and efficacy are legitimate demands upon that which a society supports.

Interestingly, neither the questioning subcommittee staff nor the queried professions assumed that the demand for hard data really was absurd. Both seemed to think it was amenable to research, although they differed noticeably in how long they thought such research might take. Moreover, the professions seemed to accept tacitly the idea that safety and efficacy were legitimate expectations of a society that supported their existence. In a sense, that was yet another awesomely wonderful idea.

Because I regard myself as a researcher, as well as a priest and a religious educator, I was fascinated by the *Science* story. Being all too human, I thought that it was nice not to be a psychotherapist faced with either of those wonderfully awesome ideas. Then I began to think about what it might mean if I *were* faced with them. When I did that, I developed a bit of empathy for the professions faced with the demand to generate hard data on the various types of heretofore accepted professional practices that showed that they were (i) safe and (ii) genuinely efficacious. All it really took for me to appreciate the can of worms was to imagine substituting "religious education" for "psychotherapy" and, then, to think about what it might mean to screen religious education for safety and efficacy!

Frankly, I reacted somewhat like the queried therapeutic professions. I found I tacitly accepted the legitimacy of the expectation that what a society supports should be both safe and efficacious. I found that, when I imagined that expectation as a demand for an assurance of safety and efficacy, I could think of no way to provide such an assurance short of research. Like the President of the American Psychological Association, I found that I had to imagine a research program that would require decades to complete. It was an intriguing exercise, and it brought me cycling back to my initial human gratitude that I was not faced with what I could imagine. At least in the United States of America, no Senate Finance Committee subcommittee was at all likely to put the question of demonstrable safety and efficacy to the field of religious education. Yet, in a way, it is too bad that the query is reserved for drugs, hospitals, medical procedures, and therapies—things most people regard as really important.

A MOMENTARY DIGRESSION: CONSIDERING CRITERIA

I shared my exercise in imagination with my wife, an almost-always practical and levelheaded person. She was intrigued with the problem, but quickly identified the all-important question: What do you mean by *safe?* or *efficacious?* She was quite right. It all turns on the criteria. While I could easily acknowledge that, I was unprepared to abort the whole exercise. I wanted to explore what the demand might mean for religious education. So I kept worrying the idea.

My large dictionary suggests that *safe* means such things as "secure from liability to harm, injury, danger, or risk . . . free from hurt, injury, danger, or risk . . . involving little or no risk of mishap, error, etc. . . . dependable or trustworthy."[3] The same dictionary suggests that *efficacious* means "having or showing the desired result or effect; effective as a means, measure, remedy, etc."[4] Once I had determined that much, I knew that the exercise was inevitably going to involve a real can of worms. Quite probably it would require the construct of paradox and, as well, the pragmatism of Zymurgy's first law of evolving system dynamics: "Once you open a can of worms, the only way to recan them is to use a larger can."[5]

Let us be both careful and honest.

It is extremely difficult to imagine that any religious educator wants to propagate an unsafe or ineffective program. It is much more likely that religious educators believe that what they do, or assist others to do, is efficacious and safe. We must not let ourselves think otherwise. If we do, we will slide into the absurdities of scapegoating. However, to engage in my exercise in imagination need involve no such belief about religious educators' intentions. Nor is that exercise one of the absurdities of that damnable act of scapegoating. Rather, the exercise is a way of being critically positive about religious education, although it may well involve some unlikely, puzzling, or even embarrassing questions about the practice.

To imagine a demand for *hard* data on (i) the safety and (ii) the efficacy of religious education is—if one will tolerate that exercise at all!—an almost certain way to appreciate the usefulness of a *tentative* approach. Still, with that caution noted, let's press on.

For instance, let's begin by considering the kinds of questions the two concepts safety and efficacy presume. In fact, let's begin by asking those questions about some unspecified, theoretical, and quite general Y. Then, a bit later, we can see what it would mean to simply substitute symbols.

Let's presume that we believe, but only believe, that Y is both safe and efficacious. Therefore, our questions imply neither a negative nor a null hypothesis of no effect. However, it would be useful to imagine generating some hard data to confirm that belief that Y is safe and efficacious. In addition, being honest, we realize that we have a basic, positive hypothesis to begin with and, so, want to be sure that we do not simply fool ourselves. Thus, we really do not want to overlook anything that might disconfirm that initial positive hypothesis.

If that were the case, we might begin to ask questions like these of our theoretical Y:

1. How can one show that Y is secure from liability to harm?
2. How can one show that Y is secure from liability to injury?
3. How can one show that Y is secure from liability to danger?
4. How can one show that Y is secure from liability to risk?
5. How can one show that Y involves little or no risk of mishap?
6. How can one show that Y involves little or no risk of error?
7. How can one show that Y is dependable?
8. How can one show that Y is trustworthy?
9. How can one show that Y has the desired result?
10. How can one show that Y has the desired effect?

Clearly, those ten questions are complex. In addition to the obvious need for criteria for the concepts of harm, injury, danger, risk, mishap, error, dependability, trustworthiness, desired result, and desired effect there is a not-so-obvious need to recognize that the nature of Y interacts with the other concepts and, thereby, determines the criteria that *are* actually applicable to Y. Thus, we might also begin to ask another set of questions about our theoretical Y.

11. Is Y an institution?
12. Is Y a service?
13. Is Y a process?
14. Is Y a procedure?
15. Is Y a therapy?
16. Is Y a unitary something?
17. Is Y a class of somethings?
18. Is Y applicable to a person?

19. Is Y applicable to all persons?
20. Is Y applicable to some but not all persons?

If we ultimately are going to consider a symbol substitution in which Y is replaced by "religious education," we had best let our purpose affect how we answer these last ten questions. We really are not interested in a Y that is antithetical to religious education. However, we are interested in any Y that is similar enough to religious education to make this imaginary exercise useful. Thus, we cannot be satisfied with some simple random selection of answers. What we want is some general-but-meaningful set of answers that describe the nature of Y in a way that is similar to but not necessarily identical to religious education.

I recognize that the ways in which one can think about religious education are quite numerous. Still, let me suggest *one* way to answer those questions about Y so that it is similar but not identical to the concept of religious education. That is, we could consider Y to be a service (question 12), a *process* (13), and a *class of somethings* (17) that is *applicable to a person* (18), although it is *applicable to some but not all persons* (20). Thus, for the purpose of this imaginary exercise, our theoretical Y is a class of processes applicable to some but not all persons as a service. Similar to religious education, but not necessarily identical to religious education. But it will do.

Notice what is now possible.

We can rephrase that first set of ten questions in a way which, potentially, will help us move toward answers. First, we can insert into the identical portion of the questions a meaningful parenthesis: for example, how can one show that Y (a class of processes applicable to some but not all persons as a service) is. . . . ? Second, we can then add to that common first portion the ten more specific concepts. Thus, our original ten questions become more specific, more limited, and more obviously meaningful. In fact, we could create four quite large queries out of those ten very specific questions. For example, we could now ask:

1. How can one show that Y (a class of processes applicable to some but not all persons as a service) is secure from liability to harm? or injury? or danger? or risk? (N.B.: How show Y is safe?)

2. How can one show that Y (a class of processes applicable to some but not all persons as a service) involves little or no risk of mishap? or error? (N.B.: How show Y is safe?)
3. How can one show that Y (a class of processes applicable to some but not all persons as a service) is dependable? or trustworthy? (N.B.: How show Y is safe?)
4. How can one show that Y (a class of processes applicable to some but not all persons as a service) has the desired result? or the desired effect? (N.B.: How show Y is efficacious?)

The first, second, and third questions concern the safety of Y; the fourth question concerns the efficacy of Y. Interestingly, there is a one-word, very general answer to all four questions. Research-as-a-method is just such a "how." Still, that really helps only a little bit in the focusing of our thinking. For instance, we could once again expand those four large queries and ask:

1. How can one show (by research-as-a-method) that Y (a class of processes applicable to some but not all persons as a service) is secure from liability to harm? or injury? or danger? or risk?
2. How can one show (by research-as-a-method) that Y (a class of processes applicable to some but not all persons as a service) involves little or no risk of mishap? or error?
3. How can one show (by research-as-a-method) that Y (a class of processes applicable to some but not all persons as a service) is dependable? or trustworthy?
4. How can one show (by research-as-a-method) that Y (a class of processes applicable to some but not all persons as a service) has the desired result? or the desired effect?

Clearly, to give a useful answer to those four questions requires further attention to the criteria for what are the controlling concepts. What do we mean by harm? What would constitute injury? What might we regard as danger? What could we mean by risk? What would be a mishap? What could we recognize as clearly an error? What do we mean by calling something dependable? What makes something trustworthy? What would be a desired result? What do we regard as the desired effect?

Once again, my dictionary proved a help.[6] While distinct, the four concepts of harm, injury, danger, and risk all turn out to be variations on a core concept: injury. Harm, for instance, is a specific instance of injury, which functions as a supraordinate category for the concept of harm itself. Danger, on the other hand, is a state of probability of injury, while risk is a state characterized by the possibility of injury. Injury itself turns out to be an act that physically or mentally "damages" or "hurts" (e.g., via an exposure to evil). Thus, that first quite large query about safety turns out to be a question of how one can, by use of research-as-a-method, show that some unspecified, theoretical, and quite general Y is secure from liability to injury, when Y is defined as a class of processes applicable to some but not all persons.

The same dictionary also proved a help with the two concepts of mishap and error. Once again, while the concepts are distinct, they turn out to be related through the concepts of intention (positive) and accident (negative).[7] A mishap is something we regard as an unfortunate and unintentional (accidental) occurrence. On the other hand, an error turns out to be an unintentional (accidental) deviation from either accuracy or rectitude. Thus, that second quite large query about safety turns out to be a question of how one can, by use of research-as-a-method, show that some unspecified, theoretical, and quite general Y involves very, very little that is unintentional or, conversely, that Y involves very, very much that is intentional or, simply, that Y is not accidental!

On yet another hand, my dictionary helped with concepts of dependability and trustworthiness. These two concepts turn out to be related to one another through the concept of reliability, whose synonyms are *trusty, authentic*, and *consistent*. Thus, that third large query about safety is, essentially, a query about how one can show, through the use of research-as-a-method, that a quite general, theoretical, and unspecified Y is actually reliable.

Notice what has happened.

Through the use of a dictionary as a tool, a conceptual analysis identifies that the idea of safety requires us to use research-as-a-method in a way that will show (or determine) whether Y is (i) secure from liability to injury, (ii) not accidental but, rather, intentional, and (iii) reliable. Actually, that is a good bit of progress. The very idea of being secure from liability to injury invites us to clarify just how secure we think a Y must be. Similarly, the idea of accident invites us to clarify our intention(s), for that will certainly contribute to our ability to be sure that Y is safe. In much the same way, the concept of reliability invites us to clarify our standards for consistency or authenticity, for that will contribute to our ability to be certain that Y is either dependable or what we could regard as trustworthy. In each of these three aspects of safety, it is evident and obvious that we are dealing with concepts that admit of degrees. Security is clearly a relative concept: one admitting of degrees. Accident or nonintention is also a relative concept, although that is less obvious. Reliability is, interestingly, also clearly relative, if we think at all about the statistical use of that term. Thus, when we engage in a conceptual analysis of safety, we are faced with a combination of relative concepts. Fortunately, we now have some tools to help us deal with just such a situation. We know some ways to deal with combinations of relativities.

Interestingly, once we identify the role intention plays in safety, we are in a position to appreciate how the concepts of safety and efficacy are related. Clearly, to define *efficacy* as either (i) having a desired result, or (ii) having a desired effect involves, through the idea of the "desired," a reference to intention. That recognition can help us understand that efficacy is also a concept that admits of degree. For example, a Y might be judged rarely, occasionally, normally, often, or always to have some desired result or effect. In fact, if we can understand that, we might also recognize that no less could be believed of the concepts of (i) security from liability to injury, or (ii) the accidental or its converse, the intentional, or (iii) the reliable. Thus, we are in a position to model a conceptual space defined by the safety concepts of injury, accident, and reliability, plus the efficacy concept of achievement. Moreover, since each of these concepts admits of degree, there is reason to consider the conceptual space so modeled as amenable to the use of research-as-a-method.

AN EXPLORATION: MODELING A FOUR-DIMENSIONAL CONCEPTUAL SPACE

One of the fundamental things about homo sapiens is that each of us lives in and perceives a three-dimensional space, across the moments of time. While it is possible to conceive of time itself as a fourth dimension to our space, it is very hard for us to visualize more than three dimensions at a time. Thus, modeling a four-dimensional conceptual space may seem like an impossibility. At least we might think there was no way to visualize it. However, that is not quite true: there is a way.

When Fuller's tetrahedron was introduced as a possible event model for G-O-D in the first chapter, it was noted that the tetrahedron "can be regarded as a four-dimensional model; it is possible to so erect four perpendiculars from its four faces that they meet in the geometric 'center' of the tetrahedron, thus defining that 'central point' in four dimensions."[8] If we use that possibility as a tool, we have a way of beginning to visualize a four-dimensional conceptual space in which research-as-a-method might help us show that some Y is safe and efficacious. Thus, let's begin this exploration with a tetrahedron and four perpendiculars that meet at a central point.

Figure 1 visualizes the condition described by Fuller. For the purposes of building a model, the central point is labeled A, and the intersections of the perpendiculars meeting at A with the four faces have been labeled B, C, D, and E. Thus, each of the faces of the tetrahedron can be associated with one of the four conceptual dimensions, as is noted in figure 1. For example: face 123 is intersected by line B-A, which represents the accident dimension of the concept of safety, so face 123 can be associated with that dimension as an "accident face" in a tetrahedral model. Similarly, face 124 can be associated with the injury dimension as an "injury face" in a tetrahedral model.

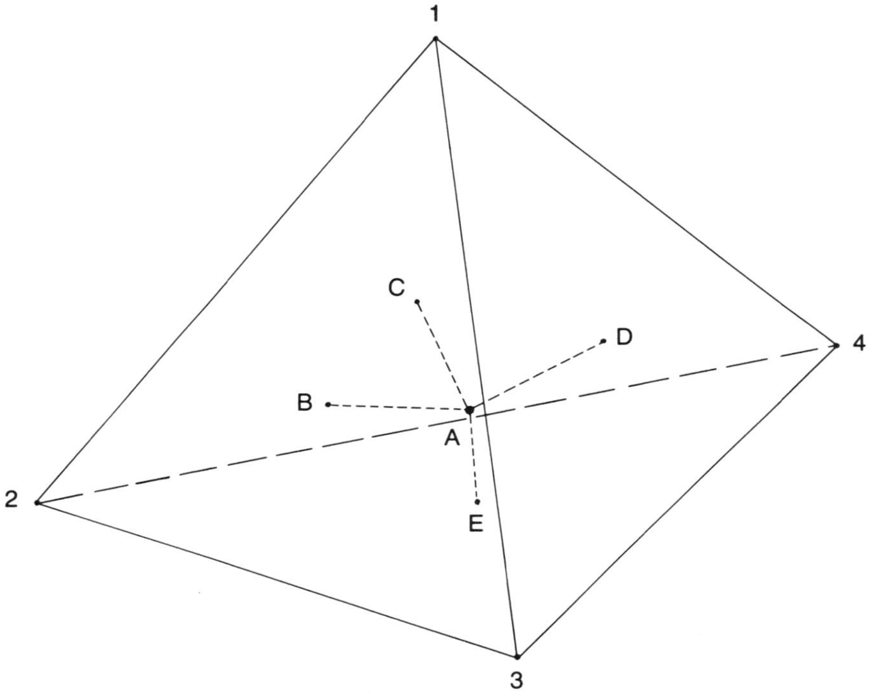

WHERE: Line B-A is 90 degrees from face 123 and B-A represents accident dimension.
Line C-A is 90 degrees from face 124 and C-A represents injury dimension.
Line D-A is 90 degrees from face 134 and D-A represents achievement dimension.
Line E-A is 90 degrees from face 234 and E-A represents reliability dimension.

AND
WHERE: Point A is the geometric center.

Figure 1. Using a tetrahedron to identify a four-dimensional researchable conceptual space defined by three safety dimensions (accident, injury, and reliability) and one efficacy dimension (achievement).

Face 134 can be associated with the achievement dimension as an "achievement face" in a tetrahedral model. And face 234 can be associated with the reliability dimension as a "reliability face" in a tetrahedral model.

The tetrahedral model of figure 1 is a help, but it is also confusing to creatures used to perceiving (and thinking) in terms of three-dimensional space. Fortunately, it is possible to create a set of three-dimensional models which will identify all of the possibilities of the four-dimensional model, but do so in a way that is much more familiar. Actually, there are only four three-dimensional models in such a set. That is because we want to use three of the four conceptual dimensions and, so, the number of models is equivalent to the number of ways one can take three of four things: a relatively straightforward question of mathematical combinations.[9] That set of four is displayed in figure 2.

The four cubes shown in figure 2 are different from one another, but also clearly related to one another. For instance, any two cubes will be found to share *two* of the four conceptual dimensions, while *one* conceptual dimension will be different. Moreover, three of the cubes make use of the one efficacy dimension (achievement) and of two of the three safety dimensions (accident, injury, and reliability). Only one of the cubes uses all three safety dimensions. That one cube (figure 2, cube #2) is a three-dimensional model of the concept of safety alone. However, the important thing about these four cubes is that they are a set; they belong together.

The essential interrelatedness of the four three-dimensional models in figure 2 can be explored by noting the pattern of edge sharing in the several cubes. Since these cube models are ways of visualizing a single four-dimensional model, such edge sharing should exist in some ordered way. As table I indicates, there is such an ordered pattern of edge sharing. Each cube has twelve edges that could be shared. Of those twelve edges, *three* are shared with three other cubes; *six* are shared with two other cubes; and *three* are specific to that one cube. The particular ordered twelve-edge sets for each of these cubes can be identified in table 2. This ordered pattern across all four three-dimensional cube models is more than just a curious occurrence; it is a

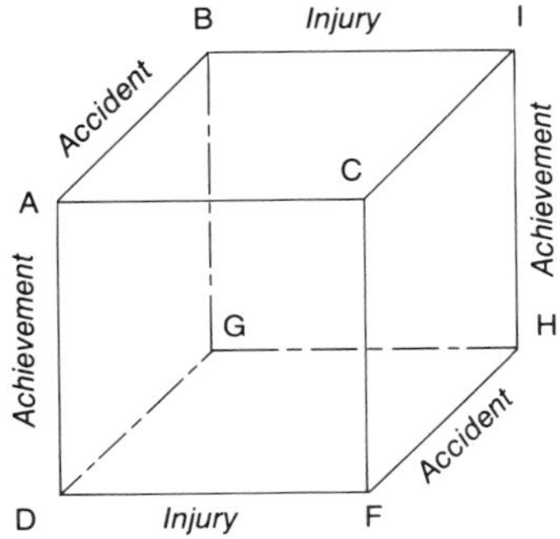

(1) Accident-Injury-Achievement

WHERE:
Accident = Safety
Injury = Safety
Achievement = Efficacy

(2) Accident-Injury-Reliability

WHERE:
Accident = Safety
Injury = Safety
Reliability = Safety

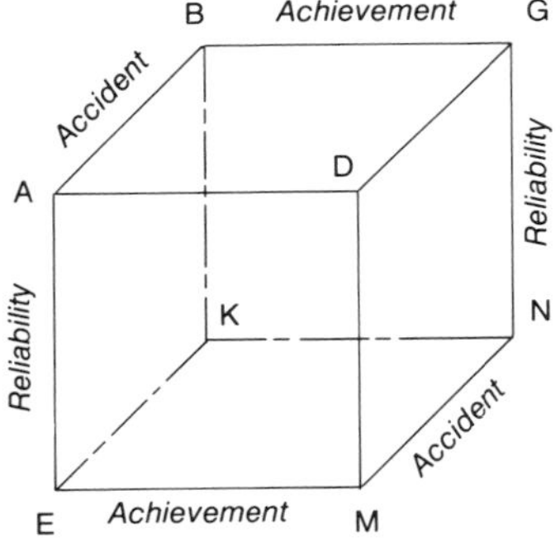

(3) Accident-Reliability-Achievement

WHERE:
Accident = Safety
Reliability = Safety
Achievement = Efficacy

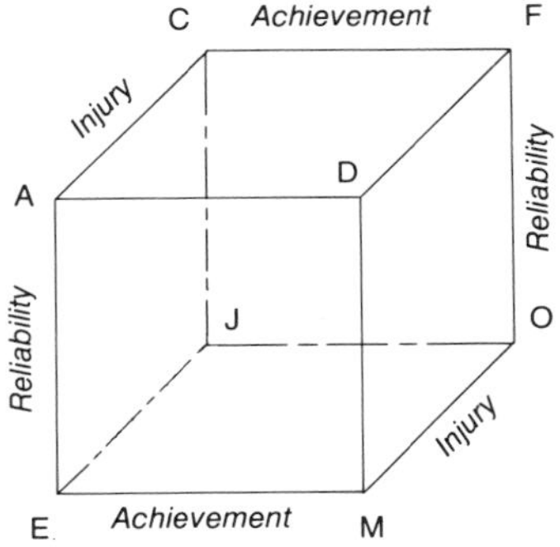

(4) Injury-Reliability-Achievement

WHERE:
Injury = Safety
Reliability = Safety
Achievement = Efficacy

Figure 2. Four three-dimensional models of researchable conceptual spaces defined by three safety dimensions and one efficacy dimension.

sign that the cube models in figure 2 are what they purport to be, a visualization in three dimensions of a four-dimensional researchable conceptual space.

Notice what is now possible.

Instead of pushing ourselves to try visualizing what is difficult, even

Table 1.
Participation of conceptual dimensions in four three-dimensional models of a four-dimensional researchable conceptual space for safety and efficacy.

Dimension:	Cube #1	Cube #2	Cube #3	Cube #4	Participation:		Conceptual Relation:
ACCIDENT	A-B	A-B	A-B	******	3 cubes	123	Safety
	C-I	C-I	—	******	2 cubes	12	Safety
	D-G	—	D-G	******	2 cubes	13	Safety
	—	E-K	E-K	******	2 cubes	23	Safety
	F-H	—	—	******	1 cube	1	Safety
	—	J-L	—	******	1 cube	2	Safety
	—	—	M-N	******	1 cube	3	Safety
INJURY	A-C	A-C	******	A-C	3 cubes	124	Safety
	B-I	B-I	******	—	2 cubes	12	Safety
	D-F	—	******	D-F	2 cubes	14	Safety
	—	E-J	******	E-J	2 cubes	24	Safety
	G-H	—	******	—	1 cube	1	Safety
	—	K-L	******	—	1 cube	2	Safety
	—	—	******	M-O	1 cube	4	Safety
ACHIEVEMENT	A-D	******	A-D	A-D	3 cubes	134	Efficacy
	B-G	******	B-G	—	2 cubes	13	Efficacy
	C-F	******	—	C-F	2 cubes	14	Efficacy
	—	******	E-M	E-M	2 cubes	34	Efficacy
	H-I	******	—	—	1 cube	1	Efficacy
	—	******	K-N	—	1 cube	3	Efficacy
	—	******	—	J-O	1 cube	4	Efficacy
RELIABILITY	******	A-E	A-E	A-E	3 cubes	234	Safety
	******	B-K	B-K	—	2 cubes	23	Safety
	******	C-J	--	C-J	2 cubes	24	Safety
	******	—	D-M	D-M	2 cubes	34	Safety
	******	—	—	F-O	1 cube	4	Safety
	******	—	G-N	—	1 cube	3	Safety
	******	I-L	—	—	1 cube	2	Safety

with the help of the tetrahedral model of figure 1, we are now able to consider a set of more familiar models. In fact, each of the four cubes in that set are a reasonably normal way to conceive of a conceptual space, in which we can imagine using research-as-a-method. Thus, we have found a way to accommodate our limitations and, yet, also transcend those limits. However, there is one more difficulty: we tend to be

Table 2.
Participatory analysis of four three-dimensional models of a four-dimensional researchable conceptual space for safety and efficacy.

3-dimensional cube model:	*Accident:*		*Injury:*		*Achievement:*		*Reliability:*		Vertices: (8/Model):
Cube #1 (fig. 2)	A-B		A-C		A-D		—		A, B, C,
Accident	C-I		B-I		B-G		—		D, F, G
Injury	D-G		D-F		C-F		—		H, I.
Achievement	F-H		G-H		H-I		—		
Cube #2 (fig. 2)	A-B		A-C		—		A-E		A, B, C,
Accident	C-I		B-I		—		B-K		E, I, J,
Injury	E-K		E-J		—		C-J		K, L.
Reliability	J-L		K-L		—		I-L		
Cube #3 (fig. 2)	A-B		—		A-D		A-E		A, B, D,
Accident	D-G		—		B-G		B-K		E, G, K,
Reliability	E-K		—		E-M		D-M		M, N.
Achievement	M-N		—		K-N		G-N		
Cube #4 (fig. 2)	—		A-C		A-D		A-E		A, C, D,
Injury	—		D-F		C-F		C-J		E, F, J,
Reliability	—		E-J		E-M		D-M		M, O.
Achievement	—		M-O		J-O		F-O		
Edges in *three* model cubes:	A-B	123	A-C	124	A-D	134	A-E	234	
Edges in *two* model cubes:	C-I	12	B-I	12	B-G	13	B-K	23	
	D-G	13	D-F	14	C-F	14	C-J	24	
	E-K	23	E-J	24	E-M	34	D-M	34	
Edges in *one* model cube:	F-H	1	G-H	1	H-I	1	I-L	2	
	J-L	2	K-L	2	K-N	3	G-N	3	
	M-N	3	M-O	4	J-O	4	F-O	4	
Edges unique to *cube #1:*	F-H		G-H		H-I		—		H = Common
Edges unique to *cube #2:*	J-L		K-L		—		I-L		L = Common
Edges unique to *cube #3:*	M-N		—		K-N		G-N		N = Common
Edges unique to *cube #4:*	—		M-O		J-O		F-O		O = Common

WHERE: — = Cube does *not* involve this conceptual dimension (i.e., row category).
A, B, C, D, E, F, G, H, I, J, K, L, M, N, O = Vertices of cube models. (N = 15)
1, 2, 3, 4 = cube numbers.

confused by the sheer complexity of considering four things at once. Therefore, let us continue the exploration of this fourfold set by picking one cube model as an example. What we discover about that one cube will, then, be true of the other three cubes, when and as we decide to attend to them. For instance, let us explore the conceptual space modeled by cube #1 in figure 2.

Figure 3 is, of course, a quite general model. However, it moves our exploration forward a step, for it also models the dimensional relativity recognized earlier in this chapter. That is, each vertex has an appropriate set of three symbols to identify the combination of dimensional states that are represented by that vertex. Moreover, the distinction along any one of the conceptual dimensions has been kept at a very simple level: that is, only a "less" or a "more." Yet that is an extraordinarily useful thing. It enables us to visualize eight threefold combinations of theoretically *extreme* possibilities for this particular conceptual space. Thus, we can identify eight possible threefold states that the use of research-as-a-method might encounter and, so, describe. In fact, from the eight corners of the cube model in figure 3 we can easily read off those logically possible albeit theoretical threefold combinations as:

A (−−−) = Less accidental and less injury and less achieve the intended
B (−+−) = Less accidental and more injury and less achieve the intended
C (+−−) = More accidental and less injury and less achieve the intended
I (++−) = More accidental and more injury and less achieve the intended
D (−−+) = Less accidental and less injury and more achieve the intended
F (−++) = Less accidental and more injury and more achieve the intended
G (+−+) = More accidental and less injury and more achieve the intended
H (+++) = More accidental and more injury and more achieve the intended

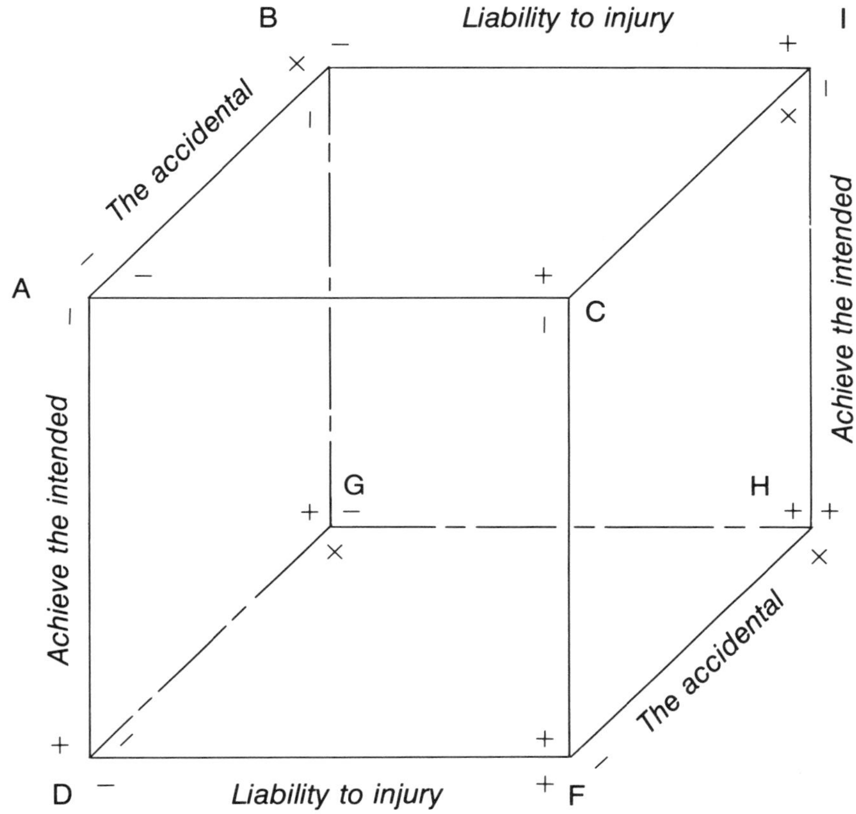

WHERE: − = Less. + = More. Of a particular conceptual dimension.

Figure 3. Three-dimensional model of researchable conceptual space.

Interestingly, these eight threefold combinations represented by the eight vertices of the cube model represent the full set of logically possible dichotomies for a set of three entities. A truth table for three entities, each of which could assume one of two states (e.g., "less" or "more"), will identify each of these corner states and, importantly, no others. Thus, the cube model of figure 3 can be regarded as a logically exhaustive analysis of the imagined conceptual space, given the simple less-more distinction along each of the three conceptual dimensions.

That is quite important; for it enables us to be confident that we can consider the full range of possible states and, if we wish, make some quite subjective judgments about our own preference for those states. We can systematically indicate our preferences without overlooking any possibility.

While I cannot predict a reader's preference, I can acknowledge my own and, so, invite a reader to agree or disagree. I find that I most prefer the threefold dimensional state represented by corner D (i.e., less accidental and less injury and more achieve the intended) and I least prefer the threefold dimensional state represented by corner I (i.e., more accidental and more injury and less achieve the intended). Interestingly, corners D and I turn out to be diagonally opposite one another in the conceptual space that is modeled in figure 3. As a result, it is possible to imagine a theoretical continuum *from* my least preferred threefold dimensional state *to* my most preferred threefold dimensional state running *from* corner I *to* corner D of this modeled conceptual space.

Moreover, if I rearrange (or redefine) the symbol system, so that the minus sign (−) means "least preferable" and the plus sign (+) means "most preferable," I find that I can specify my preferences vis-a-vis each of the three conceptual dimensions quite precisely. Then, if my preferences are at all similar to those of most persons, I will have a conceptual model of real use in thinking about what it could mean to use research-as-a-method in the attempt to show that some Y is both safe and efficacious. Therefore, consider figure 4, which is identical to figure 3 except that it now symbolizes my stated preferences.

If, but only if, one agrees that the safety of some Y involves a preference for (i) less likelihood of accidental occurrences, and (ii) less liability to injury, the model in figure 4 will be satisfactory. Also if, but only if, one agrees that the efficacy of some Y involves a preference for more achievement of that which is intended, the model in figure 4 will be satisfactory. If, but only if, one agrees that these two safety dimensions and this one efficacy dimension for some Y involve these three preferences, the model in figure 4 will be a satisfactory form of the model in figure 3. While I think my stated and symbolized preferences are clear examples of safety and efficacy, the three *conditional* state-

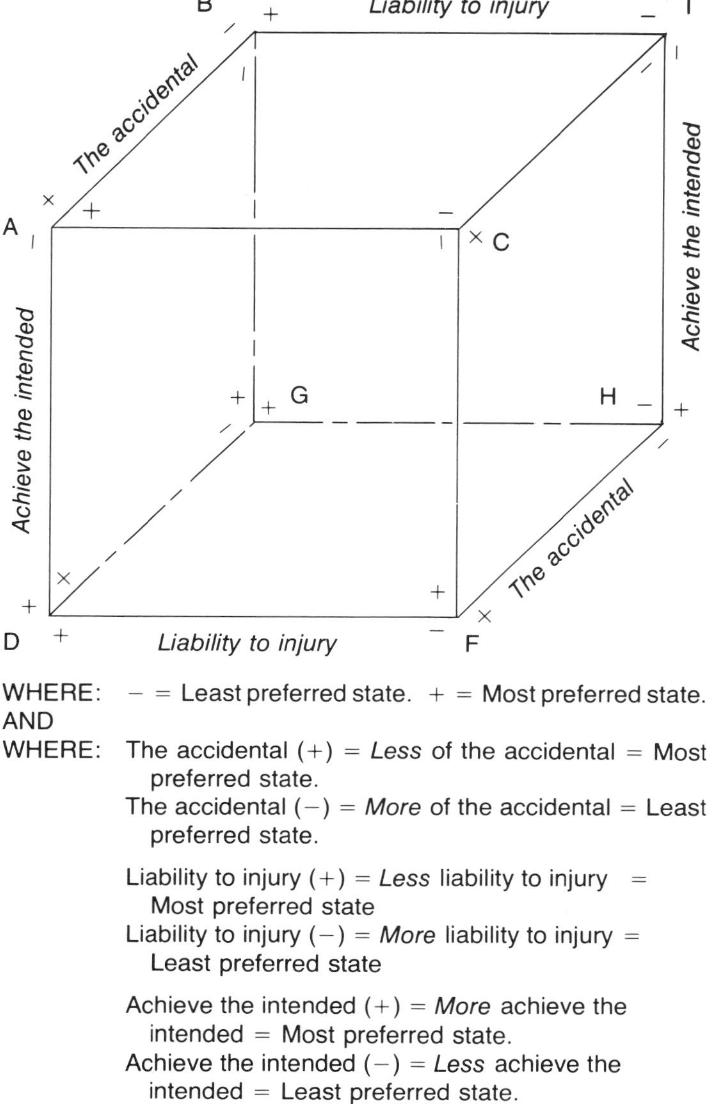

Figure 4. Three-dimensional model of a researchable conceptual space, given the problems of safety and efficacy of some given concept.

ments that precede this sentence must be stated in exactly that way, *if* readers are to recognize their own preferences, whatever they may be. I know what *I* have done, but readers need to recognize that they join me in that (if they do!), or, perhaps, choose to arrange *their* preferences differently.

Literally, all I have done is to rescale the conceptual dimensions, so that all three are in a "positive" direction (that is, match my "positive" preference). That is a common enough procedure in any of the sciences and, so, should be no sticky point for anyone. However, I do want a reader to understand *why* the eight corners (or vertices) in figure 3 and figure 4 are labeled in the same way vis-a-vis the symbols A, B, C, D, F, G, H, and I, but not vis-a-vis the combination of plus and minus signs at each corner. The rescaling has affected the meaning of plus and minus signs, but not the location or the fundamental meaning of the corners of this conceptual space.

It is still possible to imagine a theoretical continuum running *from* corner I (i.e., consistently least preferred) *to* corner D (i.e., consistently most preferred), just as it was in figure 3. However, the rescaling has now made it possible to give a reasonably unambiguous numerical value to the plus and minus signs and, so, identify a simple additive four-point scale. Such a scale could run from a least preferred state through some intermediate states to a most preferred state. In fact, through the use of the tool of a truth table keyed to the corners of this conceptual space, such a four-point scale can readily be identified. That is exactly what is displayed in table 3.

Table 3.
Truth table for three conceptual dimensions with corner equivalents in a conceptual space

SAFETY DIMENSIONS:		*EFFICACY DIMENSION:*	
Liability to injury:	The accidental:	Achieve the intended:	Corner:
− (least prefer)	− (least prefer)	− (least prefer)	I
− (least prefer)	− (least prefer)	+ (most prefer)	H
− (least prefer)	+ (most prefer)	− (least prefer)	C
− (least prefer)	+ (most prefer)	+ (most prefer)	F
+ (most prefer)	− (least prefer)	− (least prefer)	B
+ (most prefer)	− (least prefer)	+ (most prefer)	G
+ (most prefer)	+ (most prefer)	− (least prefer)	A
+ (most prefer)	+ (most prefer)	+ (most prefer)	D

Now, if we can imagine assigning a numerical value to both the plus sign and the minus sign, it will be possible to create a simple additive four-place scale. For example, imagine a rule that specified that a plus sign (+) had a numerical value of one, and that a minus sign (−) had a numerical value of zero. Then imagine replacing the plus and minus signs in table 3 with the rule-specified zeros and ones and, finally, summing each corner-specific row. That is exactly what has been done in table 4, which is identical to table 3 except for this rule-determined symbol substitution.

The four-place simple additive scale in table 4 runs from 0, through 1 and 2, to 3. It is, of course, a form of numerical shorthand. However, if one remembers what has been done, one can identify with a *single* symbol sets of possibilities that, while different, are also similar. One of these sets is symbolized by the number one (1), while another such set is symbolized by the number two (2). Each of these sets has three members, but the sets differ from one another in that the set symbolized by the number one includes only those threefold state combinations in which only one of the conceptual dimensions is most preferred, while the set symbolized by the number two includes only those threefold state combinations in which only one of the conceptual dimensions is least preferred. As a result, it is possible to determine a theoretical probability of observing any of the four sets of threefold state combinations, under the assumption of chance or randomness.

Table 4.
Truth table for three conceptual dimensions with numerical values assigned and corner equivalents identified.

SAFETY DIMENSIONS: Liability to injury:	The accidental:	*EFFICACY DIMENSION:* Achieve the intended:	Corner: (Sum)
0 (least prefer)	0 (least prefer)	0 (least prefer)	I (0)
0 (least prefer)	0 (least prefer)	1 (most prefer)	H (1)
0 (least prefer)	1 (most prefer)	0 (least prefer)	C (1)
0 (least prefer)	1 (most prefer)	1 (most prefer)	F (2)
1 (most prefer)	0 (least prefer)	0 (least prefer)	B (1)
1 (most prefer)	0 (least prefer)	1 (most prefer)	G (2)
1 (most prefer)	1 (most prefer)	0 (least prefer)	A (2)
1 (most prefer)	1 (most prefer)	1 (most prefer)	D (3)

While this last possibility may not seem like much of an achievement, it is a beginning on the important problem of researching such a conceptual space. Thus, it is only a start; but having a theoretically expected probability for any observed three-part state combination enables one to compare and contrast actual observation against theoretical expectation (assuming chance). Yet we can determine whether research-as-a-method provides evidence for something other than chance occurrences of particular states of some Y. Unless we are content to risk fooling ourselves, we need to be able to do just that.

It is clear from table 5 that a score of zero (0) identifies a state in the conceptual space that is both consistently *least preferred* and is, as well, neither safe nor efficacious. It is equally clear from table 5 that a score of three (3) identifies a state that is both consistently *most preferred* and, as well, both safe and efficacious. What we learn from table 5 is that, under the assumption of chance, both these states are equally

Table 5.
Simple four-place additive scale for a three-dimensional conceptual space with dimensions dichotomously divided.

	SCORES ON A SIMPLE ADDITIVE SCALE:				
	0	1	2	3	
Pattern:	0 0 0 (I)	0 0 1 (H) 0 1 0 (C) 1 0 0 (B)	0 1 1 (F) 1 0 1 (G) 1 1 0 (A)	1 1 1 (D)	Patte[rn:]
Number of patterns:	1/8	3/8	3/8	1/8	Number [of] patter[ns:]
Chance probability:	0.125	0.375	0.375	0.125	Chan[ce] probabili[ty:]

WHERE: Patterns are taken from table 4.

AND WHERE: 0 = − = A *least preferred* state along a conceptual dimension.
1 = + = A *most preferred* state along a conceptual dimension.

1st (left-most) position = Liability to injury (safety dimension).
2nd (middle) position = Likelihood of accident (safety dimension).
3rd (right) position = Achievement of intended (efficacy dimension).

probable. However, we also learn that the two intermediate states are (under the assumption of chance) remarkably probable: the probability of observing *either* a 2-type state *or* a 1-type state is 0.750. That is, three out of four times by chance we could expect to observe one or another of these six states. Thus, it will pay to carefully attend to those theoretically probable states and, if possible, distinguish them from one another sufficiently to understand what we are all too likely to observe.

For instance, only one of the three states with a score of one (1) is efficacious, although it not also safe. Two of the states with a score of one (1) are safe, but neither is also efficacious. On the other hand, only one of the three states with a score of two (2) is not efficacious, although it is safe. Also, two of the states with a score of two (2) are efficacious and at least partially safe. Moreover, all three of the states with a score of two (2) are, in some way, safe.

Careful consideration of these eight possible states of the conceptual space can help us (i) anticipate what *may* be observed through use of the tool of research-as-a-method, and so (ii) compare and contrast the results of our use of that tool. Thereby avoiding the risk of thinking some Y is safe or efficacious when, perhaps, it is not. There is no need for us to so fool ourselves if, in fact, we really do not want to do that. Yet, should that be our intent, less-than careful consideration will do much to ensure our actual intent: we will fool ourselves and, so, think that what is *not* actually *is*. Once again, *we* determine so much of what we "know."

A YET-NEXT STEP: REFINING THE MODELED CONCEPTUAL SPACE

What we have so far recognized is that by dichotomizing each of the three conceptual dimensions in cube #1 of figure 2, we can identify eight logically possible states, each of which can be described in terms of a threefold combination of a "more" and a "less" of each of those three imagined conceptual dimensions. Still, most mature humans tend to be a bit dissatisfied with such a gross dichotomy: they want to go further and posit more refined (more numerous) distinctions along each of the several conceptual dimensions. And, of course, that is possible. In fact, it is even useful; for doing that provides a better approximation of what we often desire—something we think of as certainty.

Therefore, let's imagine that each conceptual dimension has five (5) instead of only two (2) possible states. That is, in between an extreme "more" and an extreme "less," which we have already identified, let's imagine three more sequential states. For instance, suppose that we imagine a middle state as a "real" halfway point between the extremes. Then we can fairly easily imagine a halfway point between such a real middle and each of the already identified extremes. One will be halfway between the real middle and the "more" extreme, while one will be halfway between the middle and the "less" extreme. Then, let us imagine that our own quite subjective preference for the "more" or the "less" extreme is translated into a value sequence that parallels the degree to which, now, the preferred state of any conceptual dimension is approximated.

If we can imagine that, we are ready to imagine a logical five-part division of each conceptual dimension. For example, let's suppose that the extreme less-preferred state be called a situation that *rarely* exhibits the preferred state of that dimension. Then, moving sequentially along that particular conceptual dimension, suppose that the remaining four places be called situations that *occasionally*, *sometimes*, *often*, and *always* exhibit the preferred state of the dimension. If we can imagine that, we will have found a way to translate a simple, gross dichotomy into a finer five-place division of the logically possible states of each conceptual dimension.

In figure 5, each of the three conceptual dimensions has been marked off (or partitioned) into five sequential segments, which represent a series of states from less to more preferred. Thus, figure 5 represents what we were imagining in the previous paragraph, applied to *each* dimension.

However different it may look, figure 5 is identical to figure 4. It probably looks a good bit more complicated, because it is. Yet the two are the same: readers might well stop for a moment and determine that

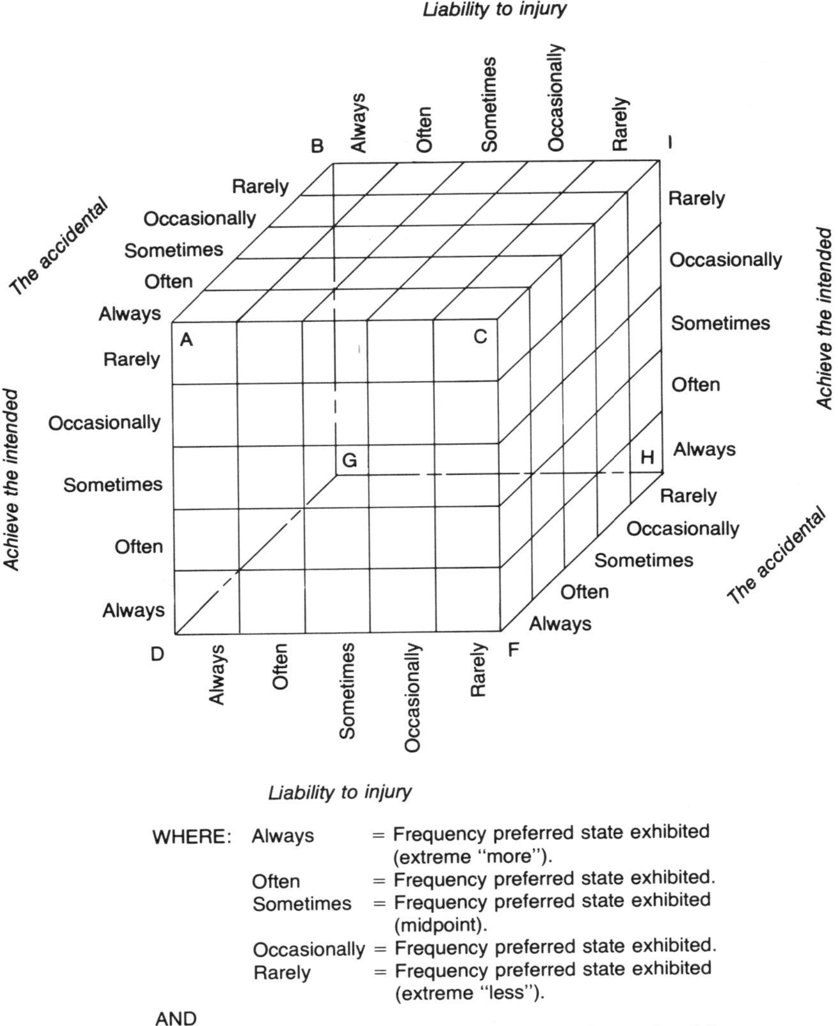

Figure 5. Three-dimensional model of a researchable conceptual space, with each conceptual dimension subdivided into five sequentially preferable states, running from "more" (always) to "less" (rarely).

Table 6.
Truth table for three items, each of which can assume five states.

ID:	State:		ID:	State:		ID:	State:		ID:	State:		ID:	State:	
001	111	03	026	211	04	051	311	05	076	411	06	101	511	07
002	112	04	027	212	05	052	312	06	077	412	07	102	512	08
003	113	05	028	213	06	053	313	07	078	413	08	103	513	09
004	114	06	029	214	07	054	314	08	079	414	09	104	514	10
005	115	07	030	215	08	055	315	09	080	415	10	105	515	11
006	121	04	031	221	05	056	321	06	081	421	07	106	521	08
007	122	05	032	222	06	057	322	07	082	422	08	107	522	09
008	123	06	033	223	07	058	323	08	083	423	09	108	523	10
009	124	07	034	224	08	059	324	09	084	424	10	109	524	11
010	125	08	035	225	09	060	325	10	085	425	11	110	525	12
011	131	05	036	231	06	061	331	07	086	431	08	111	531	09
012	132	06	037	232	07	062	332	08	087	432	09	112	532	10
013	133	07	038	233	08	063	333	09	088	433	10	113	533	11
014	134	08	039	234	09	064	334	10	089	434	11	114	534	12
015	135	09	040	235	10	065	335	11	090	435	12	115	535	13
016	141	06	041	241	07	066	341	08	091	441	09	116	541	10
017	142	07	042	242	08	067	342	09	092	442	10	117	542	11
018	143	08	043	243	09	068	343	10	093	443	11	118	543	12
019	144	09	044	244	10	069	344	11	094	444	12	119	544	13
020	145	10	045	245	11	070	345	12	095	445	13	120	545	14
021	151	07	046	251	08	071	351	09	096	451	10	121	551	11
022	152	08	047	252	09	072	352	10	097	452	11	122	552	12
023	153	09	048	253	10	073	353	11	098	453	12	123	553	13
024	154	10	049	254	11	074	354	12	099	454	13	124	554	14
025	155	11	050	255	12	075	355	13	100	455	14	125	555	15

WHERE: 1 = *Rarely* exhibits the preferred state.
2 = *Occasionally* exhibits the preferred state.
3 = *Sometimes* exhibits the preferred state.
4 = *Often* exhibits the preferred state.
5 = *Always* exhibits the preferred state.

AND WHERE: 1st position (left) = Liability to injury dimension (safety).
2nd position (mid) = Likelihood accidental dimension (safety).
3rd position (right) = Achievement of intended dimension (efficacy).

fact for themselves. The only difference is the number of subdivisions along each of the three conceptual dimensions. Each of the eight corners, however, does represent exactly the same state in figure 5 as it does in figure 4. If there is any doubt, take a few moments and determine that fact for yourself!

The complexity inherent in figure 5 can readily be appreciated when one asks and then answers the question: How many logically possible states in the modeled researchable space can now be identified? Actually, the answer is fairly simple: 5 × 5 × 5 logically possible states can now be identified. Those 125 states are many more than the 8 states that could be identified in the researchable conceptual space modeled by figure 4. However, each and every one of those states can be identified through the tool use of a truth table for three items, each of which can assume one of five possible states.

Frankly, although 125 is obviously still a finite number, it *is* a large enough number to be rather awesome to consider. However, *Table* VI contains three potentially useful things in *each* of the five major columns. First, there is a sequential identification number, which runs from 001 to 125. Second, there is a three-part identification of a logically possible combination of the numbers 1, 2, 3, 4, and 5. This combination represents a possible state of the researchable space modeled by figure 5. Third, there is the simple *sum* of the three numbers immediately to the left, which represent a logically possible state of the conceptual space modeled in figure 5. These sums run from 03 to 15, and provide a simple way to create a more refined yet simple additive scale that will summarize this large number of possible states of the researchable conceptual space. Moreover, given the truth table of table 6, we have a way of knowing exactly what *set* of possible states the numerical shorthand of a score might mean.

Just as a few paragraphs earlier we looked at eight (8) logically possible states in table 5, we can now look at the not-so-simple additive scale implicit in table 6. In fact, when we do that, as we will in table 7, we are looking at formally similar things.

The thirteen-point additive scale displayed in table 7 gives us a quasi-normal distribution for the 125 specific, theoretically possible states of the researchable conceptual space modeled by figure 5.

Table 7.
Simple additive scale from three items, each of which can assume five states.
Arranged from least to most preferred.

	03	04	05	06	07	08	09	10	11	12	13	14	15
01	111	112	113	114	115	125	135	145	155	255	355	554	555
02		121	122	123	124	134	144	154	245	345	445	545	
03		211	131	132	133	143	153	235	254	354	454	455	
04			212	141	142	152	225	244	335	435	535		
05			221	213	151	215	234	253	344	444	544		
06			311	222	214	224	243	325	353	453	553		
07				231	223	233	252	334	425	525			
08				312	232	242	315	343	434	534			
09				321	241	251	324	352	443	543			
10				411	313	314	333	415	452	552			
11					322	323	342	424	515				
12					331	332	351	433	524				
13					412	341	414	442	533				
14					421	413	423	451	542				
15					511	422	432	514	551				
16						431	441	523					
17						512	513	532					
18						521	522	541					
19							531						
N:	01	03	06	10	15	18	19	18	15	10	06	03	01
P:	.008	.024	.048	.080	.120	.144	.152	.144	.120	.080	.048	.024	.008

WHERE: 1 = *Rarely* exhibits the preferred dimensional/positional state.
2 = *Occasionally* exhibits the preferred dimensional/positional state.
3 = *Sometimes* exhibits the preferred dimensional/positional state.
4 = *Often* exhibits the preferred dimensional/positional state.
5 = *Always* exhibits the preferred dimensional/positional state.

AND
WHERE: 1st position (left) = Liability to injury dimension (safety).
2nd position (mid) = Likelihood accidental dimension (safety).
3rd position (right) = Achievement of intended dimension (efficacy).

Clearly that result is an artifact of using the conceptual invention of a logical truth table. Yet, as almost one hundred years of carefully recorded observation indicate, it is an often surprisingly accurate description of the sum of human actions or abilities or characteristics. Thus, such a quasi-normal distribution is a reasonable approximation of the way things are likely to be observed in the so-called normal state. Frankly, our problem as religious educators is that we have yet to come to terms with either that likelihood or the related notion that if something is logically possible then, sooner or later, we are likely to observe that possibility.

However, religious educators are not alone. We humans keep on thinking that if we take account of our intentions we will avoid the possibility of our actions, abilities, or characteristics (in sum) forming some quasi-normal distribution. As a result, we too often avoid an analysis of the full range of logically possible states and, so, are poorly prepared to know when or where or how or even if our intentions affect the situation. That is too bad.

I. Watch Your Step!—A Caution

I have implicitly referenced the work of Sir Francis Galton (1822–1911) on the regularity of human characteristics.[10] *That* accounts for some of the necessary and useful precision. Really, we need to recognize that, whatever merits (or demerits) we may discern in Galton's original works, what he did was to alert humankind to the observable regularity in many of its characteristics, when a considerable sample of humans are observed. In the time since Galton's works, that regularity has not disappeared, nor has it been found to be restricted to the specific examples he chose to study. Moreover, it is that regularity which, conceptually, lies immediately behind what we know as a theoretically normal distribution. *That* accounts for a bit of the useful *care*. In addition, we need to recognize that while human characteristics, in the aggregate, are often anticipatable (reasonably predictable), the specific and the individual instance is often not anywhere near so readily anticipatable. There is something like a paradox in our observations of humankind. In the aggregate, our human characteristics are often theoretically normally distributed; yet, in the specific instance, the expectation is simply unknown. We humans seem to do what we will, one by one, yet in an aggregate those individual actions often form a remarkably good approximation to a theoretically normal distribution. *That* accounts for a seemingly necessary *caution*. That paradox seems to have lurked at the edge of our collective consciousness for all too long, and it would help us all to at least acknowledge its presence.

Let us be very honest.

If we were content to encounter each situation totally afresh, without any preconceptions based on our actual or vicarious experience, we might avoid the paradox posed by Galton's nineteenth-century work. However, that would mean that we stopped thinking about such generalities as humankind or its characteristics and, instead, thought only about specific, individual cases—endlessly. To do that would mean that we never learned from experience or history, but only learned *from* specific instances *about* those specific instances.[11] Strangely, humans seem to resist such a limitation upon their learning: they rather persistently seek for some generalization which will tell them what is probable, in the aggregate, and then try to adjust that information to the encountered specificities. In a word, we humans seem to prefer living with the paradox to living without it.

II. Don't Forget the Goal!—An Encouragement

Now, let us be realistic and practical.

Very, very few humans try and keep a full set of logically possible states of anything in their mind. One of our most frequently used ways of avoiding any such necessity is to posit that we are interested only in some subset of the total set of all of the logically possible states. We put further criteria over against the mass of logically possible states, and then say to ourselves that we are only concerned with those possible states that meet those further criteria. That is an old, honorable, and quite accepted way of avoiding being overwhelmed by the sheer number of the logically possible states of almost anything. It is, also, a way of acknowledging that we are creatures of this creation, and not something other than that.

We are what we are; that is all.

And that is quite enough!

Without boring the reader with even more tables, let me report what *can* happen to that full set of 125 logically possible states which is displayed in table 5, when various *further* criteria are used. Although still theoretical, these results indicate how our use of criteria for what we tend to regard as the minimally "acceptable" simplifies the range of our options. Thus, do consider the following set of six successively rigorous criteria.

1. Suppose that we decided that we simply could not consider any Y as safe or efficacious if any of the conceptual dimensions was judged to be only rarely in a preferred state. That is, no score in any of the three positions could be a 1, or no score in any of the three positions could be lower than a 2.

Accepting this criterion would mean that we set our minimal criteria at the level of at least an *occasional* observation of the preferred state along each conceptual dimension. If we did that, we would find that only 64 of the 125 logical possibilities met our criteria. Thus, we would identify 51.20 percent of the full set as those logically possible states in which we had any interest. We would, thereby, have almost halved the full set, which is a fair simplification of our situation vis-a-vis this particular set of logically possible states.

2. However, suppose that we decided that we valued efficacy just a bit more than safety and, therefore, that we insisted on attending *only* to states characterized by at least *occasionally* preferred states of either safety dimension and by at least a *sometimes* preferred state along the efficacy dimension. That is, no score in either of the first two (safety) positions could be lower than a 2, and no score in the third (efficacy) position could be lower than a 3.

If we did that, we would find that only 49 of the 125 logical possibilities met this particular set of criteria. As a result, we would identify 39.20 percent of the full set of logically possible states as those in which we had any interest.

3. Next, suppose we decided that at least one of the safety dimensions must at least *sometimes* exhibit a preferred state, although the other safety dimension could exhibit that state only *occasionally*, while the efficacy dimension must at least exhibit a preferred state *sometimes*. That is, only one of the scores in either the first or the second position can be a 2, and the other first or second position score must be at least a 3, while no score in the third (efficacy) position can be less than a 3.

If we set our minimal criteria in this way, we would identify a yet smaller subsample of 46 out of 125 logical possibilities. Thus, we would identify 36.80 percent of the full set as logically possible states in which we had any interest. Clearly, with increasingly rigorous minimal criteria, we are increasingly successful in limiting the number of logically possible states in which (as we tend to say) we are at all interested. But the criteria are ours: we mustn't forget that.

4. Then, let us suppose that we regard all that we have considered as just so much avoiding of the issue. Thus, we might decide that both safety and efficacy require that any state of any of the three conceptual dimensions must *sometimes* exhibit the preferred state. That is, we decide that no score in any of the three positions can be less than a 3. Anything less is simply avoiding the issue.

Such a decision on our part would permit us to identify a small subset of only 27 of the 125 logically possible states as of any interest. Thus, we would identify a mere 21.60 percent of the full and complete set of logical possibilities as of any interest to us.

5. However, let us suppose that we decide to be even more rigorous. For instance, we decide to ignore any state in which both of the safety dimensions are not at least *sometimes* in a preferred state, and the efficacy dimension is not at least *often* in such a preferred state. That is, no score in either the first or the second position is less than a 3, and no score in the third position is less than a 4.

As a result of this yet-more-rigorous set of criteria, we would be able to identify a subset of only 18 out of the full set of 125 logically possible states. Thus, we would have limited ourselves to considering only 14.40 percent of the total set of logical possibilities.

6. Finally, let us suppose that none of the previous criteria match our understanding of what it means to think of a logically possible state as truly safe or efficacious. Therefore, we might decide that we could consider as safe or efficacious only those states which exhibit the preferred state on *all* three conceptual dimensions *often*. That is, no score in any of the three positions can be less than a 4.

Should we decide to be this rigorous, we will find that we have finally identified a small subset of only 8 out of the full set of 125 logically possible states. Only 8 states can meet our now quite rigorous criteria. Thus, we finally limit ourselves to considering a mere 6.25 percent of the total set of logical possibilities.

These six sets of successively rigorous criteria illustrate three important things. First, that the rigor of our criteria determine the extent to which we need to consider the full set of logically possible states in any researchable conceptual space. Second, that our decisions inescapably influence the nature of our use of research-as-a-method in any such researchable conceptual space. Third, the increasing improbability, under chance, of observing those states that meet our increasingly rigorous criteria. Thus, with increasing rigor we both know what we are doing and, as well, can anticipate increasing *difficulty* in doing that which we now know we wish to do. That may be unfortunate, but it is all too true of any exploration of any researchable conceptual space.

A PAUSE TO CONSIDER ONE MORE SIMPLIFICATION OF THE MODELED SPACE

At this point, we are like an explorer who, after struggling through steamy lowlands and up increasingly high foothills, discovers a verdant mountain valley with but one exit toward an as-yet-undiscovered "on beyond." There is a high pass to that on beyond on the other side of the valley. We have discovered a good bit of what it can mean to assess the safety or the efficacy of some Y that is similar to but not identical to the field of religious education. Like such an explorer, we can either settle in and explore *this* valley, or we can press on. But we are tired, and we need to rest before tackling that high pass.

Frankly, I have no intention of leading the reader up that steep incline to that high pass on the other side of this analogical valley. In fact, I will be content if a reader recognizes the pass's existence and acknowledges the effort that would be required to reach even its lower parts, let alone crest it, see into that on beyond and, then, explore the as-yet-undiscovered spaces on beyond.

Speculation suggests that in any such on beyond there are more definitions, more criteria, and more decisions about how one can assess the resulting states of as-yet-undefined conceptual dimensions. However, it would literally take years of hard thought before one would be prepared to assess those dimensions. Those years of thought would demand our most creative use of all our available conceptual inventions, and even the invention of some new tools. So, being a cautious but hopeful explorer, I suggest that we content ourselves with the exploration of this hidden but verdant analogical valley, while we rest and reequip ourselves for a yet-next exploratory step—an assault on that high pass, and the exploration of the possibilities that may lie on beyond. In a word, we need to be better prepared for that assault than we are now. Preparation is what we *can* do in this present.

If that seems like faintheartedness, stop and think for a moment or two. We really should admit that we are not yet ready to assess all four of the already identified conceptual dimensions . . . even for a Y, let alone for religious education. Potentially we might be able to assess the conceptual dimension related to efficacy—the achievement of the intended. Just possibly we might be able to assess the conceptual dimension related to safety that has to do with the accidental. Very probably we are not yet ready to assess the conceptual dimension related to safety that has to do with injury, except in the simplest, grossest, most obviously physical sense of the word. Almost certainly we are not prepared to assess the conceptual dimension related to safety that has to do with reliability: there are too many imponderables in that concept, and we are barely aware of their being. Thus, let us acknowledge where we are. Let us prepare for a future that is not yet within our grasp by exploring, as we can, where we are right now. Let us refine our capabilities, and develop toward ones we do not yet have. Let us explore the newly discovered analogical valley, as we prepare ourselves and our tools for a future assault on that high pass between our present and some future, other "on beyond."

If the reader has followed me through those last poetic paragraphs, then the following will make some sense. I hope the mountain valley analogy has been useful, for I am about to "settle in," use more prosaic ways, and so begin to explore the valley in which we are now. To begin that exploration, I ask the reader to consider figure 6, which is displayed below.

The two conceptual dimensions of the matrix displayed in figure 6 are the ones we are most likely to be able to presently assess: the safety dimension of the *accidental*, and the efficacy dimension of *achieve-*

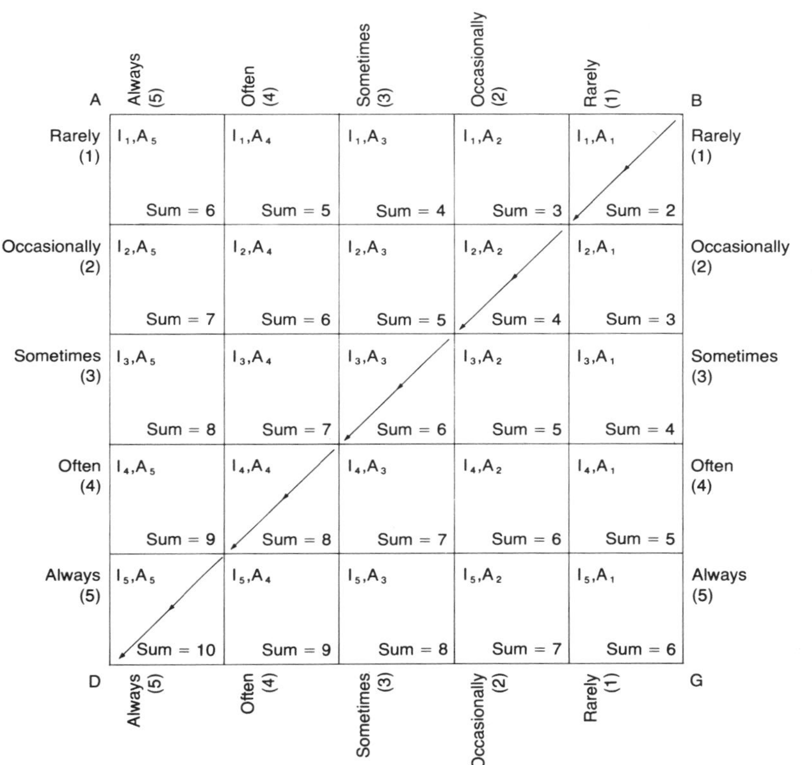

Conceptual dimension = The accidental

WHERE: Always (5), often (4), sometimes (3), occasionally (2), and rarely (1) refer to the frequency with which a preferred state is exhibited by either dimension.

Corners B, D, F, and H as in figures 1, 2, and 3.

Figure 6. Enlargement of face ABDG of three-dimensional model in figure 5.

ment of the intended. The matrix itself is like a conceptual map of that analogical mountain valley. But it is a map with a difference: it shows us a number of theoretical "wheres," but it does not yet show us any "whats." Until we actually explore that valley, we cannot know those whats, nor can we enter them onto our map. In fact, what we have in figure 6 is close to a cartographer's theoretical grid of longitude and latitude. Only careful exploration and multiple sightings enable us to know whether the cells are filled by valley or surrounding mountains. It is a challenging task to determine this valley's actual shape, topography, and dimensions.

The longitude and latitude of this conceptual map are a *safety* dimension and an *efficacy* dimension. As we noted somewhat earlier, both of these two dimensions are related through the concept of intention. The exploration of this particular analogical valley involves an exploration of intentionality. Thus, we must inevitably consider what those intentions are, and the criteria by which we could or would recognize that they had been achieved. This kind of exploration of intentionality, the thing we can be about, is usually called evaluation. In fact, that is what the yet-to-be-filled-in matrix map in figure 6 invites us to do. For it is in the doing that we begin to understand and, then, come to know. But any such knowing will involve us in careful exploration, meticulous record keeping, and multiple sightings. The accuracy of our final, filled-in map will also depend upon the care with which we explore, and the tools we have available and use. As is often the case, what *we* do with what *we* have tends to determine what happens: the result.

I. Where Are We?

The question "Where are we?" is one explorers learn to ask repeatedly. In fact, until they learn to ask and (somehow) answer that question, they are tourists, not yet explorers. Thus, it is important to answer that query vis-a-vis the exploration, the imaginary exercise, basic to this chapter. Actually, the answer is fairly clear, although it may not be all that encouraging. We are at an end of a process of simplification, which was initiated because we humans have extreme difficulty visualizing a four-dimensional researchable conceptual space and are, in fact, often hard put to deal with a three-dimensional conceptual space. It may not seem so, but that is where we are at this moment.

We have been thinking about settling into an analogical valley defined by one of three safety dimensions and the one efficacy dimension. The matrix map of figure 6 is but one of three (3) identifiably different faces of the three-dimensional cubical model displayed in figure 5. Thus, there remain two more faces of that three-dimensional cubical model to define and then explore before that one model will be thoroughly understood. Minimally, one more such face must be defined and explored before we can think of knowing how to go about the exploration of that final third face.

Moreover, the model displayed in figure 5 is but one of four identified in figure 2. Thus, all that can be imagined doing to thoroughly understand the one three-dimensional model in figure 5 must be replicated carefully three more times before we can expect to thoroughly understand the four cubes displayed in figure 2. Yet it is not until we can thoroughly understand those four three-dimensional model-equivalents in figure 2 that we will be in a position to truly, seriously consider the four-dimensional tetrahedral model identified in figure 1. That is our goal. The way from here to there is fairly clear, but it is rather lengthy. That we had best admit.

Fortunately, we can understand both where we are, and the pathway back to where we started. Our really basic, creaturely problem is not "understanding." That is reasonably possible. Our problem is that we creatures tend to want to do all things quickly: we seem to dislike the plodding, step-by-step approach. Thus, we often choose the quick and easy, rather than decide upon the slow and thorough, and almost as often find that we have chosen to follow an illusion. Yet that is an aspect of our creaturely state in this creation. What we tend to overlook is that the decisional option is also an aspect of our creaturely state in this creation. Therefore, we avoid our responsibility via ignorance, as often as not!

II. What Now?

I began this chapter with the problem of screening some set of heretofore accepted practices for (i) safety and (ii) genuine efficacy. We have moved to consider the complex of conceptual problems inherent in even imagining a demand for hard data on safety and efficacy. We have reached a form of simplification of the problem, and we have identified that we are inevitably involved in an exploration of intentionality. Moreover, we have found a word for that exploration: *evaluation*. What we have not yet found is a simple way to evaluate a Y that is similar but not identical to religious education. But we can now understand something of the nature of that task.

Maybe we can also understand the importance of that task.

Interestingly, although the specificities of each and every use of research-as-a-method for the task of evaluation differs from any other use, all such uses involve an exploration of intentionality. In fact, evaluations can be ranked along a success-to-failure continuum by the clarity with which (i) they can *specify* the intended, and (ii) they can determine *how* to assess the achievement of that which was intended. The first of these conditions is almost exclusively a problem of clear and honest thought: it is primarily a conceptual question. The second condition is, admittedly, often a problem of technical competence, but it is *always* a second condition. Too much experience in both education and in religious education over the past quarter of a century witnesses to that *order* for us to ignore it during this decade of the 1980s, or any other decade, for that matter.

While I am convinced of the importance of the general problem of measurement for either education or religious education, I also know that the conceptual problem of *what* to measure, and *why* that is what one must measure, precedes (both logically and pragmatically) the problem of *how* one will measure that *what*. However, I am not convinced that one must await a full and complete answer to the conceptual problem before addressing the often complex and usually technical specificities of the general problem of measurement. Because of both our conceptual and our practical need to evaluate what we do, it is very often well to seek to measure our best available, most nearly clarified statement of what it is that we intended. Often we find that hard; but we also learn something useful in the attempt about both our intention and our ability to assess. Such learning should send us back to two tasks, not just one. We need to attend both to our statement of our intention, and to our technique for assessing that intention.

This chapter must conclude with two related pieces of advice. First, think hard. Second, once thought reaches a level of almost any clarity, try to assess achievement. A third piece of advice is implicit in that sequence: let your experience influence your thought. In that way, you will explore intentionality, that usually hidden albeit verdant analogical mountain valley. Religious education has almost nothing worth preserving to lose from such a program, and almost everything to gain from carrying it out. For at some time, in some way, those of us who regard ourselves as religious educators may well have to conjure with that awesomely wonderful idea that a society which supports us *does* want to be shown that what we do is (i) safe, and (ii) genuinely efficacious. Without evaluation, or the use of research-as-a-method, we probably will be hard pressed to show anything like *that*.

So . . . *think*, and then *try* to *measure*.

Notes and References

1. Elliot Marshall, "Psychotherapy Faces Test of Worth," *Science*, vol. 207, no. 4426, p. 35.
2. Ibid.
3. *The Random House Dictionary of the English Language* (New York: Random House, 1967), the word *safe*.
4. Ibid., the word *efficacious*.
5. Arthur Bloch, *Murphy's Law* (Los Angeles: Price/Stern/Sloan Publishers, 1977), p. 20.
6. *The New Merriam-Webster Pocket Dictionary* (New York: Pocket Books, 1973), the words *harm*, *injury*, *danger*, and *risk*.
7. Ibid., the words *accident*, *error*, and *mishap*.
8. See chapter 1, p. 38. Also see R. Buckminster Fuller, *Synergetics: Explorations in the Geometry of Thinking* (New York: Macmillan Publishing Co., 1975), section 621.04, p. 335.
9. Allen L. Edwards, *Statistical Analysis* (New York: Holt, Rinehart and Winston, 1969), pp. 88–89.
10. For example, see Francis Galton, *Enquiries into Human Faculty and Its Development* (Macmillan, 1883); or idem, *Hereditary Genius* (Macmillan, 2nd ed., 1892).
11. See Jean Piaget, *Structuralism* (London: Routledge and Kegan Paul, 1968–1971), esp. pp. 68–69.

11

Good God! What a Help

Almost all literates have a favorite genre. Some love historical fiction. Others delight in detective stories. A select few choose to savor fantasies, old and new. For my part, I have four feet of science fiction on my library shelving. I have chosen to enjoy particular authors who are, by my standards, tellers of good tales. Thus, my collection is heavily weighted with the stories of Poul Anderson, Arthur C. Clarke, Fritz Leiber, Larry Niven, and Frederick Pohl. I know that Asimov, Heinlein, and McCaffrey are extraordinary writers. I have their stories, but I have not felt drawn to explore their work in the same way I have the tales spun by Anderson, Clarke, Leiber, Niven, or Pohl.

Almost all literates use their favorite genre for relaxation. There is something healthful and helpful about getting involved with a good story. The people and places of another time or place become interesting, and the reader relaxes. Perhaps from work. Perhaps from the simple pressures of daily living. Even perhaps from the sheer boredom of an all-too-predictable, seemingly humdrum existence. Whatever the reason, the reader's mind takes wing and finds new friends, acquaintances, and enemies. Fundamentally, the well-told story relaxes by delivering the reader (for a moment!) from the immediacy of living. Regardless of what the rigorous relevantmentalists may say or imply, relaxation *is* a human good. In fact, it may well be a human necessity.

Therefore, after challenging the reader to explore the topography of that hidden analogical valley discovered at the end of the last chapter, I now want to invite the reader to enjoy a story, "The Specialist." It is not unrelated to an exploration of that hidden analogical valley. However, it is meant to be enjoyed, as a story out of my favorite genre.

Relax. Enjoy.

Reflect, think, learn . . . afterward.

"The Specialist" is offered as a change of pace. Read it as such. Let reflection come a bit later. Actually, it may be more useful then.

THE SPECIALIST

Frederick Jameson Howard was tired. It had been a full day at the office. He had only gotten partway through his correspondence when the damn communicator had buzzed demandingly. It was another request, the fifth in the past ten terran days. So, as was his habit, he had attended to it. But it was all very tiring. He believed that there must be a better way to spend the time allotted to one. For instance, reading a book in the comfort of his den, or puzzling over a truly intriguing problem. But the requests kept coming in, and F. J. Howard was not one to turn away from those who were still intrigued by his specialty.

"Caution. Caution.

"Commuters *must* be in their seats.

"Acceleration in 60 seconds."

It was the electronically filtered voice of some nameless creature warning him of what he knew all too well. But it was a necessity. So he fastened his seat belt and nestled into the surrounding cushioning. Frederick J. Howard had made this trip for much of his adult life, so there were few surprises and little to do but relax until the shuttle reached Epsilon 45—home base, as he thought of it.

"Epsilon 45 in 180 seconds."

The electronically filtered voice again, telling him what he had already estimated. But it was a warning that commuter reveries must be momentarily stowed away, for a missed connection was nothing short of a pain where it hurt. So he glanced about, made certain he had his case and all he wanted, and waited for the seconds to pass. They did so and he felt the docking ever so slightly. Then the little blue lights came on. F. J. H. unfastened the seat belt and hoisted himself upright.

Epsilon 45 was one of the oldest commuter colonies. It went back a long way, almost to the twentieth terran century. It was no longer quite chic, just comfortable. The accommodations reflected an older standard of living. When Epsilon 45 had been built, commuters expected much more space than was now the case, and they had been willing to go a ways to get it. But that had pretty well changed now. Most of his friends wanted to walk to work, and they were willing to put up with the cubbies that allowed them to do so. But that was not for him. He would commute as long as he could. The space delighted him and, he told himself, it enabled him to have some real separation from work. Time to do what he wanted. Time even to follow out his specialty.

When he reached his accommodations, F. J. had to search his pockets for a small bit of metal, fit it into a slot, and turn it until he heard a click that told him he could enter. It was all very quaint, but he liked it. There were even manual switches that had to be flipped before his lights would come on. While his friends considered that the height of antiquarianism, he really didn't mind the bother.

He flicked the switch and the lights came on, revealing the space he thought of as home base. The ceiling was a full ten ancient feet above the floor, and the room itself was approximately square. Directly across from the doorway was an archway into his eating space, and off to his left were two sleeping spaces connected by something the original designers called a dressing room. By current standards, it was an enormous space. Only this far out could it be found. No one bothered to build on this scale any longer. But Frederick Jameson loved it.

He closed the door behind him, and heard the satisfying click of a genuine springed latch signal his privacy. No swoosh and bump: just a solid click. Then he moved through the room the original design called a living room, glanced at the comfortable antiques that filled it, went through yet another doorway, and flipped one more switch. Once again, as he shut the door, he heard the old-fashioned click of a latch. Finally he was in the very center of his private world, his den.

F. Jameson paused at his communicator, noted that there were several messages waiting for him, and decided to let them wait a little longer. He put his case down on the desk, seated himself, and swung around to his console. His fingers typed out a message and almost immediately the screen began to display a response. He shook his head, and made another inquiry. This time a yellow light on the console lit, warning him that processing would take some appreciable time. He shrugged, for he knew that inquiries which required accessing the Epsilon System Central Historical Files always took time. Well, there was nothing to do but set the console to receive and store the desired response, when it was received. So he did just that.

Since he had to wait for a response, he decided to review the messages waiting for him in his communicator. He moved across the den to the communicator and touched the review key. The faces and voices of several friends in Epsilon 45 appeared and asked him to contact them when he got in; then there were three advertisements, a request for a listing of his publications from some unknown but ingenious graduate student, a summary of his financial position from his banker, and a notice from the only bookseller in Epsilon 45 that an auction of rare twentieth-century books would be held three days hence.

Frederick Jameson Howard stored the information about the auction, directed the ingenious request to System Central for an answer, and proceeded to contact his friends. One wanted him to come over for a meal, and a day and time were agreed upon easily. One wanted to check his library for a particularly arcane subject and, after some banter back and forth, it was arranged for the next evening. A third wondered if he was planning to attend the auction, which he was, and suggested meeting for lunch before the event. Since that seemed like a good idea, they agreed on a time and place. A fourth somewhat excitedly told him that she had come across some older but surprisingly useful information stored in the Epsilon 45 substage of the Central Historical Files. She wondered when they could talk about her discovery. They agreed on midmorning at his place. Then he reset the communicator to receive and store, made certain that the buzzer was cut out, and returned to his desk.

The console was still blank, and the yellow light was still lit. His inquiry required information that was even more deeply buried than he had thought. Or perhaps it just required some manual searches of older storage tapes before the System could search them for him. Really, there was no way to know for certain, at least not until a response had been received. Well, he could wait. There was no hurry.

Slowly and methodically F. J. H. unpacked his business brief from the case, took out his alphanumeric calculator and notebook, and a pad of lined yellow paper. It was an extravagant luxury, as was the lead propelling pencil he next unpacked. But Frederick Jameson had permitted himself to grow accustomed to using both. There were things one could do with these two luxuries that the console could barely do as well. However, there was no need to flaunt his habituation before his friends. So he carefully placed his treasures in the desk drawer.

It suddenly seemed like a long, long day.

Of course, it had been tiring at the office, and there was the trip on the shuttle. No wonder he felt tired. He had every right to be so. He sighed, and went through the dressing room to his sleeping space. Frederick Jameson Howard was tired, and sleep came easily to him.

Nine and three-quarter hours later he awoke to the sounds of ancient music. The quadraphonic alarm was playing a particularly stirring passage of Mahler's Symphony no. 4 before Frederick J. managed to get out of the old-fashioned king-size bed he had inherited with the long-term lease on home base. It was a real antique. But he did so enjoy it. His feet felt the carpeted floor, and he stood upright. A glance at his bedside clock confirmed that all had happened as he planned: it was 8:30 of a terran morning. He still had a few hours to himself before his excited friend arrived. Time enough, he decided.

After completing what he sometimes thought of as his ablutions, F. J. dressed in comfortable Epsilon 45 clothing. Then he wandered out to his eating space to see what breakfast was today. Fortunately, it fit his needs exactly, and he consumed the food pretty much as it was delivered to him. Then he took a second cup of liquid caffeine and went back to his den.

There was a blue light shining on his console.

Frederick Jameson sat himself down at his desk and punched the key that let him retrieve the response to his previous inquiry. The screen came alive with text. He read it carefully as it scrolled past, nodded, and then did what he was careful not to do too often. He pushed the key that instructed the console to store for him a magnetic tape copy of what he had just read. After all, he told himself, there are times when one simply wants to check the full text without waiting all that time.

Obediently the console's reproducer whirred as it made the copy he had requested. It really didn't take very long, but few people today wanted to be bothered with even tape copies when everything seemingly was available on one's console screen. Yet F. J. knew that there was a value in having the stuff in one's own library, available for the act of picking up a tape and inserting it into a reader. Perhaps it was just another luxury he allowed himself.

For some time F. J. sat and read and then reread the text his console displayed. Now and then he shook his head in a kind of amazement. Occasionally a whistling sound escaped his lips. Then he carefully removed the copy tape and put it into his desk drawer. This would take a bit of puzzling over, he decided.

He was still sitting at his desk when the chimes announced that someone was at his door. He shook his head at the second chiming and got up. A short few moments later he opened the door of his apartment to Felicia Lucie Dodd. The excitement of last evening's message still lingered in her eyes, and there was a certain pleasure that enlivened her face. She was almost but not quite as tall as Frederick Jameson.

In a very few seconds she was seated on the antique couch in his living room. Being a decent host, he fetched a cup of liquid caffeine for her, set it on the low table before the couch, and settled himself into an old cushioned chair directly across from the couch. She sipped her drink, and then got directly to the point.

"Freddy, I located a copy-bearing segment of a very old tape in the local repository. As you had suggested, I was searching the oldest parts of our local substage of the Central Historical Files to see what, in fact, was there. That is how I happened upon an old cross-reference to your elusive friend, which I then followed out. It is no wonder that you haven't been able to find a really decent reference before. It seems that he published much of his work in several rather esoteric sources, even for the late twentieth terran century."

Felicia Lucie paused for a moment to let her news sink in. Then she continued with her tale of discovery.

"Your friend Peatling appears to have spent much of the later part of his career in an old but not too well known research center and, moreover, to have published much of his work in a journal he edited for that center. It is no wonder that your normal searches of indices of data from the later years of the twentieth century didn't turn up much of anything. He wasn't attached to *any* of the still well known university centers. The center to which he was attached was somewhere just west of the ancient Hudson River basin, a place that was then called Schenectady in the terran area then called New York."

"It seems," she continued, "that our problem has been trying to locate a direct address to his file. That appears to have been lost, if it ever existed, but a reference to the center has somehow been preserved. I found that this reference has a whole lot of primary material attached to it. In fact, I didn't even turn up the first lead until I started systematically trying out logical combinations of old descriptors three at a time."

Felicia Lucie stopped for a moment. She looked at F. J. H. and wondered what was going on in his mind. Then she sipped some of his liquid caffeine and waited for a response. She didn't have to wait long.

When he spoke, Frederick Jameson's voice was part questioning and part reaffirming. "You found a copy-bearing segment in the *local* substage of the Central Historical Files?"

"Yes," she replied.

"You have, of course, the reference recorded?" F. J.'s voice clearly conveyed the question. Her nod conveyed a positive answer.

"I'll be damned!" His voice was a mixture of exasperation and relief. "No wonder I had such difficulty in locating his work: it simply wasn't filed as we would think it should be. Instead of being filed by the name of the author, it was filed by what that terran century *must* have thought of as a prime, overarching category: occupational locus."

"Well, thanks a lot," he said. Then Frederick Jameson Howard reached over, picked up her cup and took a hearty glug of liquid caffeine himself. Then he set the cup back down on the low table separating his chair and the couch and posed two important questions.

"Do you have the reference with you?"

"Is it accessible through a console?"

Felicia Lucie nodded twice. Then she handed him her own small alphanumeric notebook. There on the screen was displayed an obviously old, old reference—a mere six characters and only eight digits.

Frederick Jameson looked at the tiny screen in wonder. Then he rose and motioned Felicia to follow him. He went directly into his den and seated himself at his desk. He turned to his console, flicked it to life, and keyed in the reference showing on her notebook. The screen told him it had accepted the reference, then it went blank and the little yellow light blinked on. There would be a wait. He knew it, and so did Felicia Lucie. So he instructed the console to receive and store the response. Then he looked up at his friend and asked how she really had managed to find the reference. She smiled, shrugged, and spread her hands wide.

"Jason and the children will wonder where I've wandered to," she said half apologetically as she moved toward the doorway. F. J. rose and followed her. At the doorway of his apartment, she stopped and turned to face him. Impulsively she reached around his neck and lightly kissed his cheek, gave him a slight hug, and went through the doorway. The sound of a genuine springed latch clicking shut brought Frederick Jameson out of his surprise. Much as he knew the history of the action, he was always surprised to find it used by his contemporaries. For so much of his life it had been but an old, old story buried in ancient history. Yet it still lived, here on Epsilon 45. Peace, that was exactly what Felicia Lucie had murmured as she kissed his cheek.

Back at his desk, F. J. H. checked the console. The yellow light was still on. No, it had just gone off. Now the blue light was on. Her reference had been correct: the local substage must have located the file without having to query the System Central Historical Files. How nice to get such service so quickly.

Frederick J. felt a certain excitement as he instructed his console to receive and store the entire data file Felicia's reference had put at his disposal. The blue light began to blink rapidly, telling him that the request was being carried out. Finally it stopped blinking. He knew that he now had available what he wanted in his own console. He could query it, explore it, or probe it to his heart's content—to use an old-fashioned phrase, as he was likely to do now and again.

Impulsively, he punched a key that let him retrieve the file's first response in hard copy. He wanted to see the index in printed form for himself. Then another thought came to him, and he keyed in another more specific request. He really was beginning to explore the contents, and his curiosity led him to wonder if his friend's picture was available. He'd been looking for some time for Peatling's work without ever knowing what he looked like. In a moment, his screen displayed the cover of a journal called *Character Potential: A Record of Research*. The issue was dated late in the seventies of the twentieth terran century, well before terra's inhabitants had ever ventured beyond their home base in any numbers. Then the screen blinked and displayed a page of what was clearly advertising, but there was a picture in the upper right quadrant. Frederick Jameson zoomed in on that picture until it filled his console's screen. He wanted a closer look at his elusive friend from the long ago. Thus, he found himself looking at a tall, bearded human male who wore his hair down to his collar and was standing before what appeared to be a set of bookshelves.[1] At first, he could hardly believe his eyes. Then he remembered that in his friend's time people had paper in abundance, and much of what they thought and said was recorded—printed—on the material and bound into *books*. Fascinating. Even though he collected books from the twentieth terran century himself, he tended to forget that they had once been so common, so prolific, so readily accessible.

As he zoomed out from the picture, Frederick Jameson caught his breath: the picture was associated with an advertisement for a book that his friend and another had written way back then. He stopped the zoom, and studied the ancient advertisement. Its approach and its conciseness caught his attention. Then his mind caught the title. He couldn't help himself; he whistled. His elusive friend and coauthor had, somehow, published a book on *the* volatile issue of *this* time and place. They had written a book about the *designing* of a self. It was exactly the problem that was being argued throughout the Epsilons at the moment. They even had chosen the category—design—which was now so topical.[2]

"Damn. Damn. Damn." F. J. H. didn't curse too readily, but the frustration was almost unbearable. Here was an early, even ancient consideration of a current topic, and he was certain there was no way to recover the text itself. Finding *any* copy from his elusive friend had been hard enough. To think he could locate this was more than he could hope to accomplish. Still, he stored the information in his mind.

He literally felt his stomach knot. Here he was, looking at a mere advertisement from the long ago, which perversely seemed to speak directly to a very contemporary question. But it was almost certainly *lost* in time. The likelihood of recovering the text was infinitesimal. The sense of simple loss affected him, he realized, almost as much as his own personal losses. Therefore, he allowed himself a minute or two of high Epsilon cursing. It relieved him but, as he knew quite well, it neither solved the immediate problem nor satisfied his curiosity.

Frederick Jameson swiveled round to his desk. He opened the drawer and took out the copy he had requested earlier. He compared it with the copy he had just received from his console. Interestingly, they *were* somewhat related. At least, he could now recognize their possible relation. Perhaps he might have traced down Felicia Lucie's reference all by himself, although he could not be at all certain that he would have done so. However, he was grateful for a reference in hand: it was much better than a dozen still undiscovered, even in an accessible file.

He now knew what he wanted from the file stored in his console. So, attending carefully to the old index, he began to review selected items in the file. As was accepted procedure in this sort of review of near-ancient journals, he called for the table of contents of issue after issue. He noted that his friend had published articles in a number of the issues, and that intrigued him. Still, what was even more intriguing was that he had written introductions to many of the issues.

Then Frederick Jameson Howard involuntarily sat erect. The journals were *not* all there was in the file. Attached to the end of the file was a set of miscellaneous manuscripts—documents that some earlier indexer had considered within the category, although not specific published pieces. It was almost too good to be true, but here they were. He let them scroll past, now and then pausing to read and reflect on what he read.

Now he knew what he wanted: hard copy.

What he had seen convinced him that he wanted, desired, needed the luxury of being able to pick up a text and read it at his leisure, when and as he wished. He punched a key, and the console's printer obediently did what he asked. His hard copy came out, page after page.

So it was that Frederick Jameson Howard came into possession of hard copy of selected portions of the writings of one John Howard Peatling, once an associate director of something called the Union College Character Research Project in someplace called Schenectady in an area known as New York. Reading the hard copy he had requested was, F. J. decided, like reading something relevant from ancient history. It didn't often happen, but now and again it did. This was one of those fortunate times when the past and the present seemed to fuse about a common concern.

HARD COPY: EPSILON SYSTEM CENTRAL HISTORICAL FILES (SUBSTAGE 45)
FILE: USISSN-0009-1669 INDEX: RESEARCH, PROCESS OF — MMS-53

Advice to a Beginning Researcher — On Sorting Out One's Actual Needs

Let me suggest that, in its most general form, the research process *begins* about where I think you are at the moment . . . with an idea. Sometimes that idea is more elegantly called a "problem." But for the moment just think of research beginning with an idea . . . your idea for research. That is the beginning of the research process, but only the beginning. The research process itself continues to the sometimes knotty conceptual work of providing answers to the kinds of questions I have listed below. In each of these questions I have used a symbol — Z — to represent your idea, your own present statement of the research "problem" that is of interest to you.

Q.1.	*WHY* does Z seem to be *the* thing to do?	Rationale
Q.2.	*WHAT EXACTLY* do I understand Z to *include*?	Description_1
Q.3.	*WHAT EXACTLY* do I understand Z to *exclude*?	Description_2
Q.4.	*WHERE* do I understand Z will *begin*?	Description_3
Q.5.	*WHERE* do I understand Z will *end*?	Description_4
Q.6.	*WHAT specific process* constitutes Z?	Description_5
Q.7.	*WHO* do I think will be *involved* in Z?	Description_6
Q.8.	*WHAT* do I think will *happen* as a result of Z?	Hypotheses
Q.9.	*HOW* will I *know* if what I thought would happen actually did happen as a result of Z?	Design: Formal

Q.10.	*HOW can I assess* what I think will happen?	Design: General
Q.11.	*HOW will I assess* what *does* happen?	Design: Specific
Q.12.	*HOW* will I *know* that what does happen was the *result* of doing Z?	Criteria for a Decision
Q.13.	*WHAT* do I think I know *after* doing Z that I did not know *before* doing Z?	Interpretation

I have purposely stated this baker's dozen questions in a very general way. However, if you will substitute your idea, your statement of the research "problem" that interests you, for my symbol Z, the general form will become quite specific to the research you want to undertake.

Some of these questions can have reasonably *short* answers, which may be easy to discover. Those questions will not take too much time. However, some of these questions will require reasonably *long* answers, which probably will take a fair amount of thought, some searching, and the expenditure of time. Answers to those questions may not be easy to discover. But do not give up; do not stop looking for an answer; do not stop thinking about the question.

At some point in the research process, almost all researchers seek advice or consult with one or more knowledgeable persons. Advisors and consultants are commonly used in almost any research project: they are a part of the extended process. However, without *easily shared answers* to questions 1–8 or 1–9, you may find it hard or time consuming to receive really helpful, useful advice or consultation. The more answers you have to these 13 questions, the easier it will be for your advisor(s) or consultant(s) to help you do what you want to do.

John H. Peatling, Ph.D.
Director of Basic Research,
Union College
Character Research Project

The first item F. J.'s console printer delivered to him came from that body of attached miscellaneous manuscripts. His experienced eye immediately identified it as a form letter, an all-purpose response to similar albeit multiple requests. He could understand that. What he found quaint was its title: "Advice to a Beginning Researcher—On Sorting Out One's Actual Needs." He knew that *he* would have used other terms, but he also knew almost exactly the need that probably lay just behind the text he now held in his hands. Moreover, he was intrigued to read what someone in the seventies of the twentieth terran century had to say in a situation he knew quite well.

The printer had delivered a neat reproduction of an old-fashioned page of print. Frederick Jameson carefully looked at it and began to read the advice of his friend from another time and place.

It was fascinating. No, actually it was intriguing. In a strange way, so little was different now. The advice was *still* good, even here on the Epsilons. Of course, it *was* rather general. Yet Frederick J. knew from both theory and experience that the kind of query he imagined this letter answering *had* to be addressed at a general level before the specifics made any sense. Otherwise, good advice became all too like a recipe—a thing too often followed slavishly and without comprehension. A low whistle of appreciation escaped his lips.

It was such a long time since the seventies of the twentieth terran century. So many terran years separated his elusive friend and himself. Yet it was evident that a good bit remained the same. Frederick Jameson found that he was wondering if his almost lost but, now, found friend had been at all appreciated in his own time. He shook his head, for it was a question he could not answer, except inferentially. Now, and here on the Epsilons, no one could answer such a question for certain. Still, someone somewhere at sometime must have thought that old tape worth preserving.

His specialty asserted itself, and he whispered, "Deo gratias."

The next items his console provided for him came from the initial body of textual materials stored on the tape. He had asked for a set of the issue introductions, and that was what he next picked up. He rapidly leafed through the sheets of printout to see what he had, then decided to read the ones from the decade which preceded his friend's form letter of advice. Frederick Jameson found that he had ten introductions. The first was dated 1974 and the last was dated at the very end of 1979. Most were two pages long, although several were but a single page in length. Actually, not very much text at all. So he started to read through the lot.[3]

HARD COPY: EPSILON SYSTEM CENTRAL HISTORICAL FILES (SUBSTAGE 45)
FILE: USISSN-0009-1669 INDEX: RESEARCH, NATURE OF—PUB-0274

APPROACHES TO RESEARCH IN THE POSSIBLE

John H. Peatling

This issue of *Character Potential* offers seven articles that, together, constitute a commentary upon the over-all theme of "Approaches to Research in the Possible." There are reports of examples of such research, plus some articles that look at the research problems from particular perspectives. In addition, there is a report in some detail of the work of researchers in one European country, Finland. The reader is encouraged both to read for information and to relate what is read to his or her own place in the educational work of mankind.

A. Explorations in Human Potential

The Union College Character Research Project has used the term *potential* for many years. It is a complex term that includes the realm of the possible, the imaginable, and that fascinating set of activities we often start to describe with the words, "If only. . . ." Jean Piaget has suggested that, psychologically, potential has a function that is somewhat more active than the word implies, that it functions as an attraction, a stimulus toward actualization, a form of facilitation. A potential is, perhaps, a rather lively possibility.

This series of articles describes something about human potential. Since one of the traditionally most honored aspects of that potential has had to do with man as a religious creature, many of these articles look at one or another aspect of man's religious nature. However, man is also an inquisitive creature, seemingly an inherent learner from the earliest periods of life. These articles also report on man-the-learner.

B. Early Childhood and Youth

Three articles report research early in the cycle of living and learning and later on in that cycle. As a unit, they remind one not only that learning goes on all the time, but that the learning that does go on can vary in both quality and quantity.

The Drs. Steward report on their continuing explorations into learning within the human family. Both their results and their methodology are of considerable interest. They are concerned with man-as-learner at an early period in the human life cycle. Their focus on early childhood and the preschool period of in-the-home learning highlights an important period in learning that becomes more formalized with the advent of the school years. Their identification of different cultural patterns of teaching and learning offers all educators information that is descriptive and can be used prescriptively.

Dr. Strommen's report of a project to help youth reach out a practical, informed, helping hand to other youth is a reminder that learning continues on well into adolescence. The three teaching-learning strategies involved in Project Youth also give educators some thought-provoking information. Perhaps this report will help educators, religious and general, to understand the possibilities (and limitations) of some differing instructional methodologies. The hopeful conclusions resulting from this project indicate that one does not have to rest content with either hand-wringing or sorrow when contemplating the reality of the "alienated" youth.

Pastor Schulz's article reports a case study of what can happen in a high school when the power of dynamic forgiveness is put to work. The author is careful to claim only that in a Christian religious community, such as a church-related school, deeply held values can be translated into effective behavior. This is a reminder that both adults and adolescents can still grow into not only knowledge but something approaching a finer character. Perhaps it is the opportunity that is needed.

C. International Research

The long article by Professor Dr. Kalevi Tamminen broadens the perspective and increases the scope of one's knowledge of research on what is possible. Dr. Tamminen reports on religious-educational research in Finland that is, to a large extent, sponsored by the Department of Religious Education of the Faculty of Theology of the University of Helsinki. This article is a reminder that good research is not solely a prerogative of North Americans! The implicit quality, plus the considerable range of the Finnish research, is almost breathtaking. The reader will find in this special international section reports of interesting, sometimes germinal research upon one or another of the cluster of researchable questions that religious educators encounter.

The concerns of Dr. Tamminen's fellow countrymen are broad. They includes the processes of study at the University level, the realities of instruction in the public schools of his nation, the parochial programs of education, and the basic, fundamental questions of how children and youth develop both their abilities to think about Biblical materials and to make ethical judgments. The research strategies reported include both cross-sectional and longitudinal studies. The analyses suggest both statistical sophistication and the ability to handle very large quantities of data. This is a record of research that, for many North Americans, probably has been hitherto unknown. As such, it is exciting.

D. Perspectives on Research

The final three articles are somewhat different from the first four articles, all of which report a kind of research into what is possible for human beings. These authors address themselves to the basic question of how one is to structure and, through structuring, comprehend the realities encountered in life. The articles are examinations of basal perspectives upon the phenomena that research into human possibilities tries to describe and, so, understand.

Dr. Earl Brewer's reflections on what is involved in any exploration of religion offer the reader the results of a year-long period of reading and thinking about a basic problem. The results of that thinking suggest a way of reconceptualizing the task of research into religion that is both creative and new. Dr. Brewer's use of the theory of complex systems to identify approaches to complexities associated with religion can be useful intellectual fodder for many a researcher. One is reminded of the remark, variously attributed, that there is nothing quite so useful as a truly good theory. Perhaps this theoretical examination of religion as a natural human activity amenable to research will prove to be such a theoretical perspective.

Dr. Ross Scherer's examination of the organizational setting of contemporary religious education reminds one that the architect's dictum that form follows function is a reversible equation: function also follows existing form or, at least, tends to do so. Therefore, the setting in which religious education takes place influences, as form, the anticipated and reasonably expected outcomes, or the function of religious education. Scherer's article looks at the shifting demands made of religious education, notices a tendency to shift some traditional elements onto college and university campuses and into public school classrooms. He looks at this shift and reflects upon what such a drastic shift of organizational locus might mean for the future. Without overlooking the possible positive results of what has been, or the potential limitations of what may be, he considers religious education in a broad, contemporary perspective. Readers interested in the future course of religious education should find his examination of the setting/form of religious education a stimulating experience.

Dr. Ernest M. Ligon's article was presented originally to the American Psychological Association some thirty years ago. In this report, Ligon proposed that the complexity of a human personality is such that the simple paradigm of stimulus-followed-by-response is quite inadequate. His proposal for a set of intermediate variables was based upon actual experience with what was then known as the Westminster-Union College Character Research Project. The insight that one needed a complex paradigm to account for a complex, organic system such as the human personality, is still important. One of the hopeful signs of progress is that now, in the 1970s, it is easy to nod in agreement. This article is a reminder that the present is built upon the past, and that in that past there are some riches that need not be forgotten.

HARD COPY: EPSILON SYSTEM CENTRAL HISTORICAL FILES (SUBSTAGE 45)
FILE: USISSN-0009-1669 INDEX: RESEARCH, NATURE OF—PUB-0375

LOOKING AT BASICS

John H. Peatling

Periodically every discipline hears the call to pause and check its direction. Usually this call involves looking, once again, at those basics that normally are merely assumed, taken for granted, or seemingly wired into one's mental circuitry. In this issue of *Character Potential* it is a privilege to present a series of articles that ask the reader to pause, to reflect upon some basics, and to check directions. The authors come from a number of different disciplines, they address several forms of the basic query to check on one's assumptions, and they do offer some challenging suggestions for future work.

A. Man and Society: Theory and Observation

In a three-part section entitled, "Man and Society: Theory and Observation," three authors look at aspects of what many assume, but do not always carefully consider: e.g., the thesis that Man and Society are in a continuing interaction in which both are formed.

R. John Huber, Associate Professor of Psychology and Chairman of the Department of Psychology at Meredith College in Raleigh, North Carolina, asks us to take a second look at Alfred Adler's theory that Social Interest is an important, distinctly human characteristic. Huber presents both the theory and a review of a considerable body of research, so that one's second look can be an informed view of a basic part of what it may mean to be a human being.

C. R. Partridge, a clinical psychologist practicing in California, next looks at his own clinical experience of treating unsuccessfully many children and adolescents as neurotics, and suggests that the clinician is seeing a strong, marked influence of societal assumptions about childrearing that requires a different treatment in the clinic. Partridge offers the reader a challenging thesis about what in the world of the 1970s it means to help children and youth reach toward the humanity that could be theirs.

Edward W. Christensen, Associate Professor and head of the Counseling Program in the Department of Counseling and Personnel Services, State University of New York at Albany, reports how in a changing culture the role of women (and men) is undergoing stress and, as well, development. Christensen reports on the relationship between Man and Society in another culture, Puerto Rico, identifies from his own research and experience there what this means to women in that culture, and so helps us to look at a basic relationship from a perspective outside our normal North American one.

B. Perspectives on the Foundations of Research

In a second section entitled, "Perspectives on the Foundations of Research," three articles respond to an article by Dr. John Wilson of the University of Oxford which appeared in the previous issue of *Character Potential*.

William E. Chapman, who now teaches in the Department of Religion at McMurry College in Abilene, Texas, has had extensive experience as a researcher in religious education, and his reflections on the issues delineated by Wilson represent an informed look at the problems posed in that article.

Bernard L. Curtis, who teaches in the History and Philosophy Division of the School of Education at the University of Birmingham in the United Kingdom, offers some reflections on Wilson's theses in an intriguing parable. The reader can read this parable as a reflection on a Wilsonian line of argument, or as a much more general reflection upon the whole process of the empirical study of religion, or religious education, or any form of education.

The final article in this section is by Ernest M. Ligon, founder of the Union College Character Research Project. The article is a kind of personal, historical note that serves to remind the reader that the issue Wilson raised is something of a perennial issue for all who try to take the research approach to values, attitudes, or religious education.

Each of these authors speaks from a unique and different perspective. Each has his roots in a different discipline. Each reminds the reader that the issue raised by Wilson is basic to a research approach to mankind and mankind's "religious" penchant, which may be another way of saying something about what it means to attempt research into things that matter "most" to some humans.

C. Cognitive Development and Religion

In a third section entitled "Cognitive Development and Religion," Charles W. Laabs of Concordia Teachers College in River Forest, Illinois, and John H. Peatling of this Project report on a comparison study which they conducted during 1971–1972. This article originally was delivered as a paper at the 1973 convention of the Religious Education Association, held in Toronto, Ontario, Canada. In this study, the performance of two different student populations on the "Peatling Scales of Religious Thinking" are reported, and the authors raise for one another some basic questions about the apparently pervasive, powerful effect of the levels of cognitive development upon the way students understand Biblical materials in programs of religious education. This report builds upon a report of Dr. Peatling's original study of students in Episcopalian schools, which was reported in *Character Potential*, 6(4). While the article in this issue focuses upon differences and similarities between students in two denominational school systems, the implications of the findings for any literature-using discipline may be fairly important, even basic. The assessment of students' cognitive levels is an objective indication of the likelihood of achieving final educational goals, something no educator can afford to overlook.

The idea that mankind must, periodically, assess where he is and where he is going is no new discovery. However, each of these ten authors offers the reader varying reasons to believe that such a periodic assessment is a good thing for mankind. Our goals surely are good if our intent is to assist children, youth, and adults to become the humane human beings they might be. Our efforts to observe that often tangled, complex pathway through research are surely also good. But there are basic questions that we cannot and should not forget. The authors pay the reader the compliment of addressing quite basic questions with all the seriousness they can muster, with the integrity that is theirs, and with a persistent attention to both detail and the overarching issue. May the reading be as rewarding, and as challenging, as the editing of this issue has been.

HARD COPY: EPSILON SYSTEM CENTRAL HISTORICAL FILES (SUBSTAGE 45)
FILE: USISSN-0009-1669 INDEX: RESEARCH, NATURE OF—PUB-0875

LOOKING AT MORE BASICS

John H. Peatling

This issue continues the process of checking directions, looking again at assumptions, and pausing to reflect upon basics that was begun in *Character Potential*, Vol. 7, No. 2 (March, 1975).

A. Child and School: Theory and Practice

In the lead article Torrance, Goldman and Torrance consider the meaning of learning readiness for religious education. Without trying to deny the complexity of the topic, the authors bring to it an objectivity that can only help educators immersed in the task of creating curricula for children, adolescents, and adults. This review existed for a decade as a fugitive document, known only to a few. However, it has been updated and, now, seeks a wider readership.

B. Discerning and Using Relevant Data

Basic to the formative evaluation of educational programs is the need to discern and use relevant data. Two articles address that problem. First, Myers looks critically at the conceptual mare's nest of religious indicators. He concludes that indicators are measures of involvement, but that little data is routinely gathered. Second, Thomas uses existing data to test hypotheses. Her use of the "Presbyterian National Sample" models a way to use available data for research.

C. Self-Concept at the Preschool Level

Freud, Jung, and Piaget all agree that the concept of self begins very early in life, even if they disagree upon how that takes place. The article by Barber is the first of a series of reports on a set of seven scales for the assessment of normal development toward a healthy self-concept. Without hiding the considerable individual variability of this process, these scales permit one to understand a complex process that is of importance to each human being.

D. Cognitive Development and Religion

In a short report Peatling, Laabs, and Newton compare three studies that used the "Peatling Scales of Religious Thinking." Since the average level of education in each sample was different, they were able to test a general developmental assumption implicit in the scales and suggested by two previous reports (See *Character Potential*, 7:1, pp. 52–61, and 7:2, pp. 107–115). Their findings for Episcopalians, Lutherans, and Methodists suggest that while religion may involve a considerable affective component, there is also a measurable cognitive component. One's "religion" may be a function of level of one's thinking, not just a matter of either dependence or counter-dependence.

This report is put into a broader context by Richard K. Gladden. As Assistant General Secretary for Research and Planning, American Baptist Churches USA, he knows both the demands of research and the pragmatic requirements of a programming agency.

E. Resources for Research and Practice: A Note

Since both researchers and practitioners use ideas, theories, and information as a resource, the meetings of professional societies are important. As this issue went to press, five such meetings were scheduled for the Fall of 1975. The Society for the Scientific Study of Religion and the Religious Research Association planned to meet in Milwaukee, Wisconsin, October 24–26, 1975. The Association of Professors and Researchers in Religious Education, the National Council on Religion and Public Education, and the Religious Education Association of the U.S. and Canada planned to meet in Philadelphia, Pennsylvania, November 21–26, 1975. Information on these meetings may be secured from: (a) Exec. Office, SSSR, Box U68A, University of Connecticut, Storrs, Conn. 06268; (b) R.R.A., Inc., P.O. Box 228, Cathedral Station, New York, N.Y. 10025; (c) Exec. Sec., APRRE, Chicago Cluster of Theological Schools, 1100 East 55th St., Chicago, Ill. 60615; (d) Gen. Sec., REA, 409 Prospect St., New Haven, Conn. 06510.

HARD COPY: EPSILON SYSTEM CENTRAL HISTORICAL FILES (SUBSTAGE 45)
FILE: USISSN-0009-1669 INDEX: RESEARCH, NATURE OF—PUB-0476

THREE-DIMENSIONAL RESEARCH

John H. Peatling

The most highly regarded research is never just description. It is always more than that. It is a simultaneous address to three fundamental human questions: What is? What was? What should be? Description based upon careful observation is the way humans arrive at a reliable answer to what is. Yet, in order to understand what has been described, it is usually necessary to know how what is came to be, which is a way humans seek to validate their observations. Humans also tend to value things, especially something as intangible as knowledge. So, the third question almost always arises and, quite inevitably, requires a theoretical context within which observations may find meaning. These basic queries can be regarded as three conceptual dimensions that give "shape" and "substance" to research, especially research into those things that seem to matter "most" to some men and women.

In this issue of *Character Potential: A Record of Research* the reader will find articles that address all three fundamental questions. The article by Barbara Hummel-Rossi, who teaches Educational Psychology in the School of Education of New York University, is a model of research directed to the answering of the first two questions. Moreover, her concern is with a valued affective outcome of the educational process. R. John Huber, who is Chairman of the Department of Psychology at Meredith College, and Robin Steier, who is a graduate student at Fordham University, collaborated on a comparison of two seemingly parallel concepts in two psychological theories. In a way, their article helps one to see how Jung and Adler proposed to answer the question of what should be. Joseph A. Browde, the Chairman of the Education Department of Meredith College, compares the work of four personality theorists, each of whom sought to specify what maturity means for humans. Maslow, Rogers, Havighurst, and Erikson seem to have a certain similar answer to the third fundamental question: "maturity." These three articles can also be understood as variations upon the theme that Man and Society are mutually formative.

The article by Ronald J. Goldman, a Professor in the Centre for Comparative & International Studies in Education at La Trobe University in Australia, provides an informal report of values and moral education in four Socialist countries. The way those countries seek to answer the third basic question, plus Goldman's observations, provides a perspective to those who seek to resolve similar issues in very different contexts.

Lucie W. Barber, the Director of Applied Research at the Union College Character Research Project, reports on the field testing of a set of seven Scales of Self-Regard for preschool children. Given a judgment that positive Self-Concept is "good," her article offers some insights into answers to the first and second questions, and holds out the promise that there is a way to follow the individual development of Self-Regard during the formative period before schooling begins.

The article by Kalevi Tamminen, Professor of Religious Education at the University of Helsinki in Finland, reports on the results of using the "Peatling Scales of Religious Thinking" with a large sample of Finnish Children and Youth. These results, but one portion of a much larger research design, seek an answer to the first fundamental question within a theoretical context provided by Piagetian theory, the work of Goldman in England and the more recent studies of Peatling, Laabs and Newton in the United States. The results reported for Finnish students are compared to those from North American studies in the article by John H. Peatling, the Director of Basic Research at the Union College Character Research Project. Apparently both Finn and American witness to a development in cognitive preferences that seems to match Piaget's theory of levels of cognitive operations. The addition of this Finnish study means that the Scales of Religious Thinking have, so far, been administered to something over 7800 children, youth, and adults.

Each of these articles clarifies one or another of those conceptual dimensions that give "shape" and "substance" to the research venture. In addition, they all have implications for formal and informal education across the human life-span. Therefore, it is a pleasure to publish them and to invite the reader to consider each one as an avenue toward an answer to basic, fundamental questions.

HARD COPY: EPSILON SYSTEM CENTRAL HISTORICAL FILES (SUBSTAGE 45)
FILE: USISSN-0009-1669 INDEX: RESEARCH, NATURE OF—PUB-1176

COMMITTED AND CONCEPTUAL: VERITIES IN SEARCH OF ONE ANOTHER

John H. Peatling

Commitment is like breakfast food: it comes in a bewildering variety. But like breakfast foods, there seems to be a market for almost every shape and size and content. Unfortunately, thinking about human commitment all too often involves more rhetoric than data. Finding an analog to the sales record for a breakfast food is no easy task. Therefore, the publication of the articles in this issue is a considerable pleasure for, in one way or another, most of them suggest that such analogs do exist.

In some ways, conceptualization is an even more varied process. Its products are often so highly individualized that they are almost like taste or preference. Still, certain *classes* of preferences do exist. Motivational research, for example, has shown such classes to be sufficiently probable to determine a variety of things, from advertising to politics. They can be labeled with religious, political, moral or philosophical phrases but, in a sense, the label doesn't really matter. There is both individual variation and a certain generality.

Perhaps humans are simply prone to both commitments and to conceptualizations. If that be so (as it seems to be!), then the two tendencies have a variety of relationships. The degree to which commitments are conceptualized appears to run from a fuzziness to a clarity that is sometimes surprising. In much the same way, the degree to which conceptualizations elicit commitment seems to run from a cool detachment to a passionate attachment. The more intermediate "positions" one imagines on such continua, the more complex the relationship betwixt them becomes. Yet, if commitment and conceptualization are human tendencies, then their interrelationship within individuals and groups is an important thing for research to probe. They are verities in continual search of one another.

Each of the articles in this issue, however, probes that relationship. Individually and together they provide some information and, not unexpectedly, raise some questions. The reader is invited to use the information, and to consider the questions. Something about human-ness may be discovered by such a dual use of the contributions of the authors.

Dean R. Hoge is an Associate Professor of Sociology at the Catholic University of America and a member of the Boys Town Center for the Study of Youth Development. His article was originally presented at a meeting of the Society for the Scientific Study of Religion held in Milwaukee, Wisconsin, in October of 1975. He suggests that opinion poll data provide a reasonably good analog to a sales record for the commitments of Protestants in the United States of America during the past 20 to 25 years. Dr. Hoge is the author of a recently published book, *Division in the Protestant House* (Westminster, 1976).

V. Peter Pitts is a young sociologist still in graduate study at the University of Iowa. The report of his initial studies of the ways children at the transition from Piaget's preoperational to concrete operational thinking conceptualize G-O-D updates a rich research technique, the analysis of children's drawings. Both the similarities and differences within and between groups remind us how individualized general concepts become as one conceptualizes. His findings also are important clues to the process whereby children construct the reality within which they live for many years.

John H. Peatling is Director of Basic Research at the Union College Character Research Project. His article reports data on an aspect of moral judgment across some 40 years of the life span. It also raises a fundamental question about just how one is to conceptualize the "development" of moral judgment across the total life span. Further reports may be anticipated.

Jack Downs is a teacher and consultant who has worked with, among others, the Michigan State Department of Corrections. His article on the sources of humanitarian attitudes toward the war-disabled in Vietnam is one of an extensive, international series of studies that have used Jordan's instrument and Guttman's Facet Theory to identify how groups conceptualize their commitments in terms of the disabled. Dr. Downs' study puts, in a poignant way, a question to a Western assumption in terms of a study of a non-Western culture. The question is certainly legitimate, even though one longs for an answer. Perhaps questioning is all that can be done at the moment.

Eric F. Rolls was, until his recent retirement, Head of the Religious Studies Department of Westhill College of Education, Selly Oak, Birmingham. He holds Master's degrees from Glasgow and Cambridge, plus a B.D. from the University of London. He has taught undergraduates for many years, both in England and in South India. His article reporting on Birmingham's new Agreed Syllabus for Religious Education should be of interest to all North American educators, for that Syllabus' topic includes "moral education," was developed to address the problem of pluralism within a societal unity, justified its proposals upon educational grounds, and sought to avert the problems of segregation. North Americans may, therefore, find much to consider in the proposals from the Heart of England for maintaining and advancing the relationship between one's commitments and one's conceptualizations of the human state, within a common educational context.

Lucie W. Barber is the Director of Applied Research at the Union College Character Research Project, and Helen C. Cernik is a Research Associate on her staff. Their article on the profiles generated by the Barber Scales of Self-Regard continues a series of articles on the development of self-concept in preschoolers (See *Character Potential: A Record of Research*, Vol. 7, No. 3, pp. 157–158, and Vol. 7, No. 4, pp. 197–205). Their article indicates how a set of multiple measures can let one "draw" something very like a "picture" of a child's unique, individual state of development at a moment in time.

R. John Huber is the Chairman of the Psychology Department at Meredith College and Lyn G. Aubrecht is also a member of that department. Their collaboration has produced a short response to an earlier, provocative article by John Wilson of the Department of Educational Studies at the University of Oxford. Drs. Huber and Aubrecht recognize Wilson's important, positive contribution to research but, also, enter some important caveats. This article initiates a new feature, *Commentary*, in this journal. Within the limits of space, and as they are received by the Editor, other such responses will be published in future issues.

HARD COPY: EPSILON SYSTEM CENTRAL HISTORICAL FILES (SUBSYSTEM 45)
FILE: USISSN-0009-1669 INDEX: RESEARCH, NATURE OF—PUB-0877

THE ADVANTAGE OF MULTIPLE PERSPECTIVES

John H. Peatling

Most everyone either knows or can readily recognize the importance of perspective, especially in Art. Aside from sheer technique, which is often a function of purpose, the difference between an Egyptian wall painting and a Chinese landscape consists in the artist's use of perspective. Similarly, the differences between Van Gogh, Monet, Sargent, and Blake are matters of technique (and purpose), for all four adopt a similar perspective, that of the viewer. The present popularity of the work of Escher, on the other hand, probably arises from the way he adopts, incorporates, and expresses the fundamental fact that perspective shifts as the viewer, an inherently mobile subject, moves. Similarly, to appreciate either a statue or a building requires one to view it from its different sides: i.e., to change perspectives. The arts of sculpture and architecture have known this for a very long time. So, they have sought to create objects that can be viewed as a totality.

Persistently the sciences of humankind are reminded that humans are whole, coherent totalities. One of the most frequent criticisms flung at those sciences, and their dependent person-serving services, is that humans are viewed as less than three-dimensional creatures. The criticism that the picture of humankind is too "flat," or not "full-orbed," or "partial," or "dehumanizing" is, in fact, no more than a complaint that Science-as-Art has failed to use perspective, whatever sophistication of technique it may have developed. In the explicitly social sciences, the renewed interest in multivariate research techniques is one response; another is the continuing interest in interdisciplinary approaches to research problems. However, the results (at the present) differ in much the same way a Monet differs from a Blake—technical difference, but a similar use of perspective. The Eschers of research are infrequent. The sculpture of research is even less frequent. Yet the desire for perspectives upon humankind persists: sheer experience continues to tell each of us that we see something different about the "same" object as we shift our perspective by walking around it, viewing front, side, and back.

It would be a rash researcher who claimed to have resolved the perspectival problem; many would be pleased to be credited with simply recognizing the problem. It would be an equally rash editor who claimed to present either Escher-type research, or a daVinci of sculptured research in the pages of his journal. This editor is not quite that rash, but he would suggest that the five articles in this issue provide (in their totality) a kind of first approximation of a "whole" view of humankind. Each article suggests something of the complexity, the three-dimensionality, the wholeness of homo sapiens. Taken as a Set of somewhat disparate items, they suggest the advantage to be gained from multiple perspectives. They also suggest that, in our present, no one researcher can (or does!) do everything. Multiple perspectives, and the reality arising from them, may inevitably require us to put into relationship things that are (in themselves) different and limited. However, like the viewer in a sculpture garden, the reader can "walk around" this Set of articles and, thereby, view the common object, homo sapiens, from several angles.

The senior author of the first article, Bernard Spilka, is a professor of psychology at the University of Denver, while his co-author, Michael Mullin, is a former student who was teaching at the College of Santa Fe. The topic they address involves a distinction Spilka made a number of years ago between the Committed and the Consensual relation to one's religion. In this article, Spilka and Mullin look carefully at the association between these measurable stances toward a religion and several measures of self-esteem, plus a measure of comfortable interpersonal distance. Their findings, allowing for the caveats which they make, suggest something about humankind that is necessary for a three-dimensional view of men and women.

Three of the authors of the second article, Lucie W. Barber, Robert W. Procter, and Herman J. Williams, are staff members of the Union College Character Research Project. The fourth, Ivan B. Stafford, was Director, Administrative Services, National Resources and Development Division, Boy Scouts of America, until his recent retirement. Their article is an all-too-rare exposure of what, in the trade, is known as proprietary research (i.e., research conducted for a client under contract). The story they relate and the results they report offer another perspective upon humankind. Specifically, they report results from a sample of male adolescents and adults, all of whom were involved in a process of gradual, designed organizational change. These results suggest that not only can such change occur but, when design is coupled with research, a good bit can be learned about adults, adolescents, and the processes of change within a continuing organizational structure. It has been four years since a final report was presented to the client (the Boy Scouts of America) for its consideration, decision, and action. Both the authors and this journal acknowledge the kind permission of Mr. John M. Claerhout, on behalf of the client, to create and publish this article.

The author of the third article, Eric F. Rolls, is the former Head of the Religious Studies Department of Westhill College of Education, which is located in the Birmingham suburb of Selly Oak in the Midlands of England. This article represents an extended example of the kind of Religious Education envisioned by the new Agreed Syllabus for the schools in the City of Birmingham. But it is more than just a specification of a new idea. Within the constraints imposed by educational realism (as those are known in the United Kingdom) the basic course on Hinduism described by Rolls presents a fascinating perspective upon humankind. Not only does it describe "another" view of the human condition, but (implicitly) it suggests that humankind can "understand" alternative views and, so, adapt to a far more radically pluralistic society. No educator should overlook this article. Its rationale is fundamentally educational. Its purpose is societal wholeness. Its approach is pedagogically sound.

The authors of the fourth article, Lucie W. Barber and John H. Peatling, are the co-authors of *A Manual for the Barber Scales of Self-Regard: Preschool Form* (Character Research Press, 1975). In this article they record what happened when curiosity, niggling doubt, and opportunity coalesced and they revisited the available data from the field testings of the Barber Scales of Self-Regard. The curiosity paid off, and the niggling doubt was laid to rest (albeit not in the way they might have hoped). Their revisit to the data has led them to report further reason to believe that the seven Scales of Self-Regard are valid. Their reanalysis of the data, using other assumptions and statistical procedures, has led them to acknowledge a technical, but important, problem in the estimates of reliability they have previously reported. However, the revisit was not a failure, for it enabled them to recognize a way (across time) to test their confidence in the reliability of the Scales themselves.

The author of the fifth and final article, John H. Peatling, continues a series of articles on the relationship between cognitive development and religion. His report expands the time frame drastically to encompass the period from late Childhood through Adolescence into young and middle Adulthood. In terms of sheer extent, this article is a companion piece to his " A Sense of Justice: Moral Judgment in Children, Adolescents, and Adults," which appeared in Volume 8, Number 1, of this journal. In addition, he reports on a seven-sample comparison that brings together results from some 10,648 administrations of *Thinking About the Bible*, to Children, Youth, and Adults in both North America and Finland. Perhaps the most intriguing results reported in this article concern the signs for two "more" cognitive levels or "stages" well within Adulthood, plus a theoretical logarithmic curve that suggests that cognitive development continues on into the later years of life.

HARD COPY: EPSILON SYSTEM CENTRAL HISTORICAL FILES (SUBSYSTEM 45)
FILE: USISSN-0009-1669 INDEX: RESEARCH, NATURE OF—PUB-0278

THE NECESSITY OF THE NINTH LETTER

John H. Peatling

The English alphabet has 26 letters. The ninth letter in that alphabet is i. In addition to serving as the first person singular, it is remarkable how many aspects of research require what one could call i-words. For example, research requires imagination, interest, integrity and intelligence. Moreover, research inevitably involves investigation, identification and leads one into the making of inferences. Rigorous, well-ordered scientific research is impossible-to-improbable without those qualities that are, in the English language, i-words. There is a kind of i-power, then, that *is* a necessity if research, or research theory, or research-based practice is to exist at all.

Of all the i-words associated with research, theory, or practice, probably the most necessary is imagination. Imagination distinguishes between a prosaic right-hand science and a stimulating, important left-hand science.[1] As the dictionary points out, imagination means: (1) the act or power of forming a mental image of something not present to the senses or not previously known or experienced; (2) creative ability; (3) resourcefulness.[2] Research as Art is simply unlikely without the exercise of imagination. Without imagination, the art of research too easily becomes an exercise similar to painting-by-the-numbers. Such "paintings" simulate Art, albeit often quite crudely, without themselves being that which they simulate. Without imagination, research, theory, or practice tend to be mere simulations of the real thing.

One of the more insidious forces tending to tame and, then, break the imagination is the power of unquestioned assumption. What everyone knows to be often keeps imagination on a very short leash. Researchers, theorists and practitioners need opportunities to have their imaginations stimulated, or exercised, or stretched. Without such opportunities, which are to be taken and relished, the imagination remains tamed, broken, and caged: a somewhat pitiful shadow, a bare analog of its possible vigor. However, imagination need not come to such a reduced state. Indeed, it must not.

A long time ago, in the late 19th century, Edwin A. Abbott created one of the most delightful, useful and lasting opportunities to stimulate, stretch and exercise one's imagination. Fortunately, two editions of Abbott's small classic, *Flatland: A Romance of Many Dimensions*, are readily available in North America.[3] Researchers, theorists and practitioners who are not already familiar with *Flatland* can secure both editions for less than the editor spent for one ticket to see George Burns in the movie "Oh, God!". The book's approximately 100 page record of an encounter of the third kind between an intelligent Square and a migratory Sphere should uncage the imagination of all but the dull. So, seek out your bookseller and buy (or order) a copy of either (or both) the Dover edition or the Barnes & Noble edition: your imagination will never be quite the same. Neither will your research, theory or practice. You and they will benefit from getting to know Abbott's Square.

The editor can not swear that the authors of the six articles in this issue know Abbott's Square. He can, and does, affirm that each of them has used imagination. In fact, singly and together, these articles represent an assault upon some all too frequently unquestioned assumptions. Thus, it is a pleasure to be able to publish Francis, Tiedeman, Veri, Peatling and Black here. Let their articles stimulate, challenge, or instruct. Imagination may be unleashed.

Leslie J. Francis is a Leverhulme Research Fellow, currently attached to the London Central YMCA. His article is based upon his recently completed doctoral dissertation at Cambridge University. Dr. Francis challenges the assumption that we know how to measure children's attitudes toward religion and, then, goes on to indicate how (in fact) he found it could be done. Although he focuses upon a fundamental issue for religious educators, the implications of his careful, rigorous study of the psychometric problem should be useful to all persons interested in measuring the attitudes of children and young adolescents.

David V. Tiedeman is Professor of Career and Continuing Education at Northern Illinois University. The first of the Tiedeman articles presents the full text of a paper originally prepared for a Symposium at the 1976 convention of the American Personnel and Guidance Association in Chicago, Illinois. It is a conceptually essential introduction to the second, shorter article, which was prepared for a Symposium at the 1977 convention of the APGA in Dallas, Texas. In both articles, Dr. Tiedeman challenges the assumptions of many who think and write about the crises characteristic of Mid-Life. With both sophistication and honesty, he addresses himself to the "I" that is in both Mid-Life and Crisis; with imagination, he identifies an alternative for Mid-Lifers caught in Career Crisis. All those who work with Mid-Life adults can benefit from these two articles.

Clive C. Veri is Dean of the College of Continuing Education at Northern Illinois University, DeKalb, Illinois. Dr. Veri is an experienced adult educator with years of experience in working with Mid-Life adults in programs of education. His article was originally presented in Dallas, Texas, during a Symposium at the 1977 convention of the APGA. Imagination, clarity of vision, and realism mark his description of how Continuing Education can contribute power to the "I" of Mid-Lifers.

John H. Peatling is Director of Basic Research at the Union College Character Research Project in Schenectady, New York. His article is an imaginative synthesis of the results of seemingly divergent results from research studies of the levels of cognitive operation and moral judgment during the adult years. The text of Dr. Peatling's article represents the paper he contributed to a Symposium at the 1977 convention of the APGA in Dallas, Texas. A revision and further extension of Dr. Peatling's Five Cry analysis is part of his chapter in Joan Marie Smith's and Gloria Durka's (Eds.) *The Other Side of Religious Education* (Paulist Press, 1978).

Percy Black is a Professor of Psychology at Pace University's Westchester Campus in Pleasantville, New York. His article challenges the assumption that now, 15 years into the Kohlberg Era, we know how to do moral education. He writes from a gestalt perspective about the "weaknesses" evident in some of the most popular attempts to engage in moral education. In addition, he applies the result of his own extended clinical research into why persons violate their own conscience to the problem of moral education. This article should stimulate one's imagination, as well as challenge one's assumptions. If so, the caged might be uncaged; imagination might be unleashed and, perhaps, moral education would be the better for it.

Each of the six articles in this issue of *Character Potential: A Record of Research* can be understood as an example of a kind of i-power. Each author has used imagination with integrity and intelligence in an effort to elicit interest from the reader. In a variety of ways, each has challenged the taming force of unquestioned assumption. However, in addition to those i-words that make the ninth letter necessary for research, theory and practice, there is at least one i-word that describes what all have sought to avoid: illusion. Imagination, strong and vigorous, is not a synonym for illusion. While research requires imagination, and both theory and practice are impoverished without it, neither research, nor theory, nor practice need illusion.

References

1. Fuller, R. Buckminster, "How Little I Know," in *And It Came to Pass—Not to Stay*. (New York: Macmillan Publishing Co., Inc., 1976), p. 48.
2. *The New Merriam-Webster Pocket Dictionary*. (New York: Pocket Books, 1971), p. 246.
3. Abbott, Edwin A. *Flatland: A Romance of Many Dimensions*. (New York: Dover Publications, Inc., 1952). (Dover 0-486-20001-9); idem, *Flatland: A Romance of Many Dimensions*. (New York: Barnes & Noble, Inc., 1963). (EH 210).

HARD COPY: EPSILON SYSTEM CENTRAL HISTORICAL FILES (SUBSYSTEM 45)
FILE: USISSN-0009-1669 INDEX: RESEARCH, NATURE OF—PUB-0878

THE IMPORTANT TRANSITION: PUTTING RESEARCH TO WORK

John H. Peatling

The late Kurt Lewin is usually credited with the observation that nothing is so practical as a good theory. His life and work, as well as that of his students, is an extended commentary upon that simple observation. Lewin was able to take common experience and build from it to theory and, then, to put that theory into research that was intended to address quite practical problems. A reading of Alfred J. Marrow's recently republished biography of Lewin, *The Practical Theorist*, indicates that he expended considerable effort not only upon research but, also, upon putting research results into practice.[1] Without ever denigrating theory, he was not content to let research be the only result of a good idea formalized into a theory. He wanted the research to be translated into an improved practice. In a word, he wanted to put research to work.

Lewin's desire to put research to work, of course, placed him in an honorable company of North Americans. In fact, the first half of the Twentieth Century in the United States was rather marked by the presence of a number of that company. As the Century began, Charles S. Peirce was still publishing in the pages of *The Monist*.[2] A vigorous John Dewey was in Mid-Life and in the midst of publishing influential books.[3] Edward L. Thorndike turned his attention from animals to humans, and influenced several generations of psychologists and educators.[4] The attempt to make Christian principles work in the real world received a tremendous impetus with the publication of Walter Rauschenbusch's *The Social Principles of Jesus*.[5] As Chapman's survey notes so well, the 1920s were a time when American educators expended a great deal of thought and effort upon what they called Character Education, which they often saw as the direct application of existing theory.[6] During these years, the first of Jean Piaget's books appeared in English.[7] By the late 1930s, Dewey was prepared to give his second Kappa Delta Pi lecture series on *Experience and Education*.[8] Vernon Jones summarized his early efforts to make students citizens.[9] Ligon initiated his investigation of the tripartite intersection of religious principle, mental health, and educational practice.[10] At the end of the 1940s, after the hiatus of World War II, B. F. Skinner's *Walden Two* was published, putting into fictional form its author's attempt to put the contingencies of reinforcement to work on humankind.[11]

The first half of the Twentieth Century bequeathed to this latter half an honorable heritage: the attempt to put the results of research to work. Moreover, there was an impetus that was incarnate in persons, as well as ideas. The effort begun in the early half of the Century still continued. New names, of course, joined the honorable company, while earlier members continued their work. In the early 1960s Kohlberg's work attracted attention and, before long, his ideas about cognitive-developmental theory and its educational implementation were woven into the fabric of educational folklore.[12] By mid-1978, the fabric may have begun to wear a bit thin,[13] yet the ideal of putting research to work, the true heritage of this Century's first fifty years, continues to intrigue, to motivate, and to provide a solid core to a considerable variety of careful work in many disciplines.

Two of the new names that have now joined that most honorable company are the joint-editors of this special issue, Norman A. Sprinthall and Ralph L. Mosher. For those with the eyes to see it, the ears to hear it, or the minds open to recognize it, their 14-page article in the October, 1970 issue of *American Psychologist* signaled the beginning of a renewed effort to attend to the important place of self-knowledge and values in American education.[14] Working with their students and colleagues at the University of Minnesota and at Boston University they have continued to explore not only the whys but the hows. With remarkable alacrity, they responded to the invitation to create or, themselves, solicit the articles that appear in this issue. Their cooperation, plus the cooperation of their colleagues and students, have made it possible for the reader to know about an effort of considerable breadth and depth that seeks to probe realistically the educational implications of a conscious reintegration of moral/ethical values and pedagogical practice in the public schools of the United States. They have revisited John Dewey, in order to find an acceptable rationale for their efforts. But they have also sought to put the rationale to the test where it matters. They have carefully worked in the elementary and secondary schools, gathering data to permit them to distinguish failure from success. They have experimented with the training and the retraining of teachers. With great care they have thought long and hard about what should be done. With equal care they are building a body of knowledge about what *can* be done, and *how* it can be done.

It is a privilege for *Character Potential: A Record of Research* to acknowledge these new names in that honorable company of those who, in this Century, have sought to put research to work for the benefit of humankind. Norman A. Sprinthall is Professor and Director of the Developmental Education Program in the College of Education of the University of Minnesota. Ralph L. Mosher is Chairman of the Department of Counselor Education in the School of Education of Boston University and, as well, is a major continuing consultant to the Danforth Foundation-supported Brookline-Cambridge Moral Education Project. Robert D. Enright is an Assistant Professor in the Psychology Department of the University of New Orleans, Lake Front campus. David E. Stuhr is an Assistant Professor in the Department of Counselor Education at the School of Education of Boston University. Philip V. Cognetta is a Counselor at the Marshall-University High School in Minneapolis, Minnesota. Sharon N. Oja is an Assistant Professor in the Department of Education at the University of New Hampshire. Paul J. Sullivan and Mary F. Dockstader are employed by the Tacoma, Washington, public school system in the supervision of a program known as The Ethical Quest in a Democratic Society, an attempt by a whole school district to respond positively to the challenge to provide an effective moral/ethical education for its students.

There is a high and clear purpose that runs throughout the articles on the succeeding pages. But there are no panaceas offered. The authors have not pandered to the all too human desire for instant gratification. They are working at effecting a very good idea, but they have not promised too much. The reader will, therefore, find stimulation and challenge in what follows, yet never feel far from the educational realities. That, in itself, is a *very* good thing.

Notes and References

1. Marrow, A. J. *The Practical Theorist*. (New York: Basic Books, 1969, and Teachers College Press, 1977.)
2. Peirce, C. S., "Issues of Pragmaticism," in *The Monist* (Vol. 15, October, 1905), pp. 481–499, for example. Text can be found in P. P. Wiener (Ed.) *Values in a Universe of Chance*. (New York: Doubleday, 1958), p. 201ff.
3. See *The Child & the Curriculum* (1906), *Moral Principles of Education* (1909), *The School & Society* (1915) and, of course, *Democracy & Education* (1916).
4. See G. M. Joncich (Ed.) *Psychology and the Science of Education*. (New York: Bureau of Publications, Teachers College, 1962) for a selection of the writings of Edward L. Thorndike.
5. Rauschenbusch's *The Social Principles of Jesus* (1916) is generally credited with being the powerful touchstone statement of the Social Gospel movement, which strongly influenced Protestant Christianity until World War II.
6. See William E. Chapman, *Roots of Character Education*. (Schenectady, N. Y.: Character Research Press, 1977.)
7. The earliest of Piaget's books to be published in English were *The Language and Thought of the Child* (1926), *Judgment and Reasoning in the Child* (1928), *The Child's Conception of the World* (1929), *The Child's Conception of Physical Causality* (1930), and *The Moral Judgment of the Child* (1932).
8. See John Dewey, *Experience and Education*. (New York: Collier Books, 1963.) This book was originally published by Kappa Delta Pi in 1938.
9. Jones, Vernon, *Character and Citizenship Training in the Public School*. (Chicago, Ill.: University of Chicago Press, 1936.)
10. Ernest M. Ligon published *The Psychology of Christian Personality* in 1935 and, in the same year, began the Union College Character Research Project as an adjunct of the Psychology Department at Union College.
11. Skinner, B. F. *Walden Two*. (New York: Macmillan, 1948/1962.)
12. An example of this influence is the report of a 1968 conference in Toronto on Moral Education. See C. M. Beck, B. S. Crittenden and E. V. Sullivan, *Moral Education*. (Toronto: University of Toronto Press, 1971).
13. An example might well be the monograph by one of the editors of *Moral Education* (1971). See Edmund V. Sullivan, *Kohlberg's Structuralism: A Critical Appraisal*. (Toronto: Ontario Institute for Studies in Education, 1977.)
14. See R. L. Mosher and N. A. Sprinthall, "Psychological Education in Secondary Schools: A Program to Promote Individual and Human Development," in *American Psychologist* (Vol. 25, No. 10, October 1970), pp. 911–924.

RESEARCH AND THE USEFUL UNS

John H. Peatling

There are times when it is very useful to use contrast. Often, the sharper the better. One way the English language has of doing that is through the simple two-letter prefix un-. The dictionary notes that un- specifies the contrast "opposite of," or "contrary to." There are times when one encounters a research study and knows that a cluster of un- prefixes exactly describes the poor thing. It is unacceptable, unclear, unconvincing, undependable, downright unethical, perhaps unimpressive, unnecessary and, even, unscholarly. Any two of these uns are damning; three or more tend to be quite destructive and, perhaps, justifiably so. Yet research is *not* an unethical, unnecessary, unscholarly, undependable, or unclear exercise. That which qualifies for *those* uns may be a human product, but it hardly qualifies as research in any self-respecting discipline. The best one can say of such a shadow of the reality is that the research effort has been bastardized.

However, there is another useful way to characterize research, and it needs some uns too. Often one discovers a study that is unusual, unexpected, unanticipated, perhaps unfamiliar or, even, unfashionable—but it *is* clear, convincing, dependable, ethical, impressive, necessary and scholarly. In this instance, the un- prefix permits us to acknowledge our discovery, via a contrast with our own expectations of what is usual and, so, anticipated, familiar, or fashionable. There seems to be something about humans that delights in such a discovery. The unexpected intrigues us. Often it serves as a doorway into an area where our curiosity, once aroused, is willing to take us. Even when we are uncertain, and just a bit frightened by the unexpected, we are likely to experience something akin to the attraction-repulsion cycles of animal psychology. Without ignoring human caution, curiosity can lead us into new knowledge and, so, into a form of continuing growth and development. When our curiosity has been disciplined, as well as freed, it can generate the sort of research that qualifies as unusual, unexpected, unanticipated, unfamiliar or unfashionable.

These reflections on the pervasively useful un-prefix relate rather directly to the five articles that appear in this issue of *Character Potential: A Record of Research*. In one way or another, each of them is unusual, or unexpected, or unanticipated, or unfamiliar, or unfashionable. Each is an invitation for the reader to free curiosity for an exploration. Each is a doorway into a different area of human experience. Each can be an opportunity for some more growth and development. None of them is unethical or unscholarly, unclear or unimpressive. Their authors represent a variety of disciplines and, so, offer the reader a variety of perspectives upon a range of human states, experiences, and possibilities.

Kalevi Tamminen is Professor of Religious Education in the Faculty of Theology at the University of Helsinki in Finland, a Consulting Editor of this journal, and the author of two previous articles (see Vol. 6, No. 4, February, 1974, pp. 188–199, and Vol. 7, No. 4, April, 1976, pp. 206–219). In this article he summarizes the results of a study carried out in 1975 by the Institute of Practical Theology at the University of Helsinki of the questions students put to life as they know it. Because the study impinges upon an oft used, muchly debated, yet persistently proposed teaching strategy (i.e., the problem-centered approach), three North American religious educators' comments are attached to this article. Fr. John T. Hiltz is Director of Religious Education for the Diocese of Toledo and is a member of the Board of Directors of the National Conference of Diocesan Directors. Charles F. Melchert is Dean of the Faculty and Professor of Education and Religion at the Presbyterian School of Christian Education in Richmond, Virginia. David S. Steward is Professor of Religious Education at the Pacific School of Religion in Berkeley, California and, with Margaret C. S. Steward, edits the periodic listing of Research in Progress that appears in this journal. The three comments are different, appreciative without being uncritical, and provide North Americans a perspective upon the work of Tamminen and his colleagues in Finland.

John H. Westerhoff III is Associate Professor of Religion and Education at The Divinity School of Duke University in Durham, North Carolina, and is also the new editor of *Religious Education*. His report on a field study of the initiation rites of two North American denominations represents an important look at an often unexamined human experience. It is also an example of the careful work cultural anthropology can accomplish and, with its methods of comparison and contrast, of the knowledge available when curiosity is disciplined. It is a pleasure to publish this article and, thereby, invite readers to consider the anthropological perspective.

Carolin S. Keutzer is an Associate Professor in the Psychology Department of the College of Liberal Arts at the University of Oregon in Eugene, Oregon. Her study of student awareness of transpersonal experiences is a good example of unfashionable research which, given a disciplined curiosity, leads to unexpected results. In addition, her study is a kind of research open to many who teach and, as well, are willing to submit their curiosity to the discipline of hypothesis testing.

Lucie W. Barber is the Director of Applied Research at the Union College Character Research Project in Schenectady, New York. Her report of one aspect of a reanalysis of data from Weissman's research led to an unexpected result, and to an unanticipated question. Many who work in the educational vineyards of moral or attitude or religious education rightfully worry about signs of success; all too rarely is the question raised of what success might mean for students.

John H. Peatling is the Director of Basic Research at the Union College Character Research Project in Schenectady, New York. His article is based upon a paper read at the founding meeting of the International Standing Seminar on Religious Education and Value Potential (ISREV) in July, 1978, at the University of Birmingham in England. In it he reports how secondary analyses led to a way to empirically address the developmental problem posed by positing potential-as-a-possibility to individuals or groups. The empirics concern Religious Thinking, but the results may have meaning for the broad field of cognitive developmental studies.

Margaret C. S. Steward heads the Section of Clinical Psychology at the School of Medicine of the University of California in Davis, California. Along with her husband David, Margaret begins in this issue to edit the periodic listing of Research in Progress, which is printed on the inside of the back cover of this journal. It is a pleasure to welcome her to this important task, and to publish an update of the previous listing (see Vol. 8, No. 1, November, 1976). Researchers who desire to be listed in this section of *Character Potential: A Record of Research* should contact the Stewards, provide a title and give an address where interested persons may write to them for more information about their research.

It is an honor to also welcome five new members to this journal's Board of Consulting Editors. Pastor Trond Enger is Lecturer in Theology and Religious Education at the Alta College of Education in Elvebakken, Norway. Professor Andre Godin is Professor of the Psychology of Religion at both Laval University in Quebec, Canada, and Gregorian University in Rome, Italy. Dr. John E. Greer is Lecturer in Education at the New University of Ulster in Coleraine in Northern Ireland. Dr. Foeke H. Kuiper is Senior Lecturer in Religious Education in the Faculty of Theology of the Vrije Universiteit in Amsterdam in the Netherlands. Dr. Brian V. Hill is Professor of Education at Murdoch University in Murdoch, Western Australia.

It is a pleasure to be able to publish these particular five articles, and to be able to include the comments of three North Americans on the Finnish work. Each article requires the positive form of at least one of the useful uns. They invite the reader to exercise curiosity and, so, grow and develop yet a bit more. Without aiming to do so, each witnesses to the potential inherent in a disciplined curiosity.

THE POSSIBILITY OF PATTERN

John H. Peatling

Humans like patterns.

In fact, we seek them out.

Chaos distresses us. So, we look for some order—some pattern. The Judeo-Christian tradition even posits that a first creative act was the patterning of a formless void. All who in any way share that tradition presume pattern. It simply is. Thus, it can be discovered. We seek for it and, often, discern it.

Reason, judgment, and decision all presume the *possibility* of pattern. Almost all developmental research is a search for those time-extended sequences of change that constitute a pattern of growth. The very concept of Character presumes a pattern of human activity sufficiently persistent to be discerned across time. However, we sometimes forget that research *per se* is a search for pattern. It is the discovery of pattern that allows us to speak of laws, or associations, or factors, or principles. Without pattern, contemporary science would collapse and the edifice of human knowledge be but a shack. Without pattern, technology could not be, and meaning would be nought but assertion. Without pattern, control would be impossible and prediction not even a fond dream.

Pattern *is* basic to human perceiving and conceiving. It is also an aspect of all human communication. We find it next to impossible to think of human activity without encountering, using, or interpreting pattern. Moreover, humankind has lived long enough with itself and with this world to recognize that pattern is often quite complex. Indeed, we have come to appreciate that beauty is often a complex of analytically disparate items which, in relationship to one another, achieve a value *more* than the sum of the parts—a pattern.

Because pattern is such a fundamental aspect of human experience, this issue of *Character Potential: A Record of Research* is built around the idea of research as pattern-seeking. However, we sometimes forget that while we presume pattern to be ever so basic, we are not always correct in discerning pattern. Thus, the search for pattern includes the confirmatory act. Both confirmation and *dis*-confirmation are of value, for pattern is no synonym for fantasy. Quite the contrary. Pattern and reality go hand in hand, and knowing what of reality we have *not yet* probed sufficiently to discern pattern is as important as discovering a *clue* to the pattern of explored reality.

The special symposium edited by David V. Tiedeman of Northern Illinois University addresses the question of the pattern of human decision-making, particularly as that was articulated in 1963 by the Tiedeman/O'Hara Decision-Making Paradigm. The article by Vincent A. Harren of Southern Illinois University reports specific, empirical research that suggests that the paradigm itself matches the reality of undergraduate college students' decision-making. Nancy K. Schlossberg's article illustrates how the paradigm can pattern the work of a counselor through reference to her own counseling at the University of Maryland. The article by Loretta C. Wertheimer indicates how Knefelkamp and Slepitza integrated the paradigm into instructional procedures predicated upon Perry's model of intellectual and ethical development, and how she used that result at the University of Maryland. Anna L. Miller-Tiedeman's article illustrates the personal power of pattern as she exposes how, in work with students at the DeKalb High School in DeKalb, Illinois, ego and values development can be integrated with decision strategies to empower students in their daily activities. Finally, the comments of David A. Jepsen of the University of Iowa (formerly of the Developmental Research Division of Educational Testing Service) and Anita M. Mitchell of the American Institutes of Research and Alternative Associates put the symposium, and its various parts, into a larger pattern and, so, identify meaning and value.

The article by Lucie W. Barber of the Union College Character Research Project identifies *when* and *where* a pattern of sex stereotyping appears in a select sample of parents. The article by William A. Koppe of the Department of Research and Studies of the Lutheran Church in America briefly but caustically identifies some *all too common and less-than-desirable* patterns which afflict some research sponsored by religious bodies. The article by Donald F. Wonderly and Joel H. Kupfersmid of Kent State University represents an extraordinarily useful form of research: i.e., the *checking* of a posited pattern of association between Kohlbergian stages of moral judgment development and general mental health. The fact that they found *very little* evidence for the posited pattern is one of the things that makes such research valuable, for sometimes our desire for pattern goes on beyond discernible reality. Of necessity, pattern-seeking research is both exploratory and confirmatory.

In addition, this issue of *Character Potential: A Record of Research* contains several English language summaries of articles originally published in Russian in the first three issues for 1979 of the journal *Voprosi Psychologii*. These "Notes From Another Quarter" are sometimes frustratingly incomplete but, perhaps, they can be parts of a pattern that otherwise we would not even be aware existed. Readers of this journal may helpfully recall Ronald J. Goldman's earlier article, "Values and Moral Education in Communist Societies," which appeared in our Volume VII, Number 4, in April of 1976.

Finally, an abstract of Kitty Greene Abraham's dissertation at Oregon State University is included in this issue for two reasons. First, because it records the use of an instrument often reported in these pages, *Thinking About the Bible* (Peatling, 1974). Second, because Abraham found an interesting pattern of response, which allowed her to distinguish her fifth graders from her sixth graders. Thus, her work witnesses to yet another way in which research as pattern-seeking may be carried out.

When he finished reading those ten issue introductions Frederick Jameson knew something about his elusive friend from the later part of the twentieth terran century. Like himself, he sometimes wrote better than at other times. Moreover, he also knew that the early indexer had been correct in suggesting that one could find a vision of what it meant to attempt research in the realms that people considered of value. It was, he felt, oddly apropos. He and his colleagues talked about that idea again and again, when they were not involved in some argument or other. Perhaps that old philosopher's idea that knowledge was an ever-expanding spiral which, periodically, reencountered themes, topics, and problems was correct.[4] Here was almost proof of it.

Suddenly he realized that he was hungry.

A glance at the chronograph on his desk indicated that he was already some past the midday food delivery. So he picked up those ten issue introductions and went off to see what was awaiting him. He decided that he would reread them while he ate his midday repast.

Frederick Jameson Howard was on his third cup of liquid caffeine before he finished his second careful reading of those ten introductions to an almost ancient journal. He slowly shook his head in wonder as he turned over the last page. So much that he had learned experientially was there. Somehow his friend had caught a vision of research as both a demanding technology and a high conceptual art. Clearly he knew that research was a useful tool, but he had pushed on toward the fundamental generalities. Research was here portrayed as a way of drawing upon *all* that was available, so one might be as rational as possible and, yet, not bow before even reason as an idol. It was amazing, surprising, and, yes, fascinating. It was so contemporary.

Then F. J. had an idea. Before he knew it, the idea had become a decision. He knew what he wanted to do right this moment. So he went back into his den and seated himself before his console. He tried the reference number that Felicia Lucie had provided once again and, to his surprise, found that he was connected remarkably quickly. Then he made a query, got a positive response, and typed in a request. When it was acknowledged, he relaxed and practically chuckled.

Tomorrow he would stop by the local repository and retrieve his order. Tomorrow by this time he would have a desk-size hologram of that old advertisement for his friend's book about *designing* a self—the one with his picture standing before those shelves of books. It would serve him well, for it would remind him that knowledge's expanding spiral does tend to recycle through sectors thought about before. Really, one should look back across the previous cycles if one hopes to understand the present encounter. Yes, it would be a very good thing to put on his desk.

Frederick Jameson guessed that his long-sought, almost lost but, now, found friend from the later decades of the twentieth terran century would be pleased at what he purposed to do here and now on Epsilon 45. While F. J. H. could never know for certain, his friend would have smiled at the very idea of winding up as a desk-size hologram in a specialist's den on Epsilon 45. In fact, had he been able to know that through some quite unimaginable foresight, he might have said, "Deo gratias!" For he, too, had been a specialist.

Notes and References

1. Frederick Jameson Howard's console screen displayed the inside front cover of the journal *Character Potential: A Record of Research*, vol. 8, no. 3 (February 1978).

2. The advertisement that Frederick Jameson found so interesting was for a book by John H. Peatling and David V. Tiedeman, *Career Development: Designing Self* (Muncie, Ind.: Accelerated Development, 1977).

3. The ten issue introductions delivered to Frederick Jameson Howard by his console were as follows:

a. "Approaches to Research in the Possible," *Character Potential: A Record of Research*, vol. 6, no. 4 (February 1974).

b. "Looking at Basics," *Character Potential: A Record of Research*, vol. 7, no. 2 (March 1975).

c. "Looking at More Basics," *Character Potential: A Record of Research*, vol. 7, no. 3 (August 1975).

d. "Three-Dimensional Research," *Character Potential: A Record of Research*, vol. 7, no. 4 (April 1976).

e. "Committed and Conceptual: Verities in Search of One Another," *Character Potential: A Record of Research*, vol. 8, no. 1 (November 1976).

f. "The Advantages of Multiple Perspectives," *Character Potential: A Record of Research*, vol. 8, no. 2 (August 1977).

g. "The Necessity of the Ninth Letter," *Character Potential: A Record of Research*, vol. 8, no. 3 (February 1978).

h. "The Important Transition: Putting Research to Work," *Character Potential: A Record of Research*, vol. 8, no. 4 (August 1978).

i. "Research and the Useful Uns," *Character Potential: A Record of Research*, vol. 9, no. 1 (April 1979).

j. "The Possibility of Pattern," *Character Potential: A Record of Research*, vol. 9, no. 2 (December 1979).

4. Only because of his scholarly interest in the middle and later decades of the twentieth terran century was Frederick Jameson aware that one Jean Piaget in his book *Structuralism* (London: Routledge and Kegan Paul, 1971, p. 34) had suggested that "rather than envisaging human knowledge as a pyramid or building of some sort, we should think of it as a spiral the radius of whose turns increases as the spiral rises."

12

God! What a Possibility

INTRODUCTION

Like many in my generation, I once learned that newspaper stories revolve around five queries: Who? What? When? Where? and Why? Somewhat later, I came to recognize that a sixth query is also involved: How? Still later, I discerned that those six queries are a set which allow one to distinguish between data and information. Somewhat later still, I was able to acknowledge that information is fundamentally neutral and noncausal: it merely provides some human being with the stuff upon which a reasonably confident decision may be built.[1]

In the beginning, there was a wonderful sense that all had been done when those six queries had an answer. Now I recognize that to be a partial truth, at best. Information must always be used by someone who, almost inevitably, works upon it (1) to see, (2) to infer, or (3) to impose some *pattern* as a necessary intermediate between information and a decision, that positable precursor of action. Information per se is simply meaningfully organized data. Action always involves an actor. There simply is no magic in information itself.[2]

The true referent for those six queries is an event, and their goal is a report sufficiently accurate and detailed to be (or become) information. That is an interesting conclusion, for event is a common category in a good deal of the recent past's biblical-theological thought. Moreover, an event *is* something that many can recognize as a kind of conceptual unit. Events, we say, occur. Events, we believe, simply are.

Still, when we think about it, we know that an event is a complex whole which is analyzable into a set of separate components, or elements. In a word or two, an event is a complex dynamic unit that can only be understood through (1) the identification of the full set of elements, and (2) a description of the interrelation of those elements.

What makes such a set of elements an event is that they are so related to each other that one simply *must* consider *all* of them together. None can be ignored. None can be forgotten. Something we quite rightly think of as set-ness distinguishes an event from its simpler, far more common analogue, an occurrence.[3]

In fact, the glorious challenge of that hidden analogical valley called evaluation is to distinguish events from occurrences and, then, use research-as-a-method to understand those events. In education and, especially, in religious education, the event is a basic conceptual unit. It is almost always *that* which comes closest to a religious educator's intention, aim, or goal. Thus, religious educators should be very interested in events and the conceptual challenge of (1) *identifying* the complex, dynamic wholes that are events, (2) *describing* such events with sufficient accuracy and detail that the details are (or become) information, and then (3) *understanding* those complex dynamic units as best we can.

The challenge is to human abilities, human ingenuity, and human skill. Research-as-a-method is available as a tool. Only the result is, in any specific instance, unknown. While a theology may set some limits, the conceptual challenge is not inherently absurd. Until we religious educators accept that fact, we will remain partially blinded by our unnecessary ignorance of the way things are in this creation. Like Toynbee's faltering cultures, we will fail to respond to our challenge.[4] Thus, we should be particularly interested in the six journalistic queries as avenues toward an understanding of an event—even an educational event, and especially a religious educational event.

As a reader may have guessed by now, six is always an interesting number in Fuller's geometry of thinking. Moreover, back in the chapter on Piaget we saw how six clues could be modeled by an octahedron, which could then be posited to be central to a larger tetrahedron whose vertices provide a set of a smaller number of more general constructs, which could in turn be used to model the meaning of a still larger, more general construct. In chapter 7 that process was used to address what I called Hickson's query ("What does it all mean?").[5] I would like to do much the same thing here, for those six journalistic queries can be taken to be clues to the meaning of an event.

While understanding an event may be useful in the biblical-theological field, that is not my reason for suggesting a parallel analysis now. Rather, it is because an evaluation of almost anything educational is to ask Hickson's query of some event.[6] We want or need to know an answer to the question, "What does it all mean?"

AN OCTAHEDRAL MODEL OF SIX JOURNALISTIC QUERIES

As we discovered five chapters earlier, octahedrons have a quality that forces us into a useful clarification of our thinking about a set of six constructs. The octahedron consists of three pairs of polar opposite vertices. Thus, we are forced to consider the interrelationship of the six constructs and decide upon (1) two sets of three "more closely related" constructs, and (2) three pairings of constructs from those two sets that seem to be "less closely related." When the six journalistic queries are examined, I think that it is reasonably evident that they concern two functions: explanation and description. Further thought can lead to the recognition that three of those six queries seem to be primarily explanatory, while the three remaining queries are primarily descriptive.

As I thought about those six queries, it seemed evident that *who*, *what*, and *where* were primarily descriptive. It also seemed evident that the queries *how*, *when*, and *why* were primarily explanatory. However, because I wanted to use an octahedron to model the set of six queries, I next had to identify three pairings of queries that could be regarded as "least" related, for they would become polar-opposite vertices. Frankly, that was not an easy task.

What I did was to construct a 3 × 3 matrix and examine the full set of nine possible pairings. As a result, I was able to decide upon a pairing scheme that seemed to involve "least" related pairs of queries. Not until that had been done could I assign queries to the six vertices of an octahedron. My decisions are displayed in figure 1.

Clearly my decisions are mine; they may not match the decisions of another. Unfortunately, that can be said of almost anyone's decisions, for any set of three pairings is but one-third of the total number of

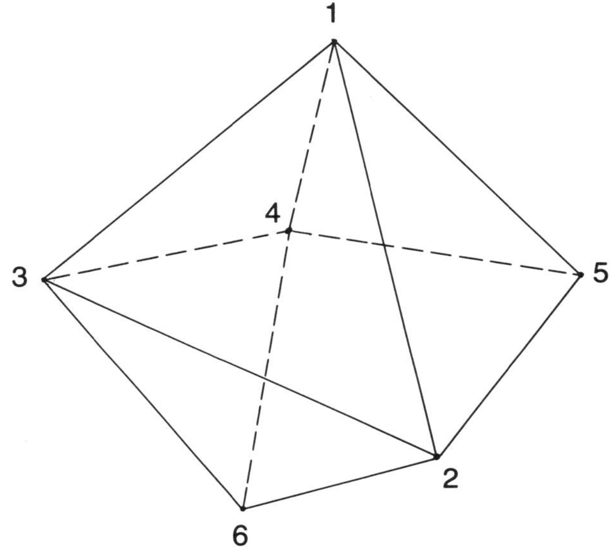

WHERE: 1 = The journalistic query WHAT?
2 = The journalistic query WHO?
3 = The journalistic query WHERE?
4 = The journalistic query HOW?
5 = The journalistic query WHY?
6 = The journalistic query WHEN?

Figure 1. Octahedron model of six journalistic queries. Regular octahedron with unit-length edges, in perspective.

logically possible pairings.[7] Thus, readers should take a few moments to identify my decisions and see if they are willing to grant them, even tentatively.

As I did before in chapter 7, I checked the results two ways. First, I checked the eight face planes defined by three edge-sharing vertex-queries. My standard was simply whether or not each trio of queries seemed to have some evident relationship to one another. On the whole, I was satisfied. Second, I investigated the pairs of face planes that connected the model-posited polar-opposite vertex-queries. Here I was checking to see if the "middle" pair, while combining with each of the polar opposites, seemed to function like a pair of conceptual transition-queries. While a somewhat more complex requirement and, therefore, a more rigorous test of the model, I found that I was satisfied with the twelve model-dictated sets of interrelationships. These last investigations are displayed in tables 1, 2, and 3.[8]

As earlier, I do not want to comment extensively upon the results that are displayed in tables 1, 2, and 3. But I do want to identify that each table posits what are best taken as a set of hypotheses about the event-ness of a complex dynamic whole, in terms of quartets of those six journalistic queries. Thus, in the three tables there are a total of twelve such relational hypotheses. Even so, I recognize that a reader must determine that *these* twelve hypotheses are satisfactory, whether or not I find them so.

Table 1.
Sequence A:
Face-planes of a regular octahedron from one to the other of a pair of opposed vertices.
Conceptual analysis via an octahedron model of six journalistic queries.

Vertex:	Query:	Vertex:	Query:	Vertex:	Query:
(1)	WHAT?	(2) (3)	WHO? WHERE?	(6)	WHEN?
(1)	WHAT?	(3) (4)	WHERE? HOW?	(6)	WHEN?
(1)	WHAT?	(4) (5)	HOW? WHY?	(6)	WHEN?
(1)	WHAT?	(5) (2)	WHY? WHO?	(6)	WHEN?

Note: Within each *row*, the conceptual analysis via an octahedron model moves from left to right. The middle *column* contains two items, which represent "intermediate" paired vertices along a connected face-plane joining the opposed vertices listed in the left and right *columns*.

Table 2.
Sequence B:
Face-planes of a regular octahedron from one to the other of a pair of opposed vertices.
Conceptual analysis via an octahedron model of six journalistic queries.

Vertex:	Query:	Vertex:	Query:	Vertex:	Query:
(2)	WHO?	(1) (3)	WHAT? WHERE?	(4)	HOW?
(2)	WHO?	(3) (6)	WHERE? WHEN?	(4)	HOW?
(2)	WHO?	(6) (5)	WHEN? WHY?	(4)	HOW?
(2)	WHO?	(5) (1)	WHY? WHAT?	(4)	HOW?

Note: Within each *row*, the conceptual analysis via an octahedron model moves from left to right. The middle *column* contains two items, which represent "intermediate" paired vertices along a connected face-plane joining the opposed vertices listed in the left and right *columns*.

ONE STEP BEYOND: IDENTIFYING AN IMPLICIT TETRAHEDRON

A potential further simplification can be achieved by determining the implicit, heretofore unidentified set of four tetrahedrons which are complementary to the octahedron and, so, together constitute a simpler Fullerian all-space-filling tetrahedral model. The experience in chapter 7 suggests that such a set of four complementary tetrahedrons should (or does) generally exist. The real problem for a conceptual geometer is *not* whether such a set exists (it almost certainly does!) *but* the identification of the four implicit, heretofore quite unrecognized vertices. In a word, it is a problem which involves determining appro-

Table 3.
Sequence C:
Face-planes of a regular octahedron from one to the other of a pair of opposed vertices. Conceptual analysis via an octahedron model of six journalistic queries.

Vertex:	Query:	Vertex:	Query:	Vertex:	Query:
(3)	WHERE?	(1) (2)	WHAT? WHO?	(5)	WHY?
(3)	WHERE?	(2) (6)	WHO? WHEN?	(5)	WHY?
(3)	WHERE?	(6) (4)	WHEN? HOW?	(5)	WHY?
(3)	WHERE?	(4) (1)	HOW? WHAT?	(5)	WHY?

Note: Within each *row*, the conceptual analysis via an octahedron model moves from left to right. The middle *column* contains two items, which represent "intermediate" paired vertices along a connected face-plane joining the opposed vertices listed in the left and right *columns*.

priate supraordinate conceptual elements. Basically, it is a "problem to find," as identified a long, long time ago by Pappus and not so long ago by Polya.[9]

The problem is displayed, in perspective, in figure 2.

In fact, since figure 2 is somewhat confusing, I simplified the "problem to find" by creating a set of four triangular faces of a regular tetrahedron, within which an octahedron model of those journalistic queries might be a central figure defining six edge midpoints. That set of four triangular faces is displayed in figure 3.

As I did earlier in chapter 7, I asked myself a series of questions with this general form: What A is relatable to what B in such a way that a midpoint is the specifiable known query? The answers I found myself giving are displayed in figure 4.

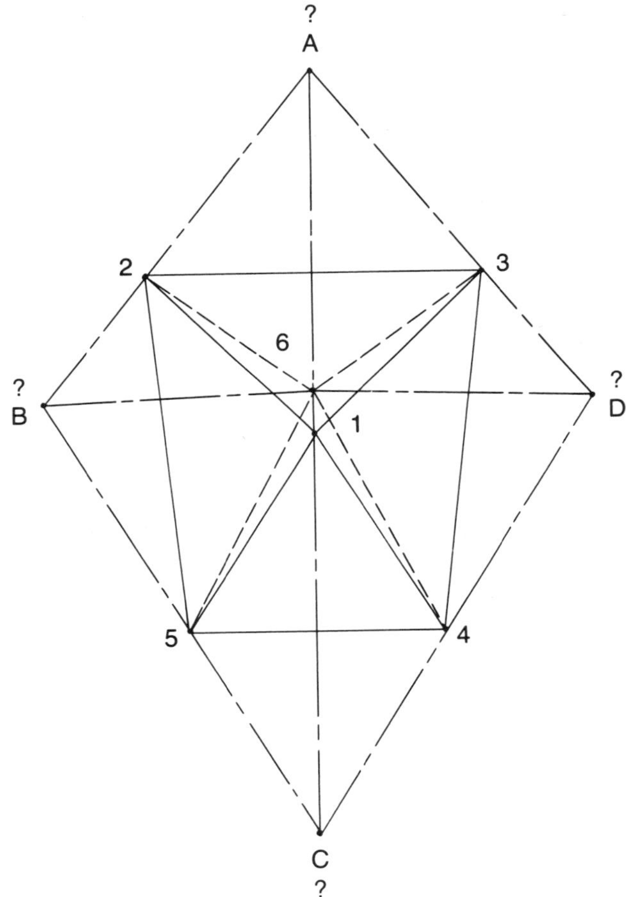

WHERE: 1 = The journalistic query WHAT?
2 = The journalistic query WHO?
3 = The journalistic query WHERE?
4 = The journalistic query HOW?
5 = The journalistic query WHY?
6 = The journalistic query WHEN?

A? B? C? and D? = Further, unidentified implications of the octahedron model of six journalistic queries.

Figure 2. Octahedron model of six journalistic queries as the center of an all-space-filling implicit tetrahedron with double-unit-length edges.

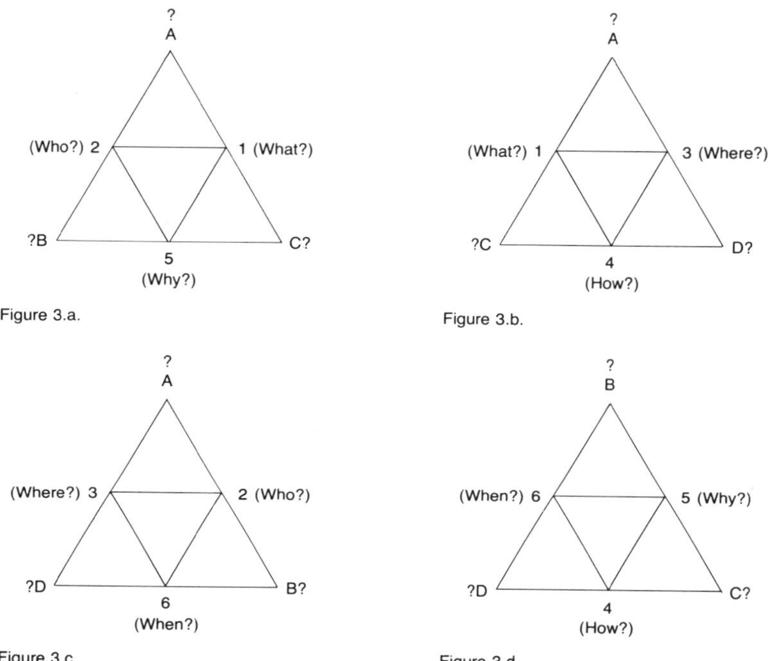

Figure 3. The four faces of an all-space-filling tetrahedron with double-unit-length edges implicit in an octahedron model of six journalistic queries as the center: octahedron vertices noted. (See figure 2.)

As figure 4 indicates, I found myself thinking that the four tetrahedral vertices could be labeled (a) act, (b) reason or rationale, (c) time or place, and (d) record or history. That is, I decided that these four concepts served well as the inescapable elements of an event, which the journalistic queries sought to describe and explain.[10] Next, just as a check on myself, I examined each of the six tetrahedron edges and asked myself if the vertex/midpoint/vertex combination for each of the six edges of the implicit tetrahedron seemed possible. While I found that I was prepared to imagine that they were possible, I clearly recognized that to be my decision. That is why I prepared table 4. Thus, it would be good to take a few moments to consider table 4 and, then, make and record some personal judgments of those possibilities.

As the *nota bene* to table 4 indicates, there are 46,656 logically

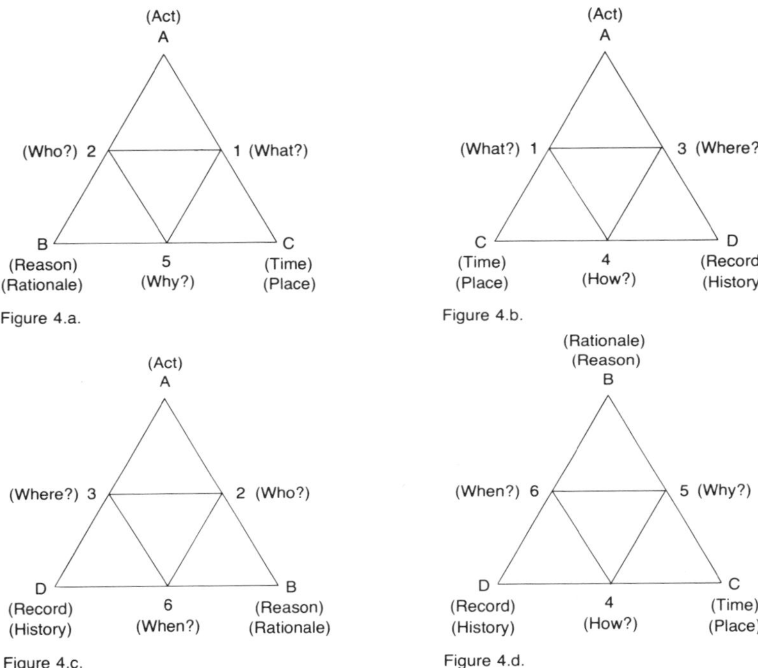

Figure 4. The four faces of an all-space-filling tetrahedron with double-unit-length edges which is implicit in an octahedron model of six journalistic queries: octahedron vertices noted and tetrahedron vertices tentatively identified. (See figure 2.)

Table 4.
The six edges of an all-space-filling tetrahedron with double-unit-length edges which is implicit in an octahedron model of six journalistic queries: vertices and midpoints noted. (See figure 2.)

Vertex$_1$:	Midpoint:	Vertex$_2$:	Personal judgment of possibility:
A (Act)—	2 —(Who?)—	B —(Reason)	Unlikely Likely : : : : : : :
A (Act)—	1 —(What?)—	C —(Time)	Unlikely Likely : : : : : : :
A (Act)—	3 —(Where?)—	D —(Record)	Unlikely Likely : : : : : : :

(*continued*)

Table 4. (continued)

Vertex$_1$:	Midpoint:	Vertex$_2$:	Personal judgment of possibility:
B (Reason)—	6 —(When?)—	D —(Record)	Unlikely : : : : : : : Likely
B (Reason)—	5 —(Why?)—	C —(Time)	Unlikely : : : : : : : Likely
C (Time)—	4 —(How?)—	D —(Record)	Unlikely : : : : : : : Likely

Note: The six-point scale of personal judgment of possibility runs from unlikely (negative) to likely (positive) and is a way of recording one's answer to the following general question:

How possible do you think it is that (midpoint query) is related to (vertex$_1$) and (vertex$_2$)?

If you think the posited relation improbable, the "unlikely" end of the six-point continuum should contain one of three degrees of unlikeliness that would approximate your personal judgment of possibility.

If you think the posited relation probable, the "likely" end of the six-point continuum should contain one of three degrees of likeliness that would approximate your personal judgment of possibility.

N.B.: The number of logically possible ways of choosing one of six degrees of possibility for six posited relationships *is* quite a large number. It is six (the number of posited relationships) raised to the sixth power (the number of possible degrees of possibility), or 46,656 ways.

possible ways to use six scales with six scale-points each to record a personal judgment of the possibility of these six vertex/midpoint/vertex combinations.[11] That is a large albeit finite number: too large, in fact, for humans readily to imagine. However, it has the advantage of being large enough to accommodate almost any combination of personal judgments we are at all likely to make, and to do so without forcing us into unreal judgments. Actually, the number of possible combinations is so large that we can quite reasonably expect the distribution of logically possible combinations to closely approximate a theoretically normal distribution.[12]

ADVANCING VIA WALTZING: A MINI-RESEARCH PROJECT

In the long, long ago I considered myself accomplished because I knew what to do when the band played a waltz and I was on the dance floor. I did not feel I had to retreat before an even-then less-than-contemporary rhythm. However, whether or not you can empathize with that memory, I want to use it for only one purpose: waltzing is an intriguing way of moving ahead while also taking in a good bit of sidewise motion. What I want to do now is, analogically, to waltz toward a useful goal. I hope you will stay with me, somewhat like a partner in a waltz. I think we can and will make it around the dance floor, and I do not think I will trod on my partner's toes. In fact, both of us may enjoy the circuit, if we listen to the "music."

If you have made use of the six six-point scales at the right-hand side of table 4, the waltz is ready to begin. If not, either do so now, or simply acknowledge that the next paragraphs may be minimally meaningful. Let me presume that you *have* recorded six personal judgments on the posited tetrahedral edges identified in table 4.

Those are *your* personal judgments: do *not* feel defensive about that. Especially, do not feel the least bit guilty if your judgments do not all reside in the extreme right-hand "likely" spaces. Whatever your judgments are, they are yours.

The important thing for this waltz is that *you* have recorded your own personal judgment of the possibility posited by the three-part "edge" displayed for you. Whatever that set of six judgments may have been, if you made them before reading this sentence, those are assuredly your judgments at a particular moment in time. They are not what researchers regard as bothersome problems: after-the-fact judgments, ratings, statements, or evaluative opinions.[13] Instead, they are "data" on you at a particular time and place, in a particular emotional state, and with a particular level of cognitive ability. Acknowledge them as such, and then use your data in a mini-research project on the degree of our agreement.

You now have a set of personal judgments of possibility. That is, for each six-point continuum in table 4 you have (1) made a judgment of the possibility of the threefold combination of vertex$_1$/midpoint/vertex$_2$, and (2) recorded that judgment by a check or tick or mark of some sort in the space between the scale's division points (the colons). Thus, you have judged and committed yourself (via recording) to that judgment.

Given that set of six personal judgments of possibility, use table 5 as an outline of a simple mini-research project on the degree of agreement between your personal judgments and my judgments. If you have taken me at my word and, in addition, been willing to follow my waltzing this far, you are ready for table 5.

I. A First Step in a Mini-Research

The first thing to do with table 5 is simply to transfer your six personal judgments from table 4 to table 5, section A. Strictly speaking, I have told you to map your judgments from table 4 onto the continua provided in table 5. The implicit rule of correspondence is that the continua in table 4 and in table 5 have an obvious one-to-one relationship, which is but another way of saying that you should transfer your record (without any change) from the continua in table 4 to the continua in table 5, section A. That is all there is to it.[14]

The sole difference in the two sets of six continua is that, in table 5, a numerical "meaning" has been given to each of the six places along each of the continua. I have given a meaning of one to the left-most place on each of the continua, and I have given a meaning of six to the right-most place on each of these continua. In a word, I have scaled (minimally and quite simply) the six continua of personal judgments, and I have done so in such a way that a low numerical value reflects a judgment placed toward the left-hand side of a continuum, while a higher numerical value reflects a judgment placed closer to the right-hand side of a continuum. What you have done is to map your judgments onto a one-to-six scale.

When you have finished mapping your table 4 personal judgments of possibility onto the equivalent continua provided in table 5, section A, you will have scaled your judgments onto a rather simple ordinal scale.[15] Since it really is so simple to do, you may not have been aware

Table 5.
Estimating the degree of agreement with six posited edges of an all-space-filling tetrahedron with double-unit-length edges implicit in an octahedron model of six journalistic queries.

A. *Transforming six personal judgments into numerical scores* (from table 4).

					Unlikely					Likely
1.	Act	—Who	—Reason		1	2	3	4	5	6
2.	Act	—What	—Time		1	2	3	4	5	6
3.	Act	—Where	—Record		1	2	3	4	5	6
4.	Reason	—When	—Record		1	2	3	4	5	6
5.	Reason	—Why	—Time		1	2	3	4	5	6
6.	Time	—How	—Record		1	2	3	4	5	6

B. *Sum the six numerical scores representing your personal judgments.*
For example: *If* your six personal judgments of possibility were transformed into the following six numerical scores

4 5 5 6 6 6

Then their sum would be 32 (i.e., 4+5+5+6+6+6 = 32).

C. *Consider the range of possible summed numerical scores.*
For example: If you consistently judged the possibility at any one of the six possible places on the scale, then your summed numerical score would be six times that place-score. Thus, the range would run from 6 to 36. The intermediate possible judgments would be 12, 18, 24, and 30 (if you were consistent in your judgments).

D. *Locate your own summed numerical score within the range.*

Unlikely — Likely

6 7 8 9 10 11 12 13 14 15 16 17 18 19 20 21 22 23 24 25 26 27 28 29 30 31 32 33 34 35 36

Probable Disagreement	Uncertain	Probable Agreement

(1) *Locate and circle* your own summed score on the 6–36 continuum.
(2) *Identify* the degree of agreement your score indicates.
(3) *Ask* yourself, "Why is my score what it is?"
(4) *Record* the answer you give yourself to the question in (3).
(5) *Consider (1)–(4) and answer Hickson's query* ("What does it all mean?").
(6) *Record* your answer to Hickson's query, as posed in (5), above.

---

of what was going on. However, you should recognize the seemingly simple thing that has been done, for we are about to make use of this minor accomplishment.

II. A Second Step in a Mini-Research

At this point, you have mapped your table 4 personal judgments onto the six equivalent scaled continua of table 5. As a result, you can now summarize all six judgments by listing six numerical values. Moreover, if you are quite careful to keep that listing in the same order as the continua in table 5, section A, those six numerical values become a sign or symbol of your six personal judgments. Thus, there is a clearly translatable meaning, for example, to the sixfold sequences 111111 or 343434 or 666666. The first sequence indicates a series of personal judgments that the posited edges are unlikely. The second sequence indicates a series of judgments that the second, fourth, and sixth posited edges are barely likely and that the first, third, and fifth posited edges are just barely unlikely—all in all, a definite "uncertain." The third sequence indicates a series of personal judgments that affirm that all of the posited edges are likely. If nothing else, being able to symbolize a set of six personal judgments so concisely has an advantage, particularly once one begins to think about comparing two or more such sets of personal judgments of possibility.

The actual second step in this mini-research is indicated in table 5, section B, where you are asked to identify a set of six numerical values that do symbolize your table 4 personal judgments of possibility, and then to take the simple sum of those six numerical values. When you take that simple sum of six numerical values, you have a single new numerical value which can function as a summarizing sign or symbol for the general meaning of the more discrete set of six numerical values. For most of us, it is considerably easier to use such a one-digit or two-digit numerical value as a summarizing symbol than it is to consider a six-digit set of numerical values. That is a simple psychological rationale. It is just as important to recognize and remember what has been done. It was a *human* act, and we should not forget that it was such an act.

Although it may seem trivial, it is noticeably easier to compare two summed numerical values than it is to compare two six-digit records of personal judgments. Probably what is most important is to recognize the compromise we humans make when we prefer a summarized one-digit or two-digit value to the far more complex yet far more precise information of a six-digit numeric code for a set of our personal judgments of possibility. Quite literally what we have done is to prefer a fairly accurate simple symbol over a noticeably more accurate but far more complex symbol (i.e., one or two digits vs. six digits).

III. A Third Step in a Mini-Research

A next thing to do in this mini-research exercise begins with that one-digit or two-digit summary symbol identified as a result of following the suggestion in table 5, section B. Whatever your summary symbol may be, it is a one-digit or two-digit numerical value between 6 and 36. If your numerical value is less than 6 or more than 36, check your calculations. In fact, check your calculations at this point, whatever your summed two-digit symbol may be. There should be no digit 0 in your six-digit code, nor should there be any digit 7, 8, or 9 in that six-digit code. Any digits other than 1–6 constitute an error.

In the strictest sense, consistency of personal judgment is not always a common human characteristic. Thus, it is entirely possible that the record of your personal judgments on those six posited tetrahedral edges indicates that some edges may have seemed more likely than others. That is, you may well *not* have checked the same space on each continuum. However, you may well have a very general sense of a certain degree of agreement, especially when you simply glance across all six continua and note where your checks are. The summed symbol is not only a simpler thing but, if you compare it to what would have been the case if you had been thoroughly consistent, it enables you to gain a sense of your general degree of agreement with the posited edges.

Within the theoretically possible range of summary symbols, certain ones can be taken to represent personal judgments which, in their total effect, are equivalent to consistency of judgment. Thus, a 6 is possible only as the result of a consistent personal judgment that the edges posited are most unlikely. A consistent use of the space given a value of 2 would produce a summed score of 12, which may represent a judgment that the edges are unlikely, but not most unlikely. Similarly, a consistent use of the space given a value of 3 would yield a score of 18, which may represent a judgment that the posited edges are only somewhat unlikely. On the other hand, a consistent use of the space given a value of 4 would lead to a score of 24, which may be taken to represent a judgment that the edges posited are somewhat likely, although the judgment is tinged with a degree of personal uncertainty. Moreover, a consistent use of the space given a value of 5 yields a summed score of 30, which can be taken to represent a personal judgment that the edges posited are actually likely. Finally, a consistent use of the space given a value of 6 would produce a score of 36, which can represent a judgment that the edges are most likely.

Actually, this third step is fairly simple and quite straightforward. Compare your summed score to the resulting summed scores for a consistent degree of agreement—6, 12, 18, 24, 30, and 36—and determine which one of those summed symbols is closest to your own summed score-symbol. Then, since the general continuum runs from "unlikely" to "likely," with low scores tending toward the unlikely end and high scores tending toward the likely end, you can determine two things: (1) a consistent judgment that is closest to your own perhaps mixed judgment, and (2) whether your judgment tends to be slightly on the unlikely or the likely side of that consistent judgment. Thus, you are able to make a reasonably fine discrimination between your own degree of agreement and the results of theoretical consistency. Of course, that may seem like quite a minor accomplishment. Still, it has an advantage for anyone into research that involves something as complex, interesting, and important as personal judgments: it enables one to decide the credibility of general, summary data, such as a summary score-symbol for six specific judgments.

IV. A Fourth Step in a Mini-Research

The full range of theoretically possible summary scores is displayed in table 5, section D. The ends of the continuum are labeled, and a certain very general three-part interpretation of ranges of scores is also suggested. Thus, if you will *circle* the one or two digits that represent your own score, you will be able to *visualize* the degree of agreement between your set of personal judgments and mine. Naturally, you have had a good notion of what *that* was for some time. However, the parenthesized suggestions (3) through (6) offer you a way to experience the *interpretative* task of evaluation research. That is a part of any use of research-as-a-method. Here, I hope it is both easy enough to do and, yet, challenging enough to seem worth doing.

For instance, the question of why your score is what it is involves more of an answer than pointing to the mathematics of adding six digits to get a specific sum. You know your reasons for those six personal judgments better than anyone else or, at the very least, you have better access to those reasons than anyone else. Just to keep the exercise reasonably precise, make a *record* (of some sort) of your answer to the question posed in (3). Then ask yourself what, in an earlier chapter, I called Hickson's query: What does it all mean?

That query is at the heart of the interpretative task in *any* evaluation. Here, an answer could be as simple as the conclusion that reader and author agree on the possibility of the six posited tetrahedral edges. Or it could be that reader and author have some degree of disagreement. Or the meaning could be spelled out in terms of what the observed degree of agreement implies for a model of an event. At the moment, and for the purposes of this mini-research, your answer can be at any level of completeness you wish. However, do record your answer to Hickson's query, whatever it may be.

At this point, we have waltzed our way through a simple, even an overly simple exercise: a mini-research project. Through a good bit of sidewise motion, we have advanced a ways toward an understanding of the use of research-as-a-method. Moreover, the basic data have been well within your control. In addition, the data have been similar to a good bit of the stuff with which the social sciences work: personal judgments which invite or permit inferences toward generalities, such as the degree of agreement with some posited construct. Finally, there was the question of interpretation, for research data without interpreted meaning remains raw and unorganized.

Without the organization of an interpretation, data per se have no way to become information. Yet without information, we humans are hard pressed to make those decisions which contribute to rational action.[16] Thus, the waltz may have been worth the effort. At least now you may have an experiential base for the further exploration of that quite luxuriant analogical hidden valley called evaluation.

GETTING EQUIPPED: WAYS TO CONCEPTUALIZE WHAT IS INVOLVED

We call ourselves *homo sapiens.* That Latin phrase is composed of two words: *homo,* which is a generic term for man, and *sapiens,* which invokes the concept of wisdom. Like almost all self-descriptions, *homo sapiens* is a positive, hopeful statement of the best case. Still, it is not a phrase to be discarded lightly. It does indicate something about humankind that is quite plain to all but the misanthropically blinded. In the best instance, humans are clearly capable of achieving wisdom. That is not, of course, to suggest that all humans do so. As yet, they do not. But it is to suggest that the genus does periodically exhibit individuals who can only be called *wise.* To think less of humankind is either to be patently blind or, perhaps, extraordinarily selective.

The dictionary defines wisdom in an interestingly provocative yet useful way. *Wisdom* is defined as (1) a noun and (2) the quality or state of being wise, which is to say (3) knowledge of what is true or right coupled with a just judgment as to action. The synonyms given for *wisdom* are terms such as *sagacity, discernment,* and *insight.*[17] That is intriguing. To call humans *homo sapiens* is to credit the genus, at the very least, with a capacity to see and know what is true or right, a knowing which is coupled with a just judgment as to action.

Wisdom involves discernment and insight. Thus, it is a complex of knowledge and judgment that is based upon some presumably high-level perceptual ability we call discernment or insight. Like so much about humankind, wisdom is intimately related to the human ability to see things in a certain way. That idea is most intriguing, for it suggests J. R. R. Tolkien's thesis, "The Primary World, Reality, of elves and men is the same, if differently valued and perceived."[18] Tolkien implicitly invoked discernment or insight in an attempt to distinguish "elves and men," while the very concept of wisdom involves the perceptually related ideas of discernment and insight. In both instances, the likely referent is what Tolkien called "the Primary World, Reality."

Therefore, to speak of or think of humankind as *homo sapiens* is not only to credit the genus with wisdom but, as well, to acknowledge the very real and very important role perception plays in human existence. What we see is involved in that high state we humans call wisdom. It is also determinative of much that we do, or are able to do, time after time in our day-by-day existence. Thus, it is no imaginative leap to suggest that *how* we humans use a tool like research-as-a-method depends upon what we perceive our situation to be and how we perceive our situation. The two are more closely related than we often think or admit.

In fact, to use research-as-a-method in a "problem to find" inescapably involves our very human ability to perceive or see Tolkien's "Primary World, Reality," in a number of hypothetical ways. Unless that happens, our human use of research-as-a-method has little creative about it and can, aptly, be more likened to cooking from a recipe than to a voyage of discovery or the exploration of some hidden analogical valley. Actually, what distinguishes important, useful, and creative research from the plethora of trivial, useless, and downright stupid studies that clog some professional journals is a matter of perception. The former has a variety of perceptual patterns available and uses them; the latter have an often unbelievable form of tunnel vision. Evaluation is almost always a problem to find; it is rarely less, and it is never done well with tunnel vision.

That is why I want to expose a number of ways of visualizing the basic nature of the phenomena accessible to the social scientist and, therefore, amenable to a tool use of research-as-a-method. Recognizing the variety of ways of visualizing the phenomena is one way to avoid tunnel vision or, even, a first step on the way toward important, useful, and creative research. So, I want to consider a series of figures. Although no one of them is without some complexity, they are very generally arranged in a sequence from the simpler to the more complex, so that we may reach a fairly sophisticated level of conceptualization without too great an effort.

I. What Is Being Studied?

It probably is overly simple to begin with the question of what it is that is to be studied. Yet, how we conceptualize that which is to be studied does tend to influence how we use the tool of research-as-a-method. For the religious educator, there is an almost inevitable interest in the individual persons constituting a group or a class or a school or some learning system worthy of study. Thus, the individual is almost always of interest. This first question concerns *how* we conceive of the individual person or, via extension, the individual group of persons to be studied.

In figure 5 several things are represented. First, it is implied that to consider the studied individual, or some group of individuals, as a theoretically free body is a good beginning. Now that may not be completely accurate, but it at least makes a rather limited number of assumptions about what "must" happen. Second, figure 5 permits one to acknowledge two things that are often not acknowledged: persons do unanticipated things and, as well, tend to respond to forces impinging upon them. Third, figure 5 invites one to combine figure 5A and figure 5B into a more complex, potentially more realistic schematic which comes close to the Piagetian idea of an adaptation cycle that is composed of assimilation and accommodation.

Clearly, figure 5 does not ask one to conceive of the individual as either a totally free body or a totally determined body. In fact, it suggests that either of those alternatives is no more than a select perspective on the individual(s) being studied. Very probably, both perspectives are somehow involved in any phenomenon to be described and understood.

II. What Could Happen Next?

Any study of individuals has to begin with some assessment of their present state. This is sometimes called *baseline data*. But one collects such data, especially in education or religious education, because of a very real interest in what happens next (i.e., across some period of time). Thus, how one conceives of the possibility of shift, change, movement, or progress from some present state to some "next" future

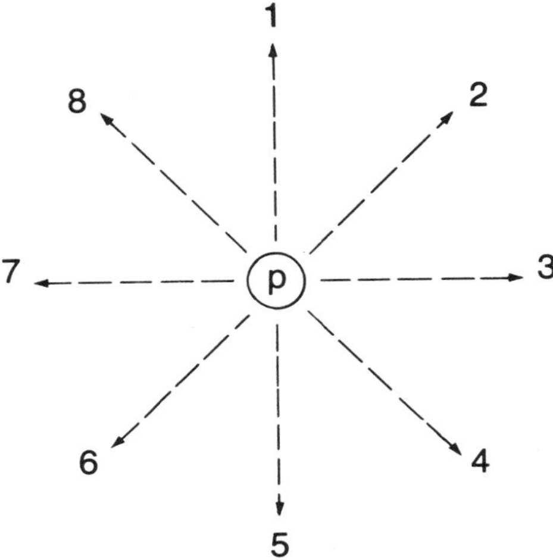

A. Schematic of the possible moves of a free body p.

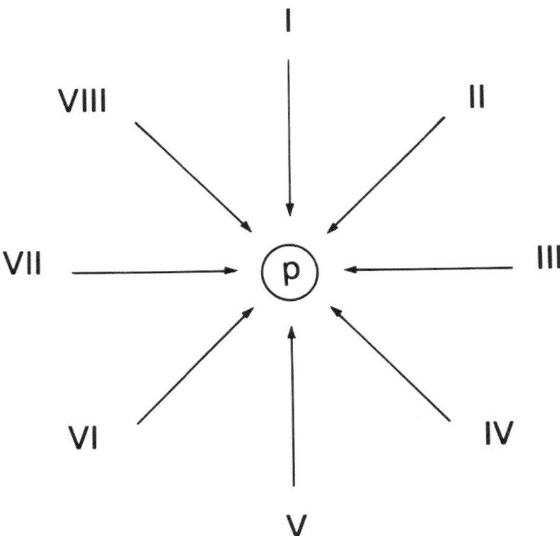

B. Schematic of the possible forces impinging on a free body p.

Figure 5. Schematic representation of the possible moves of and the possible forces impinging on a theoretically free body p.

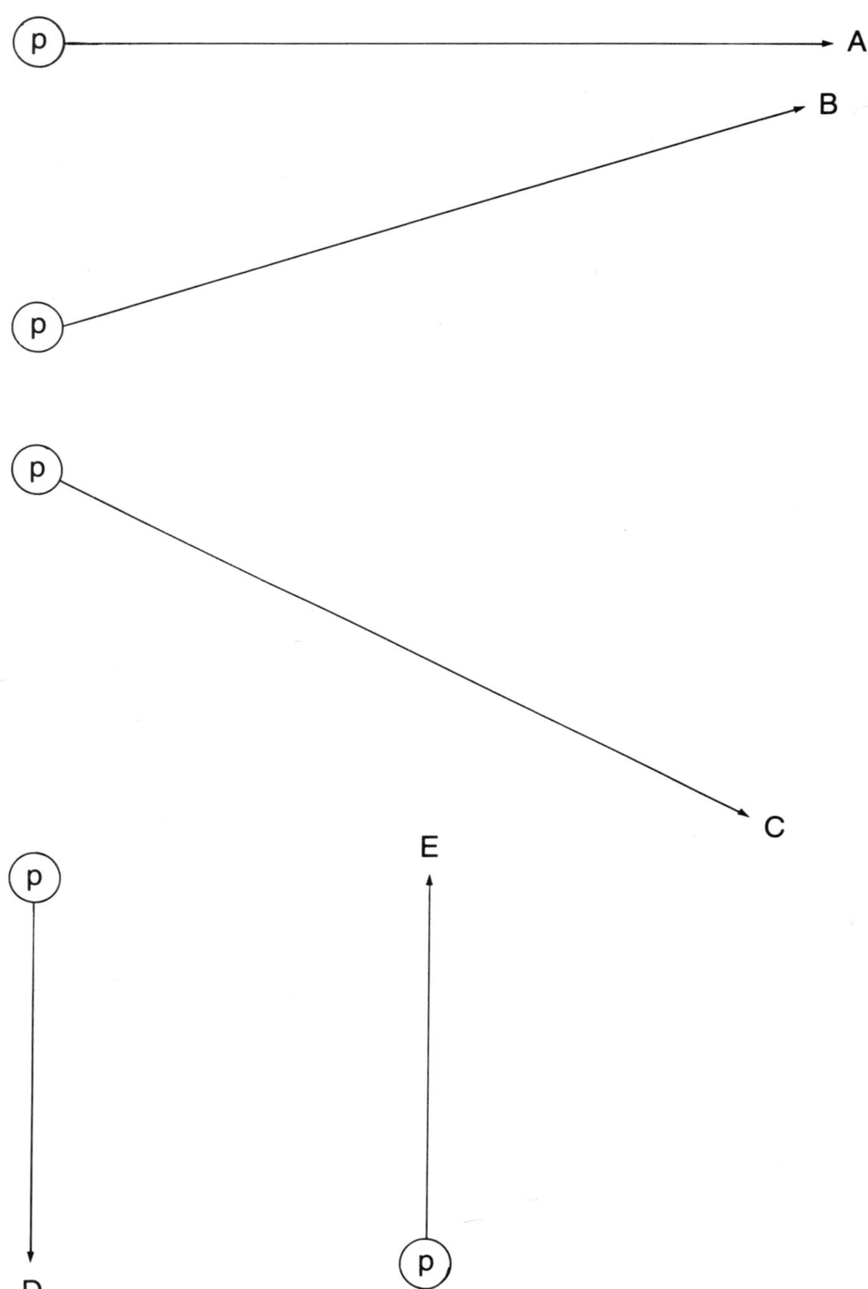

Figure 6. Schematic representation of possible rays originating at a theoretically free body p and connecting points A, B, C, D, and E.

state is basic to the study of an individual or group of individuals. One way of conceiving such a change is represented in figure 6.

In figure 6 I have used the mathematical concept of a ray to model a number of possible shifts, changes, movements, or progressive pathways.[19] It is useful to realize that all of the changes modeled in this figure are identical, until one gives meaning to up and down or right and left. Moreover, in figure 6 change is conceived of as basically (1) unidirectional, and (2) a process of successive approximation of some known or knowable goal (e.g., states A, B, C, D, or E).[20] Actually, that second idea is the very beginning of measurement theory, as figure 7 suggests.

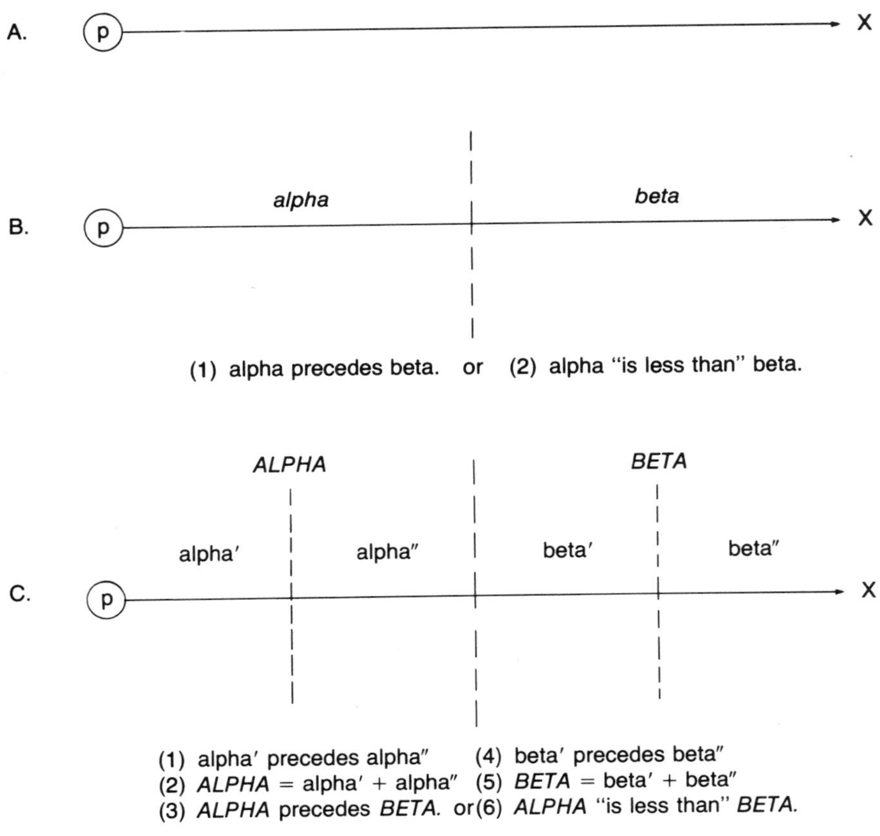

Figure 7. Schematic representation of the basic process of scaling a ray connecting a theoretically free body p and some point X via a process of successive differentiation.

In figure 7 the process of measuring is reduced to its most basic state. To measure almost any shift, change, or movement implies figure 7A, some pathway that can be identified. A first and quite simple measurement is to distinguish an early from a later portion of the pathway (e.g., to distinguish alpha from beta in figure 7B). This permits us to identify the relationship of precedence or, if we have a standard, the relationship "less than." This process of differentiation can, of course, be carried forward as many times as we desire. Figure 7C illustrates a single further differentiation of alpha into an alpha′ and an alpha″ and of beta into a beta′ and a beta″. This process can go on as long as we wish, or as long as the discriminations along the ray pX identified by the process seem to make sense.

However, not all phenomena that we may want to understand are quite as simple as the model displayed in figure 6 and figure 7. Often we know or guess that any present state of some body p is in between two seemingly opposite states. That is the situation represented in figure 8.

The situation modeled by the straight lines through body p in figure 8 is one where the question of concern is the effect of something (e.g., the effect of maturation or of an educational intervention or of a particular experience) upon body p, and it is clearly recognized that the result can be a shift toward some A or toward some B (e.g., a higher level of self-confidence or a lower level of self-confidence). Given some baseline data on body p, we are particularly interested in the effect of something, and we are willing to posit a possible shift or change toward either some A or some B. Many experiments and evaluations use this basic conceptual model. Still, it must be remembered that all four lines in figure 8 are generally identical, until we give a meaning to either up and down or right and left.

In figure 9 the process of differentiation represented in figure 7 is applied to the possible bidirectional shift, change, or movement of body p which is posited by the lines in figure 8. As was done in figure 7, the process of differentiation is carried out two cycles beyond the very general situations modeled in the previous figure.

The fourth and lowest representation in figure 9 is an addition to the schematic replication of figure 7. It can be taken as a simple example

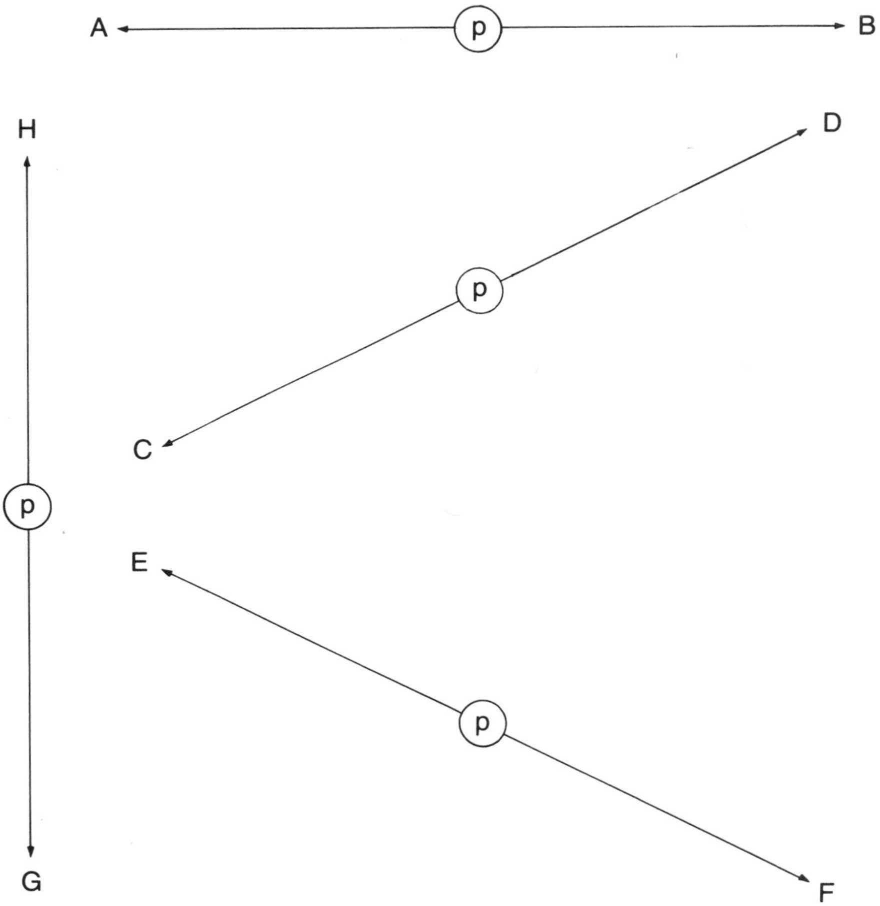

Figure 8. Schematic representation of possible straight lines running through a theoretically free body p, which occupies some "position" along lines A-B, C-D, E-F, or G-H.

of the substitution of symbols, or as a quite general instance of the process of scaling a bidirectional continuum. Numeric symbols have been substituted for the descriptive/relational differentiations of the model directly above. In addition, one direction has been assigned a negative (or less preferred) meaning, while the other and opposite direction has been assigned a positive (or more preferred) meaning. The numeric symbols have been assigned on the quite theoretical

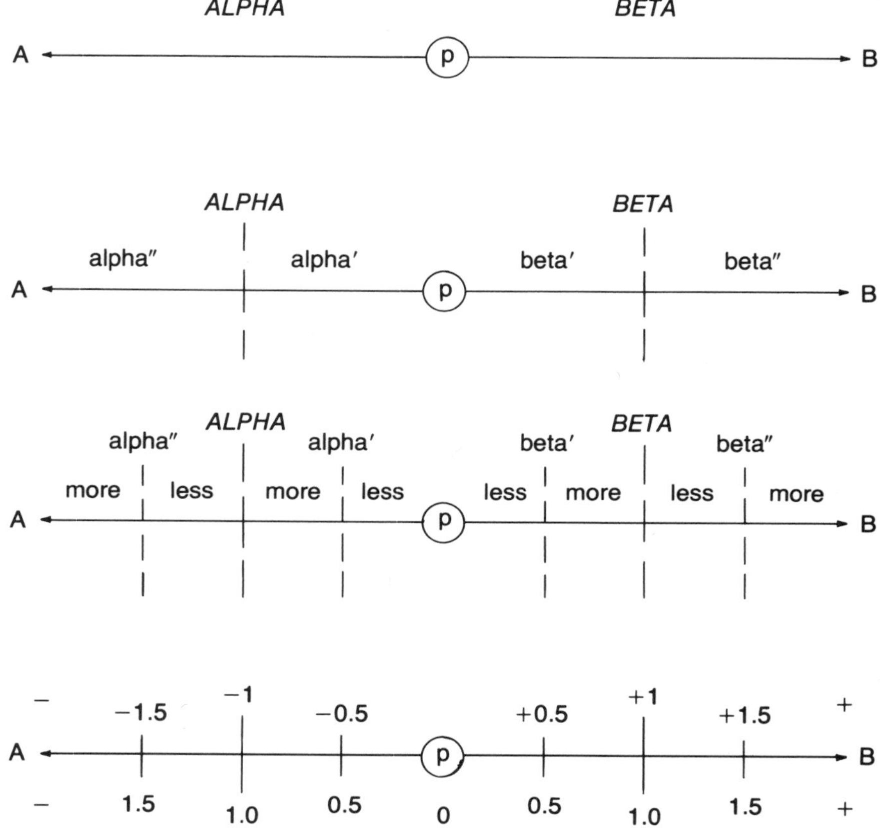

Figure 9. Schematic representation of the basic process of scaling a straight line running through a theoretically free body p toward an A and a B via a process of successive differentiation. Plus an example of assigned values for such a scale.

assumption that the process of differentiation proceeded on the basis of distinguishing a series of successive halfway points.

Basically, this fourth and lowest representation of figure 9 involves two intriguing assumptions. First, that at some initial moment of observation, body p is in (or can be presumed to be in) stasis or equilibrium and, so, can be regarded as a theoretically stable conceptual object. Second, that the possible discernible shift, change, or movement of body p can be either toward a less preferred or toward a more preferred state. Without presuming the actual frequency distribution of observable states of body p, the similarity to a theoretically normal distribution of states should not be ignored. In fact, the so-called normal distribution is but an empirical instance of this quite theoretical series of sequential differentiations, given an extremely large number of instances of very general human characteristics.

III. What about Time?

On November 10, 1979, Pope John Paul II presided over a meeting of the Pontifical Academy of Sciences in Rome that was held to honor the centenary of the birth of Albert Einstein. In an address delivered on that occasion, Professor P. A. M. Dirac noted that one of the results of Einstein's "most unusual mind" was that he showed how the common ideas of space and time had to be modified by recognizing their intimate relationship within a united four-dimensional continuum. In his special theory of relativity, Einstein introduced "a new symmetry principle between space and time."[21]

Since Einstein's theory, the importance of taking time into consideration has been evident. However, educators really do not have to invoke either the theory or the equations to recognize that fact. Educational events and learning itself occur within time and extend across time. Still, it is easy to forget or overlook that fact. Therefore, it is useful to have a variety of models which clearly presume time itself as a dimension or factor or explicit influence.

In the next nine figures, time is an explicit part of eight and an implicit part of only one. In most instances, time is modeled by a unidirectional ray because time, as we know and experience it, is a seemingly ceaseless process that flows from a past through a present toward a future. Many of the things about humankind most amenable to the tool use of research-as-a-method seem either to increase or decrease, or sometimes exhibit long-term stability and, so, inescapably involve time if they are to be understood. For example, those three typical situations can be quite generally modeled by the next few figures.

Figure 10 suggests something that is often regarded as a developmen-

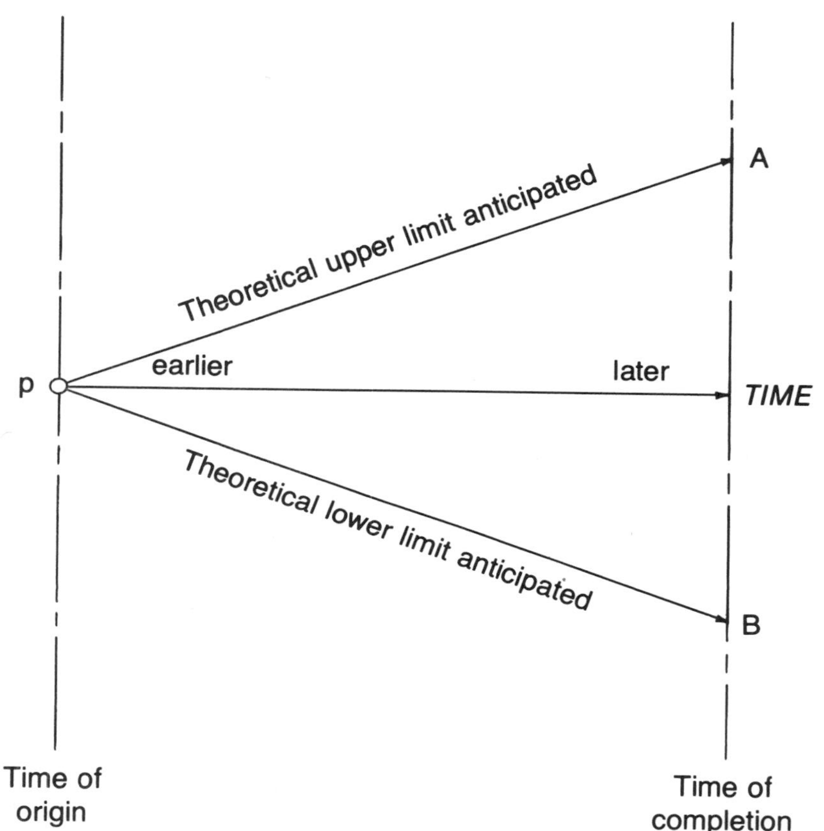

Figure 10. Schematic model of a time-related phenomenon that tends to exhibit an "increase" across time. Cone model #1.

tal learning model. The expanding cone suggests, for instance, that something like the range of application of some known or knowable characteristic tends to grow increasingly general with the passage of time. Figure 11 is both a logical inverse of the expanding cone and a sometimes overlooked developmental model. The contracting cone suggests, for instance, that across time some initially diffuse or very general characteristic becomes more refined, more specific, more limited. On the other hand, figure 12 suggests a human characteristic that is essentially stable across time, a something that exhibits little change

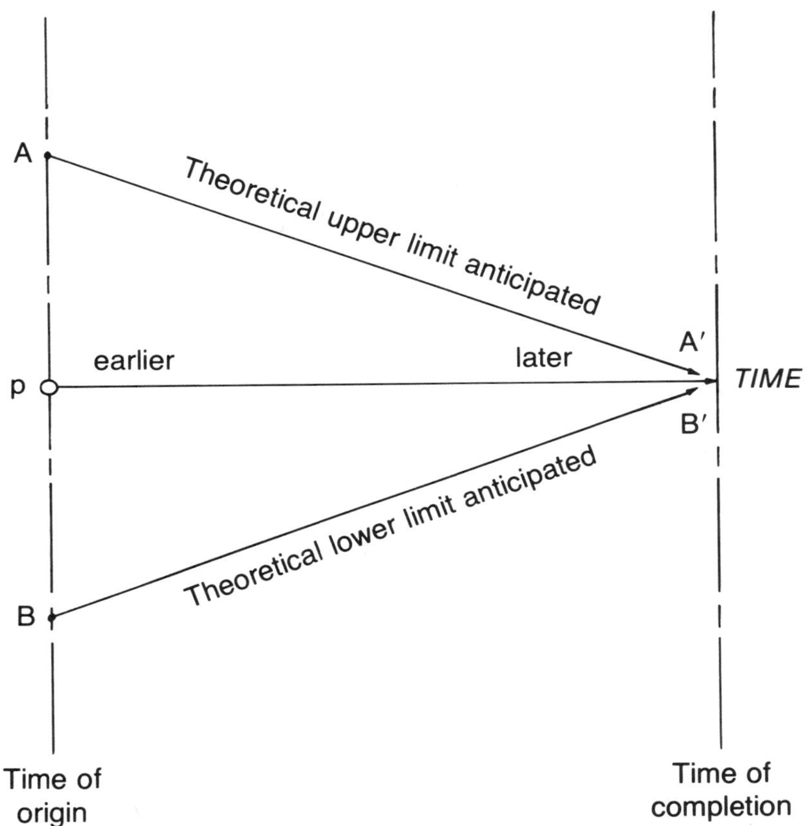

Figure 11. Schematic model of a time-related phenomenon that tends to exhibit a "decrease" across time. Cone model #2.

in either the range of application or in its refinement by specification across time. Clearly the models involve different relationships to time. Equally clearly, understanding a time-related phenomenon (e.g., anything that we suspect is developmental) depends upon matching model and data.

One of the persistent attempts that educators or developmentalists make is to distinguish a sequence of levels or stages in one or another human characteristic. Piaget's sequence of stages in the development of cognitive operations are one example, as are Kohlberg's stages of

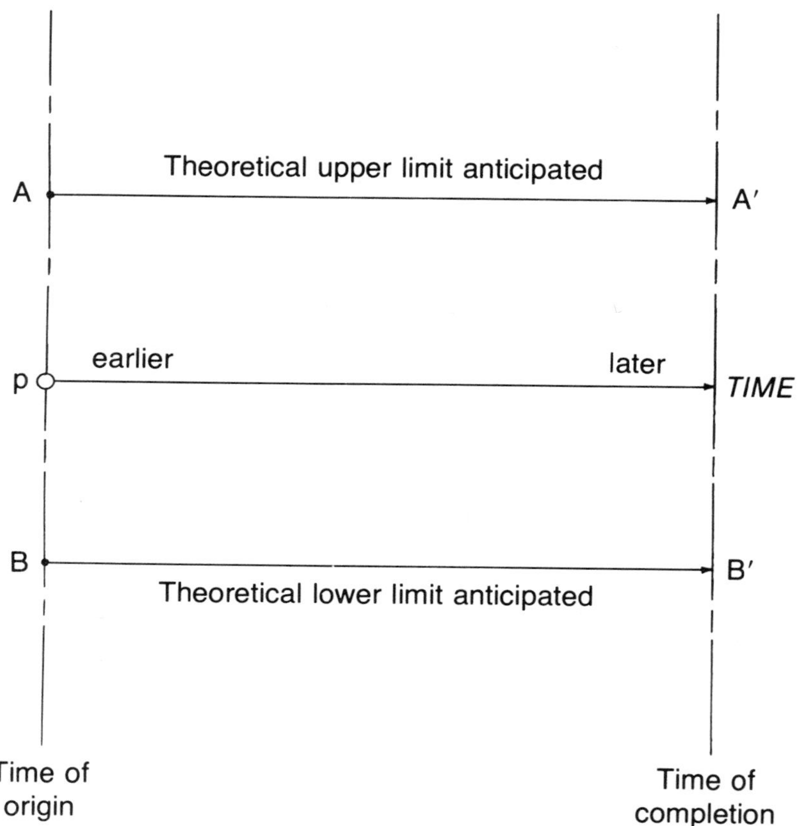

Figure 12. Schematic model of a phenomenon that is not time-related and, so, tends to exhibit neither "increase" nor "decrease" across a period of time.

moral development, Fowler's stages of faith development. Loevinger's stages of ego development, or Selman's stages of interpersonal development. The next two figures are really refinements of the basic expanding cone from figure 10 which are more easily recognized as similar to or adaptable to phenomena that exhibit a stagelike sequential growth across time. Thus, it will be useful to spend some time recognizing the interrelationship of figure 13 and figure 14.

In figure 13 the general expanding cone model of figure 10 is presented in cross-section, with two variations. First, the ray representing

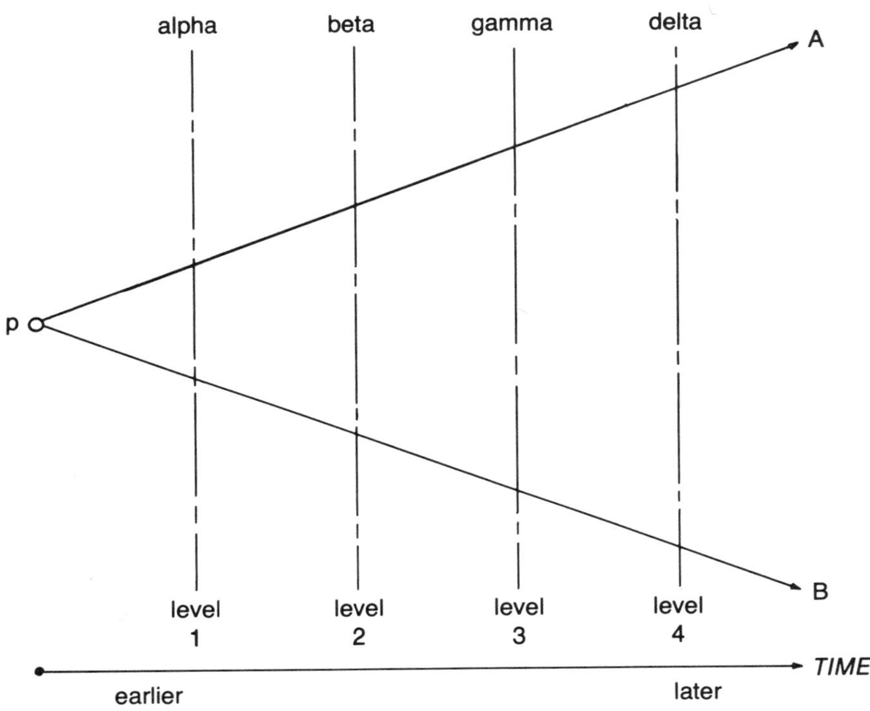

Figure 13. Schematic cross-sectional model of a time-related phenomenon that tends to exhibit an "increase" across time. Cone model #3.

time has been moved from within the cone itself to a position parallel to the cone. Second, a series of four levels or slices or planes have been added. These levels—alpha, beta, gamma, and delta—form a time-related sequence, in which level 1 (alpha) is earlier than level 4 (delta), which is sequentially later. The implication of this model is that there is some increase which is symbolized by the obviously broader base for the expanding cone supplied by level delta as compared to level beta. However, figure 13 is only a two-dimensional schematic.

Actually, a cone is a three-dimensional geometric model. The im-

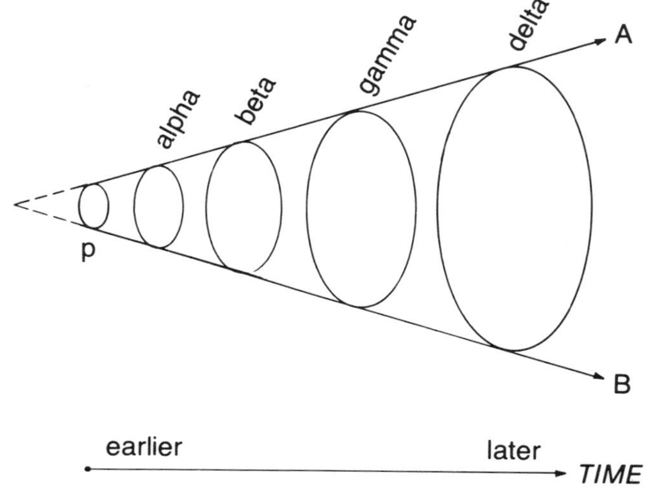

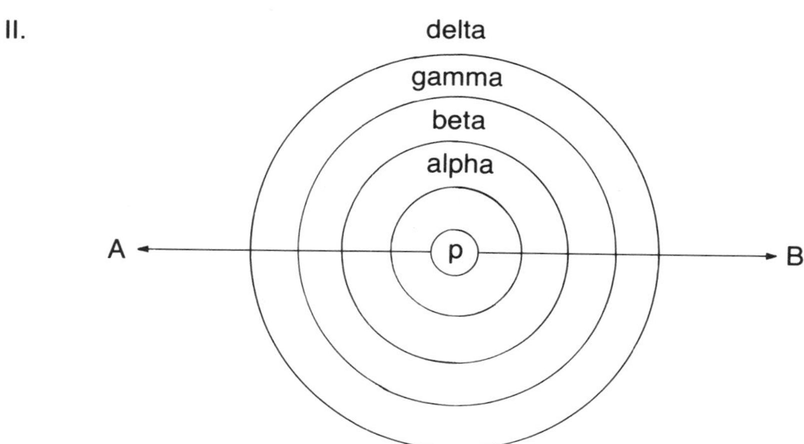

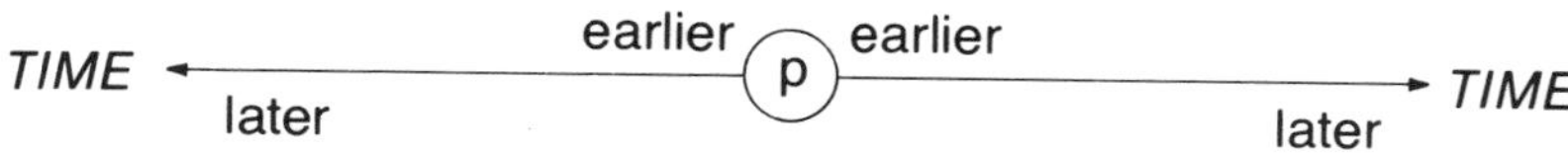

Figure 14. Variations on the schematic cross-sectional model of a time-related phenomenon that tends to exhibit an "increase" across time. Cone model #3. I. = Rotation of 20 degrees in one plane. II. = Rotation of 90 degrees in two planes.

plication of recognizing this three-dimensionality is represented in figure 14. In that figure, two different perspectives upon the cone displayed in figure 13 are displayed. The first of these perspectives simply rotates the cone a bit, so that the expanding "mouth" moves toward the observer. In figure 14(I) the four levels can be recognized as themselves cross-sections of the cone. In figure 14(II) the cone has been further rotated, and we seem to be looking directly "down" the cone. This expanding set of circles can, then, be recognized as what it is: a variation on the basic cone model. The third and lowest schematic in figure 14 suggests an interesting and important implication of this variation: time becomes a pair of rays (or a straight line) which expand from the central circle symbolizing the free body p. This implication is not always recognized when the multicircle model is used, for sometimes it is thought to be a general, time-free model. However, that is not necessarily the case. Certainly it is not inherently so.

There is also an implication of figure 14(II) which is attractive but, once again, is not necessarily so. If the set of concentric circles be taken simply as a two-dimensional model, it may be argued that delta not only presumes the existence of gamma, beta, and alpha but, as well, their inclusion. However, if that set of concentric circles be recognized as but another perspective upon a series of time-related cross-sections of the cone ApB, that presumption can be recognized for what it is—a possibility, but not a necessity. Moreover, we can also use this set of expanding concentric circles to ask an important "how" question. That is, how does the modeled phenomenon change from level alpha to level beta, and then from level beta to level gamma, and finally from level gamma to level delta? That particular how question is important for *all* models of development which identify or posit either levels or stages.

Not all the phenomena of interest to either educators or religious educators seem to exhibit a steady increase. Some seem to oscillate between periods of increase and periods of seeming decrease. The wave-form model displayed in figure 15 is one way to conceptualize such phenomena. In that figure two new concepts are introduced: frequency and amplitude. Wave-forms can be characterized by statements of the frequency with which full waves are observed and by the

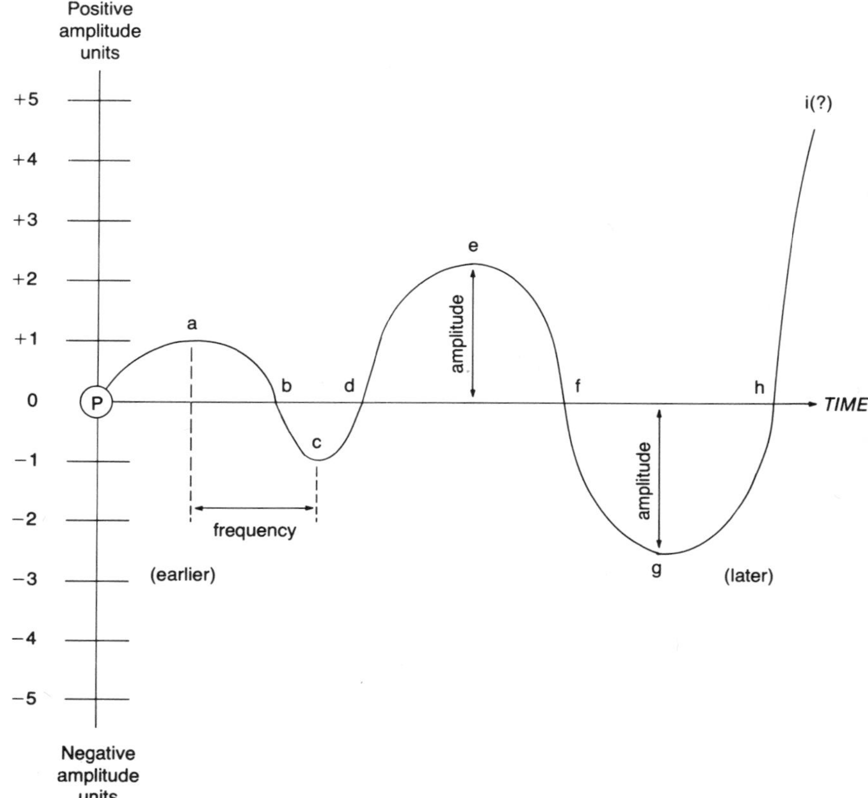

Figure 15. Schematic cross-sectional model of a time-related phenomenon that exhibits variable "increase" and "decrease" across time. Wave-form model #1. Frequency and amplitude noted.

amplitude of those waves. The actual wave-form in figure 15 is a complex one in which an oscillation is obvious within a general tendency to exhibit an overall increase in amplitude. An example of the quite general use of such a wave-form model is the anticipated result of a process of education, when education is thought to involve *both* an ability to know more and more specifically *and,* as well, to relate what is known to increasingly general principles or ideals or values.

The schematic displayed in figure 16 represents a highly structured and equally highly theoretical sequence which, at least since the works of Georg Wilhelm Hegel, has been recognized as a dialectic.[22] What

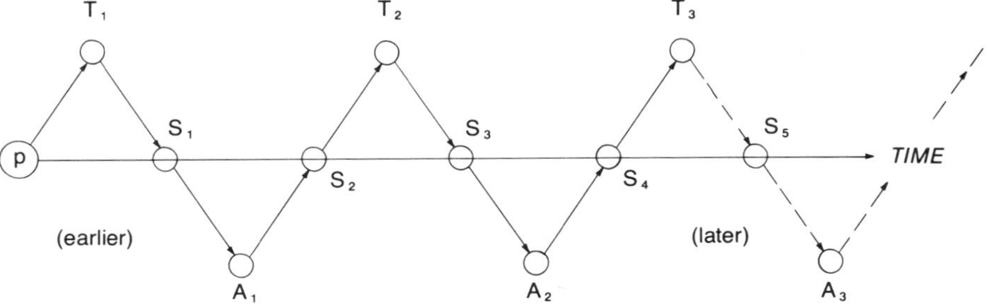

Dialectical Antitheses

WHERE: T_1, T_2, and T_3 = Sequence of dialectical theses.
A_1, A_2, and A_3 = Sequence of dialectical antitheses.
S_1, S_2, S_3, S_4, and S_5 = Sequence of dialectical syntheses.
p = A theoretical "free body" capable of dialectical "motion."

Figure 16. Schematic cross-sectional model of a time-related phenomenon that exhibits a dialectical "motion" from a thesis through a synthesis to an antithesis through a synthesis to a thesis. Wave-form model #2. Theoretical continuity noted.

may not have been recognized for quite as long is that a dialectic is but a variation on the basic wave-form model. Thus, the concepts of frequency and amplitude are (at least conceptually) applicable to the oscillatory resolution of the apparent contradiction between a thesis and an antithesis in a synthesis. The intellectual history of the century and a half since Hegel's death indicates that a number of phenomena of interest are (minimally) quite amenable to analysis as instances of a dialectic.

However, there are sequential phenomena which seem to be marked by a seeming recurrence of states. This kind of phenomena is modeled by the circle displayed in figure 17. Normally, such a sequence is said to be *cyclic*.

What is sometimes overlooked is that a cyclic model is also time-related. All too often it is thought to imply only that, in the long run, there is no progress. What once was will be. Although this model may be regarded as fatalistic, we should not ignore it. Some bodies of data may well seem to fit a cyclic model quite well. However, there is an inherent problem with the model displayed in figure 17.

In a strictly cyclic model, time presumably returns upon itself. That presumption creates its own set of conceptual problems, only one of which is that a good bit of human experience seems to suggest something else. While there is an undoubted human experience of seeming to reencounter former problems, a cyclic model is not the only solution. An alternative to that experience of seeming to reencounter problems is to imagine breaking into the cyclic motion and "pull it upward," so that the circle becomes a spiral. That is exactly what is displayed in figure 18.

The spiral displayed in figure 18 is a model capable of accommodating both the experience of seeming recurrence and the recognition that such a "recurrence" is only similar to, but not identical with some previous occurrence. The figure also introduces yet another concept,

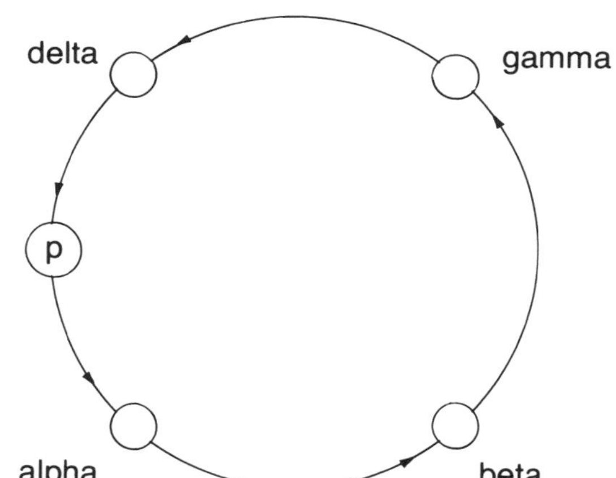

Figure 17. Schematic representation of a time-related phenomenon that exhibits a sequence of states but, periodically, seems to return to its original state. Circular model #1.

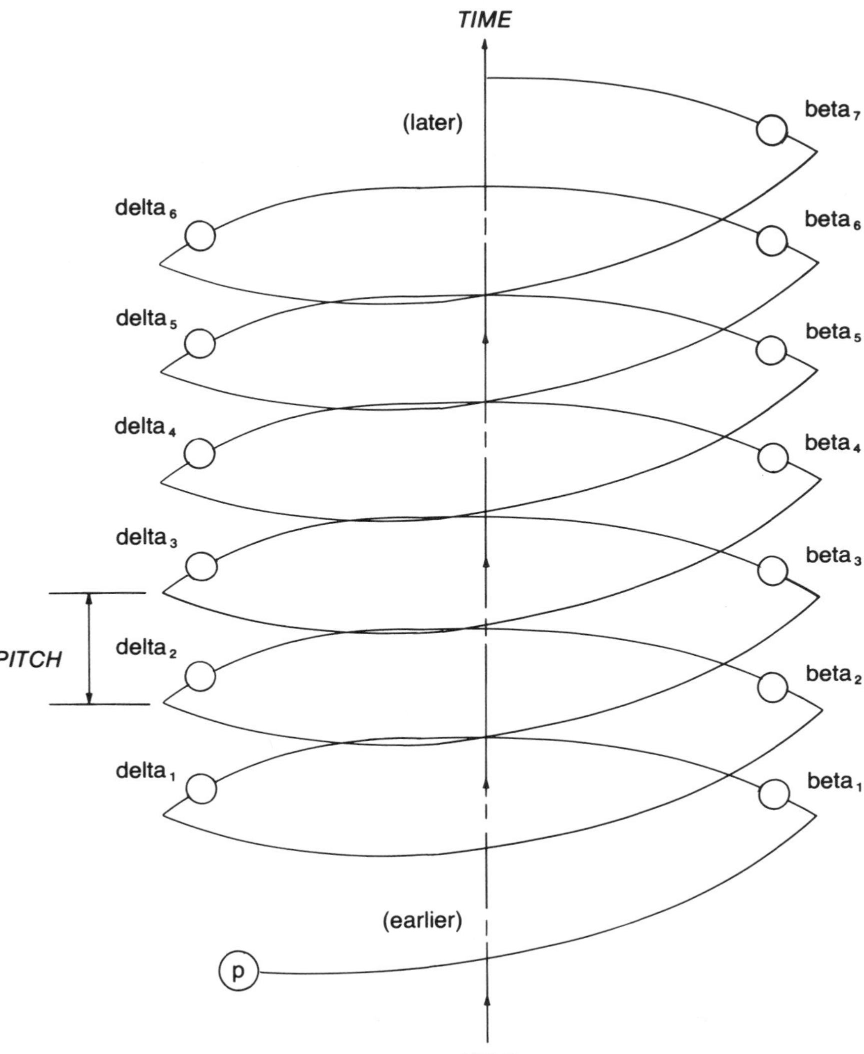

Figure 18. Schematic representation of a time-related phenomenon that exhibits a sequence of states which, periodically, tend to recur in a similar-but-different form (e.g., forms constitute a sequence of increasingly complex and inclusive states). Circular model #2.

that of pitch. In the spiral model, pitch is analogous to frequency in the wave-form model. Thus, in this particular model, it is the pitch of the ascending spiral which determines how often across a given period of time the seeming recurrence is observed. In fact, if we posit that the spiral model of figure 18 delineates a possible pathway for the successive states of a theoretically free body p, then, by also introducing the concept of rate (especially a variable rate!) it is possible to model a number of quite complex phenomena via an ascending spiral. Moreover, if one recognizes that the theoretical radius of the spiral is, itself, a potentially varying analogue of amplitude in the wave-form model, it is possible to acknowledge that the wave-form of figure 15 and the spiral of figure 18 may well be but alternative conceptual perspectives upon the same complex phenomenon.

IV. What about Multiple Effects?

Difficult as it may be to believe, up to this point the models displayed in the various figures have been primarily concerned with the possible effect of *an* identifiable force (what researchers would call a variable) upon a theoretically free body p. The only complexity acknowledged in figures 6–18 was the passage of time. Yet, while time is an important dimension for much research, humans are so immersed in time that it is easy either to assume it or ignore it. The models identified thus far did no more than identify time and, so, bring about a conscious recognition of it as an inescapable aspect of what was essentially a univariate model.

But that is *not* all there is.

Educators and, most especially, religious educators are remarkably adept at reminding a researcher of one or another "other" force, factor, influence, or variable that could (quite conceivably!) affect the observed and recorded results from some particular use of research-as-a-method. While that is less than pleasant news to any researcher, it is often a tolerably viable insight. Thus, there are relatively few problems of importance or interest to those who practice the art of education which are amenable to the use of research-as-a-method upon only one variable. Most of the time, at least two variables (in addition to time itself) are involved in a study, or are fairly operative in a situation of interest to religious educators. Thus, the "problem to find" posed by many situations of interest can be posed by some variation of the query that asks, "What *is* the relationship between A and B, in *this* group of persons?"

What that query about a relationship asks *is* amenable to the use of research-as-a-method. In fact, the query itself can be rephrased in terms of the model presented in figure 6 and scaled in figure 7. The query itself posits that some theoretically free body p (e.g., an individual or a group of seemingly similar individuals) can be, across some period of time, influenced by both a ray pA and a ray pB, each of which can be scaled after the manner of figure 7. Thus, the query itself asks, "What value of scaled ray pA tends to be or is observed to be associated with what value of scaled ray pB, in this group of persons?" Stated in that way, the query posits that *any* theoretically free body p *can* be positioned in *some* conceptual plane by referencing a scaled value of pA and a scaled value of pB. Moreover, such a positioning within a conceptual plane presumes that the plane itself is defined by pA and pB, when p itself is presumed to be previously unaffected by the force, factor, influence, or variable represented by either ray pA or ray pB, as illustrated in figure 19.

In figure 19 four possible positionings are identified. These four positionings—alpha, beta, gamma, and delta—can assume two slightly different meanings. First, they can refer to p itself; in which case they picture the complex relationship of pA and pB, given different combinations of scaled values (strengths) of those two rays. Second, alpha, beta, gamma, and delta can refer to identifiable participant components of p; in which case they form a set of components that, together, picture an even more complex relationship of pA and pB, given the individual variability of the four participant components of the group being considered as a p. However, in either meaning, what figure 19 pictures is a specific set of observations which, by visual examination, generally suggest that higher scaled values of pA tend to be associated with higher scaled values of pB. Unfortunately, such a specific set of four two-valued positionings only very generally suggests an answer to the query about a relationship between pA and pB. A

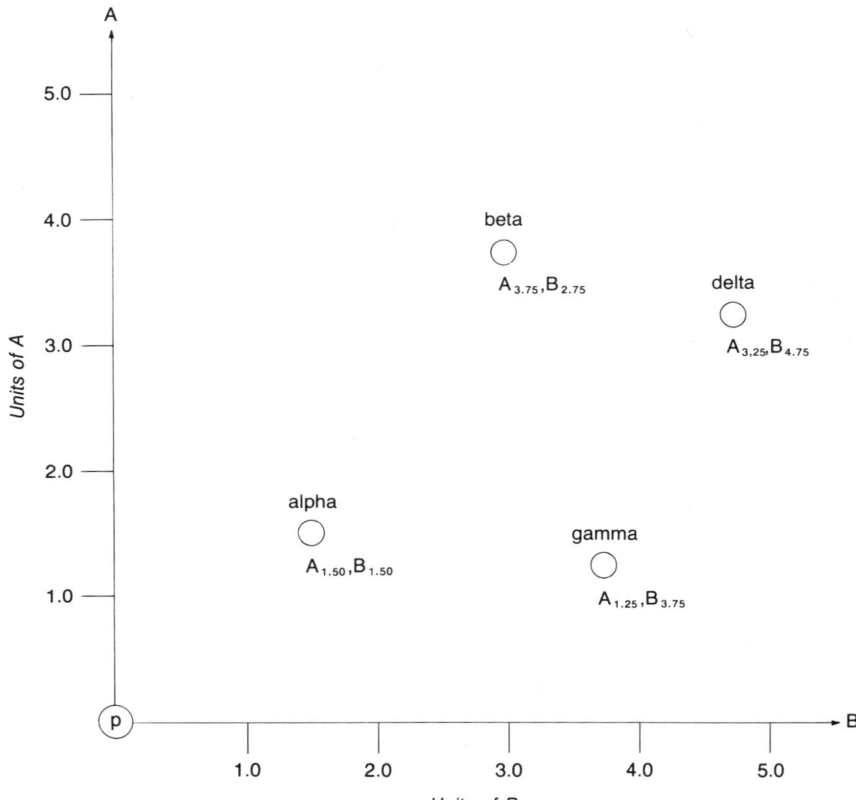

Figure 19. Schematic representation of action of two presumably independent variables (rays A and B) on a theoretically free body p, plus identification of four possible states of p, given different combinations of "strengths" of the two independent variables. Graph model #1. (Model equivalent to two rays.)

relationship is a generality, but what figure 19 provides is a specific instance, or example.

Through a somewhat complex process of determining a so-called line of linear regression and then calculating what is called a coefficient of correlation, it is possible to summarize figure 19 in a single numeric symbol, the value of the product moment correlation coefficient r.[23] That coefficient is usually taken to be a summary answer to the question concerning the relationship of pA and pB, given the observed values of alpha, beta, gamma, and delta. In fact, in the instance displayed in figure 19, the value of the product moment correlation coefficient r is a positive .3093. That value not only confirms the general impression gained from a visual examination but, as well, gives a precise albeit *average* statement of the relationship of pA and pB, given the observed positionings of alpha, beta, gamma, and delta.

The basic query about a relationship between forces, factors, influences, or variables can also be recast in terms of the model presented in figure 8 and scaled in figure 9. However, since that basic model envisions rays pA and pB as segments of a straight line running through a theoretically free body p, the determinable result of the query is equivalent to asking which ray-modeled influence is stronger. The models in figure 8 and figure 9 picture either (1) a balance of power situation, or (2) a theoretically prior state necessary for understanding a presently observed positioning of body p in terms of some scaled place on either ray pA or ray pB. This is an instance of opposite forces that can be resolved by the relatively simple process of adding a positive and a negative number if, as in the lowest straight line of figure 9, one of the opposite directional rays is given a negative meaning while the other of the opposite directional rays is given a positive meaning. This model is extremely useful, for much of human thinking involves dichotomies. However, as Osgood, Suci, and Tannenbaum report in *The Measurement of Meaning*, seeming dichotomies are not always demonstrable, empirical opposites along a theoretical straight-line continuum.[24] What they report is that, often enough to lead one to be somewhat cautious, seeming dichotomies turn out to be "opposite" ends of demonstrably parallel but not identical continua. Thus, the model posited in figure 8 and figure 9 matches much human thinking but only a portion of demonstrable human experience.

Actually, human experience tends to be surprisingly complex, once we think about it long enough to begin to analyze an experience. The models considered in figure 6, figure 7, figure 8, and figure 9 are real enough, but they are often not complex enough to serve as even acknowledgedly simplified models of human experience.[25] One way to begin to accommodate the seemingly inevitable complexity of human experience is to posit *two* straight lines, instead of one, and presume that the forces, factors, influences, or variables are distinguishably different (or, as researchers are likely to speak of it, are independent). That is what is displayed in figure 20.

In figure 20 the simple graph model of figure 19 has been increased fourfold. In addition, four possible states of body p—alpha, beta, gamma, and delta—have been identified in terms of pairs of

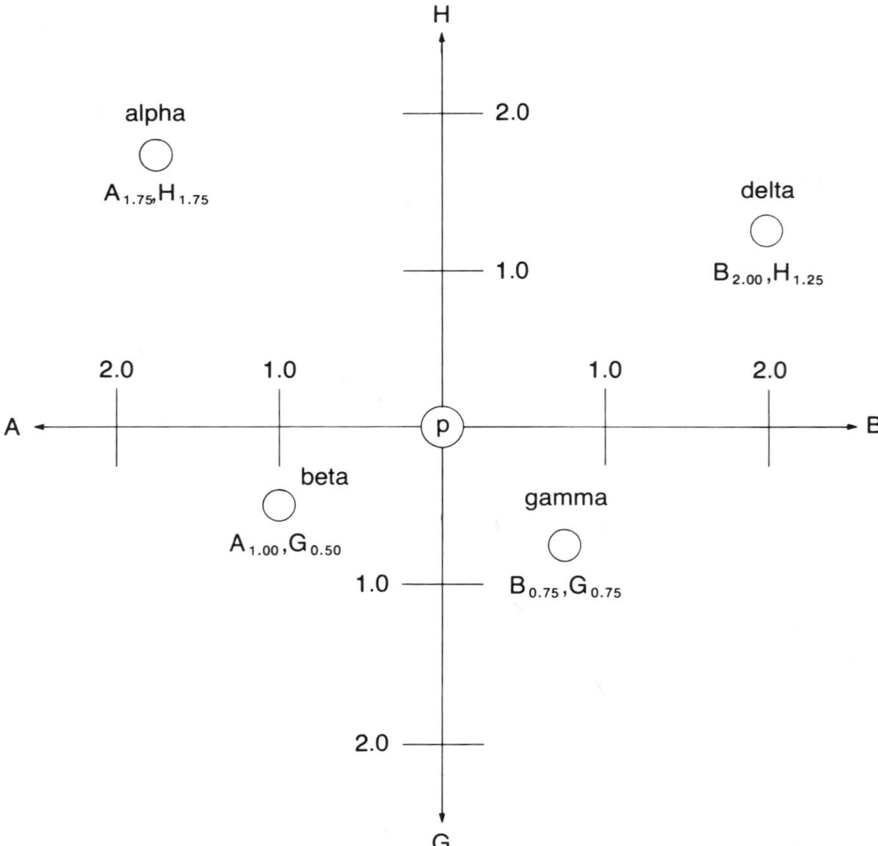

Figure 20. Schematic representation of action of two pairs of presumably polar opposite and independent variables (straight lines ApB and GpH), plus identification of four possible states of p, given different combinations of "strengths" of the four variables. Graph model #2. (Model = four rays, or two straight lines through p.)

quadrant-defining rays. Each of these states can be interpreted in the way the set of four states displayed in figure 19 were interpreted (as a picture of a relationship between a pair of identifiable variables). However, it is also possible to accept figure 20 as a way of picturing a far more complex phenomenon and, so, seek an interpretation for the full set of four positions. As was true before, two somewhat different interpretations are possible. First, the four positions may be taken to be picturings of situations in which only two of the four rays have noticeable strength. Second, the four positionings may be taken to picture a result of a fourfold combination of strengths of each of the rays. These two alternatives lead to noticeably different interpretations of the phenomenon modeled by figure 20. For example: the first way of picturing suggests simply that, depending upon what ray variables one attends to, the state or position of body p is noticeably different. The second way of picturing suggests that, depending upon the relative strength of the four ray variables, the state or position of body p shifts in an intriguingly complex yet ordered manner and, so, approximates a so-called U-shaped curve. Both of these ways of interpreting phenomena are useful, for the complexities of most interest to an educator or religious educator often require something like the model displayed in figure 20.

Although you may be wearying of conceptual complexities, there are two more models necessary to complete this survey of ways to picture multiple effects. The first of these models is displayed in figure 21, which is one way to define a conceptual space.[26] The second of these models is displayed in figure 22, which is an alternate and somewhat more complex way to define such a conceptual space. Each is worthy of some consideration.

The conceptual space modeled in figure 21 is a reasonably simple three-dimensional space. It is the space which is perceivable *from* a given point (the initial position of a theoretically free body p) *when* a particular orientation is adopted. For example, a theoretical observer at the initial position of free body p orients ahead (toward B) and to the right (toward A) and considers *only* that which is up (toward E), as many right-handed persons might do. In this three-dimensional conceptual space, only one other positioning of p has been identified—point alpha. While it may be a bit difficult to visualize, point alpha

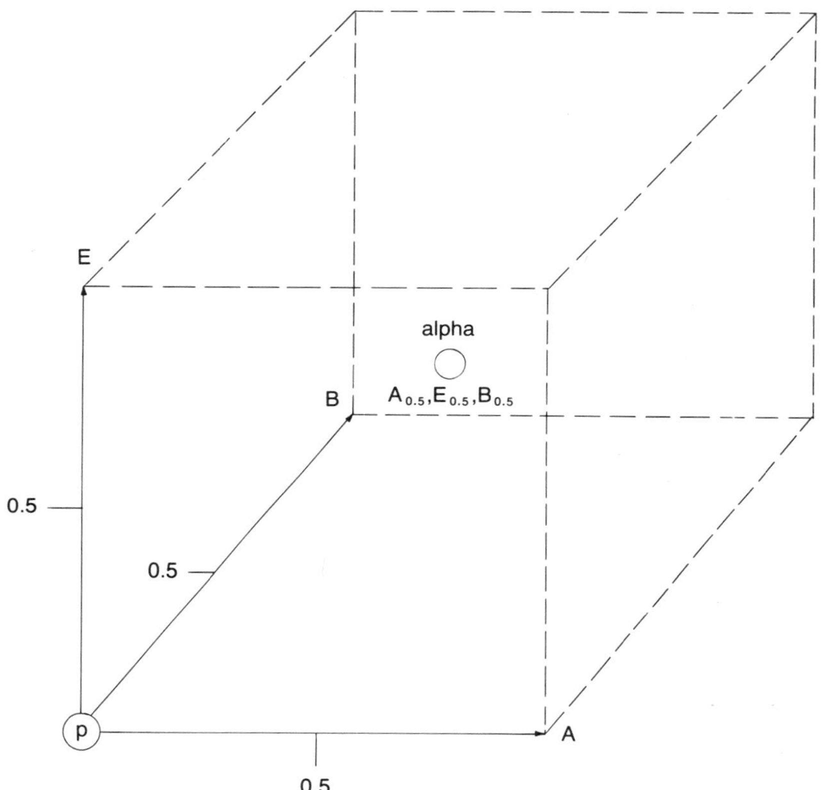

Figure 21. Schematic representations of three presumably independent variables (rays pA, pB, and pE), plus identification of a possible state of p, given an equal combination of "strengths" of the three variables. Cube model #1. (Model = three rays orthogonally related from p.)

occupies the exact geometric center of the cube of conceptual space defined by rays pA, pB and pE, when each of those three rays is presumed to be exactly one unit length. In other words, the strength of the forces, factors, influences, or variables symbolized by rays pA, pB, and pE are all equivalent and of exactly 0.5 unit strength. As a result, alpha is positioned in the exact center of the cubical conceptual space defined by those three rays.

On the other hand, the conceptual space modeled in figure 22 seems to be (and is!) considerably more complex. Instead of being at a corner of the conceptual space, theoretically free body p is at the exact center of the cube of conceptual space represented by figure 22. How-

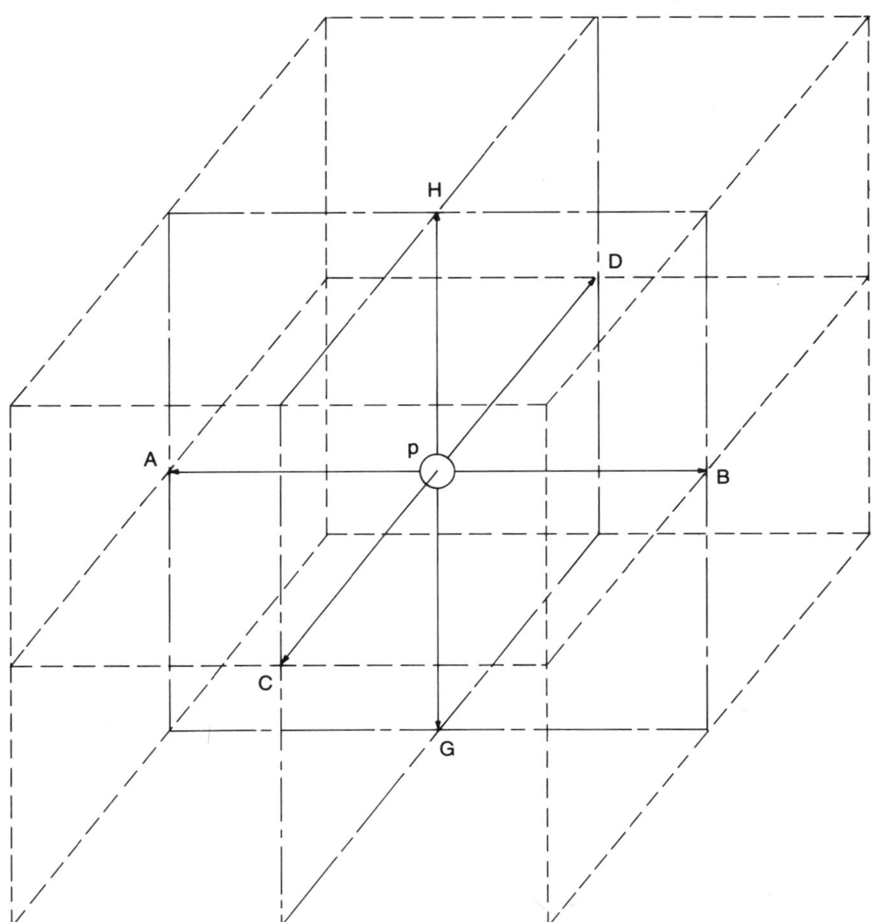

Figure 22. Schematic representation of action of three pairs of presumably polar opposite and independent variables (straight lines ApB, CpD, and GpH), plus the identification of a theoretically possible "space" determined by varying combinations of those variables, given different "strengths" of the variables. Cube model #2. (Model = six rays, or three straight lines through p.)

ever, that is but another way of saying that the position of theoretically free body p in figure 22 is an exact conceptual equivalent of the position of alpha in figure 21. Still, what figure 22 displays is that, given a position in the center of some conceptual space, the full set of possible motions determined by the variable strengths of the forces, factors, influences, or variables (or rays *from* p, or straight lines *through* p) are equivalent to an eightfold ordered combination of theoretically possible figure 21-type conceptual spaces.

While it is not mathematically elegant, figure 22 can be intuitively understood fairly simply and reasonably accurately by remembering the perceptual analogy used with figure 21. There the perceiver was oriented ahead and to the right and up. Fairly simple considerations lead most humans to recognize that there are three other possible orientations that can be thought of as, basically, ahead. Thus, one can identify a full set of simple three-dimensional orientations ahead: (1) ahead, right, and up; (2) ahead, left, and up; (3) ahead, left, and down; (4) ahead, right, and down. All that is necessary to reach the number eight is to recognize that for each of those four orientations ahead there is a mirror-image orientation behind for any observer located at a theoretical point p in the center of some conceptual space. In very direct human perceptual terms, figure 22 models phenomena where it is possible to think of describing the effect of various combinations of forces, factors, influences, or variables upon some quite theoretically free body p as "moves" either upward or downward, either to the conceptual right or to the conceptual left, either ahead or behind, or any combination of those several conceptual directions.

Within our human limits, the potential for three-dimensional movement of a theoretically free body p modeled in figure 22 is an instance of what we can recognize as maximum freedom. That is, there are no obvious three-dimensional constraints upon the potential movement of body p, nor are there the implicit yet powerful constraints there were in figures 5–21. Only by going to a four-dimensional model (or to an n-dimensional model) can the conceptual freedom of movement of a theoretically free body p be increased.

That last flat assertion is one reason why it is precise to speak of both two-dimensional planes (for example, graphs) and three-dimensional spaces as *models*, in the mathematical sense of that word. They are inevitable simplifications of some recognizably complex phenomenon. However, what can be thought of as model-ness consists almost entirely in the preservation of sufficient aspects of the real phenomenon in the admitted simplification to make the phenomenon's reality somehow understandable and acceptable. *That* is what a mathematical model is intended to do. If it does that, it is a good model. If it does not do that, it is a poor model.

Actually, the real phenomena of most interest to either educators or religious educators are almost always complex enough to require a model. In fact, such complex phenomena can *only* be modeled by a mathematical-style model.[27] The sad thing is that we humans too often forget what we have done to simplify a complexity enough to create a model and, so, assume that our simplification is an exhaustive statement of the nature of the real phenomenon modeled. *That* is a clear example of forgetting what one has done or, in balder terms, but one more example of homo sapiens's tendency toward stupidity.[28]

A model *is* a model; it is nought else. Yet it may be both useful and helpful. Therefore, it probably is both inescapable and inevitable, if we are to try to understand any genuinely interesting or important phenomenon in the field of religious education. The implicit argument of this chapter has been that to use research-as-a-method inescapably involves using models and that, when one uses research-as-a-method in religious education, *nothing* about the field itself lessens our dependence upon models. If anything, the exact opposite is true.[29]

Notes and References

1. An expression of this quite functional view of information itself is to be found in the following short paragraph:

> Ideally information is the sum total of data needed for decision-making. In practice, virtually all decisions are made with too little of some kinds of information and/or too much of others. Any item of information is needed if without it a decision would be different; leading to the conclusion that an item of information has no value if it cannot at least potentially influence a decision.

"The Value of Information," in Arthur B. Toan, Jr. and Henry Gunders, eds., *Consulting for Management* (New York: Price Waterhouse & Co., 1970), p. 19.

2. The use of the concept of magic in this sentence owes much to the

parallel views of magic suggested by Evelyn Underhill in *Mysticism: A Study in the Nature and Development of Man's Spiritual Consciousness* (London: Methuen & Co., 1911) and Jean Piaget in *The Child's Conception of Physical Causality* (Paterson, N.J.: Littlefield, Adams & Co., 1930/1960). In the author's 1973 dissertation, this parallel view was examined in some detail in a section entitled, "Differences between the RTVC and RTC Scales: Magic and the Supernatural." (See John H. Peatling, "The Incidence of Concrete and Abstract Religious Thinking in the Interpretation of Three Bible Stories by Pupils Enrolled in Grades Four through Twelve in Selected Schools in the Episcopal Church in the United States of America" (Ph.D. diss., New York University, 1973), pp. 156–168.

3. The construct of set-ness, as used in this sentence, involves the two complementary ideas of wholeness and well-defined-ness. For further useful information on the mathematical theory of sets see the following sources: E. Kamke, *Theory of Sets* (New York: Dover Publications, 1950), esp. quote from G. Cantor on p. 1; William L. Hays, *Statistics for Psychologists* (New York: Holt, Rinehart and Winston, 1963/1965), esp. pp. 13–46; and Fred N. Kerlinger, *Foundations of Behavioral Research* (New York: Holt, Rinehart and Winston, 1964/1966), esp. pp. 67–78.

4. In these sentences I have put in close proximity two ideas that deserve to be related. *First*, that theologies are often an essential wisdom that, quite appropriately, influences what a human will regard (or accept) as credible. This is an important functional contribution to the very human rational process, and no one should ignore it. However, in logical terms, determining what is credible is very, very different from presuming to determine what is researchable. *Second*, the reference to Toynbee and cultures involves: (1) a memory of the Somervill abridgement of vols. 1–6 of Arnold J. Toynbee's *Study of History* (New York: Oxford University Press, 1946), and (2) an inversion of the individual-civilization analogy, such that the anology is presumed to be *from* a Toynbean historical analysis of civilizations' response to challenges *to* an individual or group, rather than the other way around.

5. For my initial use of what I have called Hickson's query, see chapter 7, pp. 187–191.

6. Reference to my copy of *The Compact Edition of the Oxford English Dictionary* (New York: Oxford University Press, 1971), led me to recognize the following distinction between an event and an occurrence. First, an *occurrence* is defined as "an incidental meeting or encounter," while an *event* is defined (in modern usage) as an "occurrence of some importance." Second, while it is very generally true that an event is also an occurrence, the distinction of one from the other depends upon a recognizable value: the linguistically noticeable difference between that which is merely incidental and that which can be regarded as of some importance. Thus, events are more impor-

tant than occurrences, although (clearly) all events are occurrences. Clearly logic and valuing can get quite entangled in this sort of distinction, although I have posited that valuing is the more important construct and, therefore, the one that deserves priority, in this specific instance.

7. In an asymetric 3 × 3 matrix there are nine (9) possible pairings, *each* of which is different (and, so, interpretable). The problem referred to in this sentence involves the acknowledgment that, however obvious our choices may seem, those choices involve but three pairings out of nine possible pairings.

8. Compare tables 1, 2, and 3 of chapter 12 with tables 1, 2, and 3 of chapter 7, which are to be found on pages 231–233. As the reader will easily and quickly see, there is an exact parallel between the two sets of three tables.

9. See G. Polya, *How to Solve It, 2nd ed.* (Garden City, N.Y.: Doubleday & Co., 1945/1957), pp. 141–148, 154–157.

10. What is here affirmed is that without the discernible presence of all four concepts, there is *not* an event. It is also implicit in these two sentences that the six journalistic queries intend to describe and explain the specific set of (a) an act, (b) a reason or rationale, (c) a time or place, and (d) a record or history.

11. The figure 46,656 is simply the result of raising six (the number of possible scale points) to the sixth power (the number of scales having six scale-points each). Since perfect agreement or disagreement *is* logically possible, in this instance, all logically possible combinations are not only credible but possible.

12. For an example of the way logically possible combinations tend to give a reasonable approximation of a theoretically normal distribution, see table 7 in chapter 10 (p. 369).

13. Clearly after-the-fact judgments, ratings, statements, or evaluative opinions are all too open to the caveat that the judge, rater, stater, or one holding the opinion (1) already knew the result, or (2) was merely responding to an accomplished "something" by restating a bias. Thus, they are for any researcher the softest, least reliable sort of data. In fact, all of these four possibilities are subjective and, so, soft data. Even so, some problems of importance and interest in the social sciences can *only* be approached through such soft data. But there is no reason to think soft is hard.

14. For a bit more information on mapping, see Fred N. Kerlinger, *Foundations of Behavioral Research* (New York: Holt, Rinehart and Winston, 1964), pp. 80–92, esp. the section "Rules of Correspondence and Mapping," pp. 84–85.

15. For more information on the idea of an ordinal scale, see Allen L. Edwards, *Statistical Analysis* (New York: Holt, Rinehart and Winston, 1969), pp. 12–13; William L. Hays, *Statistics for Psychologists* (New York:

Holt, Rinehart and Winston, 1963), pp. 68–71; and Sidney Siegel, *Nonparametric Statistics for the Behavioral Sciences* (New York: McGraw-Hill Book Co., 1956), pp. 23–26.

16. See the section entitled "A Momentary Digression: Choosing or Deciding?" in chapter 4 (pp. 100–107).

17. *The Random House Dictionary of the English Language* (New York: Random House, 1967), the word *wisdom*.

18. J. R. R. Tolkien, "On Fairy-Stories," in *The Tolkien Reader* (New York: Ballantine Books, 1966), p. 52.

19. For the basic mathematical concept of a ray, see Robert W. Marks, *The New Mathematics Dictionary and Handbook* (New York: Bantam Books, 1964), p. 88; or Evelyn Sharp, *A Parent's Guide to the New Mathematics* (New York: E. P. Dutton & Co., 1964), p. 109.

20. In the strictest, most formal sense of the term, a ray is one-half of a line and continues from its point of origin an infinitely long way. Thus, to posit some known or knowable goal (e.g., A, B, C, D, or E) along such a ray is to posit some other point along such a ray, which is to define a segment of the ray. Such a segment of a ray is similar to a segment of a line.

21. "Address of P. A. M. Dirac," *Science*, vol. 207, no. 4436 (March 14, 1980), pp. 1161–1162.

22. Georg Wilhelm Hegel was born at Stuttgart in 1770, graduated from the university at Tubingen in 1793, and taught at universities in Jena, Heidelberg, and Berlin. The idea of a dialectical movement was developed by Hegel in his *Logic* (1816) through his analysis of the concept of relation. Hegel died during a cholera epidemic in Berlin in 1831. For a short, readable review of Hegel's life and work and influence, see Will Durant, *The Story of Philosophy*, rev. (New York: Simon and Schuster, 1933), pp. 317–325.

23. The relation of a line of linear regression to a coefficient of correlation can, in fact, get quite complex. However, one of the simpler presentations of that relationship can be found in chapter 6 of Edwards, *Statistical Analysis*, pp. 66–81.

24. Charles E. Osgood, George J. Suci, and Percy H. Tannenbaum, *The Measurement of Meaning* (Urbana, Ill.: University of Illinois Press, 1957).

25. For example, see the entry by G. W. Cussons for *mathematical models* in *Encylopaedia Britannica* (1951).

26. The idea of a conceptual space is the author's generalization of the idea of a semantic space, as developed by Osgood, Suci, and Tannenbaum in *The Measurement of Meaning*.

27. This sentence is true if, but only if, we acknowledge that any model is (to some degree) a simplification of some more complex phenomenon. That is what a mathematical model is, which is why *model* has been rather consistently qualified by the word *mathematical* in this book. Clearly, if one re-

garded a model as an exact, exhaustive representation of the essential nature of something, a model could mean something quite different.

28. While it is admittedly idiosyncratic, the author has reached the conclusion that humankind probably exhibits instances of stupidity in a way that is a close approximation to a so-called normal distribution. The author's analogue for this conclusion is the reasonably clear evidence that so-called intelligence tends to be exhibited in a way that is a close approximation to a so-called normal distribution *and* his willingness to consider such intelligence as a conceptual inverse for stupidity, and vice versa.

29. This conclusion seems to make sense if one posits that the field of religious education involves genuinely complex events that are worthy of interest and, so, of the use of research-as-a-method. If one should believe (or think) the events not so complex, this conclusion might be questionable or even clearly false. As in a number of places in this book, readers must decide whether or not they agree with the author. Either way, if there be a decision, the author can only be glad . . . even if he may not be overwhelmed with joy at the prospect of disagreement.

Epilogue

Clergy are pack rats.

I should know. However, I suspect that it really does not matter whether people call you Father or Mother, Reverend or Pastor, Brother or Sister, Rabbi or Friend. All clergypersons tend to save the notes of sermons, speeches, or lectures. They have a sense that sometime the topic will come up again, as it rather often does. In fact, lectionaries often assure that it does.

For example, my notes indicate that on August 31, 1958, I first referenced that profoundly simple work of Dr. Seuss entitled *On Beyond Zebra*.[1] I used the very introduction of Seuss's story to suggest that we humans all too often forgo humility and, so, assert of some present level of knowledge, ". . . that is all there is!" when, in fact, there is some more. Seuss's child-hero rose to the challenge. Thus, I suggested that in reading the Bible, or in hearing it read, we humans too easily think our first impression is all there is, and that there is no more. Then I tried to interpret a passage from Mark's Gospel, which had been read as a Lesson, as an instance of the principle that Seuss's child-hero enunciated when he maintained that *his* knowledge just barely *began* at the point where another confidently asserted, ". . . that is *all* there is!"[2]

LOOKING BACK: A REVIEW

In the previous twelve chapters I have repeatedly, albeit inferentially, suggested that Seuss's child-hero had a firmer grasp on that reality common to elves and men than any of us have when we think that our present school-based, experience-reinforced level of "knowledge" is *all* there is.[3] It simply isn't. There is some more.

In the first four chapters, I suggested that there was a "more" to the biblical G-O-D than first or even second pious impressions might lead us to think. I was not playing that nasty game of insulting the saints when I suggested that the Bible's G-O-D was not what we normally think of as a person, even if the saints often seem to attend far too closely and much too readily to sheer insult.[4] Insult was not my intent. Rather, I intended to cut through layers of human piety to a biblical core and, so, expose a strangely other, communicative, relating deity deserving both worship and faith. One that is worthy of the effort which is called religious education.

In the second four chapters, I suggested that there is a "more" to humankind than our first or even second impressions might lead us to believe. While I consistently viewed humans as creatures of this creation, I did suggest that a Tolkien, a Godel, a Piaget, and a Skinner are important to both you and me, for they help us to understand what it means to be the creatures we are. I particularly stressed the importance of three very human abilities—perception, decision, and cognition—for an understanding of our own creaturehood. In addition, I suggested that the effort called religious education *is* a process of helping creatures positively and joyfully accept, explore, and discover their very considerable potential in this creation, on this planet, and within the situations that are theirs.[5] As far as religious education is concerned, less is not more. It is merely less. In fact, less barely deserves to be called religious education.

In the final four chapters, I suggested that there is some "more" to the method of research than our first or even second impressions are at all likely to lead us to think. While I used Fuller's cognitive geometrics extensively, I also consistently suggested that the Fullerian tetrahedrons and octahedrons provide humans with a beautifully mathematical and satisfyingly heuristic model of meaningful conceptual space.[6] In addition, I suggested that the method of research, which is so much a part of the sciences, is nothing else than a high conceptual art—although one which religious education need fear no more than finger painting! More particularly, I invited my colleagues (e.g., you who read this sentence) to regard the sciences' basic method of research as a way to address the very important question of evaluation. Without in any way questioning the worth of the effort called religious education but, rather, because of its presumed worth, I maintained that religious education *itself* must determine the extent and degree to which it *does*, in fact, accomplish that which it intends as a very human enterprise. To do *less*, I implied, is to prefer ignorance to knowledge vis-a-vis an enterprise that *is* a way of approximating the Johannine promise that "he who has faith in me will do what I am doing; and he will do greater things still."[7] With*in* such a context, religious education is a great and hope-filled venture. With*out* it, the effort is restricted, faltering, and ultimately frustrating . . . quite literally, bedeviled.

I have neither a dislike nor a distaste for the effort called religious education. Far from it. Yet I would hold that effort to a high but *human* standard. I do not think that Christian religious educators *need* to be more than reminded that their ultimate standard is even higher.[8] Fortunately, in this creation, they make one another complete. To forget or to deny *that* is more like original sin than it is like a biblical faith.[9]

LOOKING AHEAD: A REFLECTION

There is a sense in which the Einstein session of the Pontifical Academy of Sciences on November 10, 1979, was not only a genuinely ecumenical occasion but, for those of us engaged in religious education, a tremendously important event.[10] The true ecumenical dimension of that session involved a clear recognition that the man Albert Einstein was (1) nontraditionally religious, (2) non-Christian in his religious self-identification, and yet (3) inescapably important to any contemporary view of this creation or to (4) any contemporary understanding of what it may mean to live in this portion of humankind's long, long history. For religious educators, one of the intriguing things about that session was that Pope John Paul II, speaking in French, specifically addressed himself to the question of the relationship between science and religion, including the case of Galileo.

Without raising the questions of 1870, any contemporary Christian religious educator should be able to acknowledge the importance of what a pope has to say, now, about the relation of science and religion.[11] That relation both bothers and intrigues the contemporary religious educator, whose mind may be in a past but who is, even so, still a person of this time and place. Moreover, even if a religious educator can personally manage to escape being either bothered or intrigued by that relation, sheer experience soon suggests that one's students are both bothered and intrigued by just that relationship.[12] Thus, the relation of science and religion *is* important to those who either claim or accept the identification as a religious educator.

In fact, to suggest that religious education use the tool of research-as-a-method in order to determine the degree to which it *does* what it says it intends is but another way of posing that sometimes bothersome yet quite persistently intriguing relational question. Creatures of this creation cannot really avoid that question, at this time. Perhaps in our here-and-now *how* we understand the relation of science and religion determines our ability to accept and, then, live positively with Tolkien's "hard recognition that things are so in the world as it appears under the sun." Even more particularly, how we *do* understand that relationship may well determine our creaturely ability to achieve Tolkien's "hard recognition" as just what he intended: that is, "a recognition of fact, but not a slavery to it."[13]

According to John Paul II, science, that to which Albert Einstein made an "eminent contribution," is no less than "the knowledge of the truth present in the mystery of the universe." In fact, "the search for truth is the task of basic science."[14] John Paul II also said, "Basic science is a good, worthy of being much loved, for it is knowledge and therefore the perfection of man's intelligence. Even more than its technical applications," he suggested that "it must be honored for itself, as an integral part of our culture. Fundamental science is a universal good that all people must be able to cultivate in complete freedom from every form of international servitude or intellectual colonialism."[15] Clearly, for this pope, at this time, science and truth belong together, and deserve to be beloved, respected, and free. It seems likely that much the same could be said for research-as-a-method, which is how science seeks truth in the mystery of the physical and social universe within which religious education always exists.

In addition, John Paul II seemed to identify something akin to the Tolkienian "hard recognition" when he maintained, "It is to science, among other things, that we must attribute what the Council has said concerning certain aspects of modern culture: 'New conditions have their impact finally on religious life itself. The rise of a critical spirit purifies it of a magical view of the world and of superstitions that still circulate, and exacts a more personal and explicit adherence to faith; as a result, many persons are achieving a more vivid sense of God.' "[16] That is surprisingly close to the suggestion put forth in an earlier chapter that a reason for using research-as-a-method is that it may contribute to our sanctification. Probably that suggestion was less radical than either reader or author may have thought. Certainly, it seems clear that religious educators have no lasting attachment to any "magical view of the world," or to those "superstitions that still circulate" among even those who do identify with the "religious life itself." Or so the pope's words could be interpreted.

Religious education is not and, it seems, has no real reason to be an effort in educational magic, nor is it simply a transmitter of even pious superstitions. Its task is other, and greater. That is why it needs the tool of research-as-a-method. Like basic science, religious education *must* continually be about the search for truth—including the truth about what it *is* able to do for, to, and with those who come to it.

When he spoke to the case of Galileo, John Paul II said that he hoped "that theologians, scientists, and historians, imbued with a spirit of sincere collaboration, will more deeply examine Galileo's case, and by recognizing the wrongs, from whatever side they come, will dispel the mistrust that this affair still raises in many minds, against a fruitful harmony between science and faith, between the Church and the world."[17] Then he promised personal support for such an effort, "which will honor the truth of faith and of science and open the door to future collaboration." A little later, he quoted the Second Vatican Council's document *Gaudium et spes*, No. 36, to make the further point that: "Methodical investigation in every branch of learning, if carried out in a genuinely scientific manner and in accord with moral standards, never truly conflicts with faith: for earthly matters and the concerns of faith derive from the same God."[18]

That is a point worth remembering, although we easily forget it.

At the very least, religious education should be able to claim that it *is* a branch of learning. As such, it should find that it is possible to imagine such methodical investigation in that branch of learning as would qualify for the judgment that it was carried out in a genuinely scientific manner and in accord with moral standards and, so, is capable of the discovery of truth. That is a great possibility! However, we too often seem to fear such truth, especially truth yet to be discovered by a methodical investigation.

We seem to have forgotten, or to have purposefully ignored, the challenging promise of the Johannine Christ: "You shall know the truth, and the truth will set you free."[19] Often we Christian religious educators are all too like those to whom the words were supposedly first addressed: we respond to the challenging promise by quibbling about the future tense, for we think that we already have all the truth there is. Thus, we ignore the possible "more" that is yet to be discovered, and we succeed in missing out on Tolkien's "hard recognition" as well. Like the first child-character in Seuss's *On Beyond Zebra*, we are taken aback when we are shown something of such a "more," or reminded that science's tentativeness and religion's humility are close conceptual cousins.

Notes and References

1. Dr. Seuss, *On Beyond Zebra* (New York: Random House, 1955).
2. In 1958 the lectionary used by Episcopalians listed the Gospel lesson for the 13th Sunday after Trinity as Mark 3:20–21, 31–35, and that was the passage upon which a sermon was built using the reference to Dr. Seuss's *On Beyond Zebra* as an introduction.
3. See J. R. R. Tolkien, "On Fairy-Stories," in *The Tolkien Reader* (New York: Ballantine Books, 1966), p. 52, for the passage to which this sentence refers.
4. I am following John Knox's conclusion that the word *saints* was one of Paul of Tarsus's "favorite ways of alluding to members of the community, the body of Christ." That conclusion will be found in *The Interpreter's Bible*, vol. 9 (New York: Abingdon-Cokesbury Press, 1954), pp. 384–385. Thus, the *saints* in this sentence are simply the members of the Christian churches,

many of whom seem to respond almost like Pavlov's animals to the stimulus of a sheer insult. Moreover, I am also positing that such an analysis is apropos because many of the saints seem incapable of distinguishing an intended insult from a disagreement.

The interested reader might reach the same conclusion as Knox by noting how Paul used *saints* in the introductory greeting to the letters Christians know as Romans, 1 and 2 Corinthians, Ephesians, Philippians, and Colossians.

5. This sentence concludes quite consciously with a narrowing of focus that begins with the cosmological, moves to the planetary, and then winds up with the existential and personal. In addition, the phrase "this creation" involves the not-so-theoretical possibility that there is *at least* a mirror-image antimatter creation (presently barely known and, possibly, never to be fully known) which must be posited as the result of the action of G-O-D the creator, given a firmly based biblical doctrine of creation, and present knowledge.

6. In this sentence, two standards of human acceptability are implied: the first is abstract and aesthetic, beauty, while the second is far more concrete and pragmatic, usefulness or heuristic. Specifically, the sentence advances the idea that a meaningful conceptual space, if one can imagine such, *must*, for humans, satisfy *both* standards. It also explicitly suggests that Fuller's geometry of thinking satisfies both of the standards for human acceptability, the abstract and the concrete.

7. John 14:12 in *The New English Bible: New Testament* (New York: Oxford University Press & Cambridge University Press, 1961).

8. Clearly, the sentence indicates that the religious educator's *ultimate* standard is suprahuman or, in a Christian theological context, G-O-D. The intended contrast with the previous sentence is simply that what I have called a "high but *human* standard" and what I have called "their ultimate standard" exist on a continuum in which the first is somewhat less than the second. In addition, the twelve chapters of this book have, rather persistently, advanced the idea that humans have a good bit of difficulty in ascertaining the ultimate standard (e.g., determining the deity's intention or rationale) and, therefore, might well rest content with the inevitable tentativeness involved in accepting a human best bet or best available estimate of G-O-D's intent or rationale or reason. If the two standards are not put upon such a continuum, it is very clear that this sentence is rather absurd.

9. This sentence explicitly suggests that to "forget *or* deny" that the two standards—one high but human, and one somewhat higher yet and so supra-human—are complements of one another is an example of what the Christian terms "original sin" (i.e., a constitutional, historic or seemingly

congenital human weakness or disability). The sentence, then, contrasts such an example of "original sin" to a presumedly opposite state of "biblical 'faith.'" The fundamental *contrast* in this sentence is between sin and faith, as those terms are understandable within a Christian interpretation of the New Testament documents. Moreover, it is close-to-but-not-quite explicitly stated that the complementarity of the "two standards" is an aspect of a biblical faith, while the denial of complementarity is nought but one more example of "original sin."

10. In the lectionary in use by Episcopalians in 1979, November 10 is a day of optional observance commerating "Leo the Great, Bishop of Rome, 461." The date—A.D. 461—is the year of Leo's death. A short note on his life can be found in F. L. Cross, ed., *The Oxford Dictionary of the Christian Church* (London: Oxford University Press, 1957), p. 797. Probably-to-perhaps it is worth noting that this historic variant on the celebration of Leo's commemoration and the Einstein session happened on the same day. It is doubtful if more than *that* should be made of coincidence.

11. The "questions of 1870" refer, quite specifically, to an entry entitled, "The Doctrine of Papal Infallibity, 1870," in Henry Bettenson, *Documents of the Christian Church* (New York: Oxford University Press, 1947), p. 383. The sentence itself is meant to do two things: (1) acknowledge that the question of papal infallibility is, in 1980, still a divisive question within the wider body of Christians, and (2) in specific and quite unique situations no present bar to many among that wider body of Christians to acknowledging that what an heir of Leo the Great has to say is, minimally, of considerable importance.

12. This sentence reflects a conclusion that was well put by Ronald Goldman in *Religious Thinking from Childhood to Adolescence* (London: Routledge and Kegan Paul, 1964), p. 27. In that place, Goldman says, "A major problem of religious education is to bring these separate worlds together so that when the scientific view gains ascendency the theological view is not invalidated in the child's experience." That is probably still true.

13. For this particular conclusion, see J. R. R. Tolkien, "On Fairy-Stories," in *The Tolkien Reader* (New York: Ballantine Books, 1966), p. 55.

14. For these and other quotations attributed in this epilogue to John Paul II, see "Address of Pope John Paul II," *Science*, vol. 207, no. 4436 (March 14, 1980), pp. 1165–1167. A footnote there identifies that the text of the article is based on the address, which was given in French, and which was translated for *Science* by Professor Robert Nicolich of the Catholic University of America, Washington, D.C. 20064.

15. Ibid., p. 1165.

16. Ibid.

17. Ibid., p. 1166.

18. Ibid.

19. John 8:32. The following sentences are written from within an acknowledgedly Christian frame of reference which interprets the passage, in 1980, to contrast a general human tendency to a response appropriate to the faithful Christian. There is *no* intent to express or to arouse even latent anti-Semitism. Therefore, let the reader beware of taking for granted an assumption that this author does not share.

Name Index

Name Index

Subject Index

Subject Index

Subject Index

Subject Index

Subject Index

Subject Index

Subject Index

Subject Index

Subject Index

Other Important Books From Religious Education Press

THE SHAPE OF RELIGIOUS EDUCATION
by **James Michael Lee**
No one can discuss contemporary religious education meaningfully unless he or she has read this book. Widely acclaimed as a classic in the field. ISBN 0-89135-000-4

THE FLOW OF RELIGIOUS EDUCATION
by **James Michael Lee**
A serious in-depth look at the nature and structure of the religion teaching process. This volume provides that kind of solid and systematic framework so necessary for the effective *teaching* of religion. A major work. ISBN 0-89135-001-2

AN INVITATION TO RELIGIOUS EDUCATION
by **Harold William Burgess**
A careful examination of the most influential Protestant and Catholic theories of religious education proposed in our time. An essential book for understanding the foundational issues in religious education. ISBN 0-89135-019-5

THE RELIGIOUS EDUCATION WE NEED
edited by **James Michael Lee**
A prophetic volume presenting Catholic and Protestant proposals on a viable future for religious education. Exciting chapters by Alfred McBride, Randolph Crump Miller, Carl F. H. Henry, John Westerhoff III, Gloria Durka, and James Michael Lee. This book has as its axis the renewal of Christian education. ISBN 0-89135-005-5

ABOVE OR WITHIN?: THE SUPERNATURAL IN RELIGIOUS EDUCATION
by **Ian P. Knox**
An illuminating survey of the basic theological issue permeating all religious education activity, namely: "How can the religious educator help learners of all ages meet God in their own lives?" A book centering on God's revelation in religious education. ISBN 0-89135-006-3

RESURGENCE OF RELIGIOUS INSTRUCTION
by **Didier-Jacques Piveteau and J. T. Dillon**
A well-developed theoretical foundation for the community and family model of religious education, together with concrete examples of ways in which family and community religious education programs have worked. ISBN 0-89135-007-1

CAN CHRISTIANS BE EDUCATED?
by **Morton Kelsey**
An examination from the standpoint of depth psychology of some of the most critical concerns in contemporary religious education, including education for love, education for spiritual wholeness, and education for positive emotional values. This volume integrates religious education with growth in the religion teacher's own personal spirituality. ISBN 0-89135-008-X

REGARDING RELIGIOUS EDUCATION
by **Mary K. Cove and Mary Louise Mueller**
A helpful volume for parish religious education directors striving to develop an effective program and to enhance the effectiveness of their teaching personnel. Topics include targeting instruction to here-and-now religious living, introducing accountability into all phases of the program, assessment of the learner's religious needs, and coordination of the religious education efforts of various parish and congregation groups. ISBN 0-89135-011-X

PROCESS AND RELATIONSHIP
edited by **Iris V. Cully and Kendig Brubaker Cully**
A penetrating examination of how the interactive realities of process and relationship profoundly affect the structure of religious education, theology, and philosophy. Original essays by fourteen of North America's leading Protestant and Catholic thinkers. ISBN 0-89135-012-8

CLARITY IN RELIGIOUS EDUCATION

by **Robert Yorke O'Brien**

Clear and practical treatment of some of the most vexing areas in religious education today, such as teaching holiness, teaching biblical miracles, teaching the sacraments, and teaching the church. ISBN 0-89135-013-6

WHO ARE WE?: THE QUEST FOR A RELIGIOUS EDUCATION

edited by **John H. Westerhoff III**

An exploration into the identity and special calling of the religious educator as seen by many of the most important religious education leaders of the twentieth century. Many of the most important issues facing religious education are treated in this book. ISBN 0-89135-014-4

CELEBRATING THE SECOND YEAR OF LIFE: A PARENT'S GUIDE FOR A HAPPY CHILD

by **Lucie W. Barber**

A practical guide for religious parenting and educating. This book is organized around psychologically-proven ways in which parents and members of the helping professions can successfully develop five basic capacities in the child *and* in themselves: trust and faith; a positive self-image; self-confidence and independence; a joy for learning; the ability to associate with others happily. ISBN 0-89135-015-2

TRADITION AND TRANSFORMATION IN RELIGIOUS EDUCATION

edited by **Padraic O'Hare**

Four important religious education scholars reflect on the urgent but complex issue of how religious education can transform the world while at the same time faithfully hand on the Christian message. ISBN 0-89135-016-0

IMPROVING CHURCH EDUCATION

by **H. W. Byrne**

A bible-centered approach to effective Christian education ministry. Written from an evangelical Protestant perspective, this comprehensive book explains practical and workable models for successful total church education, including models for grouping people for effective teaching and learning, models for improved instructional space, models for enriched teaching, and models for improved staffing. ISBN 0-89135-017-9

RELIGIOUS CONVERSION AND PERSONAL IDENTITY
by **V. Bailey Gillespie**
A sensitive treatment of religious conversion as a basic way of achieving personal identity and self-transcendence. This stimulating book integrates psychological findings with both the biblical perspective and theological insights. ISBN 0-89135-018-7

MORAL DEVELOPMENT, MORAL EDUCATION, AND KOHLBERG
edited by **Brenda Munsey**
A seminal volume on the interrelated topics of moral development, moral education, and religious education. An interdisciplinary treatment from the perspectives of religious education, philosophy, psychology, and general education. These original essays bring together some of the most important scholars in North America, Europe, and Israel. ISBN 0-89135-020-9

THE BIG LITTLE SCHOOL, second edition revised and enlarged
by **Robert W. Lynn and Elliott Wright**
This classic history of the American Sunday School in a revised and updated form. A superb and delightful analysis of how the American Protestant Church perceived its educational mission throughout the years, and how it actually went about bringing religion to the hearts and minds of the taught as well as the teachers. ISBN 0-89135-021-7

BIBLICAL INTERPRETATION IN RELIGIOUS EDUCATION
by **Mary C. Boys**
An illuminating examination of the way in which the bible and biblical interprétation have affected twentieth century religious education. The first part of this volume is a fine examination and critique of biblical revelation offered by twentieth century biblical scholars. The second part deals with how religious educators brought the bible into the field as salvation history. ISBN 0-89135-022-5

CREATIVE CONFLICT IN RELIGIOUS EDUCATION AND CHURCH ADMINISTRATION
by **Donald E. Bossart**
A stimulating volume centering around two major themes: the myriad possibilities for growth inherent in all conflict, and the specific procedures which can be used in religious settings to bring out the productive potential in conflict. This interdisciplinary volume deals with the theological dynamics, psy-

chological dynamics, sociological dynamics, and educational dynamics of conflict. ISBN 0-89135-048-9

THE THEORY OF CHRISTIAN EDUCATION PRACTICE
by **Randolph Crump Miller**
An elaboration on the way in which theology affects religious education in a determinative fashion, and on the manner in which religious education enfleshes theology. ISBN 0-89135-049-7

CONSCIENCE: DEVELOPMENT AND SELF-TRANSCENDENCE
by **Walter E. Conn**
A pioneering new look at the structure and growth of conscience from the interdisciplinary perspectives of theology, ethics, and psychology. Major themes include conscience as the basic form which personal authenticity takes, and conscience as flourishing in self-giving love. ISBN 0-89135-025-X

THE RELIGIOUS EDUCATION OF PRESCHOOL CHILDREN
by **Lucie W. Barber**
A holistic approach embracing all areas of the child's religious life—cognitive, affective, and lifestyle. The most significant work to date on the religious education of preschool children in home and church. ISBN 0-89135-026-8

RELIGIOUS EDUCATION, CATECHESIS, AND FREEDOM
by **Kenneth Barker**
A fine examination of the different responses given by religious educationists and catechetical leaders to the call to freedom issued by the church and by the world. A helpful book for educational ministers seriously concerned with providing learners with religious education and with catechesis in and for freedom. ISBN 0-89135-028-4

RELIGIOUS EDUCATION AND THEOLOGY
edited by **Norma H. Thompson**
This important book presents a wide variety of diverse and robust points of view on the dynamic relationship between religious education and theology. Original and seminal essays by the most important contemporary religious education scholars. A benchmark book in the sense that it provides the standard against which any future discussion of the relationship of religious education and theology will have to be measured. ISBN 0-89135-029-2